Warrior Kings of Sweden

Warrior Kings of Sweden

The Rise of an Empire in the Sixteenth and Seventeenth Centuries

Gary Dean Peterson

McFarland & Company, Inc., Publishers

Jefferson, North Carolina, and London

Excerpt from *The Story of Civilization: Vol. 6, Reformation*, by Will Durant. Copyright © 1957 by Will Durant. Copyright © renewed 1985 by Ethel B. Durant. (New York: Simon and Schuster Adult Publishing Group).

Excerpt from *The Story of Civilization: Vol. 8, The Age of Louis XIV*, by Will Durant and Ariel Durant. Copyright © 1963 by Will & Ariel Durant; copyright © renewed 1991 by Will & Ariel Durant. (New York: Simon and Schuster Adult Publishing Group).

Excerpts from *Gustav Adolf the Great*, by Nils Ahnlund, translated by Michael Roberts, published by Princeton University Press and The American-Scandinavian Foundation, 1940, © The American-Scandinavian Foundation.

LIBRARY OF CONGRESS CATALOGUING-IN-PUBLICATION DATA

Peterson, Gary Dean, 1942–
Warrior kings of Sweden : the rise of an empire in the sixteenth and seventeenth centuries / Gary Dean Peterson.
p.   cm.
Includes bibliographical references and index.

ISBN-13: 978-0-7864-2873-1
(softcover : 50# alkaline paper) ∞

1. Sweden — Politics and government — 17th century.   2. Sweden — History, Military — 17th century.   3. Sweden — Kings and rulers — 17th century.   4. Sweden — Civilization — 17th century.   5. Sweden — Politics and government — 16th century.   6. Sweden — Kings and rulers — 16th century.   7. Europe — History, Military — 17th century.   8. Europe — History, Military — 16th century.   I. Title.
DL704.7.P48   2007   948.5'034 — dc22   2007005128

British Library cataloguing data are available

On the cover: *top* Gustav Adolf the Great *(British Library)*; *bottom* ©2007 Clipart

Manufactured in the United States of America

McFarland & Company, Inc., Publishers
Box 611, Jefferson, North Carolina 28640
www.mcfarlandpub.com

To my grandparents,
Hannah Svensson and Peter Gust Peterson,
who immigrated to the United States
from Småland, Sweden,
and homesteaded in Montana

Contents

Preface

As the grandson of Swedish immigrants I have always been interested in Sweden, yet in grade school, high school and even college, any Swedish history I learned I picked up indirectly. In Roman history there were the Goths, who may or may not have come from Sweden. There were Vikings, mostly Danish and Norwegian, who ravaged Medieval Europe and reached North America — maybe. Swedish Vikings, I learned, did have something to do with the early Russian kingdoms. There was mention of Gustav Adolf's participation in the Thirty Years' War and Sweden's short lived colony on the Delaware. And that was it, except for some slurs about the country's neutrality during the two world wars.

I had not an inkling that the boots of Swedish soldiers once trod the streets of Moscow, that Swedish generals had conquered Prague and once stood at the gates of Vienna. Only vaguely did I understand that a Swedish king had defeated the Holy Roman Emperor and held court on the Rhine, that a Swede had mounted the throne of Poland, then held at bay the Russian and Turk. I missed completely the history of another Swedish king who captured Krakow and Warsaw, then reversed direction and drove the king of Denmark into a last island refuge.

It was not until later, reading on my own, that I discovered the story of Sweden's rise to power under Gustav Vasa (the first of Sweden's great warrior kings) in the sixteenth century. I learned of Sweden's military dominance of central and eastern Europe under her second great warrior king, Gustav Adolf, and Sweden's pivotal role in the Great Northern War at the beginning of the eighteenth century under her last great warrior king, Karl XII, perhaps the ablest general of his day. For a hundred years Sweden was the international military power of Northern Europe, turning the Baltic into a Swedish lake, and establishing colonies in Africa and America.

This story fills a large void in history as it is generally presented to the American student and reader. First, it bridges a geographical gap between Russian history, readily available in book and course study, and Western European history, as taught in U.S. high schools. The annals of Sweden, Finland, the Baltics, Poland, Lithuania and Prussia are little understood by Americans. Yet events in this region directly affected the course of Western European history and ultimately that of America.

Secondly, this chronicle spans a period in time generally overlooked in American history books, literature, movies and television. Medieval Western Europe has been well represented in all these media. The American Revolution and the Civil War focus attention on the late 1700s and 1800s, but it was the political and religious movements of the sixteenth and seventeenth centuries that produced the climate for European global expansion including the exploration and colonization of the New World. And it was during these centuries that great strides were made in the advancement of weapons technology, warships and military tactics. Sweden was at the forefront of this military evolution, both on land and at sea. Besides playing a major role in these military, religious and political events of the era, Sweden took a hand in the colonization of America and continued to send skilled and industrious people to the United States well into the twentieth century.

In this book I present a narrative of Sweden's age of greatness, in terms of her warrior kings, for the descendants of those immigrants, the posterity of immigrants of other Northern and Eastern European countries, students of military history, and the general reader interested in this neglected aspect of European history. A list of references, organized by chapter, is at the end of the book for the reader interested in a more detailed study.

I thank Sven Edenström of Ronneby, Sweden, for explaining details and filling in gaps, and especially my wife, Pauline, for long hours of editing and critiquing.

Here then is the story of Sweden's age of greatness, a tale of intrigues and conflicts, of power and greatness, of suffering and courage, of romance and loyalty, of kings, nobles and peasants, the story of a people, a nation and an empire.

Introduction

The origins of Sweden's warrior kings are buried in her ancient past, obscured by the mists of time. Only a vague outline can be constructed from archeological evidence and occasional references in literature from outside the country. These sources do provide enough information to paint a picture, though somewhat sketchy, of the development of the early Swedish people, their chiefs and kings.

At the height of the last ice age the Scandinavian Peninsula was pressed down under a massive ice sheet. About 13,000 to 14,000 years ago the ice sheet began to recede. As the ice melted the peninsula rose. Though the rising water from the melting ice cut off the British Isles from the rest of Europe and filled the Baltic Sea, Scandinavia rose faster than the oceans and is still increasing its height above sea level today. This elevating of the land mass means the coastline, rivers and islands of Sweden have been constantly changing during the country's history affecting harbors, port cities and river outlets.

About 6000 B.C. the first permanent settlers began to inhabit Sweden. Most of these hunter-gatherers were pre–Germanic, people crossing from Jutland into southern Sweden, but there is evidence of other people entering from the east around the northern end of the Gulf of Bothnia or across the Åland Islands. By 5000 B.C. grains were being grown in Sweden and by 1500 B.C. a bronze-age culture flourished across southern Sweden. There was extensive trade with Eastern Europe and the Mediterranean civilizations. This trade was facilitated by the use of shallow-draft boats with upturned bows at both ends, precursors to the Viking longboats. They were without sails, powered by oars and manned by warriors and merchants.

About 500 B.C. this developing culture was cut down by the Celtic invasion. The Celts, a warlike people armed with iron weapons, spread across Central Europe from the Danube to Ireland, severing the trade arteries between the north and the Mediterranean. At the same time a cold period settled over the north and Scandinavia entered a dark age.

Around 100 B.C. Northern Europe began to warm and by then the Celts had been absorbed into local populations. Trade relations were reestablished across Europe with Sweden exporting iron, along with skins, walrus ivory, honey and amber, to the south. Explorers from the Mediterranean began to visit Scandinavia and from them we get a picture of Sweden as a land of many small kingdoms.

In the second century A.D. the Goths appear in history ravaging the Roman Empire and putting an end to the ancient city's reign. There is strong evidence the Goths originated in central Sweden, and were the first of three waves of Swedes to affect Greater Europe.

The second wave was that of the Vikings, from about 780 to 1070. These warrior-merchants ranged west to North America and south to the Mediterranean. They established colonies (Greenland and Iceland), kingdoms (in Sicily, Italy, Ireland, England and Normandy), and an empire (that of Canute the Great, comprised of modern-day England, Norway, Denmark and southern Sweden).

To the east the Vikings invaded the river systems of Eastern Europe. Via the Düna, Lovat, Volga and Dnieper, they reached the Black and Caspian seas, threatening Constantinople and the Byzantine emperor. The Varangians or Rus, as the eastern Vikings were called, were primarily Swedish, though as with the western expeditions there was a mixture from all three Viking peoples in these adventures.

Varangian kingdoms were established with capitals at Novgorod and Kiev, then these kingdoms were combined into the empire of the Rus, stretching from the Baltic to the Black and Caspian seas. Merchandise from China, Persia and Byzantium passed through this empire to the Swedish trade centers of Birka on Lake Mälar, Gotland Island and Hedeby, on the Jutland Peninsula. Items excavated at Birka, at one time the greatest trade center in the Viking world, range from Rhineland pottery, English wool, Chinese silk and Arab silver to necklaces from the lower Volga and hides from the arctic. Gradually, the empire of the Rus became more Slavic than Swedish and turned toward Byzantium, adopting Eastern Orthodox Christianity.

During this Viking period, Sweden struggled toward unity. The many small kingdoms began to coalesce into a few large domains. Gradually, three states emerged to consolidate power. In Uppland the Svear (Svea, Siar or Swedes) developed a very warlike kingdom, spreading their control to the north and west. To the east, they acquired Gotland and conquered parts of Kurland along the eastern Baltic coast. As they spread south they came to dominate Birka and then encountered the Gauts.

The Gauts (Geats or Goths) probably originated in Västergötland, subjugating Dalarna, Närke, Värmland, Östergötland and, perhaps, Småland and Blekinge as well. For over three hundred years these two major powers of Sweden fought it out for supremacy. Finally, Erik the Victorious of the Svear (985–995) completed the conquest of the Gauts and is considered the first true king of Sweden.

A third consolidated area was Scania, which included Skåne, Halland and Blekinge. This kingdom grew strong on its rich farmland and fisheries. It prospered for four hundred years, even ruling Hedeby at one time. But in the ninth century Scania was conquered by the Danes, then by Eric the Victorious of Sweden.

By 995 Erik the Victorious ruled a domain that included essentially all that is modern Sweden (except the far north), territories along the eastern Baltic coast, and had nominal control of southern Jutland (Hedeby) which was again under Swedish rule. Swedish merchants dominated a trade network stretching from Greenland and Ireland to Persia and Constantinople. The country emerging during the waning years of the Viking era was a nation on the rise.

By dint of their victory over the Gauts, the Swedes of Uppland gained the right to select a king to rule both peoples. At his coronation, Olof, Erik's son, took the title "*Rex Sveorum Gothorum.*" A united Sweden seemed destined for greatness.

1. First Kings of a United Sweden

A dark and gloomy atmosphere hung over the streets and alleys of Stockholm, invading the shops and homes with a sense of foreboding. Three days of feasting and celebration in the Swedish capital had been abruptly suspended. Clergy and noblemen, staying in the great Stockholm Castle, having come from all parts of the country to celebrate the king's coronation, awoke to find themselves imprisoned in their apartments. The town's craftsmen, merchants and tradesmen ventured out into the streets cautiously, sensing that some momentous shift in circumstances had occurred, but unsure as to its nature or extent. The gray November day passed for the city's burghers, giving little indication of the crucial events taking place in the chambers of Stockholm's Great Castle, the seat of government.

Early the next morning, November 8, 1520, Danish soldiers and bailiffs began knocking on doors, forcing citizens into the streets with orders to proceed to the great square in the center of the city. Crowding into the plaza, they found themselves encircling an open space in which stood a figure armed with a single-bladed long-handled ax. Jörgen Holmuth was a German mercenary, an expert with battle ax and broadsword. This day he would serve the king as executioner.

At high noon there was a commotion at one side of the square as Danish guards brought forward a man with his hands tied behind his back. A stir ran through the crowd as they recognized Mattias, Roman Catholic bishop of Strängnäs. In the middle of the open circle he groveled, begging for mercy from two men on an elevated platform. But his entreaties were to no avail, for Christian II, king of Denmark, Iceland, Norway and now Sweden-Finland, gave the signal for the execution to proceed. The German swung his ax and Mattias's lifeless head rolled onto the frozen ground.

The execution of the good bishop of Strängnäs was followed by the beheading of the bishop of Skara. His last plea for life was to Gustav Trolle, archbishop of Sweden and the other figure on the platform next to the king; he made no move to rescue his bishop, for events were unfolding according to a plan of his design.

Following the two men of the cloth, fourteen members of the Swedish nobility were led into the square and executed by Holmuth, who used his broadsword as a concession to their aristocratic station. The ax was again employed to dispatch three city mayors followed by fourteen members of Stockholm's town council, all accused of affiliation with the Sture party. The massacre continued until nightfall, then began again the next day. Merchants and craftsmen, rumored to be Sture men, were dragged from the crowd and from their shops to be brutally killed. The massacre, known in Swedish history as the Stockholm Bloodbath, ran

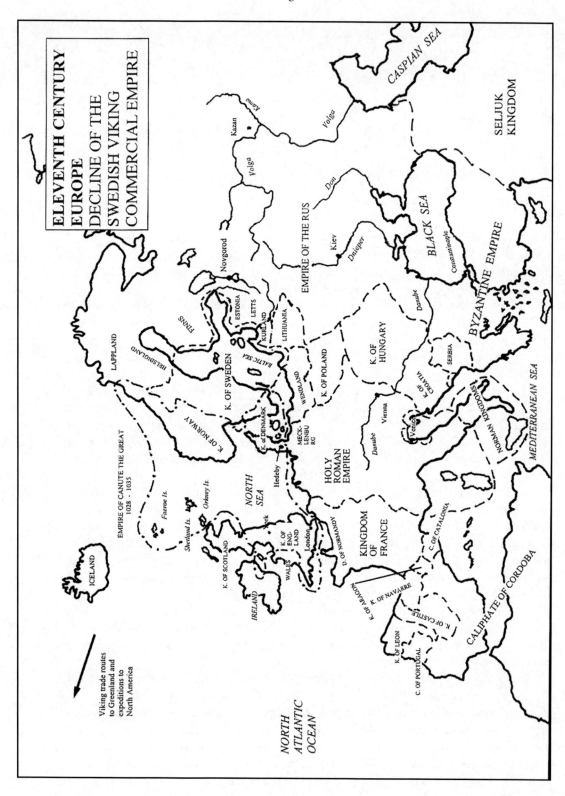

ELEVENTH CENTURY
EUROPE
DECLINE OF THE
SWEDISH VIKING
COMMERCIAL EMPIRE

CASPIAN SEA

SELJUK
KINGDOM

Kama

Kazan

Volga

Volga

Don

BLACK SEA

Dnieper

Kiev

Constantinople

EMPIRE OF THE RUS

BYZANTINE EMPIRE

MEDITERRANEAN SEA

Novgorod

FINNS

ESTONIA
LETTS
KURLAND
LITHUANIA

LAPPLAND

HELSINGLAND

K. OF SWEDEN

BALTIC SEA

WENDLAND

K. OF POLAND

K. OF HUNGARY

Danube

SERBIA

K. OF CROATIA

Vienna

Venice

NORMAN KINGDOM

K. OF NORWAY

K. of DENMARK

MECK-
LENBU
RG

HOLY
ROMAN
EMPIRE

Danube

EMPIRE OF CANUTE THE GREAT
1028 - 1035

Faeroe Is.

Orkney Is.

Shetland Is.

Hedeby

NORTH
SEA

York

K. OF
ENG-
LAND

London

D. OF NORMANDY

KINGDOM
OF
FRANCE

C. OF CATALONIA

ICELAND

K. OF SCOTLAND

WALES

IRELAND

K. OF ARAGON

K. OF NAVARRE

K. OF CASTILE

K. OF LEON

C. OF PORTUGAL

CALIPHATE OF CORDOBA

Viking trade routes
to Greenland and
expeditions to
North America

NORTH
ATLANTIC
OCEAN

into a third day with anonymous commoners being hanged. In all 94 men were executed. The Swedish nation had been brought to its knees, powerless under the heel of this foreign despot.

In 1000, Olof, king of Sweden, had defeated Olav Tryggvarson of Norway in a sea battle, successfully defending a kingdom stretching from the arctic to the Skåne-Zealand strait. His merchants plied the Baltic Sea connecting trade routes that reached from England to Persia and Constantinople. In 500 years this mighty nation had been reduced to a state of subjugation and servitude. It was indeed an ignoble state of affairs for Sweden.

This reversal in Sweden's fortunes stemmed from two conditions rooted in the Viking period. First was the state of the monarchy created with the combining of the Svear and Gaut kingdoms by Erik the Victorious. The king was to be elected by the Svear of Uppland. The right to rule was not hereditary and he was to have total authority only in time of war when he commanded the army. When the country was at peace or when the king was away campaigning, power rested with the *jarl* (earl or minister). The jarl also ruled the Mälar Lake district and would lead the expeditions to Finland. It was the jarls that conquered Finland in the twelfth and thirteenth centuries, making the land their personal fief. The united kingdom did not, therefore, have a strong government, but was ruled by three parties at odds with each other, the king, the Uppland nobility and the jarl.

The second condition was the introduction of Christianity to the kingdom. At the close of the first millennium a great struggle was commencing in Sweden, a battle for the very souls of the people. It was a contest between the believers in the old pagan gods and the new religion of Christianity. The assault was from outside the country. English missionaries were active in Västergötland, which they could reach directly from the North Sea. The Franks infiltrated from the south, across the Baltic, reaching the highest echelons of the Swedish hierarchy. There was Ansgar's visit to Birka (829–831) at the instigation of Louis the Pious (king of the Franks). He converted Hergeir, jarl of Birka. But Hergeir's successor, Gautbert, was forced to flee and his nephew killed in 839. To the warrior class Thor's hammer had more appeal than the Christian cross. The old gods would not die easily.

Most of the population was rural and exposed to the new faith much later. The rituals and sacrifices that guaranteed fertility of land and family, and protection from enemies, both natural and human, exercised a compelling hold over the people. The new, alien god and his son-come-to-earth would make slow progress among the mostly peasant population of the country.

And the merchants who had sojourned among the Greeks brought back a different version of this new church, one with an earthly ruler in the east, instead of the west. If Thor and Odin were to be displaced, which church would take their place?

Erik the Victorious had completed the conquest of the Gauts and all of southern Sweden. His son Olof (Skötkonung) of Sweden was the first to be crowned king of the Goths and Svear. Olof was also the first baptized Christian king and it is with him that the line of Swedish kings traditionally begins. The reigns of these early kings cover the period in which the fortunes of the country deteriorated steadily. During this descent Sweden degenerated from a kingdom of power and wealth to a country at the mercy of its predatory neighbors.

The line of kings had begun with promise enough as Olof, combining with Sweyn Forkbeard of the Danes, defeated the threatening fleet of some seventy ships under Olav Tryggvason of Norway (1000) in the Skåne-Zealand strait (the Sound). It was the year Leif Eriksson sailed for America, extending the Viking reach still further afield. To the east, Vladimir, king of the Rus, was trying to convert his Eastern Slavs to Greek Christianity and keep the Swedish trade routes open at the same time. But in Jutland, Hedeby was already lost and Scania, except for Blekinge, had been retaken by Denmark. By 1028 Canute the Great had established an empire that included England, Norway, Denmark and Scania. The western Viking nations would prosper a while longer, but in the east the zenith had already been reached. A line of Swedish kings from the house of Yngling would oversee the country's decline:

985–995	Erik the Victorious
995–1022	Olof of Sweden (Skötkonung)
1022–1050	Anund Jacob
1050–1060	Emund the Old
1060–1066	Stenkil of Sweden (Ragnvaldsson)
1066–1067	Erik VII (Stenkilsson)
1067–1067	Erik VIII (Hedningen)
1067–1070	Halsten
1070–1079	Haakon the Red
1079–1084	Halsten and Ingold I
1084–1087	Blot-Sweyn
1087–1105	Ingold I (the Elder)
1105–1118	Philip Halsten
1105–1125	Ingold II (the Younger)
1125–1130	Magnus the Strong

Anund Jacob was the first Swedish king with a Christian name. His efforts to convert his subjects met with only limited success, though some of the nobility had readily adopted the new religion. In fact some short reigns of this period were due to kings being forced from the throne because they refused to conduct the sacred sacrifices to the Norse gods, a duty of the Uppland kings by longstanding tradition. Västergötland became the refuge for these dispossessed monarchs; here Christianity had taken root, even among the peasants, thanks to the efforts of early English missionaries and constant reinforcement by the Franks and Frisians.

The Swedish Yngling kings were warrior kings, but, outside their capacity as commanders, they were kept weak by the nobility and were distrusted by the commoners because of the chasm that divided them in the gods they worshipped. Sometimes brothers were made joint kings, probably to reduce the power of the throne. Added to the country's problems was the declining trade to the east, particularly the loss of Arab silver on which Sweden had come to depend.

At Vladimir's death in 1019, Yaroslav became king of the Rus and ruler of the vast Novgorod-Kiev domain. He worked at maintaining his ties to the west, particularly Sweden. He married Ingigerd, daughter of Olof Skötkonung, and gave daughters in marriage to King Andrew I of Hungary and King Henry I of France. But while the crown may have been Varangian, the government, merchants and local authorities had become thoroughly Slavic. Commerce was now for the benefit of the empire and those in it, not for the Norse. Compounding the disruption was the difference in religion. An Orthodox Christian empire was dealing with a pagan Sweden. At Yaroslav's death in 1054, the connection between the Eastern Slavic Empire and Sweden dissolved in favor of closer Slavic ties to Byzantium.

The kings of Sweden struggled to maintain a semblance of control in the face of declining fortunes. Progress was hampered by the continuing three-way split in power between the crown, the nobility and the jarl. Thus, we have Ingold I becoming king in 1080 only to be driven from the throne when he would not conduct the great sacrifices to Thor, Odin and

Frey at Uppsala. Bolt-Sweyn, his half-brother, did perform the rituals and was made king. Yet three years later Ingold I was able to retake power, indicating the pagan gods were losing their grip on even the common people. Still, it was the nobility of Uppland that kept much of the political power. Either they chose the king outright or influenced the choice through the people.

As an indication of the monarchy's weak condition, consider that it had no permanent court. The king and his officers moved from place to place, making a circuit of family possessions. For the most part the king had to live off his own resources. Only in time of war did he have any real power. Again in 1105 Sweden had brothers occupying the same throne as joint monarchs, Ingold II (the Younger) and Philip Halsten. The government remained impotent and the country suffered. With the death of Magnus the Strong the long line of Yngling kings died out to be replaced by a series of kings from two well respected noble families, the Sverker and Erik:

1130–1156 .... Sverker I (the Elder) — House of Sverker
1156–1160 .... Erik the Saint — House of Erik
1160–1167 .... Karl VII of Sweden (Sverkersson) — House of Sverker
1167–1195 .... Canute I of Sweden (Eriksson) — House of Erik
1196–1208 .... Sverker II of Sweden (the Younger) — House of Sverker
1208–1216 .... Erik X (Knutsson) — House of Erik
1216–1222 .... Johan I (Sverkersson) — House of Sverker
1222–1229 .... Erik XI (Eriksson) — House of Erik
1229–1234 .... Canute II of Sweden (Knut Holmgersson) — House of Sverker
1234–1250 .... Erik XII (Eriksson — the Lame or Lisper) — House of Erik

Neither family was able to take complete control. In fact the jarls of Mälar seem to have had more power than the king. It was they who led the only successful campaign of the period. That was the conquest of western Finland in the 1150s where Sweden had had a foothold since the Viking era. This crusade included not only the subjugation of Finnish tribes, but also the colonization of the coastal region by Swedish peasants. Elsewhere, however, Swedish interests continued to decline. The once sprawling trade network was further eroded.

To the south, across the Baltic, the Germans were spreading their domination through the northern German plains to the sea and moving to the east absorbing the Slavic Wends. Formerly Viking towns, colonies, and trade centers were being replaced by German cities bent on control of Baltic commerce. A major step in the process occurred in 1143 when an old Viking town at the mouth of the Trave River was taken by the Germans and replaced by one of their own. The new town, Lübeck, quickly grew into a vibrant merchant city and came to dominate trade in the region. They founded other commercial centers along the coast, Hamburg, Wismar, Rostock, Danzig, and Elbing. German merchants gradually took over the town of Visby on Gotland and made it a German trade center, displacing the Swedes. They built Riga, Narva, and Reval on the eastern Baltic coast into thriving port cities and spread into Novgorod and Polotsk where they again took over Swedish mercantile interests. In Finland they established themselves in Åbo and Viborg. They moved west to Bergen in Norway and appropriated fisheries in Skåne from the Danes. Where they could not gain outright control of a city, they established a German merchant colony as in Kalmar and Söderköping in eastern Sweden and Lödöse on the west coast. They set up offices in London, York, Oslo and Copenhagen. Led by Lübeck, Hamburg and Bremen, the Germans organized the Hanseatic League establishing a commercial empire that stretched from London to Novgorod. By 1370 the league had seventy-seven member cities including Cologne, Brandenburg and Braun-schweig. Known as the Hansa, they had come to dominate Baltic and North Sea trade.

The league's success was due, in large measure, to the introduction of a new way of con-ducting sea trade. Cargo was carried on the Hanseatic cog, a short stubby ship, 60 or more feet in length, with two or more masts. It had more draft than the Norse longboats, but now there were port cities eliminating the need to sail up rivers and enter shallow harbors. The cog's big advantage was that it could carry many times the cargo of the longboat. The crews also changed in character. Where the longboat's captain and crew were also the owners and traders, the cog was captained by a professional sailor with a hired crew. The ship might be owned by the captain, or a company, or one of the Hansa cities. It was hired to carry cargo by merchants who often never set foot on its deck. The Swedes were slow in giving up their old way of doing business and could not compete in this new commercial world. In 1368 over 700 cogs sailed out of Lübeck in that year alone. Sweden's once pervasive and wide ranging merchant marine was displaced by the Hanseatic League cog fleets.

Completing the destruction of the old Norse trade network, the Germans sealed off the remainder of the southern and eastern Baltic by military conquest. The Teutonic Knights, originally organized as a crusader army to assault the Holy Lands, turned their attention to Eastern Europe and conquered the southeastern Baltic coast. A kindred military order, the Brothers of the Sword, extended German control through Kurland to the Gulf of Finland. Sweden was left with only Finland out of all its eastern domains. Here, at least, the Swedes could conduct their old style warfare. They raided, plundered and traded with church approval as long as it was done in the guise of a crusade to Christianize the heathen Finns.

Religion in Sweden had by this time been decided in favor of the Roman Catholic Church. Paganism was on the wane and Orthodox Christianity was confined to the east in Kexholmland, Novgorod-Kiev and Lithuania. Though Christianity was finally displacing paganism in the lower levels of Swedish society and even reaching the high mountain valleys and deep northern woods, religious conflict was far from over. Peasants were used to a high degree of control over their own lives, participating in the election of local officials and even the king through their assemblies, the *things*. Though they had accepted Roman Catholi-cism, they insisted on choosing their own priests and bishops, which did not sit well with Rome.

Feudalism never developed fully in Sweden except in Scania where it was established dur-ing Danish rule. In the early Viking period the law recognized only two classes, slaves (*thrals)* and freemen, though there was an informal class hierarchy based on the amount of land owned. As warfare became more advanced, the kings found it necessary to build an arm of the military that included heavy cavalry. The monarchy did not have the money to arm and maintain such a force so the responsibility was transferred to the largest landowners. These magnate families became the nobility. A class structure gradually developed: nobility, peas-ants (small landowners who could not field mounted armor), merchants and craftsmen, clergy and landless peasants (workers who did not own their own land). However, even the landless peasants were not serfs as in the rest of Europe. These peasants were not tied to a particular estate. They had the freedom to move at will. They had freeman's rights under the law and representation in the things. It was these landless peasants who colonized Ångermanland, in northern Sweden, as well as Österbotten and Nyland in Finland, increasing Sweden's terri-tory.

Throughout the reigns of Knut Eriksson (1167–1196), Sverker the Younger (1196–1208) and Erik Knutsson (1208–1216) the Uppland nobles struggled to retain power and carry on the raiding-trading Viking tradition though in the name of Christianity. The monarchy was kept weak. Johan Sverkersson died at 21 having become king when only fifteen (1216–1222). Erik Eriksson, who assumed the throne in 1222 at age 6, was removed seven years later before he could even come of age. He was replaced by Knut Holmgersson (1229), but regained the throne upon Knut's death in 1234. The only real advances were the jarl's crusades in Finland. He increased his domain in the interior, conquering Satakunta and Tavastland in 1238. Arrayed against the Uppland nobility were the supporters of the monarchy, the church, and Sweden's neighbors, Norway, Denmark and the German states. In this fragmented power situation the jarl came to be the dominant official in the country. He ruled the Lake Mära district, key to the trade in central Sweden, and he held Finland as a fief. Under King Erik Eriksson (the Lame or Lisper) this office was occupied by a remarkable individual. Birger Jarl was a descendant of the Sverkers and had the good sense to marry the king's sister. While on a crusade in Finland, which he began in 1249 to secure his hold in the southwest part of the country, he got word that Erik had died and that his own infant son had been chosen king (Vlademar I of Sweden) establishing a new line of Swedish kings:

> 1250–1275 .... Vlademar I (Birgersson)
> 1275–1290 .... Magnus I of Sweden
> 1290–1318 .... Birger of Sweden (Magnusson)
> 1319–1364 .... Magnus II (Eriksson)
> 1363–1395 .... Albrekt of Mecklenburg

Birger Jarl returned home to find he was regent of the throne. He held two of the reigns of power in the nation. The nobility, as well as the Germans, could see this might be a problem and began raising an army to eliminate this concentration of power. Birger with his experienced troops, which he had led in Finland, combined with additional levies from supporters in Sweden met the allies at Herrevads Bridge in 1251. Defeating the enemy force, Birger Jarl put to the sword all opposing nobility and any competitors that might threaten his son as the new king.

To counter the German threat, Birger negotiated alliances with Norway and Denmark in 1254 and 1257. To cement the relationships, he married his daughter, Rikissa, to the Norwegian heir, Häkon Häkonsson, and his son Vlademar to the Danish princess Sofia. Later he married Mechtild, widow of the Danish king Abel. He further tried to curb German commercial influence over Sweden by establishing trade agreements with King Henry III of England and making treaties with Lübeck and Hamburg.

Birger Jarl changed the law and tax system to strengthen the central government. In the Viking era each area of the country was obligated to supply a certain number of men to serve on ships. Birger converted this service obligation to a tax giving the crown an income to support itself. His legal reforms strengthened allegiance to the king and doubled penalties for crimes against women, the church, the things, and the home. He moved against the practice of killing for personal revenge, a destructive practice dating back to Viking days and clan allegiances.

As jarl of the Mälar District, Birger had recognized the strategic importance of a particular island formed by the steadily rising land. At the point where Lake Mälar flowed into the Baltic there were two streams discharging the lake's fresh water into the sea. Between these two outlets was a rocky island from which access to the lake could be controlled. As soon as Birger Jarl gained power in 1250 he began constructing a fort on this island, but his vision went further. In his treaty with Lübeck in 1252, he granted the German merchants customs and tax free status to trade at this site and allowed traveling merchants to be subject to German law. However, any person who settled there would fall under Swedish jurisdiction and be considered a Swedish subject. He made provisions for a city on this site, with one-half the council to be German. Thus, Stockholm was born.

Germans from Lübeck flocked to the new city. It quickly became the commercial center of northern and central Sweden. Although Germans made up 35 percent to 40 percent of the population and dominated trade, Birger Jarl was able to maintain political control. Stockholm never became a member of the Hanseatic League. The Germans secured a commercial advantage in central Sweden and Birger Jarl built his city.

Upon Birger's death in 1266, the nobility saw to it the powerful office of jarl was eliminated. Vlademar became king in fact as well as in name, but proved to have a weak personality. He first got in trouble by having an affair with his wife's sister, a nun who came for a visit from Denmark, which produced a child. To obtain forgiveness, Vlademar made a pilgrimage to Rome where he pledged fealty to Pope Clement IV. His penitence was to raise a tax on his Swedish subjects that would be paid directly to Rome.

Vlademar had three brothers who used this tax levee as an excuse to rebel. Aided by Denmark, they defeated Vlademar in battle. The dethroned king fled to Norway. Magnus, next in line, became king. Eric died. Bengt, the third brother, was made duke of Finland, the position being vacant since the elimination of the office of jarl.

Magnus I (Ladulås) had many of the qualities of his father. He made some concessions to the German merchants, but maintained control of Stockholm. He turned back a drive by Visby Hansa merchants to take over all of Gotland. Magnus advanced Sweden's political position by negotiating new treaties with Riga and Lübeck, and arranged family marriages to neighboring kingdoms. He consolidated crown power by marrying kin to Swedish nobility and ruthlessly putting down a rebellion, executing the conspirators.

Magnus codified many of the laws, particularly those dealing with land ownership (the important Magnus Eriksson Land Law). It was in his reign that knighthood was established along with the associated frälse (freedom from taxation for providing heavy cavalry to the king). Church properties were also exempt from taxes which laid more of a burden on the remaining landowners. Society became even more stratified with the creation of other titles, *hertig* (duke), *drots* (vice king), *kansler* (chancellor), and *marsk* (marshal). Swedish society was becoming a complicated hierarchy of rank and privilege, taking on some of the trappings of feudalism.

Magnus extracted a promise from the nobility and the *Thing* that upon his death his oldest son, Birger, would be anointed king. In 1290 Birger, at ten years of age, received the crown. A younger brother, Erik, was made duke of Sweden and the other brother, Valdemar, duke of Finland. Birger would marry the Danish princess Märta and Erik was promised to Ingeborg, the daughter of Häkon, king of Norway. This three way division of authority was certainly a recipe for intrigue and political chaos. To make matters worse all of the brothers seem to have been somewhat unbalanced.

The only stable personality in the picture was the regent, Marshal Torgils Knudsson. He campaigned successfully in Finland, taking the western part of Karelia and building a fortress at Viborg which would become key in Sweden's defense of her possessions against Novgorod. In 1306, however, the three brothers combined to get Torgils executed. They then went after one another, Norway backing the dukes, and Denmark, the king. The power struggle seesawed back and forth. The dukes imprisoned the king and queen, then were forced to release them.

Erik's union with the Norwegian princess produced a son, Magnus, which Birger saw as a threat to his line. In 1317 he invited the dukes to a banquet, after which he had them thrown into the dungeon. The treacherous act came to be known as the Nyköping Banquette. This was too much for the Swedish people. They rose up in rebellion and assembled an army to overthrow their king. The army finally took Nyköping a year later, but not before Erik and Valdemar had died of starvation. Birger fled to Denmark where he died in 1321.

In 1319 King Häkon died leaving his son, three-year-old Magnus Eriksson, heir to the Norwegian throne. That same year Magnus was also elected king of Sweden at Mora Meadows. For the first time Sweden and Norway were under the rule of one monarch. Complicating things, Magnus's mother arranged a marriage between the king's sister, Eufemia, and Albrekt of Mecklenburg. What seemed to be a good political move at the time would later become a problem for Sweden and a disaster for Magnus. Events, at first, unfolded in the new king's favor. The king of Denmark, Kristofer, found himself in financial trouble and was looking for relief. By the Treaty of Varberg (1343) Denmark ceded Scania (Skåne, Halland and Blekinge) to Sweden for 34,000 marks. Magnus was, thus, the ruler of an empire that included Sweden, Norway, Finland and Scania. With the last came the fertile Skåne coastal lowlands, the thriving city of Mälmo and at least partial control of the Sound which could be used to tax ships passing between the North Sea and the Baltic. Sweden seemed to be once more in a position to take control of her own destiny becoming the leading power of northern Europe. But problems soon developed.

Raising the 34,000 marks for the latest acquisition put a terrible tax burden on the population. Again, the exempt lands of the nobles (frälse) and Catholic Church properties came into play. At the same time the Black Death devastated Sweden in the late 1340s, reducing the population by one-third. The plague sapped the energy and spirit of the people. Cities were decimated. Lands lay uncultivated. Churches were filled with bodies, then abandoned. The country was on the verge of collapse.

In the meantime, Denmark had recovered under a new king, Valdemar (Atterdag) and now regretted the loss of the Scanian lands. The Hanseatic League was suspicious of Sweden's control of the Sound and worried about her increased power. The Swedish nobles, meanwhile, were searching for a way to regain power. With all these factions about to pounce on the country, Sweden's empire would have a short life. Magnus, in an attempt to gain more control over Sweden, turned Norway over to his son Häkon in 1356. His other son, Eric, who was to inherit his father's Swedish throne, decided he couldn't wait and joined the nobles in a rebellion.

This was the opportunity Valdemar had been waiting for. He invaded Skåne where the inhabitants joined him, having more allegiance to Denmark than to Sweden. He also attacked Gotland, but here the going was a bit tougher. He was able to defeat the farmer-fisherman militia of the island, inflicting horrific slaughter. Valdemar followed up this victory with a campaign of extermination and devastation reducing all of the island except for Visby. He could not take the port city with its stout fortifications and Hans-German defenders. Finally, Valdemar settled for a large ransom from the city and called off the campaign. The havoc he wrought on the island destroyed its prosperity. Centuries of rich farming, fishing and trade extending back to before the Viking age were ended; the island would never again reach a high level of affluence. It would slide into anonymity. Sweden and Denmark would fight over her and pirates would use her harbors as bases to raid the Baltic Sea. Gotland would never again be master of her own destiny. By the late fourteenth century the Hanseatic League and Teutonic Knights had gained control of the unfortunate island.

Eric died in 1359 leaving the nobles without a champion. They looked around for another to lead them against their king and found Albrekt of Mecklenburg, the son of Magnus's sister Eufemia. Twenty-year-old Albrekt and his father, the Duke Alberkt, arrived off the Swedish coast with a German fleet carrying soldiers and adventurers. Magnus gathered his troops along with soldiers sent to him by his son Häkon, king of Norway. The Swedish king mounted a stout defense but in the end was overwhelmed by the combination of German forces, Swedish nobility and the Hanseatic fleet. Magnus was taken prisoner by the Mecklenburgers, who proceeded to take control of not only the central government but the provinces as well. Then they began the systematic takeover of the large estates. Too late the nobles realized the mistake they had made inviting in the Germans.

Next the Hanseatic League turned on Valdemar Atterdag. After a two year war they forced Copenhagen to surrender in 1370, acceding to Hanseatic demands. The Hansa seized the Skänian fisheries and fortified ports securing free and open passage through the Sound for all Hanseatic ships. Sweden was reduced to the status of occupied state. The Hanseatic League was at the height of its power, wealth and influence.

The nobles, finding themselves dispossessed, joined the peasants in a war against the oppressive German foreigners. There was little they could do, however, without outside help. They appealed to Norway and Häkon responded, invading Sweden with a Norwegian army. Picking up support from both commoners and nobles as he crossed the countryside, he arrived outside Stockholm with an army that the Mecklenburgers could not defeat. A compromise was negotiated. Albrekt would retain the crown, but the nobility would be restored their estates and the provincial governments would be returned to Swedish control. However, before the conditions of the agreement could be carried out, Häkon died (1380). Once more at the mercy of the Germans, the Swedes cast about for a new champion and found one in Häkon's seventeen year old son Olov. The Norwegian heir would be the figurehead and rallying point, but the real power would be exercised by his mother, Häkon's wife. The widow Margareta would prove to be one of the most remarkable women in European history.

2. The Kalmar Union

Margareta was the daughter of Valdemar Attardag, king of Denmark. At the age of ten she was given in marriage to Håkon, king of Norway and son of Magnus Eriksson, king of Sweden. The marriage was not consummated for six years. The intervening time was spent with her Swedish foster-mother, Mareta Ulfsdotter, daughter of Saint Bridget. This was Bridget of Uppland, canonized in 1391, founder of the Bridgettine Order, who recorded her revelations in the widely read *Revelationes Celestes*. She was the most famous Swede of her day. From her foster mother, Margareta gained a thorough religious education and close contact with the Swedish people and nobles. Her intimate association with all three courts and royal families gave her unusual access to internal and external affairs of state, commerce and the military. She seems to have taken advantage of her position.

Margareta was religious, disciplined and intelligent with boundless energy. Her father said of her that she was an error in nature — she should have been created a man instead of a woman. Her main protagonist, King Albrekt, nicknamed her Kung Braklös (King Trouserless). She was said to be the perfect mistress of the art of diplomacy and statesmanship. She seemed to know instinctively what was politically attainable and when. Combined with these talents were a sincere Christian faith; she took the Vadstena Monastery, creation of her foster grandmother, under her wing and supported it as long as she lived. Margareta was, without question, one of the great monarchs of European history.

At seventeen Margareta left Sweden to live with her thirty year old her husband, King Håkon of Norway. She moved to Akerhus Castle, just outside Oslo. In 1370 she gave birth to a boy, Olov. At first she ran only the household, but with the king absent most of the time on tours of the country and military campaigns, she gradually assumed more and more power in local politics.

Then, in 1375 her father, Valdemar, died. Margareta rushed to Denmark to try and secure the throne for her son. It would be a difficult task. The Mecklenburgers were already there with a compelling case. Their candidate, Albrekt, was the grandson of Valdemar and Duke Albrekt. What's more, the Germans were in a strong military position, having Sweden on the Danish northern border and Mecklenburg on her southern frontier. But all this proximity was just what worried the Danish nobility. They could see themselves becoming a Mecklenburg fief as had happened to Sweden. Margareta was quick to take advantage of these concerns and received the backing of most of the nobility. She then turned to the Hanseatic League, which had its own doubts about Mecklenburg's rising power in their region of influence, and made agreements with them. Outmaneuvering the Mecklenburgers, she was able to get Olov named future king of Denmark.

In 1380 Håkon died, leaving the Norwegian throne vacant. Margareta hurried back to

Norway to ensure Olov would be heir to this throne as well. Again she was successful. Her son was now the future king of two Scandinavian countries. Margareta turned her attention to Sweden, the home of her youth.

She renewed contacts with the Swedish nobility and to them Olov looked like the rallying point they needed to throw out Albrekt and the despised Mecklenburgers. She negotiated with the league again. Using their fear of Albrekt's power, she gained control of the forts in Skåne. She was in the midst of negotiations with the Swedish nobility when the seventeen year old King Olov took sick and died, throwing Scandinavian politics into chaos.

Two thrones were now vacant and the scramble for power began all over again. The Danes were once more faced with having a Mecklenburg prince for king, a prospect they did not relish. They considered, instead, breaking all the rules and customs of throne succession. Margareta was savvy, capable and far preferable to the Germans. They made her regent of Denmark and gave her the responsibility for selecting the next king. She was in fact, if not in name, monarch of Denmark.

Norway came to the same conclusion and made the same arrangement. To ascend the throne of both countries, Margareta selected her niece's son, Eric of Pomerania, then seven years old. This was a calculated choice leaving her mistress of both countries for a good long time.

In Sweden, meanwhile, Albrekt was initiating another campaign to consolidate his hold over the country, which meant gaining control of the nobility. They were forced to act or be crushed. Following the example of the other two Scandinavian countries, the Swedish nobility drew up a document appointing Margareta "all powerful lady and rightful mistress" of all Sweden. This included the right to select the country's next king. The nobility pledged fealty to Margareta, turning over all castles and fortresses under their control, creating a civil war.

Albrekt brought in an army from Mecklenburg and Margareta fielded an army of Danes and Norwegians with such Swedish contingents as were able to join the force. The decisive battle was fought on the flats east of Falköping in Västergötland on February 24, 1389. Legend says that the heavily armored German knights' horses foundered on the swampy ground, allowing the more lightly armored Scandinavian cavalry with their smaller horses to outmaneuver and defeat them. Though Margareta's general was killed in the battle, the Scandinavians won the day. Albrekt and his son were taken captive. It would require more than a year for the Swedes to retake all the castles in the country, but the reign of the Mecklenburgers in Sweden was ended.

The significance of this battle should not be underestimated. It was the turning point for Sweden and all Scandinavia in terms of the influence of the German states over the region. German merchants had controlled Baltic commerce and, in the case of Sweden, the government. German states now dominated the entire southern and eastern Baltic coast except Finland. Had Margareta's forces not prevailed, all Scandinavia might have succumbed to German vassalage. Though it would be some time before these countries would themselves control the region, the tide had been reversed and, gradually, the Scandinavian countries began to direct their own destinies.

Margareta was now ruler of an empire that stretched from Lake Ladoga, next to Novgorod in the east, to the west coast of Greenland. She purchased Gotland from the grand master of the Teutonic Order in 1407. Margareta arranged the marriage of Eric to Philippa, daughter of Henry IV, king of England. She ruled the domain she had created until her death in 1412. Under the united kingdoms, which became known as the Kalmar Union because of a treaty negotiated at that Swedish fortress, there was not a blending of cultures. Each country retained its own individual laws, institutions, and customs. It was a confederation for mutual protection, mainly from the Germans, which ushered in a period of peaceful co-existence. Although there were many treaties and marriages to cement the union, there were still three separate nations held together by a skillful ruler and a common threat. When either of these elements was removed the union would begin to fall apart.

With the death of Margareta, Sweden entered a century of political turmoil. Instead of a monarch of the union, the rulers became progressively more Danish in viewpoint, treating Sweden as an occupied territory. At the same time Sweden was evolving as a country with a rising spirit of nationalism replacing the old medieval system of allegiance to a person or office. The Swedish people began to develop a consciousness of themselves as a nation. To the south the Hundred Years War between France, England and Burgundia alternately smoldered and raged contributing to the instability further north. In Scandinavia the Kalmar Union, with all its promise of peace and prosperity, its effective defense against outside influences, particularly German encroachment, began to disintegrate. But it would not go easily.

Eric of Pomerania had been the king of the Kalmar Union for several years when Margareta died in 1412 though she had wielded the real power. Still, Eric was established with the reigns of government firmly in his hands and no complications from a possible challenger. His first act was to consolidate his grip on the union by taking an extensive tour of his domains, even visiting Finnish territories. He quickly stirred up trouble, however.

His first problem was with the church in Sweden. He continued a practice, started by Margareta, of appointing his own church officials and priests, then going directly to the Holy See in Rome for conformation instead of letting local church authorities make the selections. Swedes had hoped local control would be returned to them after Margareta's death. Secondly, he outraged the nobility by appointing Danes and Germans as lawmen (judges), bailiffs and provincial officials. By Swedish law these offices were to be filled by Swedes, providing jobs for the nobility and petty nobility.

Thirdly, he raised the ire of foreign factions. His ambition was to make the Baltic his domain. He already held Norwegian, Swedish, Danish, Finnish and Pomeranian coasts, why not the whole Baltic? The Teutonic Knights had finally been defeated — by Polish and Lithuanian forces at Tanneburg (1410) — and were in decline. It seemed a good time to strike. Eric put together an army and attacked at Schleswig, but was driven off by the determined Count of Holstein. This aggression alerted the Hanseatic cities to his potential danger and they became wary of his purposes.

Eric exacerbated the situation by fortifying the Öresund narrows (the Sound) and taxing non–Scandinavian shipping passing through the channel. He also imposed restrictions on the Skåne markets in an attempt to limit Hansa control. The league retaliated by blockading various Scandinavian ports. All this crippled Swedish commerce. Stifled trade combined with the heavier taxes to support Eric's military adventures caused resentment against the union to run high in Sweden.

Eventually, distrust and anger spilled over into an open revolt headed by Engelbrekt Engelbrektsson, a petty noble from Dalarna. He led his Dalesmen against Eric's Danes and the tough, independent miner-farmers earned a reputation as ferocious fighters. Engelbrekt was eventually murdered and become a legendary hero in Swedish story and song, a symbol of Sweden's fight for independence. Gradually leadership passed from commoner and petty noble to the aristocracy, the great families (the magnates). Soon three peasant armies commanded by men from Sweden's nobility marched though the country taking royal lands and fortifications. Eric sailed to Stockholm with a fleet. A battle was averted and compromises were made. Eric sailed home only to continue the same oppressive practices. Soon he was faced again with a rebellion in Sweden, but now he had other problems as well. A revolt broke out in Norway and even the Danish Council turned against him.

In 1439 the Danish *Rigstag* removed Eric as king and replaced him with his nephew, Christopher of Bavaria. This was an unusual move by Denmark where the hereditary right of kings was honored, unlike Sweden where kings were elected. Sweden followed Denmark's lead and in 1442 Norway did the same. Long live King Christopher.

But he did not live all that long, dying in 1448. The joint kingship was thrown into confusion once more. Karl Knudson, *dots*, administrator of Finland and one of the architects of the last rebellion, quickly raised an army and marched on Stockholm. He was elected king of Sweden and was accepted by Norway also. But Denmark chose Christian of Oldenburg as king. The union was at least temporarily split. Eric, the deposed union king, conspired with the nobility of Norway to obtain Karl's removal in that country and have himself reinstated. Intermittent wars broke out between the three kings and Karl was forced to raise taxes in Sweden to pay for the armies.

The situation under Karl was turning out to be as bad as that under Eric. Rebellion broke out in Sweden once again. This time the revolt was led by Jöns Bengtsson, the archbishop of Sweden and a member of the powerful Oxenstierna family. Karl was defeated and fled to Danzig. Jöns appealed to the other two countries to find a solution to the constant warfare that had resulted from having three independent kings. A new Kalmar Agreement was reached in which Christian would be king of the union, but all three countries would maintain a certain autonomy. Before long Christian was scheming to consolidate his hold over the three countries and taxes were raised to pay for troops. Jöns again rebelled and this time he was joined by Kettil Karlsson, a bishop from the Vasa family. Together they raised an army and attacked the royal troops stationed in Sweden. Christian's forces were defeated and driven out of the country. Karl was invited back to rule as king. He returned old, tired and sickly. In 1465 he withdrew to Finland. Although he kept the title of king, Jöns and Kittel effectively ruled Sweden.

The two aristocratic families ruling Sweden were challenged by a third, the Axelsson family. Originally Danish, they had established large land holdings throughout Sweden and Finland. They built a political organization among the nobility. Supported by enough of the nobility and well organized, they took over key government offices, displacing the Oxenstiernas and Vasas until they controlled the government. They recalled Karl Knutsson as a figurehead and ruled in his stead.

In 1470 Karl died and Axelsson's cover evaporated. King Christian quickly took advantage of the confusion to reinsert himself into Sweden. He built up his military while at the same time he sent feelers out for support in Sweden. Meanwhile, a new leader of the growing Swedish nationalism emerged. Sten Sture was Karl Knudson's nephew, executor and guardian of his young son. He was married to an Axelsson. Thus, he inherited support from the nationalistic movement Karl had been part of and from the powerful Axelsson family with connections in both Sweden and Denmark. Sten himself was a man of means, having inherited family holdings in southern and central Sweden. In operating these estates and associated businesses, he had gained experience in farming, commerce and politics.

Sweden was now clearly divided into two parties. Among the unionists, supporting King Christian I, were the Uppland peasants and much of the nobility including the Vasas and Oxenstiernas. The nationalists (though they would not have called themselves such), led by

Sten Sture, were backed by the Axelsson, Trolle and Posse aristocracy, the provinces of Västergötland, Östergötland, Småland and the miners from Dalarna. The Bergslag (the mining area) followed Nils Sture (not a close relation of Sten's) and was in the Sture camp. A notable exception to the Vasa allegiance to the Danish king was Johan Vasa, grandfather of Gustav Eriksson (Gustav I of Sweden).

Christian raised a new army of Danish knights supported by German and Scottish mercenaries. He ferried his force to Stockholm where he was joined by the Upplanders and troops of some of the Swedish nobility. The Danish king laid siege to the city. Sten Sture had gathered an army among the nationalists, mainly from southern and central Sweden. He advanced on Stockholm to engage the Danish army. One of the bloodiest battles in Swedish history took place at Brunkeberg outside Stockholm (now part of the city). On the morning of October 10, 1471, Christian took up a good defensive position on Brunkeberg Ridge outside the city walls. Sten Sture drew up his Swedish army in front of the ridge. Christian had about 5000 men, mostly professional soldiers well armed and armored. Against this formidable force, Sten had a mostly peasant militia with little armor and only the essentials in arms. The one effective weapon they carried was the crossbow. Where the weapon of the English infantry was the longbow, in Sweden it was the crossbow. Every farmhouse had at least one, used for hunting and home defense. So Sten's footmen were expert with this device and could make it devastatingly effective.

Sten led his troops up the slopes of the ridge into a withering barrage of arrows, bolts, bullets and shells. They advanced up the hillside taking heavy losses. Finally, the bowmen, crossbows, arquebuses and field guns were too much and the surge ebbed and then receded. The Swedes tried again, but were once more repulsed by the determined Danes. Sten next led an attack on positions around Klara Monastery at one end of the ridge where the ground was more even. Christian, seeing the heavy hand-to-hand combat, took reinforcements into the melee. It was a close pitched battle with the outcome in some doubt. But then a force of Stockholm militia commanded by Knut Posse broke through the siege lines around the city and attacked the Danish flank. At the same time Nils Sture with his Dalesmen, having swung around the other flank, attacked the Danes from the rear. Christian was surrounded and fighting on three sides. The Danish lines begin to collapse and the unionists were forced to cut their way out. The retreat turned into a rout as Christian's troops headed for the port and their ships. A bridge was sabotaged by the Stockholm citizens and collapsed as troops fled over it. A number of men drowned or were captured including the Danish commander. Uppland troops who made it to the ships were forced overboard by the mercenaries and many drowned. Some 500 Danish knights perished in the battle. Perhaps as many as 2000 Swedes fighting with Sten Sture died, but the battle was a total Swedish victory. The Danish occupier was driven from Swedish soil.

Trading on his popularity after the Battle of Brunkeberg, Sten Sture gathered in the reigns of authority in Sweden. He was named national administrator and effectively ruled the country for the remainder of Christian I's monarchy. However, with Christian's death in 1481, the question of Swedish rule was raised anew. A three way struggle ensued between the new Danish king, Hans, the Swedish National Council and Sten Sture. At the same time a new and ominous threat was developing in the east; a nation once dominated by Swedes was reconstituting itself and would soon loom large on the Swedish frontier.

The old Viking era empire centered at Novgorod and Kiev had become the Empire of the Eastern Slavs separated from the rest of Europe by a Lithuanian kingdom stretching from the Baltic to the Black Sea. The Eastern Slavic Empire had close ties to Byzantium, but had lost contact with Western Europe.

This empire was smashed by the tidal wave of the Mongol invasion in the 12th and 13th centuries. Kiev, along with the rest of the Eastern Slavs, was crushed and reduced to a near slave state. Novgorod, however, escaped the Asian inundation, providing a buffer between the Mongol invaders and Sweden's possessions in Finland, as well as the Hansa cities, Teutonic knights and Brothers of the Sword domains along the eastern Baltic.

In the late 13th century the Mongol tide began to recede, giving local Russian principalities the opportunity to reassert themselves. By 1300 Moscow, beginning as a city-state, was able to establish its independence, although it still paid a tribute to the Tartar khanate further east. It grew to the status of a duchy (1400) by subjugating its neighbors and by 1465 had extended its territory to Lake Onega in the north, to the Don in the South and to the Volga in the east, resembling the Russia of modern times.

By 1488 Russia had absorbed Novgorod completely, placing itself in direct competition with Sweden for territories in Finland and along the eastern Baltic. Sweden suddenly had a new, aggressive and very powerful neighbor.

In 1493 Denmark formed an alliance with Russia and Tsar Ivan III attacked the Swedish stronghold of Viborg on the Finnish frontier. He was repulsed, but the ensuing war provided the opportunity Hans had been waiting for.

With Sweden distracted in the east, King Hans sent Danish armies north from Skåne into Småland and the Götlands. He loaded another army onto his fleet and sailed north, dropping anchor in Stockholm Harbor. Sten was forced from office by a combination of Danish military might and a jealous nobility acting through the National Council (*Råd*). Hans gained control over Sweden and the Kalmar Union was restored in 1497. But by 1501 Sten Sture had made a comeback, inducing the Råd to renounce Hans as Swedish king and reinstate him as national administrator. And so the power struggle continued with first one side gaining the upper hand, then the other.

In 1504 Sten Sture died but was immediately replaced by a family member, Svante Nilsson. When he died (1512), he was replaced by Sten Sture the Younger. The next year King Hans died and was succeeded by his son Christian II, and the three-way struggle continued.

Two new factors were introduced along with the Russians and the nationalist movement. First was the declining power of the Hanseatic League. The Scandinavian countries were beginning to recover a bit of their own commercial power and the Dutch were providing more and more direct competition to the league.

The second factor was the increasing role the Catholic Church was playing in politics. The situation was brought to a head when Gustav Trolle, the Swedish archbishop, was given orders by the pope to create a four hundred man force to protect church properties.

At issue was a castle north of Stockholm called Stäke which the church said it owned. Sten claimed it for the Swedish government with the argument that to have it held by anyone else was a threat to the capital. In 1517 Sten, backed by a council of representatives from all over Sweden (a primitive *Riksdag*), captured the castle and burned it to the ground. Then he deposed Gustav Trolle and selected his own archbishop of Sweden. These actions challenged church authority beyond anything tolerable; these were crimes calling for a punitive response.

The church in Rome condemned the acts and encouraged the Danish king to punish the Swedes. Christian II assembled another force and sailed for Stockholm. He landed his army and was met by Sten and his Swedes. The Danes were repulsed at the Battle of Braenukyrka and a truce was arranged. As part of an agreement, Christian insisted on being given six hostages, persons of importance, before he left the country. One of these hostages was Gustav Eriksson of the old and great family of Vasa. Christian sent the prisoners to Denmark, then weighed anchor.

Church officials decided a stronger response was required if it was to be effective. The Holy See excommunicated Sten Sture and placed the country under interdict. Christian could now mount a crusade with full church backing and the authority to not only punish Sweden, but also to conquer and completely crush the country. He raised a serious mercenary army and sent it into Sweden from Skåne. Sten Sture assembled his Swedish forces and moved south to meet the Danes. They collided at Åsenden on New Year's Day 1520 at the Battle on the Ice. The Swedes were defeated and Sten Sture was wounded. He died a few days later. Danish forces swept north, meeting little resistance. Only the great castles held out. Christina Gyllenstierna commanded the stronghold at Stockholm and Ann Bielke held Kalmar Castle, the two strongest fortresses in the country. Christian now crossed over from Denmark and marched north from Skåne with additional forces smashing any remaining resistance. He left troops at Kalmar to invest the castle, then marched on to Stockholm to lay siege to the capital.

Christina held out until September with the help of commoners who had come to her aid, but in the end Christian's Danish troops and German mercenaries were too much for the unskilled defenders and the castle surrendered. On November 4, Christian II was crowned king of Sweden not by election (the Swedish law), but by heredity. The traditional three day banquet followed. Archbishop Gustav Trolle was reinstated and immediately charged the Sture supporters with heresy for acts of violence against the church and its representatives. Christian seems to have been only too willing to carry out the prescribed sentences.

On the night of November 7, the coronation festivities were halted, and Christian summoned his captains to his quarters in the palace. They were given orders to arrest a number of patriots: clergymen, nobles and burghers (men and women) on a list compiled by Gustav Trolle. The next day a council headed by Trolle pronounced the death sentence on two bishops and fourteen men of the Swedish nobility. The infamous Stockholm Blood Bath or Stockholm Massacre began on November 8, 1520. The coffin of Sten Sture (the Younger) was dug up and his body burned along with many of those executed. Messengers were sent to Finland and leaders there connected with the Sture party were also executed. Other nobles, burghers, and citizens on Trolle's list were imprisoned and several women of the aristocracy were sent to prison in Denmark. Christian II must have thought he had stamped out Sweden's nationalism for some time to come. The leaders were dead, the commoners thoroughly cowed and the remaining nobles were on his side with fear to keep them there. The Danish occupation of Sweden was secure and the Kalmar Union resurrected under Christian II's rule.

An independent and powerful Sweden was a dim memory of her distant Viking past. The country had traded foreign German overlords for a Danish tyrant. The Sture party's dream of a Sweden that could stand on its own among the European nations appeared to be finally and irrecoverably crushed. The Swedish-Finish territory seemed destined to be a satrapy in the Danish Empire along with Iceland and Norway.

3. *Gustav Vasa's Rise to Power and Swedish Independence*

In late May 1520, a merchant ship owned by Henrik Möller of Lübeck quietly slipped into the port of Kalmar on the coast of Småland in southern Sweden. There was nothing particularly remarkable about this German carrack except that in addition to its cargo, the vessel carried one singularly noteworthy passenger. Stepping onto Swedish soil for the first time in almost two years was Gustav Eriksson Vasa, just 23 years old, the son of Swedish noblemen, soldier, hostage, and most recently, escaped prisoner. After sojourns in Danish captivity and as a refugee in Germany, the young aristocrat was finally home.

Shouldering his way along the crowded wharf, Gustav would have picked up the voices of foreign merchants, Kalmar burghers, farmers and stockmen from Småland speaking his native Swedish. The familiar language, dress and customs must have been comforting and reassuring. He might have encountered a Danish customs official or one of the king's bailiffs. These the young Vasa would have avoided for he had come to loath his country's oppressors; the yearning for freedom and independence swelled within him and the fire of rebellion burned in his soul. Surely there were still others of his countrymen who shared his vision of a Sweden free of Danish domination. These were the people he was looking for, the men and women he had to find.

But the Sweden he was returning to was far different from the country he had been forcibly removed from in 1518. With the defeat of the Swedes at Åsunden and the death of Sten Sture, organized resistance against the Danes had collapsed. Christian II's forces had swept through the country establishing Danish rule in all the provinces. For Sweden, the Kalmar Union had become a Danish occupation, and Christian II was projecting his power into every corner of the realm.

The Swedish people had not succumbed entirely, however. Guerrilla bands still operated in forests and remote areas. Many of the castles had not yet fallen, two of the strongest being commanded by a couple of remarkable women. Kristina Gyllenstierna, Sten Sture's widow and Gustav's aunt, held Stockholm with a garrison of Swedish commoners. Anna Bielke, backed by mostly Germans, commanded at Kalmar Castle, the key to Sweden and its strongest fortress. The spark of nationalism had not been completely extinguished; if Gustav could rally the countryside as the Stures had been able to do, independence might yet be achieved. But the refugee, mingling with his own countrymen for the first time in months, was an unknown quantity. At twenty-three, Gustav Eriksson might be just another aristocratic ne'er-do-well. Even if he possessed purposeful determination, did he have the energy, talent, even genius the struggle for independence would require? His young life to this point had shown no particular promise.

Born May 12 in either 1496 or 1497, Gustav was the oldest boy in a large family of the Swedish nobility. The family estate, Rydboholm, was located in Uppland where his father, Erik Johansson, was a knight and councilor of state.

Erik was a hard and violent man. Records show he killed a Stockholm man for cutting trees on Rydboholm and fishing in its waters. He is also supposed to have looted the Frösunda rectory near his estate and later plundered a church on one of the Mälar islands. For these crimes he seems to have gone unpunished. Perhaps family connections provided protection.

Both Gustav's mother, Cecilia, and father were related to noble families in Sweden and Denmark. The Vasa family was one of less than a couple of dozen families in all Sweden that would have been considered true European nobility, the great magnates of Sweden. These families had extensive land holdings scattered throughout the country to protect against agricultural disasters in any one area ruining them. Gustav's grandfather had married the sister of Sten Sture the Elder so the family had direct connections to the capital. As a child Gustav was sent to the court of Sten Sture the Elder for formal education. At thirteen he attended the University of Uppsala where he learned Latin, some German, and became expert in both written and spoken Swedish. After four years he left school. His departure spawned the first of many stories about this semi-legendary figure. At least two versions of his exodus are told. According to one, Gustav just got tired of a particularly boring instructor, marched up to him and stabbed a knife into a schoolbook, then announced that the teacher and his school could go to the devil. Another version has it that Gustav was struck by his professor who was Danish. Gustav stormed from the class in a rage, implying the young Vasa developed a hatred for Danes early in life.

There followed a few years in which Gustav participated in the operation of the family's extensive farm holdings. He learned management skills and developed a knowledge and interest in agriculture which he maintained the rest of his life. Again his father sent him to the Sture court, this time the court of Sten Sture the Younger who was now chancellor of Sweden. He learned fencing, the soldiering arts, politics, court intrigue and international affairs. From Hemming Gadh, the shrewd old court advisor, he learned the Machiavellian style of statecraft.

At the time Sture the Younger fought the Danish king in 1515–1517, Gustav experienced his first taste of battle. When Christian II struck again in 1518, Gustav was a flag bearer at the Battle of Braenukyrka conducting himself with conspicuous bravery, it is reported. At negotiations following the battle, Christian demanded hostages. Gustav, Hemming and four other important Swedes were turned over to Christian who promptly imprisoned them and sent them back to Denmark, to Kalø Castle in Jutland. Here, under minimum security conditions, the prisoners were cajoled, enticed, threatened and bribed into changing sides. All succumbed except Gustav. Hemming Gadh would even become an advisor at the Danish court.

Gustav, however, resisted all persuasions until, in 1519, he got a chance to escape. Seizing the opportunity, he fled Jutland. Disguised as a cattle driver, he made his way to the German city of Lübeck where he renewed some old acquaintances, made new friends and contacts among the German princes and city burghers. In particular, Karl Konig, the Stures' old benefactor, and the merchants Henrik Möllar, Markus Helmstede and Herman Iserhal would become his close friends.

These merchants and burghers were much concerned with rising Danish power. Christian's tightening grip on Sweden would give him an empire stretching from Finland to Iceland with a secure hold on the strategic Danish Sound and associated, unrestricted toll privileges. In addition, his connection to the Hapsburg queen of the Netherlands, his sister, could mean more competition from the Dutch for the North German trading cities (Lübeck, Hamburg, Bremen, Wismar, Rostock, Stralsund, Danzig) in particular and the Hanseatic League cities of the Eastern Baltic (Riga, Reval, Narva) especially.

Lübeck and the other German Hanseatic League cities would have much preferred dealing with an independent Sweden than a united Danish empire. Lübeck, in particular, felt it could influence, if not dominate outright, a weak Sweden, gaining special trade status and access or even a monopoly on her rich resources. With the leading force in the Swedish drive for independence, Sten Sture, dead, the Lübeck city council was looking for a replacement they could support. Gustav, they knew, was untested, but he talked a good fight and was at least worth the price of the passage back to Sweden to see what he might accomplish.

Thus, Gustav Eriksson stepped off the Hanseatic carrack onto familiar soil determined to reinvigorate the Swedish nationalist movement. The task before him was certainly daunting, but there were the rebel bands and the great castles still resisting. Gustav's greatest impediment to organizing a unified resistance movement seemed to be Christian II himself, who had landed, earlier in May, with an army of mercenaries in Danish Scania (Skåne, Blekinge and Halland) and was marching north in a mopping up operation. The last strongholds were being taken and the guerrilla bands hunted down. Danish bailiffs and sheriffs were being positioned in the towns and parishes to enforce Danish law and collect taxes for Christian.

Kalmar Castle was cut off by Christian's Danes and Gustav's message of nationalism would not sell well to the mostly German garrison anyway. So Gustav went to work trying to arouse the small landowners who populated the rocky and forested province of Småland. This frontier territory, whose clans were interrelated with the families of Danish Skåne and Blekinge, refused to participate. These farmers had for generations encouraged cross-border marriages and signed numerous local agreements between border clans promising to keep the peace in spite of their central government's declarations of war. None of this proved very effective of course. So for the last hundred years, armies and raiders had plundered estates and small farms alike on both sides of the border. The wars of the Christians and Stures were just the latest conflicts causing homes to be burned and crops destroyed. The call to arms by Gustav seemed to be just one more invitation to further devastation and these nearly impoverished people had had enough. He would raise no army in this quarter.

Gustav's attempts to build a revolution in Småland only served to alert the Danes as to his location and activities. Now instead of being a nameless passenger emerging from a Lübeck merchant ship, he was a hunted fugitive with a price on his head. Worse off than when he arrived, he left Småland and made his way to Södermanland, one of his ancestral homes, where he could find friends and relatives willing to hide him and where, perhaps, the prospects for revolution were better. However, here too he found people exhausted and battered from the long struggle against the Danes. It was in Södermanland he received word of the surrender of Stockholm Castle and the nobility's agreement to accept Christian as Sweden's king. The traditional three day coronation celebration was being arranged to be followed by another festival. Gustav was offered amnesty to attend the celebrations.

He must have pondered the offer and his prospects. His attempts to foment rebellion in southern Sweden had come to nothing. The people, it seemed, didn't have the stomach for more fighting. The guerrilla movements had been destroyed; Kalmar and now Stockholm castles had capitulated. Christian was in the capital and had won over the nobility and burghers with what appeared to be reasonable terms — Sweden would be ruled under Swedish law, the king to be elected according to Swedish tradition. If he were to attend, he would see again his mother and father and others of his family. Yet Gustav could not bring himself to trust the Danish king; he had had first hand experience at the court of this foreign prince. He rejected the invitation and remained in hiding. His misgivings would soon be substantiated.

Christian had laid a trap. In one symbolic gesture Swedish law and tradition were swept aside; Christian, Gustav learned, had claimed the crown by heredity, dispensing with the agreed to election. Then the young fugitive received word of the almost incomprehensible Stockholm Bloodbath. As reports filtered in he learned that his father, two uncles and a brother-in-law had been beheaded. His mother, grandmother, three sisters and his aunt, Sten Sture's widow, were imprisoned. This must have been stunning and devastating news. With one stroke, Christain had wiped out a good share of Gustav's family and then proceeded to confiscate all of his family's property and titles. Bereft of much of his family, the young former nobleman was also penniless and now the price on his head was raised and the manhunt intensified.

Gustav reacted with strengthened resolve. He left Södermanland disguised as a peasant woodcutter, so the story goes, and headed for Dalarna. With ax in hand, he trudged the paths leading north constantly on the lookout for the Danish jacks intent on running him to ground. Here, fact becomes mixed with myth elevating a historical figure to a legend. He has become a combination George Washington and Robin Hood. Like the chopping down of the cherry tree and splitting the arrow at the archery tournament, some tales are folklore only, but others, like the crossing of the Delaware and the collection of money for the ransom of King Richard, are based on fact.

As the story goes, Gustav arrives in Dalarna in his disguise as a *bönder* and seeks refuge in the house of an old Uppsala classmate, Anders Persson, but he does not reveal his identity. He is taken in as an indigent traveler, fed and boarded until work can be found for him. But within a day or two a servant girl notices a gold embroidered collar sticking out from under his homespun outer garments. She reports the discovery to her master who confronts his guest. Gustav has to admit his identity whereupon Anders asks him to leave, fearing Danish retribution should the association be discovered by authorities.

Once again Gustav is on the road, homeless and friendless. He next seeks shelter at the farm of one Arent Persson of Ornäs. The old acquaintance graciously invites Gustav to stay, dines him and puts him up for the night. When all is quiet, the friend sneaks out of the house and makes for the local Danish bailiff. The mistress of the house, Barbro Stigsdottor, becomes suspicious, however, wakes Gustav and helps him escape through the privy just as twenty Danes rush through the front door. While the king's men are searching the house, Barbro helps Gustav harness a horse and he escapes with his friend's horse and sleigh over the frozen Lake Runn.

Gustav next looks for asylum with a priest and old friend, Jacob Jacobsson of Svärdsjö, where he works as a field hand helping with the grain threshing. One afternoon, Jacob is observed by one of his maid-servants holding a towel for Gustav while the nobleman is washing himself. The girl spreads the story and Jacob advises Gustav he should make his escape before he is discovered. Jacob sends him to a friend, Sven Elfsson in Isola, a royal forest warden. Though never betrayed by Sven, Danish soldiers and informants are searching everywhere and break into the warden's house while Gustav is warming himself in front of the fireplace. Sven's quick-thinking wife grabs her bread spade and smacks the nobleman while yelling at him to quit staring at the strangers and get outside to the threshing loft and get to work. As the Danish jacks can't find anyone hiding around the place, the king's men eventually leave. But the authorities are getting too close, Sven hides Gustav in a load of hay and heads for Lake Siljan. Danish soldiers patrolling the roads run their spears through the hay wounding Gustav, but do not discover him.

Another version of the story has Gustav actually being discovered, cornered and partly crippled by Christian's soldiers at Isola. Though wounded in the knee, he fights his way out and escapes. In both stories Gustav makes his getaway by hiding in Sven's hay wagon. The Danes, systematically searching all the roads and paths in the area, find blood from Gustav's wound on the trail the hay wagon has taken. The Danes run down the hay wagon in short order. Meanwhile, Elfsson has also observed the occasional blood spatters on the roadway and when he hears the charging men-at-arms on his trail, he quickly takes his knife and cuts the leg of the horse pulling the wagon. The Danes arrive to find Sven ministering to the bleeding wound on his horse's leg. After running spears through the hay a few times, barely missing Gustav, the Danes leave and Gustav escapes.

Sven eventually gets Gustav to trustworthy friends in Rättvik who hide him under a fallen pine tree for three days until the soldiers move their search concentration elsewhere.

Recovering from his wound, Gustav then takes the risk of coming out in the open and speaks to the bönder of Rättvik. The peasants are friendly but cautious, and spies quickly report Gustav's presents to Danish bailiffs.

Gustav moves on to Mora, one of the more populous areas of the province. Again Danish jacks are hot on his trail and Gustav is forced to hide in the cellar of one Matts Larsson of Utmeland. Soldiers enter the house looking for him, but Matts' wife, who is brewing Christmas ale, rolls a large brewing vat over the cellar trap-door, hiding the entrance. Again the Danes are foiled and Gustav escapes.

True or not, these exiting stories have lent Gustav's legend a wild west flavor and were once a staple of Swedish elementary education just as American school children once read the stories of Abraham the rail splitter, and the discouragement and desperate hardships of Washington at Valley Forge. As in America, these charming stories have become a casualty of realism and historical correctness.

What we do know is that Gustav intended to rekindle the nationalist movement in Dalarna. He knew the farmers and miners of this mining region were a tough lot. It was the workers from the iron bogs, copper mines and smelters that had so often provided the backbone for the struggle against Danish domination. With no large aristocratic estates or major church holdings, it was a region of fiercely independent farmer-miners, who owned their own land and bowed to no one. It was here that the Stures had found their strongest and most dependable supporters in their battles against the Danes. Gustav delivered fiery speeches of nationalism to assemblages of these people. He reminded them of better times past, of Swedish heroes and Swedish pride in past accomplishments. He appealed to their patriotism and sense of nationalism. He pointed out wrongs suffered under Danish oppression, heavy taxation, the interruption of trade so vital to this metal-producing region. He spoke to individuals and to groups throughout the province, but especially the peasants in Rättvik and finally Mora.

Though he swayed many, he could not quite produce the spark that would ignite the flames of revolution. The Dala people were drained by the years of constant war with the Danish crown, wars in which they had contributed so much, especially to the Stures' struggle of the last few years. They had pledged fealty to Christian and were not ready to go back on their word. Finally, with the king's men getting ever closer and even the Dalesmen resisting his best efforts, Gustav left the province. His only option now was flight. So, in the closing days of 1520, Gustav made his way west, away from the Danes and from the Sweden he loved, toward Norway, perhaps to search for support there.

But now Christian II made two strategic blunders. With all his successes, he must have felt secure in his control of the country. The leader of the nationalist movement, Sten Sture, was dead. Christian had imposed Danish rule and law in all the provinces, taken the last castles, stamped out the last embers of insurrection and literally decapitated the body politic of the country. He was in control.

His first mistake was to open Swedish trade to the Dutch, breaking the near monopoly the Hanseatic League, particularly Lübeck, had had on Swedish imports and exports. Christian did have ties to the Netherlands, but mainly this was an attempt to reduce the power of the Hansa cities. This act insured German support for whatever rebellion might still be smoldering in Sweden.

His second blunder was his decision to extract one last pound of flesh from the defeated Swedes. On his way back to Denmark he would make a grand tour of his Swedish domains. This was an old Swedish tradition for a new ruler of the country. But instead of a celebration, as was the tradition, Christian made it a march of brutal oppression. Heavy taxes were collected en route, fines levied against all families suspected of having a hand in the resistance. All weapons were to be turned in on pain of losing a hand or foot if found in noncompliance. Individuals and whole families who were known to have fought the Danes were summarily executed. Scaffolds were erected in the towns and cities Christian passed through so he could witness the hangings firsthand. Even monks and children were not exempt from the hangman's noose and the headsman's ax.

This final act of retribution was too much for the people of Mora. They had had enough of this cruel, foreign tyrant. They were ready to rise up and rid themselves of the vicious despot, but who would lead the fight? The one Swede preaching revolution and ready to head such a struggle had been turned out by these same people. It was decided they would appeal to Gustav to lead them. Two of the fastest cross-country skiers of the area, Engelberkt and Lars of Kettilbo, were selected to track Gustav down and try to convince him to return and lead a war of liberation. Legend tells how these two swift skiers raced from town to town inquiring after Gustav. Finally, they overtook him in the desolate wastes of the Norwegian frontier near the town of Salen.*

Gustav returned to Mora to find a corps of determined men ready to follow him. In a month he had a small army of 400 Dalesmen. From their ranks would come the leaders of his peasant army, men who would stay with him through the bitter struggle ahead. Anders Persson, Mans Nilsson, Ingel Hansson and Peder Svensson would prove loyal comrades through the coming triumphs and setbacks.

By February 1521 they were ready and they struck the mining headquarters of Stora at Kopparberg. The raid netted them money taken from the fines and taxes collected by the royal bailiff, and supplies from the German merchants including cloth which they used to make banners giving the little army a sense of pride and esprit de corps. The show of force resonated with the tough miners, and men of the copper district joined Gustav's revolt.

Next they raided the Dalarnian capital of Falun, capturing the provincial seal, an ax and bow. Now they could issue official proclamations that would carry the weight of the province giving the revolutionary group at least a particle of legitimacy. More men of the

Each year, in Sweden, this event is commemorated with a ski race from Mora to Salen, some 57 miles. It is the longest public cross-country ski competition in the world and everyone is welcome to participate, not just elite athletes, making it an event of the people, altogether fitting as a memorial of this turning point in Swedish history.

province flocked to Gustav's banner. With an army of over 1,500 men, Gustav moved into the southern part of the province.

Meanwhile Christian II had left Sweden. After his heavy handed and bloody royal tour, he had returned to Denmark, handing over control of Sweden to Archbishop Gustav Trolle, the German Didrik Slagheck (appointed bishop of Skara), and Jöns Andersson Beldenak (now bishop of Strängnäs) as administrators of the country. Christian left only a small force of soldiers to garrison the castles, disbanding his army of mostly German mercenaries to save money. Supervision of the fortresses he placed in the hands of trustworthy Danish and German commanders: Stockholm to Henrick Slagheck (brother of Didrik), Kalmar to Soren Norrby (also captain of Viborg on Gotland), Stegeborg to Berent von Melen and Vesterås to Henrik von Melhen.

From Denmark he went on to the Netherlands for three months to promote his dream of a Scandinavian trading company that would break the Hanseatic League's power once and for all. Unfortunately for him, Christian was not very careful about keeping his activities secret and soon the Hansa was well aware of his plans. Now the league cities, particularly Lübeck, resolved to do what ever was necessary to stop Christian. It was beginning to look like Sweden might provide the means to that end.

Besides the insurrection in Dalarna, there were now revolts in Småland and several places in Västergöttland and Östergöttland. With Dalarna completely committed to him, Gustav had set out for Hälsingland and Gästrikland in the north to bring them into the war. But in Stockholm Christian's proxies were finally beginning to move. They were able to put together an army of some 6,000 men, a conglomerate of Danish regulars, German, Scottish and even French mercenaries. The interim regents decided the Dalarnian outbreak was the most dangerous and had to be stopped first. Jöns Beldenak and Gustav Trolle led their army into the field to smash this peasant uprising. The Dalesmen, under Peder Svensson since Gustav was in the north, met the Danish army at Brunback's Ferry on the Dal River.

There is a story that Jöns, upon finding himself facing a larger force, asks Peder how many men the Dalesmen can field. He is told that the province can muster 30,000 men if needed. Jöns expresses some surprise that such a large number can even be fed in the field. Peder responds that his men can live on only water and bark bread if necessary. The astonished Dane is supposed to have said, "People who can live on bark and water can be subdued neither by the devil nor by any man. Brethren, let us speedily take ourselves hence."[1]

In any case the Danish professionals armed with guns and modern weapons were routed by the peasant army armed with bows and arrows, crossbows and farm tools. The retreating soldiers were overwhelmed and cut down by the aroused bönder, eliminating the only major field army available to the Danish regents. Christian's supporters had lost their army, but still held the major castles.

The victory brought more men flocking to the Vasa banner and when Gustav returned from the north, he had a 15,000 man army to lead. In April 1521 he invaded Västmanland and attacked the fortified city of Västerås, garrisoned by Christain's soldiers. The city fell and this region also joined Gustav.

Next Gustav marched to Stegeborg Castle and it capitulated. Christian's commander of the fortress, Berend von Melen, came over to Gustav's side without a fight. Von Melen was a German soldier of fortune, a type common in sixteenth and seventeenth century Europe. In U.S. history we have Miles Standish of Plymouth and Capt. John Smith of Jamestown who were examples of the soldier for hire serving many masters. Von Melen was of this ilk and decided Sweden offered better prospects than Denmark, at least for the moment. Gustav gave

ARMS AND ARMOR OF THE 16TH CENTURY

Used by Danish Troops and Gustav's Mercenaries

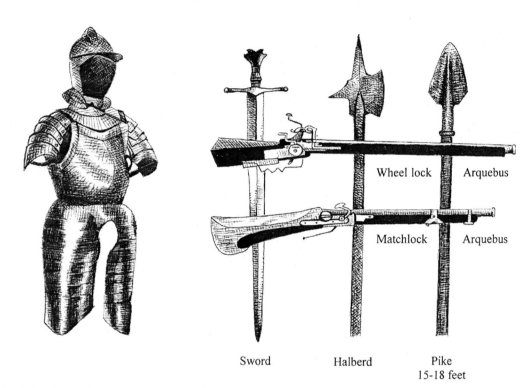

Wheel lock   Arquebus

Matchlock   Arquebus

Sword   Halberd   Pike
15-18 feet

Used by Swedish Peasant Militias

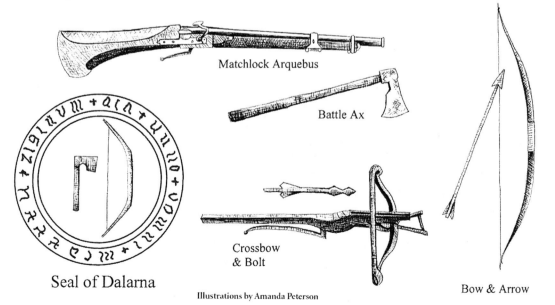

Matchlock Arquebus

Battle Ax

Seal of Dalarna

Crossbow
& Bolt

Bow & Arrow

Illustrations by Amanda Peterson

him command of an army in the field and appointed him one of his inner circle military advisors.

By May Gustav had pushed into Uppland and driven to the sea providing access to supplies from the outside world, notably from his old friends in Lübeck. From this position of power, he now made overtures to Gustav Trolle, as a Swede, for a peaceful conclusion to the war. Trolle reacted by sending a raiding party into Uppland to try and capture or kill this Vasa upstart. The attempt failed, but it put the rebel leader on notice that this would be a contest to the death. It would be Gustav Vasa as head of a free Sweden or his head on a Danish spear.

On the coast Gustav made contact with Sture privateers who were already plundering Danish shipping in the Baltic. He enlisted their help in attacking supply ships feeding Danish forces in Stockholm and elsewhere along the coast.

Gustav's leadership was now accepted by most of the rebel groups in all parts of the country. By the end of May, Gustav had taken Uppsala, and stood at the gates of Stockholm. His fame and power spread nationwide. He sent one of his lieutenants to Finland and soon this region, except for the castles, was in his hands. By midsummer he was the recognized leader of the Swedish nationalist movement. On August 23, 1521, Gustav Eriksson Vasa was named regent of Sweden at a national meeting in Vadstena. Though he now had been given official sanction to rule Sweden by the Swedes, Gustav's position was far from secure.

Gustav's power base was the common people, the farmers, miners and townspeople whose volunteers had made up, by far, the majority of his army. The nobility, however, was divided in its support with the opposition being led by Ture Jönsson Tre Rosor of Västergötland and Bishop Brask of Linköping. To gain their support, Gustav was forced to give Jönsson a role in government appointments and decisions of state. To Brask he granted guarantees of church property and privileges. Strengthening his political position with the nobility was necessary because militarily Gustav still had much to accomplish.

With his peasant army Gustav had been able to conquer the countryside, towns and small fortifications, but the great castles were still in Danish hands including Stockholm, Kalmar, Älvsborg and Viborg. In addition, his citizen army wanted to go home. These men had crops to harvest, families to attend to and property to ready for winter. Gustav, perhaps because of his understanding of agriculture, let many of these men return to their homes. But with his popularity at a peak throughout the country, he was able to find replacements and more. However, to take the castles, Gustav needed professional soldiers skilled in siege operations.

In 1522 Gustav approached Lübeck with a shipload of silver and promises of special trade privileges, but the city council hesitated in becoming involved officially, its relations with Christian and his brother-in-law, the emperor, being somewhat strained. So a consortium was formed consisting of Gustav's friends and contacts made during his 1519 stay in the city. The consortium provided the rebel leader with arms, supplies, 750 trained German mercenaries and a fleet of ten warships, all on credit. This gave Gustav something the Stures had never had, a navy of warships. He already had privateers, as the Stures had had, but these were merchant ships merely used to attack other merchant ships. Sea battles were still fought as infantry contests at sea with small arms used while one ship closed with another. The attacking ship would try to grapple itself to the defender and board that ship with soldiers. Warships, though often converted merchantmen, were constructed with forward and aft castles built high so that soldiers could shoot down on the other ship. Also, their sides were raised to prevent boarding by enemy ships and to facilitate boarding from the warship. The Stures had never had this kind of naval advantage.

With these reinforcements, Gustav increased pressure on the castles and cleared the seacoast so he could receive outside supplies in large quantities. He laid siege to Stockholm Castle, driving Christian's supporters from the city and occupying many of their buildings.

Encouraged by these successes, the Lübeck City Council accepted Gustav's silver and promises of preferential trade relations, delivering a second fleet of warships which promptly captured a Danish supply fleet headed for Stockholm Castle. With the Swedish coastal shipping secure, the Lübeck City Council insisted the fleet be used to attack Denmark. The ships approached Copenhagen, but were outmaneuvered by the Danish admiral, Soren Norrby. The invasion of Denmark by sea was lost, but the battle on land was going better for Gustav, putting Christian on the defensive.

Gustav had made Berend von Melen commander of an invasion of Danish Skåne and Blekinge, increasing Christian's problems. Making his situation more precarious, the Danish king had antagonized Frederick of Holstein, his neighbor to the south, and he eventually made enemies of the holy Roman emperor, Charles V, his brother-in-law. Christian had also pushed through legislation favorable to the burghers and peasants. Finally, he had made contact with the Lutheran movement in Germany. This was too much for the Danish nobility and clergy who now rose up and forced their king out of Denmark. Christian fled to the Netherlands with his family and part of the Danish fleet. Frederick of Holstein was placed on the Danish throne with potential claim to both Norwegian and Swedish crowns. Sweden was threatened anew by a Danish king.

The Swedish council moved quickly. On June 6, 1523, the Estates of Sweden gathered at Strängnäs, a town on Lake Mälar in central Sweden. Represented were the miners, burghers, peasants, the council (5 clerics and 25 laymen) and much of the nobility. Berend von Melen was present as were two other Germans, official observers from Lübeck, Berut Bombouwer and Hermann Plonnies. The occasion was indeed momentous and pivotal in Swedish history. The business at hand was to be the election and crowning of Gustav Vasa as king of Sweden.

There seems to have been some hesitancy on the part of Gustav at the last moment. Perhaps it was show, maybe he did have some qualms about his abilities, or was he extracting some last commitments and promises from particular members of this austere group? Whatever the hold up, after conferring with members of the council and the Germans, Gustav preceded with the election. He was proclaimed king by acclamation and took the oath of office that day. The following day the coronation was sealed with a solemn Mass celebrated in the Cathedral of Strängnäs.

Over the next four days Gustav worked out the terms of his agreement with Lübeck. Sweden would limit its foreign trade to Lübeck, Danzig and other Hanseatic cities as Lübeck dictated. Trade with other countries was forbidden. There would be no Swedish navigation through the Danish Sound or Belts. Lübeck and the other Hansa cities would be free of all tolls, customs and tariffs in Stockholm, Kalmar, Söderköping and Åbo. The Hansa cities could trade directly with Swedish nobility and clergy. In short, Gustav had agreed to allow Lübeck and the other Hansa cities control over Swedish foreign trade without tax or toll. This circumstance, Gustav must have realized, could not be tolerated for long.

Cut off by land and by sea, the German mercenary garrison of Stockholm Castle surrendered on June 17, having been given the promise of safe conduct out of Sweden. Gustav entered the Swedish capital on the 24th as master of the nation. Frederick withdrew his claim to the Swedish throne; the Kalmar Union was finally and irrevocably dissolved and Sweden's independence, for the moment at least, was secure.

It was indeed a new age. While Gustav was battling for Swedish independence, the *Vic-*

toria, the last of Ferdinand Magellan's original five ships, sailed into Sanlucar de Barrameda Harbor, completing the circumnavigation of a world only guessed at a decade earlier. Hernando Cortes finally subjugated Tenochtitlán, one of the great cities of the world and capital of the Aztec Empire. The gold, sought so long by the conquistadors, would finally begin to flow into Spanish coffers. Francisco Pizarro was organizing his first expedition to Peru where he would conquer the Incas, rulers of the largest empire on earth. Gold, silver and emeralds from the New World would make Charles V, king of Spain and ruler of the Hapsburg domains including the Netherlands and Holy Roman Empire, the richest monarch in the world. Wealth from the Americas would change the economies of Europe.

Earlier, England and France had joined Spain in the search for a route through or around the new land mass blocking quick passage to the rich orient being exploited by Portugal. The Cabots and other explorers probed the coast of North America. The riches found were not gold or spices, but fish. The Grand Banks off New Foundland proved to be the richest fishery in the world. These early explorers and their regular voyages across the Atlantic to take advantage of the Grand Banks laid the groundwork for colonies soon to be founded along the North American coast. Among those vying for territory here would come adventurous Swedes and Finns.

Closer to home and of more immediate import to Sweden was the religious controversy brewing in Germany. As Gustav rose to power in Sweden, a Saxon monk was being excommunicated by Pope Leo X. He was then called to face the German princes, nobles, and clergy at the Diet of Worms by Charles V for his heretical writings and teachings. Martin Luther's dissent was about to create a storm of conflict in Germany. This storm would inevitably crash on Sweden's shores and eventually draw her armies back into Germany's religious maelstrom.

4. King Gustav I

By the end of June 1523, Sweden was a fully independent country, ready to claim her place among the rising European nationalist states and Gustav Eriksson Vasa was her recognized sovereign. It would fall to him to shepherd this still medieval country into the Renaissance, a period generally considered to have begun about 1500. Gustav had proven himself a leader and revolutionary, but could he build a nation?

Real Swedish independence, which the Stures had striven for, had been achieved. But to accomplish the rest of the Sture ambitions for Sweden would be at least as difficult, that is, a strong, secure central government and a sense of nationalism among the Swedes.

The challenges were formidable, but in Gustav the Swedish people had a king of considerable talent and determination. His triumphant entrance into the shattered Stockholm was not the end of the struggle, there would be merely a shift in focus. The common enemy had been defeated, at least temporarily, but now there would be enemies both from within the country and without. To the east, Swedish Finland was threatened by the rising power of Muscovite Russia which had driven to the Finnish frontier with its conquest of ancient Novgorod in 1488. The key to the region's defense was the Swedish fortresses of Åbo, Olofsborg, and especially Viborg on the Gulf of Finland. Across the gulf, along the eastern side of the Baltic, the domination of Semgallen, Ingria, Estonia, Livonia and Kurland by the German Livonian Brothers of the Sword was weakening. Control of the area would soon be contested by Poland, Russia and Lithuania, as well as native princes. Lithuania itself was in decline having lost much of its medieval empire that once stretched from the Baltic to the Black Sea. Further west along the southern coast the Livonian Brothers' confederate and kindred order, the Teutonic Knights, who ruled Prussia, were collapsing, producing opportunities for Poland and some of the surrounding Germanic states. All this instability meant potential problems for Swedish holdings in Finland and for her Baltic commerce.

Finland itself consisted mostly of sparsely populated forests. However, the coastal areas had received significant Swedish immigration until a substantial peasant population thrived there. Little of the area had fallen into the hands of either the church or the nobility. Indeed, 96.4 percent of the land was held by taxpaying peasants, revenues important to the crown.

To the north of this populated area stretched Österbotten along the Bothian Gulf, an area with only a scattered population of Finns and recent Swedish settlers along the coast. At the head of the gulf and northward ran Lappland, an expanse of wilderness with ill-defined frontiers between Russia, Norway and Sweden, a region inhabited by nomadic reindeer herders owing allegiance to no king or country.

South of Lappland, on the west side of the Gulf of Bothnia, ran Västerbotten, a remote area with the far northern port of Umeå. It stretched south to Ångermanland where Sweden

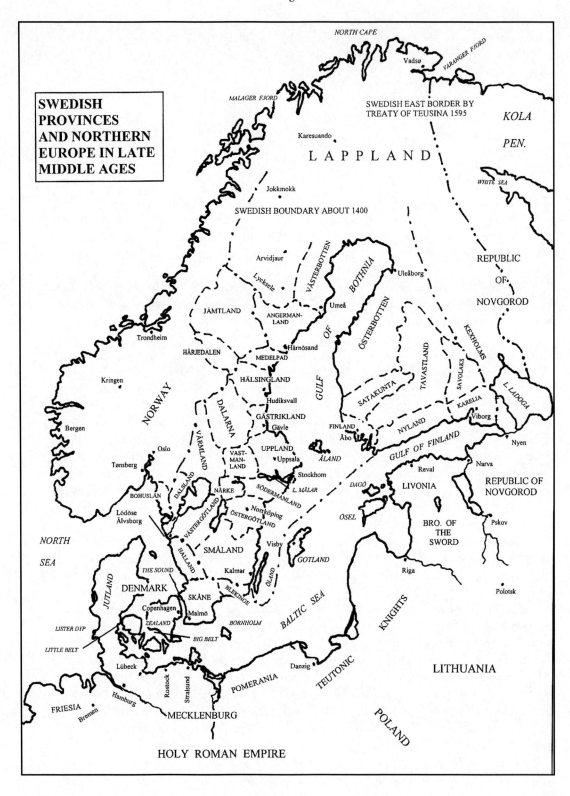

SWEDISH
PROVINCES
AND NORTHERN
EUROPE IN LATE
MIDDLE AGES

narrowed to less than fifty miles at its border with more southerly Medelpad and remained tenuously slim through Hälsingland. Finally, at Dalarna and Gästrickland with its important Bothnian Gulf port of Gävle, Sweden spread to a respectable land area. Here was Sweden's ore producing region, the Bergslag, encompassing the provinces of Dalarna, Närke, Värmland and much of Norrland.

Mining in Medieval and early Renaissance Sweden was not the deep tunnel or open pit operations we usually associate with mining today. A better analogy might be the 1800s gold miners of Western United States. Individuals, maybe two or three, digging into bogs or hillsides, perhaps excavating a shallow tunnel into a mountain to follow a particularly rich vein of ore. These men were peasants working on their own or minor gentry with a few servants that could be employed in the digging, washing and the refining of the ore. The products of their efforts were traded in local markets for grain from the plains provinces. They hunted and fished to supplement the earnings made from the earth to pay their taxes and sustain their families.

Three minerals were mined in the Bergslag. Of overriding importance to Gustav was the silver produced at Sala. This intrinsically valuable metal was especially liquid with ready markets in almost any quarter. Production had started in 1510 and remained significant during Gustav's reign, but fell off by late century. Subsequent administrations tried to revive production, but after that the mines consumed more resources than they ever returned.

Copper from Kopparberg had been an important export since ancient times and continued to be a mainstay of trade with Lübeck via Stockholm. However, it was iron that was the real Swedish stock-in-trade. Since the beginning of the Iron Age in northern Europe, when the iron bogs of central Sweden were first tapped for their unglamorous but essential mineral, the Bergslag was famed for its production of particularly pure and malleable iron. The ore, wrested from the bogs, was slow smelted to produce pellets of *osmund* that sold for a premium in the German markets. By the late Middle Ages ore was also being extracted from rock in Utö (an island in the southern Stockholm archipelago) and Västmanland by a faster smelting method that produced a primitive pig iron.

Chief in the Bergslag was the province of Dalarna. Here, neither church nor nobility had acquired much land. These independent, tough-minded peasants had formed the backbone of the Sture resistance and had thrown in with Gustav Vasa to begin the drive to oust the Danes. Famed as crossbowmen, with their characteristic heavy bolt called a dalapilar, they formed the nucleus of his early peasant army. But with independence won, they also expected special consideration in maintaining a free and open trade for their products and representation in the new government. Their outlook was less parochial than the people of other regions because of their dependence on trade, and they were closely tied to Stockholm economically and often allied with the city politically. A valuable friend in war, they could also be real trouble if not appeased at the end of the fighting.

On the borders of the Bergslag were the densely populated provinces of Uppland, Östergötland (with its grain producing plains), and pastoral Västergötland. Västergötland, like rocky, forested Småland, paid most of its taxes in butter and in oxen that could be driven to markets at ports, Stockholm, or the Bergslag. Butter and hides from these provinces were important Swedish exports.

At the southern end of the peninsula Sweden was cut off from the sea by Danish Scania. Three provinces made up this part of Denmark occupying the mainland: Halland, Blekinge (with its close family and trade ties to Småland) and rich, grain producing Skåne. Only a narrow strip of Swedish territory touched the North Sea and that was along the Göta

Älv River between Danish Halland and Norwegian Viken. At the mouth was the port of Lödöse, protected by the Swedish fortress of Älvsborg. There were three passages from the Baltic to the North Sea, the two straits (the Belts) and the Sound between Zealand and Skåne. In ancient times east-west trade had passed across Jutland at Hedeby, but as boats improved, the route shifted to the Little Belt. With bigger boats, the Great Belt had become the main waterway. But the larger cogs needed the deep channel of the Sound to travel back and forth between the Baltic and North seas. The Danish crown derived a great deal of revenue from fees and tariffs charged merchant ships passing through these waterways, money the king used to finance his armies and navies. He could even stop traffic from a country or port altogether if it served his purpose.

Sweden was, therefore, locked out of access to the west except for the single port of Lödöse and it was not connected by water highways to her major export areas. Sweden, quite literally, faced east, not west. Even here Danish control of Bornholm and German rule of Gotland gave them the ability to disrupt and harass Swedish maritime trade. Gustav's options were severely limited and none available without a price. Although Frederick had given up, at least temporarily, his claim to the Swedish throne, the Danish nobility still looked upon Sweden as a Danish possession and there was Christian II lurking about in the courts of Europe pressing for help in regaining his Scandinavian empire.

Sweden of the Middle Ages never fully implemented the feudal system, certainly not to the extent that its more southerly European neighbors had. In England, France, Germany and even Denmark, this hierarchy of fealties built on a foundation of an almost slavelike serf population was pervasive. But in Sweden over half the peasants owned their own land, paying no rent to lords, only taxes to the crown. Still many of the trappings of feudalism had been adopted.

At the top of the pyramid was the king, although the position was not hereditary. By tradition, approval, even selection, was made by the Råd, the Council of Nobles. The king held his position, if not by consent of the people, at least by consent of the aristocracy.

Next in line were the great magnates (*län på tjänst*) who owned many estates scattered about Sweden and often in Denmark and Norway as well. Thus, they protected themselves from crop failures in any one region, solidifying their family's hold on their social and economic positions. The Vasas, Oxenstiernas, and Posses belonged to this class. These families moved from estate to estate so as not to place too much burden on any one of their holdings. They were members of the Råd and actively involved in national politics as a way to look after their interests. By carefully husbanding their resources, they could build considerable surpluses in the form of butter, hides, grain and, if holding lands in or adjacent to the Bergslag, osmund iron. A share of these surpluses was traded for family and estate needs, cloth, spices and arms. Materials of war were needed to defend their own lands and to answer the call of the king for as much as a company of men-at-arms. The remainder of their surpluses was invested in land.

Earlier monarchs had built and maintained fortress castles at strategic locations around the country. The development and steady improvement of artillery increased the cost of maintaining defensible castles and fortresses to the point that their administration was often turned over to these great nobles in exchange for rights to the associated fief lands. The very largest of these grand nobles, perhaps a half dozen, even had their own ships with which to carry goods, mostly to the markets of Danzig and Reval.

In 1396 all agricultural land was designated as either frälse (free of taxes) or *ofrälse* (tax paying land). A petty nobleman might get his land redefined as frälse land if he supplied the king with an armed horseman in time of war, but for the most part, land retained its designation. Since peasants working ofrälse land were already paying a tax to the king, the noble landowner could not levy much of a rent on the peasant. These terms were established by law. If the noble used his own servants to work the land, then he had to pay the taxes on the land. Peasants on frälse land, on the other hand, paid the noble a full rent. Thus, frälse land was much more desirable than ofrälse, as far as the landowner was concerned. There was bitter competition for this land when it came up for sale, not only amongst the nobility, but also between the nobility and the church. If the real estate was in a city, particularly Stockholm, burghers were added to the mix, making the acquisition of municipal land a three-way contest. Land was wealth and its pursuit was creating conflict between segments of Swedish society, particularly the nobility and the church.

Below the great magnates were the rest of the nobility with land holdings ranging from a single estate to a few in number. Some were members of the Råd. Many acted as judges at the provincial landsting or the county häradsting.

Barring confiscation of property by the king, as happened to the Vasas, or some catastrophic general series of disasters like war, famine and plague, the great magnates were fairly secure. This was not the case, however, for the general nobility. The dividing of family lands among sons over and over could reduce holdings, removing the noble to the status of petty noble or even peasant. A series of crop failures or devastation due to war might have the same effect, forcing a noble to sell land in order to sustain the family or meet his *rusttjänst* (levy of armed horsemen to the king). Thus, social mobility was another unfeudal-like characteristic of Medieval Sweden.

Below the true nobility were the petty nobles or gentry (*kngar*). The dividing line might be the rusttjänst and the holding of frälse lands. Petty nobles would not contribute the armed horseman, but did pay taxes, though this line was often blurred. With astute management and good fortune a petty noble might rise to the rank of true nobility, acquiring frälse property or building surpluses to the point where he could provide rusttjänst. It was from the gentry that the king usually obtained his local representatives, his bailiffs.

The distinction between petty nobles and taxpaying peasants was even more ill defined and often changed from generation to generation. These peasants were masters of their own land, which generally met their family's needs for sustenance and to pay the taxes. Taxes were usually paid in kind: butter, grain, cattle, furs, or the osmund of the Bergslag. Agricultural production was often supplemented by hunting, fishing, trapping or logging, products of the ubiquitous forests, lakes and streams of early Renaissance Sweden.

Finally, at the bottom of the social scale were the rent paying peasants. But even these tenant farmers had certain rights by law, making their lot better than the true serfs of central and southern Europe.

Paralleling the secular social-political structure was an ecclesiastic hierarchy. The Catholic Church in Sweden was headed by an archbishop appointed by the pope. In some cases nominations were made by the Swedish crown. However, the archbishop generally operated completely independent of the head of state and at times the two were at odds, as witness the Gustav Trolle scrap.

In Sweden, unlike most of Europe, bishops were to be chosen from recommendations from the crown and priests were to be selected by parish or county officials.

The church owned over one-fifth of the arable land in Sweden, more than the nobles, and was constantly buying more property in competition with the gentry and nobility. Once acquired by the church this land almost never came back on the market. In addition to rents and surplus products, the church also received tithings. Though much of this money from the people went to the Holy See in Rome, a sufficient amount was kept by the church in Sweden so there was seldom the resource squeeze that forced secular landowners to sell their property.

In some ways the archbishop, bishops, and abbots operated like the nobility, living in fortified monasteries and rectories, maintaining armed servants to guard their property and escort excursions through the countryside. There was the Bishop's Cavalry that gave the church a military option in resolving certain types of problems. This company of men-at-arms, last commanded by Bishop Hans Brask of Linköping, often ranged the countryside requiring maintenance from the peasantry. In terms of real estate, gold and silver, the church had more wealth than either the nobility or the crown. Much of the gold and particularly the silver was in the form of church and cathedral decorations, candlesticks, communion pieces and other church devices that the parishioners considered theirs, as part of the parish.

At the same time there were the priests, friars, monks and nuns at the base of the church hierarchy. For the most part these were hard working, sincere clergy with their devout flocks, parishioners who donated the tithes and offerings that built the churches and decorated them with paintings, tapestry, silver and gold objects. Parish churches in Sweden, by the end of the Middle Ages, were mostly constructed of stone or brick, replacing the earlier wooden structures that were subject to incineration every few years. They tended to be small and of unremarkable construction. Likewise, the interiors were usually simple, perhaps reflecting a simple, unpretentious congregation who, nevertheless, prized what decorations and precious items they were able to furnish their churches with.

Besides this feudal system of church, nobility and peasants, there was, in the Sweden of the early Renaissance, a governmental structure that had developed through the Middle Ages. At the county level, there was an assembly, sheriff, and administrator (*häradshövdingar*) combining executive and judicial offices. The officials were usually from the petty nobility, but all taxpaying peasants had the right of representation in the assembly (the häradsting).

The provinces acted much like independent states, exchanging emissaries and making agreements even with foreign provinces and governments. In the eleventh century, during a war between King Olof of Sweden and St. Olaf of Norway, Västergötland concluded its own peace treaty with Norway. In 1381 Skåne signed a peace treaty with Sweden during a Swedish-Danish war. Skåne repeated the act in 1434 and in 1436, concluding an armistice with Engelbrekt of Sweden in defiance of the Danish king Erik of Pomerania who was waging war with Sweden. Later, in 1505, the Smålanders of the Varend, More, Sunnerbo and Västbot counties signed a peace treaty with Blekinge during Svante Nilsson's war against King Hans of the Union. Apparently this was not considered treasonous as a copy was sent to Svente Sture's court.

Again the governors (*lagmän*) combined executive and judicial functions and were usually nobility, but as in county government, all taxpaying peasants could take part in the provincial assembly (the landsting). This was especially important because, by law, any new laws or new taxes had to be passed by the landsting.

At the national level the *Råd*, an assembly of nobility representatives, had been able to exert considerable influence through the late Middle Ages in selecting the king or regent and apply pressure on the crown. In 1441 the Råd forced Kristoffer to promise that no new members would be appointed to it without the body's consent. In 1457 Christian I was forced to agree that the crown would not acquire more frälse land. If additional support was needed a *herredag* might be called, that is a Råd with representatives from one or more of the other classes. Finally, the king, or regent, found he could dilute the power of the nobility by calling a meeting of all the Estates, an embryonic Riksdag. Christian II did this twice to reinforce his authority and Sten Sture the Younger called one meeting of all the Estates in 1517 to endorse his action against Gustav Trolle. So, by the early Renaissance the idea of a national assembly with representatives from all classes, except the church, was established if not practiced with any regularity.

To deal with this hodgepodge of a semi-feudal system and developing governments, Gustav had inherited a woefully inadequate civil government system. At the local level were the king's bailiffs. During the Danish occupation, Danes had filled this office, and it had been used successfully to gather taxes and maintain Danish control of county and provincial governments. Although Gustav had now turned these positions over to Swedish gentry, they were still looked upon by the peasants with suspicion and distrust.

The castles and associated fiefs were looked after by the great nobles, but the king reserved for himself certain high production fiefs, the larder-fiefs (*fatu-burslän*). And he always kept Stockholm Castle as the very symbol of throne and power. The royal court, that is the king's civil service, had traditionally been made up of trusted servants. If Gustav was going to create a strong central government, he would need to expand the number of these administrators, but he found a dearth of material. The nobles were not interested nor did they have the training. True, Sweden did have the University of Uppsula founded in 1477, prior even to the University of Copenhagen, however, education here was almost strictly ecclesiastic in nature. Little was available in terms of training for business or government. So Gustav was forced to turn to the clergy and foreigners to augment his administrative workforce.

The king did inherit a chancellor, two in fact. One was the old Sture personal officer. This was Peder Jakobsson Sunnanväder, who had escaped the Stockholm Bloodbath, being on a diplomatic mission in Danzig. The other, an office of the Råd, was, by tradition, the bishop of Strängnäs. Neither of these would be acceptable to the new king.

During the period of the Kalmar Union, Sweden had, in many respects, stagnated. Her industrial growth, political progress and mercantile development had all been stifled. A formerly vibrant and progressive people had fallen behind the rest of Europe. Early Renaissance Europe would certainly have considered Sweden backward, a country out on the fringe, geographically as well as developmentally, a nation of little consequence. Gustav Eriksson Vasa was about to set his people on a path that would change all that. True, he ruled a land without the great cities of his southern neighbors, without a large, highly developed class of tradesmen, burghers, merchants or a merchant marine. His realm was almost entirely agrarian. Still, it was not a nation without resources.

About half the land was arable, providing sufficient food for the people and supplying some surplus for trade. Grain was mostly barley, though rye was growing in popularity. Hard bread and salt-fish were the staples. Butter and hides augmented the export of copper, iron and furs. These were exchanged for cloth, beer and, most importantly, salt. Furs came from the great forests that touched all parts of Sweden. The forests also supplied lumber for fences and buildings, birch bark for roofing, fuel for home fires and smelting. There was game and in the event of crop failure, certain barks and mosses could be used as grain substitutes to make bread. This bark bread was a common staple and was made from the inner bark of the pine, oak and some other trees. It was stripped in the late summer, dried, and pounded into a flour. Though difficult to harvest and process, and not particularly appetizing, it did provide excellent nourishment and was a food source well into the 1800s.

Roads were poor, often impassable during periods of heavy rain or snow. However, as in colonial America, waterways facilitated transportation. Boats and barges plied Sweden's ubiquitous lakes and rivers in the summer, and sleighs and sledges traversed the winter ice.

Gustav's subjects numbered less than a million people with only about 5 percent living in towns and even these towns were tied to the soil. Generally villages were surrounded by a high wall with fields and meadows, belonging to its citizens, laid out around the town. Villages generally developed around ecclesiastic centers, in areas of dense population, or at major markets.

The only real city was Stockholm with perhaps six to seven thousand inhabitant, but could claim both burghers and merchants, and boast a class of craft and trades people. Perhaps half the houses and commercial buildings were now of brick instead of traditional wood. This was the main trade center between the Bergslag and the Hanse cities with copper traded primarily to Lübeck and iron going to both Lübeck and Danzig. It was also the nominal seat of government and featured Stockholm Castle, an impregnable citadel never taken by storm.

During his war of independence with Christian II, Gustav had sent forces into the Danish-Norwegian provinces adjoining southern Sweden causing the Danish king great consternation. Some progress was made in Blekinge, Halland and Viken, but for the real prize, the breadbasket province of Skåne, Gustav put together a serious force. Three thousand German, mercenary men-at-arms and a large contingent of Swedish peasant foot soldiers were placed under the command of Lars Siggesson Sparve and the German Berend von Melen. In January 1523 this army crossed the Lagan River from Västargötland into Skåne where no opposing force near its size existed. Yet within six weeks this expeditionary force was in full retreat, withdrawing back across the Lagan River. What had happened?

Von Melen claimed he had been stopped by the spring flooding of the rivers. The army was back in Swedish territory by the end of February, a little early for spring runoff. Actually, the invasion fell victim to the border people's peace treaties, in this case, the long-standing agreement between Skåne and Västargötland not to attack each other or aid those that did. The companies of Swedish foot from Västargötland refused to fight their Skånean neighbors. Border clans on both sides of the frontier collaborated in sabotaging communications and supply lines. Von Melen, whose heart may not have been in the expedition in the first place, pulled out giving Gustav one more defeat at the hands of the border people.

This failure did not, however, dampen Gustav's enthusiasm for his German general. As we've seen, he played a prominent role in Gustav's election and coronation at Strängnäs later that year.

In Stockholm, Gustav set about restoring the war ravaged city. The population of a few thousand had been reduced to a few hundred and most of the structures destroyed. Burghers, merchants and laborers were ordered into the city from other parts of his realm. Construction boomed and trade began to build to its former level of activity. However, the disruption of commerce due to the war was having its effects across the country. Exports of Bergslag metals had been interrupted. The importation of salt, necessary for the preservation of the fish, a staple all across Sweden, was slow in coming back. Gustav's rebuilding of Stockholm added to the huge debt to Lübeck. This, on top of a shattered economy, had brought about a debasing of the currency. These grievances produced smoldering resentment, especially in Småland and in Dalarna, a province also unhappy at not getting more consideration in Gustav's government. To exacerbate the situation Peder Jakeobsson Sunnanväder, former chancellor under the Stures, arrived from Danzig expecting a high place in Gustav's government, but was rebuffed and given the disappointing office of bishop of Västerås. He settled in Dalarna, combining forces with a Master Knut Mickilsson to lead a revolt already brewing there.

Gustav moved quickly to contain this new menace. Threatening and cajoling the Dalesmen, he was able to stifle the revolt. His old allies Mans Nilsson, Ingel Hansson and Anders Persson again stuck by Gustav and helped him quell the insurrection. The two leaders escaped to Norway, finding safe haven with the archbishop of Trondheim. The good archbishop, however, succumbed to Gustav's entreaties and returned the two men, thinking they would be tried by an ecclesiastic court. But Gustav wanted to make an example of the pair and had them tried by the Råd where he acted as prosecutor. They were found guilty and sentenced to death. According to Peder Svart, they were led into Stockholm, "clad in old threadbare tattered cloaks, riding backwards on famished horses, Peder Sunnanväder with a coronet of Straw on his head and a broken wooden sword by his side, Master Knut with a crosier of birchbark."[1] Both men were executed in the Stockholm public square.

There was still some mopping up to be done from the war with Denmark. The fortress at Stockholm had fallen when Lübeck had refused to resupply the defenders and the Danish-German garrison had been given safe passage out of the country, but Kalmar Castle, Sweden's strongest fortification, still resisted. Gustav turned to his German commander, Berend von Melen, to take the fort. Von Melen arrived at Kalmar Castle with a large force and threatened a siege, then talked the garrison into surrendering. Kalmar was taken in the name of Gustav and Sweden. As reward for all his efforts von Melen was given Kalmar County and Uppvedinge Hundred as fiefs and made counselor to the king. Gustav gave him his second cousin, Margareta Eriksdotter Vasa, in marriage, probably in the hopes of securing permanent loyalty from this soldier of fortune. If that was Gustav's intention, it did not work.

Von Melen immediately set about creating his own barony. He took over Kalmar County and used the fortress to guard it, putting his brother Henrik in command. He had the garrison and county officials swear fealty to him instead of crown and country. Gustav either was unaware of what was going on in Kalmar or turned a blind eye, for he next put von Melen in charge of an expedition against Gotland Island to root out Soren Norrby and his nest of pirates causing much damage along Sweden's Baltic coast.

During the Swedish war for independence Admiral Norrby, after defeating the Swedish-Lübeck naval force off Copenhagen, had set up headquarters on Gotland. From here he attacked Baltic shipping and raided the Swedish coast, acting more like a condottiere of the sea than a Danish admiral. This activity was becoming intolerable to both Gustav and the Lübeck merchants. Even after Christian's ouster in favor of Frederick, Norrby continued to support the former Danish king, making him a danger to both Gustav and Frederick.

To complicate things, Kristina Gyllensteina, Sten Sture's widow, was released from Danish prison in 1524 and returned to Sweden, settling at Kalmar. She immediately began scheming with the Sture party in an attempt to put one of her sons on the Swedish throne in place of Gustav. She was certainly plotting with von Melen against Gustav and there were rumors she was planning to marry Soren Norrby, laying the groundwork for an invasion of southern Sweden. The marriage rumor was not at all ridiculous as the two had met while Kristina was a prisoner in Denmark. Norrby had been kind to her, perhaps interceding on her behalf with the Danish king. Norrby also happened to be a widower at this time. At the very least, these conspiracies may have led to the actions Norrby would take a year later.

Norrby's continued Baltic piracy finally drove the Lübeck merchants to propose lending Gustav additional funds to assemble an expedition to wipe him out of his island base. Gustav turned to von Melen to command the assault.

Von Melen landed on Gotland and made good progress until he reached the fortress of Viborg. Lacking siege equipment, he entered into negotiations with Norrby, very possibly plotting further mischief against Gustav.

With von Melen in Gotland, Gustav made a move to secure Kalmar Castle. He ordered the gates opened to him for a state visit. Henrick refused, presumably on von Melen's orders. This rebuff combined with rumors coming back from Gotland began to place doubts in Gustav's mind as to the loyalty of von Melen.

To make matters worse, Norrby now decided to change his allegiance from Christian II to Frederick, making Gustav's invasion of Gotland a war on Denmark. A Danish war was more then the merchants of Lübeck had bargained for and they quickly applied pressure on Gustav to negotiate an end to hostilities. At a conference in Malmö, with Lübeck mediating, the state of Danish and Swedish affairs following Sweden's break with the Kalmar Union was finally settled. By the terms of the Malmö Recess of September 1, 1524, Sweden seeded all rights to Gotland, Bleking, Halland and Skåne. Denmark gave up Viken (the modern Norwegian province of Bohuslän). For her efforts in arranging the peace, Lübeck obtained new trade concessions from Denmark and a cordial relationship between the two countries. Gustav felt he had been outmaneuvered by von Melen, Norrby, Frederick, and especially by the Lübeck merchants. This seems to be the point at which Gustav began to develop a different attitude toward his Lübeck benefactors. The Swedish king may have come out second best in this round, but he was learning and he generally didn't make the same mistake twice.

Upon von Melen's return from Gotland, Gustav ordered his general to Stockholm and there he extracted a promise from the German adventurer that he would proceed to Kalmar and have the gates of the castle opened for the state visit. However, upon arriving at the fortress, von Melen threw off any pretense of loyalty to Gustav. He placed Henrick Jute, a soldier who had fought under Sten Sture, in command of the castle and had all the German and Swedish soldiers renew their vow of fealty to him. He then departed Sweden with his family, including his brother Henrick, returning to Germany where he immediately entered into intrigues against the Swedish king. For many years to come von Melen would be a focal point for conspiracies and plots against Gustav in Germany. Swedish outcasts, German mercenary opportunists and rebuffed Lübeck merchants would float in and out of these conspiracies, waiting for a crack in Gustav's power, a chance to reenter Sweden and reassert control.

Gustav, furious at von Melen's treachery, was now faced with retaking "the key to Sweden" himself. In July of 1525 Gustav left Stockholm with four companies of his finest foot soldiers bound for Kalmar Castle. His fifteen hundred men were opposed by a far inferior force in numbers, but the fortress proved to be every bit as formidable as its reputation promised.

Gustav stormed the walls and lost half his troops in the first few days. The moat was said to be red with the blood of the Swedish soldiers. Bodies lay everywhere at the foot of the walls and many of those surviving were missing arms or legs, a common result of warfare in the early Renaissance. These were losses Gustav could ill afford. Peder Svart records in his chronicle of the period that the king wept tears of grief at the terrible losses. Still Gustav could not leave the fortress so close to Danish territory in enemy hands.

He threatened to lead the troops himself up the scaling ladders and began to don his armor. His officers begged him to stay clear of the fighting, that they would lead another effort and this time would carry the wall. They did not. They only succeeded in getting more precious soldiers killed.

Still, the battle had taken its toll on the defenders also, so eventually a truce was arranged followed by capitulation. The terms of the surrender are not known. It is possible that the defenders' numbers were so depleted that surrender became the only option. But it seems likely that safe conduct to Germany would have been insisted upon by the defeated.

However, following their surrender, the garrison was seized and held for court-martial, found guilty of treason and sentenced to the wheel, a nasty form of execution whereby the victim was beaten until enough bones were broken so that he could be threaded through the spokes of a large wheel. His body was then raised on a post of the wall and left to die and rot. In this case the defenders had their sentences commuted to beheading except for two who were freed. The remainder, some sixty to seventy men, went under the headsman's ax, ending the last holdout from Swedish crown control.

Kristina Gyllensteina eventually reconciled with Gustav. She married a supporter of Gustav's and disappeared from the Swedish political scene.

While Gustav had his hands full dealing with von Melen on the Swedish side of the southern border, Frederick and Lübeck were having their problems with Norrby on the Danish side. Early in 1525 the former Danish admiral switched allegiance back to Christian II and invaded Blekinge from his base at Viborg. He called for a general uprising in the name of the deposed Danish king and was rewarded with a peasant revolt in Skåne allowing him to lay siege to Hälsingborg. He appealed to Christian to send reinforcements and turn the insurrection into a war for the return of his throne. Fortunately, for the parties to the Malmö Recess, the exiled former king was in no position to take advantage of this opportunity. In April Lübeck sent its fleet to crush Norrby's squadron and Rantzau, Frederick's general, with his German mercenaries cut Norrby's peasant army to pieces in Skåne. But the Viborg Castle on Gotland would be a challenge to take so Frederick bought Norrby off by granting him Blekinge as fief-for-life in exchange for Gotland. He pacified Lübeck by handing over Bornholm. However, Norrby seems to have been incorrigible. No sooner had things settled down than he put together another fleet and began indiscriminately attacking Baltic shipping from the Blekinge sea ports.

Once more the Malmö partners combined to rid themselves of this persistent nuisance. In August 1526 a Danish-Swedish fleet met and annihilated Norrby's ships, sending most to the bottom. Norrby escaped and made his way to Russia where he was imprisoned for not accepting service with the tsar. Emperor Charles V negotiated his release in 1529 and sent him to fight in his Italian campaign. Soren Norrby was killed a year later in the siege of Florence, a soldier of fortune to the end.

The revolt was over. Sweden had won her independence from Denmark and was beginning to have a sense of itself as a nation. Gustav was the key to this transformation, but his trials were far from over. He had, at best, a tenuous hold on a people that still thought of themselves as Dalesmen or Smälanders more often than as Swedes. Rulers had come and gone with such frequency that the idea of any particular king being long term was foreign to them. Sweden had its independence, at least temporarily, but it would take a civil war and religious revolution to make this country a nation.

5. War Debt and the Reformation

At the same time Gustav was dealing with military and external matters, he had to find the money to satisfy the country's war debt owed primarily to Lübeck and its merchants. Sweden was encumbered with a staggering debt of 114,500 marks (about $1.5 million) to various factions in Lübeck. Gustav had literally won his crown on credit. A letter from Herman Iserhel illustrates the situation: "I sit here in great sorrow. My creditors press me hard. Send at once as much wares as you can — salmon, lard, oil, furs, silver, copper, iron."[1] Likewise Henrick Möllar, whose ship had taken him to Småland, pressed Gustav, as did others. Exercising the tools available to him would aggravate already volatile situations, particularly with the peasants, Dalesmen, Smålanders and clergy.

Gustav's conventional means of raising money were severely constrained by the partial feudal system Sweden had acquired and the strong position of the Catholic Church, which owned 21.3 percent of the land and was exempt from taxation. The nobility, also not taxable, held 20.7 percent, leaving only about half the land (52.4 percent) owned by taxpaying peasants (*skattebonder*). In Swedish Finland 96 percent of the arable land was occupied in this manner. However, skattebonder were mostly subsistence agriculturists, generally growing enough to provide for their families, but not accumulating any real wealth. They simply did not produce a lot of excess to tax. The king did have his own lands, and 5.6 percent of Swedish arable land was occupied by peasants who paid rent to the king (*kronobonder*). In addition to the crown lands and the peasant tax, the king received a portion of the court fines (*sakoren*) and duties on imports and exports which was negligible because Gustav had turned over nearly all trade with the outside world to the Hanseatic League cities, primarily Lübeck. According to law, the king could ask for a special tax on all subjects to meet an emergency, but the amount was set by the landstings of each province (*landskap*). Gustav would have to be resourceful if he was to find the money he needed to repay the debt to his German creditors.

Gustav's Sweden was overwhelmingly agricultural and even this population was scattered with much of the country being forested. Only the fertile plains of Västergötland and Östergötland, the basins of Lake Mälar and Hjalmar, and the south coast of Finland had any kind of a dense peasant population. Only in the iron and copper producing region of the Bergslag was there any non-agricultural industry and this was poorly developed. The only city of any size was Stockholm and that had been decimated by the war. Gustav had ordered merchants and burghers back to the city, but it would take time and money to rebuild this commercial center to its prewar level.

Gustav did what he could to raise taxes on the peasantry then turned to the church, the source of real wealth in the country. With Gustav Trolle in exile, Hans Brask, bishop of Linköping, was nominal head of the Church of Rome in Sweden. Brask was an astute politician. He had managed to stay in the good graces of Trolle while maintaining relations with the Stures and keep his head through the Stockholm Bloodbath, yet had not antagonized the new king. With Gustav's ascendance to the throne, Brask joined the Gustav party, supporting the crown with grants and loans from church coffers. However, as the new king pressed the monasteries, cathedrals and even parishes for more revenue, Brask became increasingly less ardent in his support. Besides the pressure from Gustav for money, Brask was alarmed by the number of positions being held by Lutherans in Sweden.

After rejecting the two sitting Swedish chancellors, Peder Jackabsson Sunnänvader and the bishop of Strängnäs, Gustav had selected as his chancellor and chief counselor Laurentius Andreae in 1523. Laurentius was the archdeacon of Strängnäs and had studied in Germany before Luther's time, had been to Rome three times, and was a supporter of the Lutheran cause. In 1524 Gustav appointed Olaus Petri secretary and chaplain of Stockholm. Petri was becoming known as the voice of Lutheranism in Sweden. Gustav certainly had no far ranging plan to bring the Protestant Reformation to Sweden. Indeed, his first acts upon taking the throne had been to reconcile differences with the Holy See in Rome. At Strängnäs, he had vowed to uphold and protect the church. He accepted the pope's envoy, Johannes Magnus, a Swedish commoner by birth and noted scholar at the Vatican. The terms conveyed by Magnus were that Gustav Trolle be reinstated to his position as Swedish archbishop and that Rome retain the right to appoint foreigners as Swedish bishops. Gustav could not accept either of these conditions. Finally, he proposed that Magnaus himself be appointed archbishop of Sweden and sent him back to Rome to plead his case. Gustav's letter to Pope Adrian VI (1523) provides a glimpse into the king's thinking and an indication of what was to come:

> If our Most Holy Father has any care for the peace of our country, we shall be pleased to have him confirm the election of his legate ... and we comply with the Pope's wishes as to a reformation of the Church and religion. But if His Holiness, against our honor and the peace of our subjects, sides with the crime-stained partisans of Archbishop Trolle, we shall allow his legate to return to Rome, and shall govern the Church in this country with the authority which we have as king.[2]

Time passed. Gustav received no answer and the ties between Gustav and the Church of Rome remained strained. The situation in Germany, however, was even worse.

The Reformation sparked by the Saxon monk was in full flower. Martin Luther was born in Eisleben, Saxony, in 1483. Early on he showed ability as a student. His industrious father had been able to get him into the University of Erfurt to study law, but his interests leaned more toward theology and at 22 he entered the monastery at Erfurt. Three years later he became a professor at the new University of Wittenburg and visited Rome on monastic business at least once. Gradually he became more and more concerned with many of the practices of the church of his day and in 1517 he posted his 95 Theses on the door of the castle church in Wittenberg. In 1520, he publicly burned the pope's bull condemning his teachings. He was summoned to appear before the Diet of Worms in 1521 where he was denounced for his heretical preaching, but here a minority of delegates protested, casting dissenting votes and earning the label Protestants. This was followed by Charles V's edict condemning Luther as a heretic, authorizing his capture and trial, and demanding the burning of his books and pamphlets. For his own protection Luther was seized and hidden by the elector of Saxony. Luther continued to write, translating the Bible into German along with the catechism and composing several hymns.

His teachings spread throughout Germany, bringing about a peasant revolt in 1525 that was suppressed ruthlessly by the nobility. The Schmalkaldic War began in 1546 (the year of

Luther's death) and ended a year later with Charles V defeating the Protestant princes. Despite these military setbacks, Lutheranism continued to spread. Sometimes its propagation was due to sincere religious beliefs, but often it was for political or economic advantage. Religious wars continued on and off in Germany until the Peace of Augsburg in 1555, by which Charles V granted each German state the right to choose between Catholicism and Lutheranism. This peace was to last for over fifty years, until the outbreak of the Thirty Years' War, a war that was to involve Sweden directly.

Martin Luther's counterpart in Sweden was Olaus Petri (Olof Persson or Petersson in Swedish, but better known as Petri, the Latin form of his name). Like Luther, Petri came from the lower classes, the son of a blacksmith in Örebro. He also showed early aptitude in letters. After schooling in Sweden, he went to the University of Wittenberg where he studied under both Luther and Phillip Melanchthon, the theologian of the German Reformation. After receiving a magister degree, he returned to Sweden in 1519 imbued with the ideas and enthusiasm of the early movement. He was appointed chancellor to the bishop of Strängnäs and immediately began collecting about him others of his belief, including his brother Laurentius Petri. Soon their preaching and publications drew the attention of Bishop Brask, who was building a coalition of bishops, priests, nobles and laymen to fight the "German heresy." Brask would no doubt have moved against Petri, but the king's chancellor, Laurentius Andreae, interceded and arranged the appointment of Petri as town clerk of Stockholm. In 1525 Petri married. In 1526 a printing press was brought to Stockholm and the new town clerk almost monopolized it publishing a Swedish translation of the New Testament and many of the German Lutheran hymns. He and his followers published and circulated pamphlets and books on the new theology. Through his prolific writing and wide distribution, thanks to the new printing press, Petri reformed the Swedish written word from its clumsy ancient form to a much more readable, useful style. Although he was certainly an advocate of making changes in the Church of Rome, he did not accept the German Lutheran teachings uncritically. He put his own stamp on them based on his Swedish background and what he saw as the needs of the Swedish people. He retained those early Lutheran ideals all his life and in the end was bitterly disappointed they did not bring about a recreation of a truly righteous, humanitarian society.

Even as religious foment brewed in his realm, Gustav was faced once again with an outbreak of the continually smoldering revolution in Dalarna. This time it was the high taxes and objections to the new religion that drove the rebellion. The instigator is known in Swedish history as the *Daljunker*, an energetic and charismatic figure who first gained support among the Norwegian nobility, even marrying the daughter of a Norwegian lady who was proud of her dashing son-in-law and had visions of him occupying the Swedish throne. Crossing into Sweden, in 1527, he fanned the flames of discontent in Dalarna claiming to be Nil, the elder son of Sten Sture the Younger and Kristina Gyllenstierna. He was not. The real Nil died a year later and his brother Svante remained loyal to Gustav, even serving foreign missions in the king's behalf. The impostor may have been an illegitimate son of Sten's. Whoever he was, he managed to set the province ablaze with attacks on the king's men.

Gustav used this outbreak as an excuse to gather a Riksdag. He called a meeting of all the Estates and bade the nobility to come armed and ready for action. The Riksdag was held in a monastery in Västerås within striking distance of the uprising. Though the reason for the Riksdag was ostensibly to quell the rebellion, Gustav knew other grievances would be presented. Bishop Hans Brask of Linköping made the journey to voice his concerns. The clergyman had no independent vote, but he could speak as part of the Nobility Estate. He would be backed by a faction of the aristocracy that felt the king was concentrating too much power in the central government. Their leader was Ture Jönsson Tre Rosor, *lagman* and great landowner in Västergötland, the same Jönsson Gustav had acceded to during the revolution. Representatives from the peasantry and miners would be there denouncing high taxes and the heretical preaching emanating from Stockholm.

It seemed Gustav's only allies would be the burghers from Stockholm and other towns, a faction of the nobility concerned with the loss of lands to the church and the delegates from Lübeck who had no vote.

The general format for a Riksdag was that the king presented his proposals to the assembly, which discussed them, then approved or disapproved them. In this case Gustav had read to the Estates assembled his proclamation, a stinging indictment of his subjects. The king had fulfilled his obligation to the people, but the people had not reciprocated. He had driven out the Dane, he said, and secured their freedom, but he had not received sufficient resources to defend the country or to pay the Lübeck debt. The problem, he went on, lay in the loss of properties by the nobles and gentry to the churches and monasteries through sale, donation and foreclosures. Now they wanted compensation from the crown, but the king could not even pay the war debt let alone return property or money to the nobles. He ended with an offer to abdicate and let the Estates deal directly with the Lübeck debt owners, who had representatives right there at the assembly.

Hans Brask could see where this was going and replied that no church property or possessions could be turned over to any lay faction without express permission from Rome. Ture Jönsson and his party of nobles applauded the bishop of Linköping's response and offered their support.

Gustav then retorted with a scathing attack on those assembled as to their ingratitude, disloyalty and open rebellion, no better than the Dalarnian outlaws they had come to suppress. He announced that he would consent to have such subjects no longer and asked for appropriate compensation so that he could leave the country and never return. He then left the monastery and took up residence in the Castle of Västerås.

Discussions and arguments rang in the halls of the monastery and schisms began to develop between the factions. As the days went by, the peasants swung into Gustav's camp, believing it was vital to keep Gustav as king. This left the great nobles backed by the clergy as the holdouts.

Finally a couple of the bishops broke ranks and urged the nobles to reconsider. These were the same clergy who had split with Gustav Trolle over his wholehearted support of Christian II. Eventually the promise of church lands overcame the nobles' fear of a too powerful king and they capitulated. Gustav had won.

The Västerås Recess was drawn up, with a great deal of help from the king no doubt. The provisions were first, all assembled promised to cooperate to stamp out sedition and rebellion. Secondly, all castles owned by the bishops would be turned over to the crown. The king was to determine the number of soldiers church officials needed — namely none. Sufficient revenues were to be retained by the cathedrals, bishops and parishes to sustain them; all surpluses would go to the state for maintenance of a standing army and other national services. The monasteries would be turned over to the nobles intact as fiefs, and lands lost to the church through donation or sale since the mid–fifteenth century were to be returned. Finally, it was agreed that accusations of heresy against preachers would stop, and that the word of God would be preached plainly throughout the kingdom. This last came to mean Swedish would replace Latin in church services.

Later, a corollary of ordinances to the recess was issued with council approval. These ordinances, probably drawn up by Olaus Petri and Laurentius Andreae, clarified the structure of the church. The old organization of archbishop, bishops and priests remained, but it was no longer subject to the authority of the pope in Rome. In 1531 Laurentius Petri was chosen to be the Swedish archbishop by Gustav. He was consecrated by Petrus Magni, bishop of Västerås, who had been consecrated in Rome in accordance with canonical law in 1524. Thus the apostolic succession was maintained unbroken in Sweden. Ecclesiastical courts were to be confined to issuing church discipline. Finances of the church would be administered by the crown. It made clear that the main duties of bishops were to oversee the clergy in looking after the spiritual needs of the people, and to see that children were taught the fundamentals of the faith and morality.

These ordinances were too much for Bishop Brask and he asked leave to visit Gotland Island. Though Danish territory, it was part of his diocese. He traveled with a large amount of money to Viborg and from there escaped to Danzig. Gustav was relieved to be rid of him, but unhappy about all the money that had slipped from his grasp, money that was destined to be used against him in the future.

Having handled ecclesiastic matters at Västerås, Gustav turned again to the *Daljunkern* revolt in Dalarna. He first issued a series of letters and proclamations to the provincial officials and leaders denouncing the imposter, and reminding the inhabitants of their obligations to and advantages in remaining loyal to the crown. Again, he was aided by his old allies Anders Persson, Mans Nilsson and Ingel Hansson who took the lead in convincing the miners to stand with the king. Support for the insurrection fell away until the Sture pretender could only flee the country. He escaped to Germany where, under pressure from Gustav, he was captured and executed.

Next Gustav entered Dalarna at the head of an army. There he called a meeting of the people, rounded them up, placed them in the middle of his soldiers and threatened them with cannon fire. The ringleaders were selected out and summarily executed. Dalarna was once again subdued, but the implementation of the provisions of the Västerås Recess continued to be deeply resented in many parts of the country, especially the rural areas.

Upon his return to Västergötland, Ture Jönsson began to incite an uprising against the new power of the king and the heretical new church practices. He found a ready confederate in Bishop Magnus of Skara. In 1529 a rebellion erupted and spread to the ever-restive Småland. Led by the nobility, the outbreak was picking up adherents in Östergötland and Hälsingland, but now Gustav had the nucleus of his planned standing army. He recalled additional troops from Finland. Again Gustav's propaganda machine was employed and the peasantry was persuaded to drop out of the fight. Then he moved aggressively against the rebellious nobles. Jönsson and Bishop Magnus escaped the country, but most of the other leaders were captured and brought to a Riksdag at Strängnäs that same year. All were found guilty of treason and executed, their properties confiscated and turned over to the crown. Gustav was learning to be ruthless in dealing with rebellion and also how to turn adversity to his advantage.

In 1530 Gustav decided on a unique approach to settling the remainder of the Lübeck debt. He ordered the monasteries and city churches to give up one of their bells to the state for this purpose. This worked so well that the next year Gustav extended the bell tax to the country churches. The outcry was tremendous. The pious country folk, already reeling from changes in the church so central to their spiritual and social lives, were now being asked to give up the bells that called them to service and drove away the evil spirits. The clear clanging purified the air and gave a sense of community to the housewife in her kitchen and the farmer in the field. They had seen decorations and service pieces confiscated and now they were to lose their bells? It was too much. In Dalarna the king's agents were met with sledgehammers and ax handles. The borders were sealed off. The miners of that province would not give up their bells. Among the leaders of this latest uprising were Gustav's longtime friends and supporters Andres Persson, Måns Nilsson and Ingel Hansson.

In the middle of the Bell Revolt, Gustav received word that Christian II was making his move. He had finally gotten the backing of Charles V, assistance he had sought for so long. Charles, as head of the Hapsburg Empire, now ruled the largest empire the world had ever seen. Gold from his American domains and silver from Spanish Asia were pouring into his coffers. The holy Roman emperor was holding his own against the French and had stopped the advance of the Turks coming north through Hungary. His war against the Lutheran princes of Germany was going well. He could afford to finance his brother-in-law's expedition. He might arrest the spread of Protestantism in these northern countries and even make this territory the northern flank of his Hapsburg Empire.

In October 1531 Christian II set sail from the Zuider Zee with 7,000 men and thirty ships purchased with Spanish gold. With him were Gustav Trolle and several of the nobility that had escaped capture after the collapse of the Västergötland revolt. Upon landing in Norway they picked up popular support from the Norwegian aristocracy, but the force failed to take Fort Akershus at Oslo. Having added a strong Norwegian contingent, they pushed on into Viken on their way to Skåne and Västergötland. Here, however, the expedition bogged down. For once the border clan's opposition to an invading army favored Gustav. Communication and supply lines were cut and foraging parties ambushed. Roads and trails were barricaded and made impassable. Gustav rushed all the troops he could spare from the Bell Rebellion to help the peasant guerillas. Then in early 1532, Christian's fleet was defeated by a combined Lübeck-Danish fleet that landed Danish reinforcements at Oslo. Cut off in the rear and bogged down at the front, Christian disengaged and pulled back from Swedish forces on his front leaving Ture Jönsson's decapitated body behind. Cornered on foreign soil and now cut off from supplies, Christian succumbed to an offer from Frederick to come to Copenhagen and work out a peace. Upon his arrival, however, the former Danish king was thrown into prison at Sønderborg Castle where he remained until his death in 1559. The war had forced an alliance between Denmark and Sweden for the first time in the modern era. Sweden had come a long way from being merely a Danish possession.

Having dispatched a contingent of troops to fight Christian's invasion, Gustav turned to dealing with the insurgent Dalesmen who had called a Riksdag at Arboga. Gustav outmaneuvered them by calling his own Riksdag in Uppland and applied pressure on Stockholm to cut off all support to the rebellious miners. The Stockholm burghers and merchants, now dependent on the king for the continuation of the Protestant practices they had become accustomed to, obliged. Gustav had broken the traditional Bergslag-Stockholm tie by exploiting their religious differences. By the end of 1531, Dalarna had capitulated, paying the king 2,000 marks in place of the bells demanded.

Gustav accepted the payment and let the matter rest until the threat from Christian was removed, then he exacted retribution upon the offending Dalesmen. Perhaps he was stung by the defection of his longtime allies or just fed up with Dalarnian intransigence. In any case, in February 1533, he marched his army through the province to Kopparberg where he convened court and summoned the peasant miners. The leaders were taken to Stockholm where they were tried and condemned to death. Among those executed were Gustav's old supporters and early leaders of his war against Denmark, Andres Persson, Måns Nilsson and Ingel Hansson. The effect on the province was profound. Never again would Dalarna rise in rebellion against the king.

Gustav Eriksson Vasa was now in firm control of his realm. Rebellion had been crushed; the powerful and wealthy church state-within-a-state had been smashed. The nobility had been brought to heel. Much of their property had been confiscated. Crown castles and fiefs that had been parceled out to the noble magnates to oversee were back under the king's control, administered by his bailiffs. Gustav had a standing army and the beginnings of a navy at his disposal and the resources to pay for them. The central government was now the strongest entity in Sweden. Gustav had the luxury of turning his attention to his country's debt and trade restrictions, and in these matters he was about to get some help from events unfolding outside Sweden.

As early as 1525 Gustav had encouraged trade between the Netherlands and his only western port, Lödöse, in defiance of his treaties with Lübeck. Cooperation between Denmark and Sweden had loosened the restrictions on shipping through the Danish straits from the Baltic to the North Sea. These changes along with rising Dutch mercantile power meant Lübeck and the Hanseatic League were losing their control of northern commerce.

These stresses plus some internal matters led to a change in government in the German merchant city. The old conservative council was thrown out in favor of a more progressive, Protestant leaning group headed by an enterprising if somewhat unscrupulous Jörgen Wullenwever. His ambition was to lead the city back to dominance of the northern maritime trade. Conflicts with the Netherlands soon led to open war and Lübeck appealed to Sweden for help. Chafing under Lübeck's trade constraints and the continual undervaluation of goods sent to pay the debt, Gustav saw his chance to settle accounts. He refused to support the warring city and what's more, declared the debt paid. Even Gustav's counselors objected to such high-handed tactics. Johan av Hoya, Gustav's brother-in-law and governor of Finland, had personally pledged this repayment and felt so strongly he left his position in Sweden and went to Germany where he joined the anti–Gustav group in exile.

Meanwhile, events in Denmark were also moving precipitously. Frederick I had died in 1533. The nobility favored his son, Christian of Holstein, as successor, but he had shown decidedly Protestant leanings opposed by the strongly Catholic ruling Danish Council. The towns and particularly the burghers on the council also objected to the strong hand Frederick had given the nobles. The council deferred his coronation and ruled in his stead. There were now three potential heads of government in Denmark: the de facto ruler (the council); Frederick I's son, supported by the nobility; and Christian II (still in Danish prison), supported by the towns and serfs. Jörgen saw this confusion as an opportunity to strike. He concluded a peace treaty with the Netherlands and attacked Denmark. Thus began the so-called Count's Feud, named after the Lübeck army commander, Christopher, the count of Oldenburg. Lübeck had raised a large mercenary army to augment its powerful navy. These forces were thrown into invasions of the Danish Baltic islands, Holstein, Halland, Skåne and Zealand, whereupon Copenhagen and Malmö rose in support of the return of Christian II. The Lübeck navy next moved to take control of the Sound, capturing most of the Danish navy. The serfs of the eastern counties revolted, spreading terror and taking bloody revenge for years of repression.

In the western counties of Jutland, however, the nobles held onto power and pushed the hard pressed council into accepting Frederick's son as Christian III. Before he left Holstein, Christian defeated the invaders and was able to conclude an agreement with Lübeck to remove their forces from the country, leaving the insurgent peasants in Jutland, to the north, at the mercy of the Danish nobles. The council also appealed to Sweden for help and Gustav responded with loans, troops and ships.

In February 1534 the Danish Council made a treaty with Gustav. In exchange for military assistance and money, they granted a guarantee of non-interference in Swedish governmental affairs, dropping any claim to the Swedish crown. Swedish forces invaded Halland in the spring of 1534, capturing Halmstad by October, then pushed south taking Häsingborg early in the new year, recovering Halland for Christian III. Though receiving setbacks in Holstein and Halland, Lübeck still controlled both sides of the Sound (Malmö and Copenhagen) and most of Skåne, while Zealand was in chaos. Driving westward, Lübeck landed Christopher and the main body of their army on Fyn supported by their fleet, positioned to threaten Jutland.

At the same time, Gustav sent his fleet into the southern Baltic. In addition to the armed merchantmen he had purchased from Lübeck, Gustav had added four major warships of 500 to 1700 tons displacement and armed the entire fleet with cannon. The Swedish fleet was joined by a Prussian fleet and a Danish squadron still controlled by Christian, although most of these ships were poorly armed converted merchantmen. A squadron of Dutch merchantmen also joined the fleet. This combined force met a Lübeck fleet off Bornholm on June 9 in a battle in which the Swedish heavy guns were decisive. Many of the Danish captured ships and much of the Lübeck fleet was scattered or destroyed. A week later the combined allied fleet attacked the main Lübeck fleet in the Little Belt strait. Again, Gustav's naval guns proved the difference. Much of the Lübeck navy was destroyed, eliminating it as an effective force for the rest of the war. The allied navy was now free to recover the Sound, and blockade Malmö and Copenhagen.

Count Christopher's army was finally forced to battle and was decisively defeated by Christain and his nobles at the battle of Øxnebjerg on June 11. Captured was a seriously wounded Gustav Trolle, who died a few days later. Also killed in the battle was Johan av Hoya. Two more of Gustav's enemies had been dispatched.

With the death of Gustav Trolle, Sweden's official Catholic archbishop, the pope appointed Johannes Magnus as Swedish archbishop. However, Gustav had made Laurentius Petri archbishop at Uppsala in 1531. Johannes would never return to Sweden, but would travel Europe and spend his time writing in Rome. It is interesting that two of Sweden's great literary works should be written at this time, Johannes's *A History of the Goths and Svear* and Olaus Petri's *Chronicles of Sweden*, two quite different views of Sweden's past.

Lübeck had made a determined effort to regain control over Baltic shipping and had lost to the united Scandinavian monarchies. As a result of the war, Lübeck's military power was destroyed. The Hanseatic stranglehold on northern maritime commerce was broken. The Swedish debt to Lübeck was canceled and new trade privileges for merchants negotiated. Under the new terms Sweden retained the right to tax all imports and exports. Swedish ports were open to all nations and Swedish merchants were free to trade throughout the Baltic and beyond. Gustav had obtained the economic and commercial freedom Sweden needed to develop as a modern European nation.

In Denmark the Zealand peasant revolt was put down mercilessly. Malmö and Copenhagen were blockaded and starved into submission. Christian III's crown was secure, except for the constant worry that Charles V might at some point decide to take up his brother-in-law's cause again. To mitigate this possibility both Sweden and Denmark sent feelers to Frances I of France, Charles V's primary enemy in Western Europe.

As the country gained strength, it was obvious that Sweden would play an increasingly important role in international politics, but Gustav still had internal problems to deal with that would test the limits of his capabilities. There was the question of who would succeed him as regent of the realm and a civil war would test the very fabric of that realm itself.

6. Succession and Civil War

As Gustav's throne became more secure and the central government stronger, he began working on another of his goals, a change in the succession process. The traditional Swedish method of election from among members of one or more aristocratic families was too unwieldy and put too much power in the hands of the electorate, namely the nobility. The elected king was then beholden to the factions who put him in power. Gustav wanted to establish a straight hereditary monarchy which could rule independent of the aristocracy, but to do this he needed an heir.

The recent instability in the Swedish government and the almost constant revolutions he faced caused Gustav difficulties in making proposals in the courts of Europe. His early attempts were rebuffed. However, in 1531 Gustav won the hand of Catherine of Saxe-Lauenberg, a German princess. Her family had neither wealth nor power, which indicates the extent of the problem Gustav was having in obtaining a bride. Catherine's sister later married Christian III of Denmark, promoting ties between Christian and Gustav. By all accounts Catherine was delicate in terms of health and not happy in her new northern home. Gustav and Catherine had one son, Erik, born in 1533. His mother would die two years later.

Gustav's second wife, Margaret Leijonhufvud, was from an old Swedish noble family. This marriage, in 1536, seems to have been a happy one producing ten children including three sons, Johan, Magnus, and Karl. Upon Margaret's death, Gustav married her niece, Catherine Stenback. There were no children from this union, but Gustav had sons now with which to construct his new method of succession.

Stern and exacting in public, energetic, demanding and authoritarian as monarch, Gustav was warm and charming in private with family and friends. He had the ability to leave the pressures of state in the council room to pick up and play with a child a moment later in his private quarters. Yet the strain of the constant struggle to maintain power and build a free, strong nation certainly took its toll even on a strong man like Gustav.

Through the 1530s he suffered from bouts of depression and exhibited outbursts of erratic behavior. An example is the time he chased one of his state counselors through the courtyard with a drawn dagger because of some perceived offense.

A more serious event nearly cost the lives of Gustav's two former chancellors, Olaus Petri and Laurentius Andreae. Laurentius had been Gustav's first chancellor and close confidant since his election in 1523. Olaus followed as chancellor in 1531, but left the position two years later to return to his ecclesiastic and scholarly activities. He didn't like being closely controlled and Gustav found him to be ill-suited to the highly political position.

In 1531 Olaus discovered a plot against the king through a parishioner's confession. He could not divulge the treasonous information except to another clergyman, so he confided in

Laurentius. Between the two of them the plot was foiled, but word of the incident eventually reached Gustav. The king was angry he had not been informed, but did nothing about it until years later. In 1539 Olaus and Laurentius were maneuvering the now independent Swedish church into a position of self-determination disapproved of by the king. Gustav had the two men arrested and tried for treasonous activities relating to the earlier plot against him. He influenced the trial so that both men were found guilty and sentenced to death. Gustav pardoned them, but imposed heavy fines that broke Laurentius financially and the citizens of Stockholm had to raise the money to free Olaus. Both men escaped with their lives, but they lost much of their influence in state affairs and the church movement toward independence from the state was arrested.

With the declining fortunes of the church, monastic and other ecclesiastic schools disappeared including a Greyfriars school in Stockholm. The University of Uppsala, weakened by the revolution, closed its doors in the early 1530s. Particularly promising students and some young men were sent to Germany for education, but these were few in number.

Unable to find qualified administrators in sufficient numbers in Sweden, Gustav brought in foreigners, mostly German, to fill civil service and advisory positions. This period is referred to as Gustav's German era. As his new chancellor, Gustav appointed a German, Konrad von Pyhy. As tutor for his children, he imported another German, Georg Norman, but the ambitious Georg soon moved into Swedish politics.

Fortunately for Gustav the 1540s began with some triumphs in foreign affairs and relative quiet at home. In the spring of 1541 Gustav met with representatives from the Hanseatic League cities to renegotiate trade agreements. He could now play the cities against each other and dictate his terms. He met with Christian III at Brömsebro on the border just south of Kalmar. The two kings seem to have developed a warm personal relationship. On September 15 they signed the Treaty of Brömsebro providing for friendship and an alliance between the two countries. Denmark also repaid the loan Sweden had made during the Count's Feud war. Thus, final recognition of Sweden as an independent nation was achieved.

After a period of quiet, new problems began to appear. The Swedish church, now severed from Rome, with its independent archbishop, began to slip from under Gustav's control. In the Västerås Riksdag of 1544 the church was represented as its own estate, separate from the nobility for the first time. Gustav organized a system of government superintendents, one for the archbishop and one for each bishop, which usurped the church prelate's authority. Georg Norman was appointed to head this agency with an office corresponding to the archbishop, essentially a minister of ecclesiastic affairs. But Gustav's German administrators were about to cause him real problems.

First it was his chancellor. In November 1541 Denmark concluded a treaty with Frances I. The next year Gustav sent Konrad von Pyhy to the French court as head of a mission to negotiate for Sweden. The ever-conservative Gustav cautioned Pyhy to conduct proceedings carefully and with restraint. Once in France, however, Pyhy was apparently overwhelmed by the French court's magnificence and tried to present an inflated picture of Sweden's status. He spent money lavishly and promised Frances twenty-five thousand troops and fifty ships in support of his war against Charles V. On his return trip he hired a number of German knights to bolster Sweden's army.

As the bills started piling up and word of his obligation to France arrived Gustav became worried and bewildered. This quickly changed to anger as the German knights began to disembark and he learned Pyhy was also being accused of bigamy. As soon as Pyhy arrived in Stockholm, he was removed from office and imprisoned for life.

At the same time Georg, the minister of religious affairs, was conducting an austerity program in the Swedish church. All unnecessary church valuables were to be turned over to the crown. The people complained that this final removal of bridal crowns, church plate and other ornaments was too much. Soon the chapels would be stark and bare. One might as well worship in the forest, it was said. Indignation and anger spread through all of Sweden's rural areas, but in Småland this last act of sacrilege led to open hostilities.

The Dacke Rebellion was the most serious uprising of Gustav's reign, indeed, the largest popular revolt against a native ruler in Swedish history, Sweden's civil war. Georg's act of removing the last of the church ornamentation and service pieces may have been the final straw, but the peasants of Småland had other complaints against the crown that weighed heavily on them. The religious reforms themselves were odious to these pious peasants who began and ended each day with family prayer. The tax burden certainly seemed excessive to this province of mostly taxpaying peasantry and minor nobility. In addition to taxes paid throughout the country, the small farmers and stockmen of Småland were paying fines imposed because of the 1537 revolt.

The king's proclamation that "None shall hereafter drive oxen or horses out of the realm whether small or large, at the risk of their neck"[1] cut off the border folk's traditional trade with Blekinge and Halland. Prices were much higher at Ronneby and the other markets in the Danish provinces and the roads and waterways led in that direction as opposed to Kalmar where they were now forced to trade.

The king's decree against killing deer and cutting trees impacted the people's hunting and lumbering practices that helped sustain them. Also, the wild animals now ravaged their crops with impunity and the small farmer was prevented from wresting additional land from the ever present Småland forest.

Finally, the bailiffs themselves, the king's men, were becoming more and more oppressive. By law they had a right to the hospitality of households they were visiting. But this had come to mean helping themselves to livestock, grain, hay, cloth, even a portion of bridal dowries. Bribes were often needed to clear the way for land and livestock sales, and other transactions. It was precisely this kind of corruption that led to the crime that would first make the leader of the Småland uprising an outlaw.

In 1536 Nils Dacke and Jon Andersson, peasants from the border country, hunted down and killed Inge Arvidsson, a particularly hated bailiff of the Möre area. At the time, Nils was living on Södra Lindö farm in Torsås parish of the Möre county with his wife and young son. Feelings against this man must have been running very high for the two men to risk everything in this desperate crime.

As was the practice, Nils and Jon took to the woods, losing themselves in the trackless forests of Småland and Blekinge. Here they would have run across other refugees from the law, indigents, all sorts of political, social and legal outcasts. They could slide back and forth across the Swedish-Danish border at will, avoiding capture, yet staying in contact with friends and relatives in both countries.

Nonpayment of taxes and fines, and the occasional killing of a bailiff had become such a problem in Varend and Möre, Småland, that Gustav sent his marshal, Lars Siggesson, to the province to bring this area into line. He was instructed to be particularly hard on the border clans. Delinquent debtors were thrown into the Kalmar Castle dungeon and their properties confiscated.

Led by Jon Andersson, the peasants of Möre rose in revolt, calling for an assembly with the men of Varend to make plans for action. Just in time, Ture Trolle, lord of Bergkvara and chief nobleman of Småland, stepped in, calling his own assembly of the disaffected peasants. He was able to quell the revolt and placate their anger with promises to address their grievances. Further bloodshed had been averted for the moment.

Following the aborted rebellion, Nils and Jon were relieved of their debt to society for the bailiff's killing by paying a fine. Interesting that the theft of a horse or ox meant the gallows, but a murder, even of a king's man, could be rectified with money, although in this case, a great deal of money. The fine was 40 oxen apiece. At the market in Kalmar an ox would bring about sixteen marks, higher at Ronneby in Blekinge. Forty head would be 640 marks, about the price of a sizable farm.

Nils was destitute, having lost everything while he had been in hiding the last two years. His extended family was obliged to come up with the money. This was common and the reason such fines were called clan fines.

Nils moved back to Södra Lindö, but stayed less than a year. He probably didn't own the farm anymore and only returned long enough to make other arrangements and gather his family. He moved to a very small farm called Flaka, still in Torsås parish, but closer to the Danish frontier. It was an outcropper's smallholding, newly cut out of the forest, belonging to the crown. Nils was now paying rent to the king. The farmstead was too small to make a living on, but it lay beside Lyckeby River, which had an abundance of fish, particularly eel, highly prized at the markets of Ronneby. The river also formed the boundary between Småland and Blekinge (Sweden and Denmark), but Nils' neighbor on the other side claimed all rights to the river's fish. The neighbor, Sven of Ledja, took his complaint to court and Nils lost.

Unable to make a living on the farmstead alone, Nils picked up his crossbow and, in early 1542, killed the bailiff who rented the farmstead to him, then fled into the forests once again. This time the outcropper turned outlaw was about to shake the throne of Gustav Vasa.

By May 1542, Nils had gathered about him a partisan fighting force. On June 20, he attacked Voxtrop, a bailiff's farm, with 30 men. The bailiff, Nils Larsson, and a courtier, Arvid Vastgote, were stripped, tied to trees and shot full of arrows. A week later he called a thing at Inglinge Mound, the traditional assembly place for the border clans, and was able to attract a thousand men. Two weeks later he marched on Växjö, the main town of Varend, with over three thousand followers.

Meanwhile, Gustav had not been idle. He had appealed to Christian III for help under their Treaty of Brömsebro and sent what forces he had in the vicinity to the point of conflict. About 200 Swedes under Gustav Olofsson Stenbock invaded Värend from Västergötland, joining a small Danish contingent under Peder Skram. Their combined force, however, was vastly outnumbered and Stenbock called for a meeting with Nils on July 22. The royal army was forced to withdraw, leaving Nils in control of a good share of Småland.

The rebels were getting weapons, halberds, arquebuses, and ammunition, lead, shot and gunpowder from the mayor and citizens of Ronneby. Peasants on both sides of the border supplied food and clothing to the growing army. In addition to conventional weapons, Nils employed the traditional fighting methods of the forest people: felled trees to block roads and trails, ambushes from the thick undergrowth and the tree pull where a series of standing trees were cut nearly through then toppled at the same time with ropes as the enemy passed. But the most common weapon was still the one that every peasant had hanging on his wall at home, the crossbow. They were made by the peasants themselves. The bow was steel or horn and it shot a two foot, two and a half ounce bolt. At a hundred yards it could penetrate chain mail and all but the heaviest plate armor. Used for hunting, Nils' commoners were practiced and deadly with this weapon. Nils and his peasant army met with continued success through the summer, driving out the king's men from all corners of the province.

Gustav, now fully alarmed, recruited a peasant army from Gästrikland, Hälsingland, Uppland and even Finland. He received additional troops for his Danish contingent and mobilized the nobility's heavy cavalry. He spent large sums of money to import German mercenaries. By late summer he was ready and sent his army into the rebellious province.

The lead element of this army, some 1,000 to 1,500 German mercenaries, crossed the border from Östergötland into Småland and were immediately attacked at Slatmon near the town of Kisa. Nils' men surrounded and cut them off by felling trees in front and behind. Gustav's advanced corps was annihilated. The few who escaped straggled back into Linköping on September 15. Nils, with an estimated 14,000 men, then drove into Östergötland and holed up only three miles from Linköping where Gustav was camped. The rebel army was also within reach of the great forests of Kolmarden only 30 miles away. These forests are on the border of Södermanland and stretch to within striking distance of Stockholm. Gustav seems to have feared the possibility of Nils getting to this forest more than the danger to his own army or even his own safety.

Småland was lost and Östergötland hung by a thread. Gustav had no choice but to sue for peace. By the terms of the treaty, Nils pledged fealty to Gustav and the king promised to send agents to investigate the complaints of oppressive taxes and corrupt bailiffs. Nils would withdraw his forces back into Småland, but would be left to govern the province as he saw fit.

At one point the throne or governorship was offered to Svante Sture, but he turned it down. Again, Svante Sture and his mother remained loyal to Gustav throughout the rebellion. So Nils set himself up as ruler of Småland. In late 1542 he took over the royal castle of Kronoberg situated on an island in Lake Helgasjön some four miles from Växjö. With a garrison of a thousand men, he made this his capital of Småland. On November 25 he called a provincial assembly at Växjö declaring his rule. The terms of the armistice were to be strictly obeyed and the pillaging of noble estates was to cease. He appointed his own bailiffs in each district to enforce his rule, and maintain law and order. Local leaders were called to hold assemblies in each county, establish local control and make new laws.

The Catholic faith was restored as the church of the realm. Once more, Mass would be celebrated by priests, some of whom, not willing to take up the new religion, had been forced from their parish churches to become wandering vagrants. The familiar Latin verse and song were heard again by the faithful country people. What could not be restored were the gold service pieces, silver candlesticks, church ornaments and decorations. These now resided in Gustav's treasure vaults.

And finally, he rectified the financial situation, canceling royal fines and lowering the tax burden. He opened the border so Småland could again reach the markets of Blekinge and Haland where access was easier and prices higher. Through the late fall and winter of 1542–43, it was indeed a return to the good old days for the people of Småland.

Nils' insurrection caused a great excitement in Germany. The anti–Gustav party was sure this was their chance to retake Sweden. Gustav's former general and later avowed enemy Berend von Melen, Duke Albrekt of Mecklenberg and Count Friedrich of Palatinate offered support in exchange for money or political considerations. Even the emperor, Charles V, issued a proclamation calling upon the Swedish people to rise up and overthrow the usurper, and replace him with the count of Palatinate, husband of Christian II's daughter (Charles V's niece). In the end none of these schemes came to anything, but they might have had Gustav allowed the rebellion time to mature. He did not.

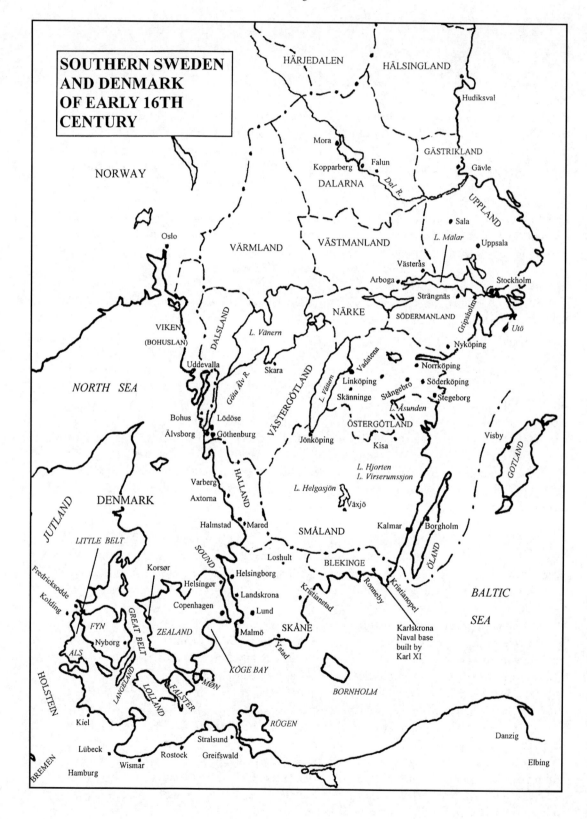

SOUTHERN SWEDEN AND DENMARK OF EARLY 16TH CENTURY

HÄRJEDALEN

HÄLSINGLAND

Hudiksval

NORWAY

Mora

Kopparberg Falun

DALARNA

GÄSTRIKLAND

Gävle

Dal R.

UPPLAND

Sala

L. Mälar

Uppsala

Oslo

VÄRMLAND

VÄSTMANLAND

Västerås

Arboga

Stockholm

Strängnäs

Gripsholm

SÖDERMANLAND

Utö

NÄRKE

L. Vänern

DALSLAND

VIKEN
(BOHUSLAN)

Nyköping

Uddevalla

Skara

Göta Älv. R.

VÄSTERGÖTLAND

L. vättern

Vadstena

Norrköping

Linköping

Söderköping

NORTH SEA

Skänninge

Stångebro

Stegeborg

L. Åsunden

Bohus

Lödöse

ÖSTERGÖTLAND

Visby

Älvsborg

Göthenburg

Jönköping

Kisa

GOTLAND

L. Hjorten
L. Virserumssjon

Varberg

HALLAND

L. Helgasjön

Axtorna

Växjö

JUTLAND

DENMARK

Halmstad Mared

SMÅLAND

Kalmar

Borgholm

LITTLE BELT

Loshult

BLEKINGE

ÖLAND

Korsør

Helsingborg

BALTIC

Fredricksodde

Helsingør

Landskrona

Kristianstad

Ronneby

Kristianopel

SEA

Kolding

Copenhagen

Lund

SOUND

FYN

ZEALAND

SKÅNE

Karlskrona
Naval base
built by
Karl XI

Nyborg

Malmö

GREAT BELT

Ystad

ALS

LANGELAND

KÖGE BAY

HOLSTEIN

LOLLAND

FALSTER

MØN

BORNHOLM

Kiel

RÜGEN

Danzig

Lübeck

Stralsund

BREMEN

Wismar

Rostock

Greifswald

Elbing

Hamburg

Nils apparently hoped and perhaps even believed that Gustav would grant him Småland in fief in exchange for his vow of loyalty, and allow the province to operate as a semi-independent state. Gustav would not. By mid-summer it was obvious Gustav was marshaling all his forces. He had launched a blistering propaganda campaign. By pamphlet and word of mouth he hammered away at the Smålanders: "You want the good old times, do you? What were the good old times? With 400–600 soldiers, when the land lay open to invaders, merchants were robbed of ships and goods, people thrown overboard and drowned like dogs, fishing stopped, cattle taken, houses burned? Was it really so good?" he reminded the populace. Then he stated his case: "Now we have 4,000–6,000 soldiers, with deadly guns and swords, harness and horses, good ships and sailors. And no one has lost a chicken."[2]

This was intended for Småland. In other parts of the country he launched a campaign to slander the rebels. The province was reported to have not done its part in the revolution against the Danes. They were rumored to be making big money trading with the Danish provinces and were forcing prices up everywhere. Finally, Nils, himself was accused of incest, of lying with "two sisters of his own flesh."[3]

Gustav appealed again to Christian III and was rewarded with an army of three companies of horse and foot, about 1,500 men. Commanded by Peder Pederson, they crossed into Småland on February 24, but never managed to join forces with Gustav's troops or engage Nils' peasant army. They accomplished little accept to rape and plunder peaceful farms and villages.

By midwinter Gustav had finally mobilized all his nobility's quota of knights and men-at-arms. He had imported thirteen companies of German infantry and cavalry, some 6,000 mercenaries, troops who fought well enough in the open but which had proved ineffective in the Småland forests. To carry the fight into the woods, Gustav needed Swedish troops with a core unit of the toughest and the very best in the kingdom.

His propaganda machine went to work in Dalarna, circulating a letter bearing the provincial seal asking for volunteers to subdue the "pack of thieves"[4] in Småland. Gustav picked up 500 Dalesmen to add to his peasant conscripts from the other provinces. He was ready to move.

Although Nils had forbidden the continuation of savagery against the Småland nobility, there were independent bands of guerrillas, or more properly, just outlaws, that were still attacking these estates. This provided Gustav with all the pretext he required and he gathered his army, minus the Danes, and pushed south toward Småland.

Nils was forced into action. In late January he advanced on Kalmar Castle, the one part of Småland still in royal hands. He assaulted the walls with his peasant army. He had no heavy artillery, no siege equipment, no trained storm troops and no chance of carrying this indomitable fortress commanded by the quite capable Germand Svensson.

Repulsed at Kalmar, Nils summoned all the Småland peasants who would follow him into Östergötland to intercept Gustav's army. Here on the plains, the heavy cavalry was too much for the untrained peasant infantry. Beaten once again, Nils withdrew into the forests of north-eastern Småland. The royal army pursued. Nils selected for his final stand a narrow pass, deep in the woods, between Lake Hjorten and Lake Virserumssjon. Here was the perfect defensive position and here, in the forest, Nils' Smålanders were in their element. But Gustav, too, had brought his Swedes accustomed to woodland warfare and at its heart were the 500 Dalesmen.

The battle was joined on March 20, 1543, when the lakes were still frozen over. The water that should have protected Nils's flanks instead turned out to be his undoing. While the main body of the royal army attacked the Smålanders head on, a detachment crossed the lake ice and took the peasant army from the rear. In addition, Nils was carried from the field early in the fight with an arquebus ball in either thigh. Pressed front and rear with their leader down, the peasant army broke. Five hundred Smålanders were left lying in the field.

The rout of the Småland peasant army was complete. It broke up, each group returned to its parish and county to carry on the fight as guerilla bands. One by one Gustav's troops recaptured these areas, returning Småland to crown control, treating the province like a conquered and occupied territory.

Nils recovered from his wounds, only to be hunted down and finally killed not far from Flaka, once his home. His body was taken to Kalmar Castle where, according to castle records, it was "quartered and in four pieces, was placed on stake and wheel and on his head a copper crown."[5]

Gustav had had a very close call and the lessons of this last great Swedish rebellion were not lost on him. He did what he could to slow the pace of the Reformation in Sweden and lightened the tax burden on the peasantry. He cracked down on the unlawful practices of his bailiffs. Gustav had always despised incompetence and corruption in his government, but his cleansing had been done at high levels, ministers and provincial governors, officials he had personal contact with. Now he went after lower members of his civil service and had some success in correcting the injustices.

In 1544 Gustav called a Riksdag at Västerås, not to deal with some crisis, but to plan for the peace and prosperity of the kingdom. He pushed through his reforms of the succession process. The throne would go to the eldest son. The younger ones would be granted duchies with some degree of independence.

At this assembly Gustav set forth the reorganization of the military. Levies from the nobility would still provide the cavalry. Infantry would still be drawn from the peasantry, universal service in wartime, but only one in six would be required in peacetime. Peasants would be issued imported steel weapons. Besides conscripts, Gustav needed a ready reserve of trained soldiers that could be called upon at a moment's notice. To fill this need Gustav recruited the *fänikor,* units of foot soldiers organized by district. These volunteers would live on their own small parcels of land and maintain themselves for the most part. Their pay would be minimal except when called up. These fänikor, about 500 men to a unit, were the beginning of what would grow into the Swedish system of provincial infantry regiments.

There would still be a standing army of professional soldiers, but as much as possible these would also come from the Swedish population instead of importing mercenaries. The Stockholm guard was 64 percent German in 1545. This had dropped to just 10 percent by 1553. The army was to become a Swedish fighting force.

Gustav continued to build his navy. In addition to the armed merchantmen and large sailing warships, he added a considerable number of galleys to his fleet in which he could use his standing army and new fänikor as both rowers and landing force. On all his ships Gustav emphasized the use of cannon and the new modern style of fighting at sea. Instead of the traditional method of closing on ships so small arms and boarding parties could be employed, Swedish ships would maintain a separation and fire their onboard artillery. At first these guns were the wrought-iron straps laid side-by-side to form a tube, held together by bands much like a barrel. These early siege type guns threw a very large ball or stone at a high trajectory only a short distance because the barrel was short; the powder charge had to be small to keep from blowing up the gun and they were breach loaded with no good way to completely seal

VASA ANCESTRAL LINE - MONARCHS OF SWEDEN AND POLAND

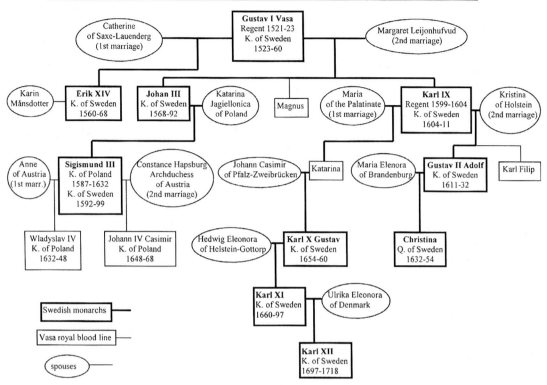

the breach. The firing rate was slow and accuracy poor, but the effect of hitting a wooden ship with one of these missiles could be devastating.

Gustav imported the early guns and their crews from Germany, but gradually the Swedes learned to cast their own "copper" cannon made of bronze (copper and tin). These guns were superior. Using a large powder charge, they had more range and accuracy and, although muzzle-loading, could be fired rapidly. By the end of his reign, Gustav was replacing most of his naval artillery with the modern cannon. The superb showing of his infant marine force against the Lübeck fleet in the Count's Feud indicates just how far Sweden had come.

Although Gustav was constructing the foundation for what would become a powerful military, he did his best to stay out of wars with foreign countries. However, in 1555 Russia attacked Swedish Finland, breaking a 1537 Novgorod armistice. The Russian aggression was in response to Swedish-Finnish settlement encroachment in Karelia and continuing clashes along the Finnish-Russian border.

Gustav went to Finland to lead the war effort and was able to maintain control of Viborg and Nyslott. Neither side could claim any major victories and the affair was finally settled with a somewhat humiliating peace agreement signed, this time, in Moscow. Thereafter the tsar turned his attention to the Baltic States south of the Gulf of Finland where Gustav refused to get involved.

At his last Riksdag in 1560, Gustav made final arrangements for his succession. Erik, his oldest son would be king. Johan would be duke of Finland. Östergötland would go to Magnus, and Södermanland, Närke and Värmland to Karl. The king would die later that same year. He had done his best to see that the nation building he had so carefully nurtured would be carried on.

Gustav had handled his kingdom as he would an estate. He dabbled in the agriculture of the realm, made rules and regulations on when to plant and when to harvest. He brought in new blast furnaces for the Bergslag and made rules regulating hunting and fishing. He changed the character of land ownership. One-half of the land was still owned by taxpaying peasants, but now the church and nobles combined owned one-fourth instead of one-fourth each. And the rest, one-fourth, belonged to the crown.

Much was written about Gustav by those outside Sweden, mostly his enemies. He was characterized as a usurper, evil, greedy, power hungry, cruel and treacherous. In the first couple of centuries after his death, Swedes lionized him as the father of modern Sweden, brave, clever, inspirational, wise, a great leader of men, an almost legendary figure. The truth, of course, lies somewhere in between. Though not a highly educated man, he was obviously very intelligent and he had a practical sense of what he could and should do for his people. He was a gifted orator, charming and persuasive when dealing with individuals, ruthless and unscrupulous when treating with enemies. Above all he was pragmatic and always proceeded with a single purpose, the building of a strong Swedish nation.

In America the construction of our nation, from the outbreak of rebellion to final consolidation at the end of the Civil War, took almost 90 years. In Sweden this same process took less than 25 years and occurred under the leadership of one man, Gustav Vasa. Perhaps his most fitting epitaph was written by his grandson Gustav Adolf: "This King Gustav was the instrument by which God again raised up our fatherland to prosperity. By his wisdom he gave peace and good government to the land."[6]

7. Erik XIV and the First Northern War

Gustav Vasa had worked hard to provide for the stability of his kingdom and at the same time establish suitable positions for each of his sons, two objectives at odds with each other as many a monarch has discovered. At the Riksdag of 1544 the Estates had accepted the Succession Pact by which Erik would become king and they had agreed, in principle, that the other sons would each gain a duchy, details to be set forth in Gustav's testament. This Testament of 1560 confirmed Johan as master of Finland, a position he had in fact held since 1556 with his own chancellery, exchequer and appointed government officials. Magnus received Östergötland and Västergötland while Karl was allotted Södermånland and Västermånland. Each duke was to receive all the revenues from his duchy ordinarily passed to the crown including fines, taxes, tariffs and tolls. They could make some limited international agreements, but were bound to be faithful to the king and provide all the armed men they could muster for his military needs. Great decisions of national importance were to be made by all the brothers in consultation. This arrangement was a prescription for trouble if any of these siblings turned out to be overly ambitious and at least two were certainly that.

All four brothers were handsome, physically strong and intelligent. In addition, they had had educational opportunities not available to their father. They had been raised as heirs to the throne with all the advantages of any other European prince.

Of the four, Erik certainly considered himself the superior. Not only was he the eldest and in line for the throne, but he was the only one of royal blood on both sides. As the only child of Gustav and his first wife, Catherine of Saxe-Lauenburg, he felt apart from his siblings and the Swedish nobility, more on a par with European aristocracy in general. This was to color his pursuit of a suitable match in marriage.

At twenty-seven, Erik had for some time held his own court at Kalmar Castle, spending large sums to make it into a palace fit for a European prince. He was a patron of the arts, playing the lute and composing music. He was fluent in Latin, French, Spanish, Italian, Finnish and German. He read Hebrew and Greek, and was well versed in history, both ancient and modern. He had an understanding of science and mathematics, and his mind turned to the abstract easily rather than to the practical as was his father's trait. He understood the nuances of the day's theological discussions where Gustav had not. He could be eloquent, a family trait, although his rhetoric tended to be classical in composition and delivery rather than earthy and emotional as were his father's speeches that connected with the people. He had studied military theory and tactics, and would put into practice his own ideas as king. He inherited his father's organizational and administrative talents, but also Gustav's suspicious nature which in Erik became pathological. He showed a spark of genius, but lacked his father's good common sense and ability to weigh the pros and cons of an issue and come to the best conclusion. For all his accomplishments, he lacked his father's sense of humor and common touch especially among those he would have to socialize with and depend upon, namely, the Swedish nobility. In temperament he was high strung, nervous and could be quite violent when provoked. His passion was astrology, which was to get him into difficulty more than once.

Well before his father's death Erik had begun his quest for a suitable wife. From his stylish court at Kalmar, the heir to the Swedish throne surveyed the courts of Europe for a proper match. Marriage projects were begun with Poland, Hess and the Electorate of Saxony, but none came to fruition. Erik's standards were high. To be eligible, a princess had to be of proper royal stature and provide political advantage, as well as be beautiful and charming. He demanded a portrait and reports on interviews from his negotiators on each potential candidate. Then a chain of events was started at the other end of the Baltic that would affect Erik's marriage schemes, his royal reign and the destiny of Sweden.

For some time the power of the Livonian Knights (The Brothers of the Sword) had been disintegrating. They were still operating much as they had in the thirteenth century when they had Christianized the tribes of the eastern Baltic south of the Finland Gulf at the point of the sword. Their grand master still recruited new members only from Germany for this military-religious medieval state. But its crusading spirit had long since died and its organization was behind the times. Poland and Lithuania, united from time to time, were threatening from the south and Russia was steadily advancing from the east, conquering Ingria and taking Narva in 1558, giving Ivan IV a port city on the Baltic. The effect on Russian trade was immediate. Dutch, Danish, Hansa and English merchants could trade directly with Muscovy without passing their goods through the Livonian Knights' ports, chiefly Reval. In retaliation, the order unleashed its merchantmen as privateers on ships passing through the Gulf of Finland. The Russian encroachment continued breaking the final resistance offered by the German order. Desperate, the knights, bishops and cities of this Baltic state appealed to the northern nations for help. In 1559, the grand master ceded his southern territories to Poland in the treaty of Vilna. Sigismund II Augustus sent in troops to garrison the important castles and cities of southern Livonia.

That same year, the bishop of Kurland and the regent of Ösel Island negotiated their protection with Denmark as a fief under the king's brother. Frederick II was only too happy to get rid of a troublesome younger sibling to a distant land. Magnus landed on Ösel in 1560 and took over the fortress of Sönnenburg from the order's commander.

Meanwhile, the city of Reval was petitioning Gustav for his protection. The old king had spurned these advances in the past, but by 1560 he was reconsidering because of the Russian advance through Ingria, Estonia and northern Livonia toward Reval. With Estonia and Ingria in the tsar's hands, Finland, across the gulf, would be threatened. Besides, there were close ties between Reval and Finland. About a quarter of the city's population was Swedish. However, by the time the city's emissaries arrived, Gustav was on his deathbed and negotiations had to wait.

The fluid trade situation in the eastern Baltic was compounded by the discovery of the White Sea route north of Scandinavia to Russia by Richard Chancellor in 1553. As early as 1557, Gustav had sent a mission to the English queen Mary I encouraging that nation to use Viborg as the path to Muscovite trade and suggested an Anglo-Swedish commercial venture. The envoy accomplished nothing except to learn something of the state of English politics since Henry VIII's death in 1547 and introduce a new candidate into Erik's calculations.

Henry's heir and only legitimate son was from his third wife, Jane Seymour. Edward VI took the throne at age nine and died seven years later of consumption. Mary, Henry's daughter with Catherine of Aragon, his first wife, then ascended the throne in 1553 and tried to re-establish Catholicism, but met with resistance at every level of society. Almost 300 people, many prominent social members, were burned at the stake. It seemed quite possible that she would cause a civil war or be forced from the monarchy allowing Elizabeth, Henry's daughter by Anne Boleyn, his second wife, to be crowned. Erik considered a marriage proposal to Elizabeth, but this would be a gamble. Mary could hang on and relegate Elizabeth to royal oblivion providing no advantage to Erik. Nevertheless, the idea struck Erik's fancy and he sent his tutor, Dionysius Beurreus, to England in November 1557 to ask for Elizabeth's hand. The mission failed, as did another in early 1559. A third embassy, headed by Prince Johan, left that year to carry the proposal to now Queen Elizabeth I (Mary having died), but was likewise fruitless and returned in 1560. Erik determined to go himself and received permission from his father and the Estates. He had preparations in full swing when Gustav's death canceled the voyage.

Erik assumed the reins of state at twenty-seven years of age in 1561 confident, but wary of his brothers and the aristocracy. He immediately set about consolidating his position. The sharing of power as set forth in Gustav's testament would have to be changed. At his coronation in July — ostentatious to say the least — Erik created the first hereditary noble titles in Swedish history, three counts (one of these was Svante Sture) and nine barons. There had been for some time, a difference in the lesser nobility and the great magnates, but this difference was economic and to some extent social. The titles of steward and martial, et cetera had existed, but these were earned by the individual and not passed on. The new titles, however, were hereditary and later would be given special privileges and status under the law. Erik's purpose may have been to elevate Sweden's position among European nations by recognizing its noble class or elevating his own situation or simply currying favor with the aristocracy. In any case he set in motion a movement with lasting effects.

Within only a few months of his coronation, Erik called the 1561 Riksdag of Arboga, the first meeting of the Estates to actually be called a Riksdag. Here, Erik had an amended Gustav's Testament approved. By the new terms the dukes would forfeit their inheritance if found guilty of any conspiracy against the king, all duchy military forces were placed under direct command of the king, all ecclesiastic appointments and policy were reserved to the crown, ducal court decisions could be appealed to the king's courts, and all high government official appointments had to have crown approval. The dukes were forbidden from calling local meetings of the Estates and conducting foreign policy except for arrangements of marriage — an important exception as it turned out.

Finally, Erik initiated a legal process by which the nobles, particularly the great magnates, could recover land lost to Gustav and the Vasa family. During the old king's reign, Gustav had built up his family's holdings through litigation, confiscation, bargaining and forced sales. These lands had been split between the four sons providing each with large estates. Much of the nobility was bitter about the loss of these holdings and Erik now gave them the opportunity to sue in an attempt to recover titles of questionable validity. Out of 5,000 manors, over 2,600 were judged to have been improperly acquired by the old king. Erik lost little in these proceedings as the crown was one of the major plaintiffs acquiring not only Vasa lands, but also some church property the nobles had taken when the church estates were broken up. The aristocracy was happy at recovering lands they thought lost forever. The real losers were the dukes who saw much of the family property melt away in litigation.

Through a series of actions Erik had strengthened his position immeasurably vis-à-vis his brothers. He now felt reasonably secure. He was generally popular with the masses of the people as he had interceded in their behalf against both the nobility and government servants. His actions to gain favor with the nobility, especially the magnates, had paid off with at least outward support. Duke Magnus would be no problem. He was already showing signs of the insanity that would eventually completely overtake him. Karl, at ten years of age, was not a threat for the present. Only Johan remained as a major concern and the king's brother was about to use the one avenue Erik had left open to him to cause the new monarch problems.

After Erik's acquisition of the throne, the Reval emissaries approached the new king petitioning for protection from the Muscovite Empire practically at their gates. In addition to the advantages Gustav had seen, the city would put Erik in a position to oppose any ideas his brother might have about expanding across the Finland Gulf. In January 1561 he accepted the emissaries' offer. By March Klas Kristersson Horn was in Reval negotiating terms. In June the city burghers swore fealty to the Swedish crown as did the nobles of Harrien, Wierland and later Jerwen. Reval was now Swedish, but other areas would have to be secured. This was surely a major turning point in Swedish history. With this one move, the country could lay claim to central and western Estonia, the first territory outside traditional Swedish-Finnish lands, placing her irrevocably on the path to empire.

King Erik XIV ruled not only Sweden and Finland, but had his own waterway as the Danish kings had their Sound. Could he make it pay the way the Danish monarchs did? First Erik tried to induce foreign merchants to trade at Reval or Viborg instead of the Russian Narva. Both were better ports, but Narva offered direct access to the Russian trade and therefore received a great deal of traffic from the western merchants. Next he threatened to charge a toll on cargoes bound for or returning from Narva — ships trading at Reval or Viborg would be exempt. In April 1562, with Russia and Poland at war, Erik informed Denmark and the Hansa that he would enforce his demands for shipping tolls with his navy. In June his warships captured a merchant fleet of 32 ships returning from Narva. Danish and Dutch merchantmen were released once they had paid the toll, but the eleven Lübeck ships were detained and harassed. The blockade antagonized not only these nations, but also England and the emperor, all of whom felt they had a right to free and open trade with Muscovy through Narva.

Meanwhile, Erik's general in Estonia, Klas Kristersson Horn, had taken Padis in September 1561 and had pushed on to attack Leal, securing eastern Estonia. However, this territory was claimed by Magnus as his Danish fief. To make matters worse, Erik conspired with factions in Riga to have that city turned over to him as Reval had been. The attempt failed and served only to antagonize Poland, which held the city.

In November 1561 the Livonian Knights finally dissolved their order, turning their territory over to Poland which could then lay claim to all of Livonia, Estonia and Ingria putting Sigismund II Augustus in direct competition with Erik. The young Swedish king's adventures in the Baltics were creating more enemies for him than he could possibly handle. Erik needed some allies.

In spite of their differences, Sigismund had made overtures to the Swedish king. In January 1561 and again in the spring of 1562, Polish emissaries had been sent to Stockholm offering an alliance in return for Sweden's suspension of military actions in Estonia. Erik agreed to a truce only to learn that on June 2 his army had taken Pernau, a fortified city deep in Polish Livonia. Sigismund was furious over the betrayal and immediately sent an emissary to Denmark proposing joint action against Sweden in the Baltics. As the storm of war gathered strength in the eastern Baltic, Erik would have one more act of treachery to deal with.

Soon after Gustav's death, his son Johan had become interested in marriage to Polish royalty. Overtures by the duke of Finland were reciprocated by an offer of proposal to Katarina Jagiellonica, one of Sigismund's sisters, all perfectly legal under the Articles of Arboga. Erik raised no objections, but as relations between Sweden and Poland became more and more strained, the wedding seemed more and more in jeopardy. In spite of this situation, or because of it, Johan loaned his prospective father-in-law 30,000 *dalers* in January 1562 without telling his sovereign. Eventually, Erik found out about his brother's loan to a foreign monarch which should have put him on guard.

As Swedish-Polish relations deteriorated, Johan resolved to hurry the wedding along. In June of 1562 he left for Danzig and on October 4, he married Katarina in Vilna. He promised his aid in Sigismund's war with Russia, loaning Sigismund another 120,000 dalers. In return Johan received seven castles in Livonia and Estonia. One of these, Weissenstein, was just coming under attack by the Swedish army. So Swedish forces laid siege to a fortress garrisoned by Polish troops fighting for Erik's brother. It fell in November 1562.

These acts of treachery were too much for the Swedish king. The duke had at least violated the Articles of Arboga if not committed outright treason. Erik called a Riksdag to try Johan in absentia. On June 7 a guilty verdict was rendered and Johan was to forfeit property, hereditary rights and his life. Johan, holed up at Åbo Castle, surrendered August 12. The prince and his Polish wife were imprisoned at Gripsholm Castle for the next four years.

On August 13, 1563, Frederick declared war on Sweden. In addition to the incidents in the Baltics and the Finland Gulf, three events finally brought about the Seven Year Northern War (the First Northern War). First, Frederick II adopted the Three Crown symbol of the old Kalmar Union. The device stirred up all the old hatreds felt by the Swedes toward the Danes. A Swedish embassy on its way to Hesse was captured in Copenhagen and thrown in prison. Finally, a Swedish-Danish naval engagement was fought off Bornholm.

On May 30 a Danish war fleet met a Swedish naval fleet and demanded the Swedes provide the traditional salute of respect to the Danes in their waters. The Swedes refused. A four hour battle ensued. The Swedish ships armed with "coppers" outgunned the Danes mounting the old wrought-iron breechloaders. The Danish admiral, his flagship and two others were captured. Two more ships were damaged. Two months later the two countries were at war.

Lübeck and Poland joined Denmark in a coalition. Lübeck hoped to regain her dominance of Baltic shipping and free access to Narva. Poland looked to expel Sweden from Livonia altogether, but Denmark wanted to conquer Sweden, canceling Gustav's achievements and his country's independence. Erik and Sweden were quite literally fighting for their lives.

Though vastly outnumbered, Sweden was not unprepared for the coming struggle. Her successes in the Baltics and at sea owed much to Erik's military innovations. Since he had taken office, he had worked hard to strengthen his three key fortifications: Älvsborg, to protect his western outlet to the North Sea; Viborg, the key to holding Finland and one side of the Finland Gulf waterway; and Reval, to secure the opposite side of the gulf.

He reformed the army drawing inspiration from the Roman model, especially Caesar and Vegetius. The infantry was divided into a basic unit called the fänikor corresponding to the Roman cohort. This was an extension of the military organization his father had started. A number of fänikors were grouped into a tactical division corresponding to a legion. He armed the infantry with pikes, halberds, body armor and the latest in firearms, the last being the matchlock arquebus. Erik agreed with the latest military thinking, in that the day of heavy cavalry on the battlefield was over — though the Poles would prove this wrong — and concentrated on his infantry as the centerpiece of his army. They were trained to fight in combined formations, arquebus with pikemen, halberds with pikes, etc. These combinations were deployed in a linear fashion instead of the block formations (the tercio) generally used in Europe at that time. He continued his father's practice of purging the army of mercenaries, relying as much as possible on native troops.

He reorganized the artillery, standardizing the calibers of his coppers. He expanded the royal foundries for the production of these bronze cannon for use in both the army and the navy. Here Sweden had the advantage of being able to produce all of its own copper for its artillery.

Erik was no less an innovator with his navy. Beginning with a powerful fleet left to him by his father, he added to it, especially large warships. He is credited with introducing the *tumblehome* hull design and double hull type of construction to the Swedish navy. This innovation solved a couple of problems created by the new style of naval warfare. Small arms, hand to hand combat by boarding parties had given way to shipboard artillery which meant mounting cannon on the decks above the waterline. More cannon and more decks led to the great ships of 500 to 700 tons displacement or even larger. But more weight placed higher and higher in the ship's structure above the waterline along with the tall masts moved the center of gravity of the vessel well above the waterline making the ship inherently unstable. Secondly, the powerful new bronze and iron cannon fired a ball with a relatively flat trajectory instead of lobbing a large stone onto the enemy ship as the old wrought-iron stave type guns had done. Now hulls could be pierced at or near the waterline, sinking a ship in minutes.

To mitigate both these problems the tumblehome construction featured an expanded lower hull with narrowing sides above the water line. In addition, large ships were built with double hulls. Erik had the space between the hulls filled with iron ore for added ballast. Swedish great warships were reputed to be the most stable in northern waters. The new Baltic maritime power was building some of the largest warships in the world.

Erik completed the conversion from wrought-iron naval artillery to coppers begun by his father. Further, he introduced new tactics. Early shelling between gun mounted sailing ships proved surprisingly ineffective. Several hours of fighting might see few hits because so few shots were actually fired. Maneuvering the ships into a position so the guns could be trained on the enemy vessel was proving difficult. Swedish battle fleets were divided into squadrons of one great ship and two smaller ships. The great ships formed the forward line followed by a second line of smaller vessels. The leading large ships were to engage the enemy then the two smaller vessels would move in to support each great ship. All these reforms were possible only because of the huge treasury Gustav Vasa had accumulated. Thus, the Swedish army and navy had been effective in both Estonia and the Baltic. Erik's main deficiency was in experienced officers, generals and seamen. In some cases he would turn to professional mercenaries for generals and the results were not always favorable.

The Seven Years Northern War or First Northern War opened auspiciously for the coalition. Frederick, having close contact with Germany, could quickly build an army of professional mercenaries. By August 1563, he had assembled 27,000 men and twenty-seven warships which were sent against Älvsborg, the fortress guarding Sweden's only western port. The strong fortification was manned by 700 troops with two months' provisions and 148 guns. Nevertheless, its walls were breached after only three days of shelling and the garrison surrendered in early September.

SHIPS OF THE BALTIC

Early
Hanseatic
Cog

16th
Century
Cog

Swedish
Major
Warship
17th
Century

Illustrations by Amanda Peterson

Erik had 3,400 troops stationed in Livonia, but he did have 18,000 infantry and 4,500 cavalry available in Sweden and with these he led a counterattack, invading Halland laying siege to Halmstad in October. Overcoming supply and artillery transportation problems, he was able to breach the walls in November, but two attempts at storming the city were beaten back and Erik finally turned over command of the army to a French mercenary, Charles de Mornay.

Meanwhile, Frederick rushed a relief force to Halmstad that was intercepted by de Mornay. The Swedes met the advance guard of a small cavalry force and 2,000 arquebusiers at Mared. The Swedish horse was driven off, exposing the flanks of the infantry, resulting in a Swedish defeat. Had the Danish infantry been brought to bear, the defeat might have been a rout. Fortunately, the mercenary foot did not arrive for another day and de Mornay was able to slip away under cover of darkness, but he was forced to leave behind his guns.

Victorious twice, Frederick prepared two more campaigns. In Jämtland, Norway, he ordered a force be assembled and sent into Ångermanland to cut Sweden in two and open a backdoor to an invasion of Finland. This attack never got off the ground, but the risk was noted by Erik.

Frederick's second campaign was in the south of Sweden. Here he sent his ablest general, Daniel Rantzau, through Skåne into Småland to capture the fortress and port of Kalmar, an attack that was supposed to have coincided with the advance against Älvsborg, but had been delayed by Erik's move into Halland. In Småland, Rantzau got a taste of the border people's defensive methods of delay, sabotage and ambush. Unable to reach Kalmar and with winter fast approaching, he withdrew to Skåne after pillaging the border area, spreading as much havoc as possible. It was only a prelude of things to come.

Now Frederick found himself with a large mercenary army he could not afford and that was not fighting. By spring he had reduced his mercenaries to two incomplete infantry regiments and seven companies of cavalry, less than 8,000 men.

While Frederick's army was resting during the winter, Erik again took the offense sending Klas Horn into Bohuslän to besiege the castle at Bohus in the hopes of breaking through to the sea in February 1564. A second army under a French mercenary, Claude Collart, invaded Jämtland with 4,000 foot and horse, and 300 ski troops. Horn was unsuccessful and had to withdraw, but Collart broke through, capturing Jämtland and Härjedalen, then crossed the mountains taking Trondheim on the Norwegian coast. Erik would hold Jämtland and Häjedalem through the war, but in May a Danish rescue force of over 4,000 men landed at Trondheim and Collart was forced to surrender.

In 1565 the Swedish forces operating in Scania took most of Halland and captured the port of Varberg. It was put into service as the main western Swedish port, replacing Älvsborg. Records show the quantity of goods passing through this port surpassed normal traffic through Älvsborg. Frederick called upon Daniel Rantzau to recover the lost seaport. The Danish army lay siege to Varberg, but could not dislodge the Swedes. Erik countered by gathering all his remaining troops and moving in that direction. With winter coming on and the threat of a relief force intervening, Rantzau raised his siege of Varberg and set out for winter quarters in Skåne. His main objective achieved, Erik turned over command to Jakob Henriksson Hästeskog and departed with a 1,200 man escort.

Hästeskog pursued the Danish army, catching up with them near the small town of Axtorna. The ensuing fight would be the only major land battle of the Seven Year Northern War. Rantzau had 7,500 infantry, 1,600 cavalry and 21 guns, nearly all German mercenaries with a sprinkling of Scots. Hästeskog's Swedish army consisted of 8,000 foot (peasant conscripts), 3,000 horse (Swedish rusttjänst and some German *reiters*), and 42 pieces of artillery.

On October 16, 1565, Rantzau took up defensive positions and waited for the Swedes to attack. Hästeskog hit the Danish army with light artillery then pushed forward with his first line of infantry. Rantzau counterattacked with cavalry, which silenced the Swedish guns, then turned on the infantry. Hästeskag ordered in his cavalry carrying a 2 to 1 advantage. Nevertheless, the Danish horse broke the Swedish cavalry charge and scattered the troopers.

The distraction of the Swedish cavalry attack did allow the infantry to press forward driving the Danish foot backward. However, once the Danish horse had destroyed the Swedish horse, they returned to the attack on the infantry. Bielke, the front line infantry commander, ordered his troops to fall back and retake the artillery, then join up with the rest of the infantry. But without cavalry support, the Swedish foot could not hold against the Danish foot and horse. They were soon in full retreat leaving their artillery behind. Again, the Swedish conscript infantry had aquitted itself well against the German professionals, but the poor showing of the Swedish cavalry had lost the day.

While the land war was grinding to a stalemate, it was the sea blockade that could bring Sweden to her knees quickly. Älvsborg had been taken in the first months of the war, cutting the country's traditional opening to the west, though Varberg was proving a good substitute. Danish and Lübeck fleets now threw up a blockade cutting Sweden's eastern ports off from the German and eastern Baltic ports. Without imported commodities, particularly salt, the population would soon face starvation. Fortunately, Gustav had foreseen such circumstances and stockpiled salt in the a isles of the Great Church in Stockholm, allowing the county to get by for the first two years of the war when the blockade was fairly effective.

During the summer of 1563 Denmark and Lübeck had put together great fleets by buying and converting large numbers of merchantmen into warships and manning them with German mercenary soldiers. These were added to the few built-for-war ships already in their navies. The coalition navy was commanded by Danish admiral Herluf Trolle, who introduced his own tactics whereby the fleet was divided into squadrons of three ships, one major vessel of 300 tons or more supported by two converted merchantmen. If attacking with the wind, the squadron would form a wedge with the major ship leading. If downwind and being attacked they formed a line with the major ship in the center.

A combined fleet sailed for Stockholm to enforce the blockade with 20 major Danish ships and 5 from Lübeck. On September 11 the coalition ships were joined by the Swedish fleet of some 12 major ships, but even the smaller Swedish vessels were warships and were better armed than the coalition's merchantmen. Again the Danish-Lübeck ships attempted to close and board, but Erik's ships were faster and able to hold them off while hitting them with cannon fire. Yet, the Swedes were not able to inflict a decisive blow and eventually withdrew into the Stockholm Archipelago. The coalition fleet was left to cruise the northern Baltic enforcing the blockade.

The next summer, 1564, the coalition fleet again appeared off the Swedish coast, this time with 16 Danish and 10 Lübeck major ships. On May 10 it was attacked by an increased Swedish fleet of 16 major warships. Again, even the smaller Swedish craft were warships while all but the largest allied vessels were converted merchantmen. Running with the wind, the Swedish fleet inflicted some damage the first day, but the second day the wind changed in favor of the coalition. One by one the Swedish ships withdrew leaving the giant flagship *Mars* (about 1,800 tons) to carry on alone. It sank one Lübeck ship and damaged several Danish vessels. Coalition gunfire finally smashed her rudder allowing the Danish-Lübeck ships to close and attack at close range. Eventually, the giant was set afire and destroyed.

Erik ordered the fleet back to sea that same summer to destroy the enemy fleet and this time they intercepted a Lübeck convoy of merchant ships, capturing the lot. This prize was brought to port where it was discovered a major portion of the cargo was salt, enough to supply Sweden for a year, a great triumph, but it still did nothing to raise the blockade.

Exasperated by his navy's timidity and lack of confidence, Erik now put his general from the Estonian campaigns, Klas Kristersson Horn, in command of the fleet and sent them out once more. Again the two fleets collided, but under Horn the Swedes did not run. A series of battles were fought between Öland and Gotland from August 11 to the 15, 1564. Again the coalition tried to close and board, but the Swedes outran and outmaneuvered them while firing their coppers. The effect, however, was slight. No decisive kills were made all though three Danish ships were captured in a night action. In the fall the Swedish fleet was able to put in at Kalmar, leaving the northern Baltic open to commerce. The coalition cruised the southern Baltic still able to interrupt trade with Germany, but had to leave the Swedish-Finland traffic unmolested.

By spring 1565 Erik had built his fleet to 25 major warships of 300 tons or more, a tremendous achievement due again to the treasury he inherited from his father. In early May he sent Commander Horn to duel with Admiral Trolle and the coalition navy once more. Horn sailed into the southern Baltic catching an enemy fleet of ten ships by surprise. Badly outgunned, the ships were burned by their crews or escaped to the German coast where the duke of Pomerania interned them for the duration of the war.

The coalition hastily pulled together a fleet of eleven Danish and ten Lübeck ships. Under Trolle, they met the Swedish fleet between Mecklenburg and the Danish islands on June 4. Again the Swedes held the coalition off with their shipboard artillery. One of the casualties of this battle was the Danish admiral Herluf Trolle.

The blockade was broken and the Swedes cruised the south Baltic, even stopping neutral merchant ships in the Sound and extracting a toll. The symbolism was clear; a new naval power now controlled the Baltic, if only for the time being. Sweden had served notice that from now on her sea power would have to be considered in Baltic naval calculations.

But the coalition wasn't through yet. On July 7 a combined fleet of some 27 major warships met the Swedish fleet of about the same size off Börnholm Island. This time the Swedes allowed the coalition ships to close where their cannon were more effective. Horn lost three ships, but took the Danish flagship and sunk two others, one Danish and one Lübeck. Casualties were heavy on both sides, but it was the coalition fleet that retreated, leaving the Baltic to the Swedes. Again in the spring of 1566 Erik sent a still larger fleet with 30 major warships into the southern Baltic. It blocked the Sound and extracted tolls, even forcing some merchants to port in Sweden to sell their goods. Among these was a Dutch fleet of 52 merchantmen whose cargo was mainly salt. Coalition resources were nearly exhausted, but by midsummer they were able to scrape together something approaching the size of the Swedish fleet. The coalition had also acquired iron cannon from English foundries to replace the old stave and hoop breechloaders. The iron artillery was an improvement, but they did not cool as fast as the Swedish coppers and therefore could not be fired as fast. The two fleets met off Öland in an indecisive action of all cannon fire on both sides. Withdrawing, the coalition fleet made for Gotland where it ran into a fierce summer gale. Nine Danish and three Lübeck major ships were lost off Visby, losses that could not be made up. Nature had finished the job begun by the Swedes; the coalition navy had been irrevocably crippled. In 1567 the Swedish navy cruised the Baltic unchallenged.

By 1567 Erik had accomplished most of his objectives for the war. He had held onto nearly all his Swedish territory, even taking two Norwegian provinces and a good share of Danish Halland. His admiral Klas Kristersson Horn had broken the blockade and now controlled the Baltic. Successes in the war, however, were not enough to sustain his troubled reign.

Many of the land campaigns Erik had led in person, leaving government administration to his secretary, Jöran Persson. He was the first of what came to be known as the "rule of secretaries," a long line of powerful administrators in the Swedish government.

Persson was the son of a parson of Sala, educated in jurisprudence at Wittenberg under Melanchthon, a schooling financed by Gustav Vasa under his plan to educate Swedes for his civil service. Upon his return in 1555, he entered government service rising to the position of secretary. After 1560 he attached himself to Erik, becoming his confidant and chief advisor. He was intelligent, efficient, capable, arrogant, ruthless and greedy for power. The aristocracy was jealous of his position. He had in effect replaced the Råd, the king's council of noblemen. He was the government's chief prosecutor among other things. It was Persson who managed the case against Johan in his trial before the Riksdag. He brought to trial those of the nobility whom Erik was suspicious of. One of the tools he used was the new High Court created by Erik when he first took office.

During Gustav's reign the king was the court of last appeal. This required a great deal of the monarch's time. The High Court was intended to take much of this burden from the crown. At first it was made up of 16 nobles and functioned as intended. But before long the nobles were replaced by commoners more easily manipulated and Persson became the crown prosecutor. Then it increasingly became a court of first instance, trying matters of treason, sedition and charges of negligence. As the Seven Years War dragged on, it became a kind of court-martial board hearing cases involving accusations of incompetence or lack of enterprise. Charges against the nobles' failure to meet their rusttjänst obligations were brought before this court. Between 1562 and 1567, 300 death penalties were handed down by the court. Many of these were commuted to heavy fines and were pronounced only so the accused could be tortured to reveal co-conspirators — by law only a man condemned to death could be tortured. Persson used this means to collect information on political enemies, particularly the aristocracy, which came to fear and hate this high secretary and his high court.

By 1567 Erik's marriage problems had become a state problem. He had had a series of mistresses and a band of illegitimate children, but no heir. He had made overtures to princesses in Poland, Saxony, Mecklenburg, England, Scotland and Hesse to no avail. At 34, his heir, or lack there of, was becoming a matter of state. For Erik it had become an obsession.

The strain of the war, paranoia toward just about everybody, especially the aristocracy, personal and national pressures to provide an heir, and his own mercurial personality were steadily crowding Erik to the edge of mental collapse. His frustrations and anxieties gradually began to center on one person. His astrological readings had told him he would lose his throne to a light-haired man. Erik interpreted this to mean Nils Sture, eldest son of Svante Sture. Of all the nobles, Erik feared the Sture family the most, a fear he now focused on Nils as his imagined nemesis.

In 1565 Nils was recalled from his position with the army in southern Sweden. He was given the special assignment to go to Halland and coerce the local peasants into doing the labor to strengthen the fortress port of Varberg. He apparently did not carry out his instructions very well for he was soon recalled and scolded for his derelictions. There the matter seemed to rest until June of 1566 when he was arrested and put on trial before the High Court with Persson prosecuting. He was found guilty and sentenced to submit to an act of degradation. He had to ride through the streets of Stockholm in a humiliating manner similar to the mock triumph inflicted on Peder Sunnanväder by Gustav Vasa. Erik figured this disgrace would remove Nils as a potential candidate for his replacement. What it did do was cement the distrust and hatred the aristocracy felt for their king, especially the Sture party, and it prompted a conspiratorial meeting.

In July 1566 there was a secret gathering of the magnates on an island of the Stockholm skerries. Included among those present were Nils Sture, Abraham Stenbock, Ivar Ivarsson Lillieörn, Hogenskild Blielke, Klas Fleming (from Finland), Sten Bauer and most interesting of all, Karl, the king's youngest brother. It was here that fear and hatred turned to organized resistance.

Later that same year Erik once again sent Nils on a special mission. This time it was to secure the hand in marriage of Christina of Lorraine. Christina was the daughter of the former Danish king, Christian II, and therefore related to the Hapsburgs. She was now the duchess of Lorraine, having married and outlived the duke. She was also a schemer laying plans to reclaim the Danish throne. In truth Sweden was not part of her plans, at least not the first step and the mission had no chance of success. This failure piled on top of other evidence of aristocratic conspiracies, including the revelation of the meeting on the island of the Stockholm skerries, drove Erik nearly to the breaking point. But the pressure was not about to abate.

Now his old problems with Russia resurfaced. Caught up in the Northern Seven Year War, Erik had considered it imperative to keep the tsar in at least a neutral position. In 1564 he had signed a treaty with the government of Novgorod acting for Ivan IV by which Russia agreed to recognize Sweden's rights to Reval, Pernau, Karkus and Weissenstein, but had to accept Russian rights to all other territories of the old Livonian Order except Denmark's under Duke Magnus. But as the First Northern War dragged on Ivan saw a chance to pick up a pawn he might use against his adversary in Poland. He demanded Erik hand over Johan's wife, Sigismund's sister, a former princess of Poland.

Erik's back was truly against the wall. New negotiations were opened and a treaty written by which Katarina would be turned over to Ivan, Narva to be freely open to all merchants and Sweden would get Russia's recognition of sovereignty over Estonia. In May Russian emissaries arrived in Stockholm demanding the treaty be signed and the Polish princess be given over to their care.

Under circumstances that would have been difficult for even a strong and stable personality to handle, Erik turned to his only trusted confidante. This was Karin Månsdotter, his latest mistress. She had been with him for two years. The daughter of a prison official and former barmaid at an inn, she was kind, good humored, good hearted and possessed a good deal of common sense. She was the only one who could deal with Erik's fits of depression and he loved her deeply. He was tormented still more because he wanted to make Karin his wife.

Erik called the Estates to meet at Uppsala on May 19, 1567, to deal with the conspiracy charges against him, real or imagined. Before the Riksdag even met Erik had Svante Sture and Sten Eriksson arrested, along with other attendees to the Stockholm skerry meeting, and charged with treason before the High Court. By the time the Riksdag met, Abraham Stenbock and Ivar Ivarsson Lillieörn had received death sentences along with Erik Sture, Nils's brother. At the meeting Jöran Persson demanded the court's sentences be confirmed. On May 21 Nils Sture arrived from Lorraine and was promptly imprisoned.

Erik was to speak to the assembly, but lost his notes and broke down when he tried to ad lib. By this time he was crossing in and out of sanity.

On May 24 he visited Svante Sture in Uppsala Castle taking Sten Eriksson with him. In Svente's cell Erik fell to his knees and begged forgiveness, actions certainly out of character for the king. Upon leaving the cell Jöran Persson caught up with him and engaged Erik in conversation. Erik then left the castle, but returned a couple of hours later, entered Nils Sture's cell and stabbed him to death. As he rushed from the castle he ordered that all the prisoners be executed except "Herr Sten." Within hours Svante and Erik Sture, Abraham Stenbock and Ivar Ivarsson Lillieörn were dead. Only Sten Eriksson Leijonhufvud and Sten Bauer survived — the guards didn't know which Sten the king intended to exempt.

Before Erik could get to Uppsala he was overtaken by his old tutor and servant Dionysius Beurreus, who tried to calm him. Erik, now quite mad, ordered him killed also, then fled into the Uppsala forests. For the next six months the king remained in a state of confusion, divorced from reality. The Råd assumed control of the government and arrested Jöran Persson. He was condemned to death, but the council did not carry out the execution. During that summer Erik secretly married Karin Månsdotter. In October he had Johan and Katarina released from prison. By Christmas he was showing signs of improvement. By New Years he seemed fully recovered. It was none too soon.

With the Swedish government in chaos and its military paralyzed, Frederick II had seen his chance to gain his objective, the conquest of Sweden. He assembled a picked army of his best German mercenaries and put them under the command of his most competent general, Daniel Rantzau. The small army of 4,000 men crossed over from Skåne into Småland and marched to Jöuköping. It hacked its way through the forests of Hålaveden onto the plains of Östergöttland. On their way they burned the cities of Vadstena, Linköping and Söderköping, then retreated to Skänninge where they encamped for the winter.

Rantzau sent word to Frederick that with another 2,000 men he could take Stockholm in the spring and end the war. Fortunately for Sweden the Danish king did not have the resources to hire even 2000 more mercenaries. Trying to keep pace with the growing Swedish navy, paying for the expensive German mercenaries and the interruption of the Sound toll by Horn had exhausted the Danish treasury. He couldn't even resupply the troops Rantzau had led deep into Swedish territory and the army prepared to pull out altogether.

Erik resumed command of Swedish forces, organized an army and set out to destroy the invaders. Rantzau's men needed little encouragement to evacuate and were soon in full retreat with Erik in close pursuit. With the Danes expelled, Erik returned to Stockholm and internal matters. He freed Jöran Persson and reinstated him as secretary. On July 4 he publicly married Karin, legitimizing her two children. Erik had returned to sanity and seemed to have regained complete control of the country, but in reality his authority was only superficial.

By midsummer the dukes, fired by their own ambitions and stung by Erik's marriage to a commoner, led an aristocracy outraged by Persson's return to power. A week after Karin's coronation a force gathered at Vadstena and began marching north, gaining support as it moved along. Erik's commanders and troops deserted him, some joining the opposing army. What loyal troops he could find he personally led into the field. At the battle of Botkyrka just outside Stockhom, the advance was slowed momentarily, but the tide was moving and its momentum would not be denied. By September the dukes and their supporters were at the gates of Stockholm. Now the city burghers deserted Erik as did the Råd and even his half-sisters and their families. The Stockholm garrison turned Jöran Persson over to the dukes who promptly put him to death. The gates were opened and Karl led the rebels into the city. In Erik's last stand in the city center, Sten Eriksson was killed and Ivan's treaty embassy barely escaped with their lives. Finally, on September 28 Erik surrendered and Johan entered the city the following day to take over the government. Erik's tortuous reign was over.

Erik would live another nine years in confinement with Karin and their family. He bequeathed to Sweden an improved military, naval dominance of the Baltic, an exhausted treasury (which Gustav had so carefully built), a war that had drained all its participants, deep enmities between the crown and the high aristocracy that would last for decades and a program of imperial expansion that would last for a hundred and fifty years.

Gustav had freed his country. Erik had expanded Sweden's borders and created a navy to rival any in the Baltic Sea. A new power was emerging on the northern frontier of Europe.

8. King Johan III and the End of the First Northern War

With Erik now a prisoner, the Riksdag met in Stockholm on January 24, 1569, to decide the succession question. The situation harkened back to the old days of the Råd selecting the king. Gustav's efforts to establish a hereditary monarchy were not entirely cancelled, however, for the Riksdag considered only three candidates: Johan, Karl (Erik's two half brothers) and Erik's son Gustav (still a minor and therefore not a serious contender).

Karl conferred with members of the Råd to assess his support, but the nobility had had enough of instability. The council was of one mind and that was to lay out a clear line of succession and they would adhere to Gustav's Testament in doing so. Karl acquiesced and signaled his support for his brother to become king and his nephew, Sigismund, to be next in line.

On January 26 the Estates called Erik to appear before them. No prisoner before the bar on his judgment day ever felt more anxiety. He came with two prepared speeches, ready to accept return to the throne or recognition of the worst, the headsman's axe.

Neither was required. In fact Erik was not even allowed to speak. The Riksdag merely renounced their allegiance to him, officially removing him from the throne. Johan was declared the new king of Sweden with his son, Sigismund, next in line. The succession Pact of 1544 was reaffirmed in spite of the election that had just occurred. Johan's coronation took place six months later, a particularly subdued and austere ceremony befitting the circumstances.

Johan now ruled Sweden as Johan III, yet he did not rest easy as he had inherited the paranoia which seems to have run in the Vasa family, perhaps with good reason. There were constant rumors, some of them probably true, of Erik supporters conspiring for the return of the deposed king. Johan moved Erik from place to place, Stockholm to Åbo, to Gripsholm, to Västerås, to Orbyhusin in an attempt to stay ahead of plans for a breakout. At first he even kept Erik and Karin separated to prevent more progeny that might threaten his or Sigismund's throne, and at times Erik's jailers treated him very inhumanely. Erik finally died February 24, 1577, after falling ill. (Recent tests of his exhumed body show he had a high level of arsenic in his system when he died. He was probably murdered although arsenic was commonly used in medicines of the time and that could account for the presence of the poison.)

Karin Månsdotter remained loyal to the crown and lived to see her daughter marry into Swedish nobility. Erik's son, Gustav, went to Poland in 1575 to be educated in a Jesuit school and later moved to Russia where the tsar, Boris Godunov, tried to use him to advantage in dealing with Sweden and Poland, but found Gustav uncooperative. He died in Russia in 1607.

While keeping one eye on Erik, Johan also had to deal with the war he had inherited from his half-brother. All parties were by now completely exhausted from the struggle. Frederick could not even take advantage of a Swedish civil war and a government in chaos. His one potentially lethal thrust into Sweden was stymied because he had no money to pay his German mercenaries. With Johan's ascendance to the throne the coalition quickly fell apart. Johan inherently favored Poland as a potential partner or ally rather than Russia as Erik had done. Ties were further fractured by Poland's desire to become a Baltic sea power, aspirations that neither Denmark or Lübeck could abide.

Even before his official instatement, Johan sent a commission to negotiate a peace with the belligerents. In November 1568 they signed a peace treaty at Roskilde decidedly partial to Denmark and Lübeck. By its terms Danish and Swedish territories would be returned to the prewar status except Swedish Estonia would be turned over to Duke Magnus and Lübeck would recover its trade privileges of 1523 over Sweden. Johan could not ratify such a treaty and began to arm for a final campaign he hoped would give him a better bargaining position. It would not.

Johan put his dominating fleet to sea in 1569; it captured several Danish and Lübeck merchantmen, but did not make contact with either country's war fleets and in the end accomplished little. In July of that year, however, a Danish-Lübeck fleet shelled Reval, putting pressure on Swedish forces there. In November Frederick sent a small army against Varberg, which fell after only weak resistance. This was a particular blow to Johan as he planned to use the Halland fortress to exchange for Älvsborg. No other important battles were fought along the Scanian frontier between the two countries, but raids and counterraids continued to decimate an already impoverished population on both sides of that border.

Finally, in 1570, Frederick and Johan agreed to a congress of arbitration to end the war. The mediators, meeting in Stettin, Pomerania, included Duke John Frederick of Pomerania presiding, Maximilian II (the new emperor replacing Charles V), King Charles IX of France, Sigismund II Augustus of Poland and the elector of Saxony with delegations from Denmark, Sweden, and Lübeck. It is interesting that Sigismund managed to represent Poland as one of the arbiters and not one of the belligerents.

The Peace of Stettin was concluded on November 30, 1570, with terms that seemed to be a defeat for Sweden on every point. Johan was to renounce his claims to Jämtland, Härjedland and Gotland. Sweden got back Älvsborg, but was to pay 75,000 dalers in 1571 and 37,000 a year for the next two years. The three-crown issue was to be arbitrated later, but in the meantime both countries could display the symbol. Johan was to cease his attempts to extract tolls on Gulf of Finland shipping. Lübeck's trade privileges granted by Gustav in 1523 were to be restored except the guarantee of the monopoly of Swedish foreign trade and Sweden was to pay 75,000 dalers to Lübeck as a settlement for claims going clear back to Gustav Vasa's war debt.

On the matter of Livonia-Estonia, Maximilian took the opportunity to insert himself into this already complicated equation. Poland's acquisition of most of Livonia was recognized, but the rest of Livonia and Estonia was to be part of the empire. Maximilian would reimburse Sweden and Denmark for money spent in defending the former holdings of the Livonian Brothers of the Sword against the encroachment of the Russians. This territory would be entrusted to Frederick II as fief to protect for the emperor except for the towns of Reval and Weissenstein which would remain in Swedish hands.

In exchange for all these concessions, Johan III received only Frederick's recognition of Sweden's sovereignty, but this was no small matter. After all, Denmark entered the war with the objective of conquering and reestablishing control over the Swedish-Finnish realm. In this he had utterly failed, thanks to Erik's ingenuity and the immense treasury Gustav had left. Sweden immerged from the war with a much improved military. Her fleet dominated the Baltic. Her improved infantry, weapons and tactics had stood up to the best in German mercenaries. Only Sweden's cavalry seemed woefully inadequate. What's more, she retained at least a foothold in Estonia and as to the punitive terms of the Stettin Peace, it remained to be seen whether all of the odious provisions could be enforced. Here Johan's most effective weapon would be simple procrastination.

The end of the devastating Seven Years Northern War (First Northern War) allowed Johan time and energy to deal with Swedish internal matters which were coming to a head. Perhaps the most pressing was a crisis developing within the Church of Sweden driven to a large extent by forces outside the country.

Since the beginning of the Reformation, much had happened in the world of the once unified Western European Latin Church. The breakaway of the Church of England initiated by Henry VIII to facilitate his divorce from Catherine of Aragon and marriage to Anne Boleyn was now firmly established under his daughter Elizabeth I. Following Henry's death, Parliament had passed several laws during the reign of his only son Edward VI (1547–1553) reforming the church along Lutheran and Calvinist lines, but all this had been reversed by his daughter Mary I (1553–1558) who had reinstated Catholicism as the state religion. Her early death brought the succession of Elizabeth (1558–1603) who restored the independent Church of England which was never again seriously threatened.

Across the channel, Spain was in a struggle for supremacy over the Low Countries. Controlled by Burgundy since the 14th century, today's Belgium and the Netherlands absorbed the Protestant movement in the early 1500s at the same time its maritime commercial power was gaining strength. In 1516, the Low Countries came under Spanish rule when Charles, duke of Burgundy, became king of Spain and part of the greatest empire in the world when he was elected emperor of the Holy Roman Empire as Charles V (1519). Charles first made his sister Maria queen of the Netherlands then set about persecuting the Protestants just as he did in Germany.

Upon Maria's death in 1555, Charles turned over rule of the Netherlands to his son Philip II of Spain who stepped up the pressure against the Protestant movement. Finally in 1568, the nobles led by William I (the Silent) of Orange revolted against their Spanish overlords. In the wars that followed, the Spanish had the advantage on land, but the Dutch dominated the sea. By 1579 the southern provinces (Belgium) had returned to Spanish rule, subject to the Holy See in Rome. The northern provinces (the Netherlands) formed the Protestant Union of Utrecht which declared their independence in 1581. Wars continued intermittently until Dutch independence was recognized by Spain in 1648. These wars for Dutch independence would eventually affect Sweden's drive for empire in Germany.

Switzerland, likewise, was caught up in the Reformation and here the fractious nature of the movement quickly became evident. No sooner had Lutheranism been introduced into the German speaking cantons than a more radical form was established by Zwingli in Zurich. French speaking Switzerland developed its own version led by John Calvin centered in Geneva. From Switzerland these new sects of Protestantism spread into France, then back into Germany.

In France, the Reformation movement was based primarily on Calvin's teachings. His French followers became known as Huguenots. They were particularly strong in southern France, although by the 1550s, they had communities in Paris, Lyons, Orléans, Angers and Rouen. Attempts to suppress the movement were made by King Frances I and Henry II, but with only limited success. At Henry II's death (1559) France crowned Charles IX, still a minor, with the queen-dowager Catherine de Medici as regent. The Huguenots took advantage of the weakened central government to further expand and in January 1562 Catherine issued an edict of toleration allowing the Huguenots to practice their religion freely outside the towns as long as they didn't carry weapons, but all Catholic church properties forcibly taken by the Huguenots were to be returned. This did little to calm the conflicts between Catholics and Protestants, however, and in March of the same year the first of a series of Huguenot wars broke out. These wars continued intermittently until Henry III issued the Edict of Nantes in April 1598 which granted the Huguenots full religious freedom and admission to all public offices.

Meanwhile, Calvinism had also spread into Germany with a strong center in Emden in lower Saxony across Ews Bay from the Netherlands. From here its influence had a major effect on the Dutch Protestant movement and spread to England where its adherents were known as Puritans. In Scotland the Calvinist form of Protestantism became firmly established by 1555 under the leadership of John Knox and was supported by the nobility.

In Germany the Protestant movement was becoming badly divided. The original Lutheranism had subdivided into Lutheranism and Melanchthonism. In addition Zwinglian-ism and Calvinism had emerged from Switzerland and new forms like the Unitarians (Socinians) and Anabaptists appeared. From Germany Protestantism spread into Poland and Hungary.

In Hungary the Reformation was backed by the nobility and grew rapidly though again there was much dissent as to which form to adopt.

King Sigismund I (1501–1548) energetically suppressed the spread of Protestantism in Poland, but footholds were established in the University of Krakow, at Posen and in Danzig. Sigismund II Augustus was not as vigilant and under his rule the Reformation gained strength until the Religious Peace of Warsaw in 1573 granted equal rights to Catholics and dissidents.

Denmark was wrestling with Lutheranism at the time of Christian II (1513–1523). In fact his bias toward the movement was one of the factors in his removal by the nobles. However, Frederick II, though he professed allegiance to the Catholic Church at his coronation in 1523, soon afterward threw his support behind the reformers. At the *Rigsdag* of Odensee (1527), he granted freedom of religion to all in the kingdom and took over the appointment of the clerical hierarchy. Under Christian III (1534–59) Lutheranism was established as the state religion and he forced the remaining reluctant nobility into acceptance. At the *Rigsdag* of Copenhagen in 1546, the last rights and vestiges of the Catholic religion were removed. Christian then moved to establish Lutheranism in the rest of his domain, namely Norway and Iceland (the Greenland colony was lost in the early 1400s, the last recorded contact being 1408).

Though the Reformation reached Sweden in Gustav's time, in the form of Lutheranism, this tumult in the Protestant movement was sure to have some effect on Sweden. Under Gustav the Swedish church was closely controlled and religious thought constrained. He created government offices to oversee the church. Erik subordinated these offices and allowed the church to develop its structure, educational system and theology. This development was pushed to completion in response to outside influences.

To further trade relations with East Friesland, particularly Emden, Gustav had encouraged immigration by promising religious tolerance to the persecuted Calvinists of that area. Erik continued this practice, but found the new Protestant communities were attracting large numbers of Calvinists from all over Germany, the Netherlands and France. Soon they were spreading their propaganda and preaching in areas outside their communities. The Swedish church, led by Archbishop Laurentius Petri, became alarmed. He issued a pamphlet in 1562 laying out arguments against their theology. In 1663 Erik XIV curtailed immigration of these reformers and two years later he issued a mandate restricting their proselytizing activities. The Calvinists never gained a strong presence in Sweden. Rather, the religious conflicts in Sweden would be within the Lutheran framework, Melanchthonism versus Lutheranism and what parts of Catholic practices, liturgy and theology to retain and what to change.

By 1561 Laurentius Petri had a draft of church ordinances drawn up. However, he and Erik disagreed on many points. The church generally accepted both the elevation (of the host and chalice), and adoration of the host (bread) during the sacrament. Petri was ambivalent about elevation, but felt adoration was essential. Erik rejected both. These fine theological points would have been lost on Gustav altogether, nor would he have cared. Erik and Johan, on the other hand, not only understood them, but took a deep interest in these matters.

At the Riksdag of 1561, Petri tried to obtain official recognition of his ordinances, but Erik would not let them pass. Recognition by the government would wait another ten years, until Johan had firm control.

Johan III was better educated and more deeply interested in church matters than even Erik and seemed to have a real appreciation for service music, rich furnishings, even some of the old saints' days to provide holidays for the people. Indeed, Johan sponsored a revival of church and cathedral rebuilding, improvement and beautification. Petri thought he finally had a kindred spirit to work with on the throne. But Johan saw himself as a reformer, the king who would reconstruct the church in his country in the form he envisioned. It must be remembered he was married to a Pole, a devout Catholic who kept her own chapel and priests. During his visit to England he had been exposed to the Anglican reforms and during his long imprisonment at Gripsholm, he had read extensively on the early Christian Fathers, particularly the first centuries of Christianity. He observed the fractious nature of the Protestant movement in Germany and seems to have longed for what he saw as the unity and accord of the ancient church.

Johan III began to bring about his vision as quickly as he took office. He handed Petri a list of thirteen articles he considered matters the church needed to address. Several of these Petri incorporated into his Church Ordinance, which was approved by the council in 1571 and presented to the clergy and bishops at Uppsala in 1572. Here all church representatives took an oath to follow its precepts.

This Church Ordinance of 1571 allowed for a state church independent from the crown although the king retained the right to confirm the bishops who were to be chosen by a diocese electorate composed of clergy and laymen. The ordinance accepted exorcism, vestments, the chalice and paten, the sign of the cross, adoration and elevation, canonical hours and singing of parts of the Mass in Latin. It provided for a system of church discipline and called for improvements of the church education system. In the final paragraph the ordinance allowed for additional provisions to be made as would become necessary. As far as Johan was concerned this clause meant that since the clergy had vowed to uphold the ordinance they were bound to support any additional provisions, an assumption that would soon be put to the test.

The adoption of the Church Ordinance of 1571 was Archbishop Laurentius Petri's great and final achievement. He died in 1573 having served patiently yet resolutely in directing the church he held so dear. A year later Johan presented to the new archbishop, Laurentieus Petri Gothus, and the clergy, an additional ten articles. The king presided over the debate of these reform measures which included such things as: the clergy were to abstain from drunkenness and immoral acts just before Mass day; the Elements were not to be handled with unclean hands, and the vestments were to be clean for Mass. Church officials were hard put to argue against these new restrictions and the king carried the day. His next set of changes would be much more controversial, however.

In 1575, Johan brought to the clergy his New Ordinance which he presented as merely an explanation of the original Church Ordinance. It was much more than that. It, first of all, attempted to reconcile the difference between the Lutheran salvation by grace alone and the Catholic necessity for works. The argument was that our salvation depends on our love of God which stems from our faith in him; the greater our faith, the greater our love. But our love is demonstrated by our works. If this rational was not disturbing enough to the Lutheran Purists, there was the call for the retention of at least one monastery or nunnery in each diocese and the extension of the authority of the king to veto church appointments. Further, at Laurentius Petri Gothus' archbishop consecration ceremony, he was forced, by Johan, to carry a crook (bishop's staff) and miter (bishop's pointed hat), and submit to unction (anointing with oil), symbols generally condemned previously by the Swedish Lutheran Church.

Next Johan presented what he considered his ecclesiastic masterpiece, a new liturgy prescribed in his book which came to be known as the *Red Book*. In his work, Johan combined the Roman and Swedish masses describing a rich celebration with the use of some eight vestments for one ceremony. The work created much consternation among the strongly Lutheran clergy when it was presented to the Riksdag in 1577. It was accepted by the Church Estate only after considerable arm twisting, threats and promises.

At this same time Pope Gregory XIII was making a move to try to recover Sweden for the Roman church. Through contacts with the Swedish queen's personal Catholic staff by way of Polish cardinal Hosins, Gregory was encouraged that there existed this possibility. In 1576, he sent to the Swedish court one Father Laurentious Nicolai, a Norwegian Jesuit priest. He arrived in Stockholm disguised and did not reveal his true position. His mission was to begin the recovery of the country for Rome.

Johan quickly found an official position for him. The king had been looking for a place of education that he could use to train and indoctrinate the next generation of clergy. Since the closing of the University of Uppsala in Gustav's time, both Erik and Johan had worked to restore the institution, but the faculty now proved to be hostile to his religious ideas. So Johan opened a school in Stockholm in the facilities once used by the Greyfriars. Laurentius was placed as rector of the college and thus picked up the nickname *Klosterlasse*.

As Klosterlasse schemed in secret to turn the country, Johan worked to gain acceptance for his *Red Book* by Rome. In 1576 Johan sent an embassy to Rome to explore the possibility of a reunion of the churches and in the process Johan hoped his *Red Book* would be recognized by the Holy See. Gregory XIII saw hope in this reopening and returned a mission headed by Antonio Possevino, former secretary-general of the Jesuits. He and his embassy members arrived in Stockholm in layman's dress and contacted Klosterlasse, still disguised as a Lutheran at Greyfriars. This group then set to work proselytizing peasants, gentry and working hard at developing allies among the nobility, particularly members of the Råd. They felt they were making good progress until the Henriksson scandal blew open the whole clandestine operation.

This affair was one of those personal misadventures that, under ordinary circumstances, would be of no consequence to anyone except the immediate participants. But in this case events would take on international implications. Johan Henriksson was one of the king's secretaries who had been living with the wife of another man. This situation came to the attention of Archbishop Gothus who took the secretary to task for his unseemly adulterous activity. Henriksson's solution was to have a servant murder the husband, then apply to Klosterlasse for dispensation to marry the widow. The college regent turned to Possevino, who appealed to Rome, but in the meantime authorized Klosterlasse to give an oral dispensation to the disreputable civil servant. Henriksson, however, was able to extract the dispensation in writing from Klosterlasse. He then showed his exoneration to the archbishop exposing Klosterlasse for who he was. The connection was quickly made to Possevino and the role of the whole delegation as agents of Rome was clear. The Swedish church hierarchy was stunned to find that their associates and in some cases close friends had been working to undermine Swedish church independence. The nobility, especially the Råd members who had been so carefully cultivated, recoiled in indignation and in some instances genuine horror at the degree of infiltration accomplished by the Catholics.

Even after this setback Johan and Possevino seemed to think reconciliation was still a possibility. Johan composed a letter which he sent with Possevino to Pope Gregory outlining his demands for reunion, sacrament for laity, priest marriage, the Mass in Swedish, clergy subject to Swedish law and abolition of Holy Water. Worship of saints and prayers for the dead would not be obligatory. Possevino left for Rome on March 1578 and five months later Gregory XIII's answer came back rejecting all points.

When Possevino returned to Sweden, it was in clerical dress and he ordered all the Catholic priests in the country to make themselves known. He then made a grand visit to the nunnery of Vadstena that Katarina was having rebuilt.

This demonstration was the last straw. Johan could no longer assist or even condone Catholic activity in the country if he hoped to retain his crown. There were anti–Catholic riots in Stockholm. The Råd told the king to make clear his support of the state church. The Riksdag in March 1580 condemned Klosterlasse and the Jesuits. Klosterlasse openly denounced the *Red Book* and was deprived of his rectorship. In August Klosterlasse, Possevino and a few converts left the country. Greyfriars was closed once more and in 1583 Queen Katarina died, ending the last connection between the crown and Rome.

At her passing Katarina was mourned throughout the country for her kindness, virtue and her devotion to her religion. Even detractors who, during her life, had blamed her for much of the Catholic activity in their country, now honored her. Katarina, at least, came out of the incident with her dignity and loyalties intact. She had made no pretense of being anything other than a devoted Roman Catholic, unwavering in her faith and for this she was respected. Johan, on the other hand, emerged broken, with his dream of a Swedish church united with Rome shattered. He had succeeded only in creating fear and suspicion of the Catholic Church and now he had to worry about his son's succession to the throne.

He had tried to persuade Sigismund to at least consider or even show tolerance toward Swedish Lutheranism, but the heir to the throne would have none of it. He steadfastly refused to attend Lutheran services and by 1579 made clear his intention to remain a devoted Catholic putting him at odds with the Råd. Though both the Råd and the Riksdag had proclaimed his right to succession in 1569, Johan knew Sigismund's throne was now in jeopardy. As early as 1572 Johan had pressured the clergy to formally endorse the succession and in 1574 he got the Estates to do the same. In 1582, after the Klosterlasse-Possevino affair had settled out, Johan persuaded the clergy to renew their pledge of support. As late as 1587 Johan had the Riksdag of Vadstena once more promise fidelity to Johan's line of succession. Johan's concerns were not misplaced for always hovering in the background was his brother Karl.

During the upheaval in church affairs, Duke Karl had maintained a core of resistance to any encroachment by the Church of Rome in his duchy. Where Johan's Lutheranism leaned toward the traditional and even the Catholic fringe of the church, Karl's inclinations were nearer a Puritanism form of the church, closer to a Calvinist type of Protestantism. Johan's vision was a reunion of the Swedish church and the Church of Rome. Karl's vision was for a united Protestant movement. He was disgusted with the division and bickering going on among the Reformers in Germany.

Karl operated his duchy as a semi-autonomous state within a state. This extended to religious matters as well as political. After Johan's failure at any kind of a rapprochement with Rome, the king turned even more resolutely to gaining acceptance of his liturgy in Sweden, as described in the *Red Book*. Dissenting clergy were persecuted, harassed, even imprisoned or escaped to Karl's domain where they found refuge and support. Meanwhile, Johan pressed his agenda in the church.

When Laurentius Petri Gothus died (1579) Johan left the position of archbishop vacant for three years, demonstrating the office was subservient to the crown. When he finally did appoint a successor, it was a man of his ecclesiastic philosophy, one Anders Lars Björnram. At his consecration in 1583, the bishops affirmed their support for both the New Ordinance and the *Red Book*. Johan also carried out a program of church building, repair and beautification. Church government was reorganized and made more efficient. Clergymen were better educated and better trained albeit according to Johan's vision of the church.

Karl fought just as hard on the other side. In 1587 his duchy's clergy issued the *Confessio Strengneusis* which denounced the liturgy of the *Red Book* and accepted the *Augustana invariata* for the first time in any Swedish church publication. Johan retorted with the Hard Patent of 1588 calling his enemies liars, scatterers of the faith, bunglers, and traitors and outlawed the entire clergy of the duchy. But his position began to weaken. In 1590 Johan and Karl reached an agreement that the duchy was free to practice religion as it saw fit. By then defamers of the *Red Book* were rising in power and in 1591 Johan's real champion, Archbishop Björnram, died. Once again Johan's religious vision was crumbling before his eyes and he was powerless to stop it.

The differences between the royal brothers extended to more than religion, of course. Karl, with his nearly independent duchy, refrained only from conducting independent foreign affairs. He ruled from Nyköpping, had his own chancellor, Råd, bailiffs, secretaries and called his own meetings of the Estates within his realm. His taxes and tariffs differed from those in the rest of Sweden and at times he coined his own money. Indeed, when Karl went to Germany to court the daughter of the elector of Palatine, he assured the ruler that within the duchy he was an independent sovereign using Gustav's testament and Johan's letter of confirmation as evidence. In 1578, Maria of Palatinate became his first wife.

In consolidating his control, the duke took care to ingratiate himself with the nobility of his realm. However, his efforts were not universal. He favored the nobles who had lands within the duchy in every way, while ostracizing those with lands elsewhere. Nobles with holdings solely within the duchy tended to be lesser nobility while those with lands within and without were some of the great magnates of Sweden. So, very early, Karl began to make enemies among the great families of the kingdom, families who were the members of the king's Råd. A three way power struggle developed between the king, the aristocracy represented by the Råd, and the duke. Each suspicious of the other, each trying to carve out as much political power as possible.

Karl seems to have been more like his father than either of his brothers. He had his father's love of business and commerce, his suspicious and untrusting nature and attention to detail. His duchy flourished under his rule.

Johan on the other hand was preoccupied with religion, and with his other passion, architecture. Not only were churches and cathedrals repaired and beautified during his reign, but castles, government buildings, and even cities were built or rebuilt. All this, along with his continuing war in Livonia and the ransom of Älvsborg, had emptied the royal coffers already drained by Erik's Seven Years Northern War. The country's financial peril was of constant concern to the Råd, which tried to keep some kind of account if not control. In 1574 and again in 1583 careful accounting was made of government revenues and expenses. These figures show income in 1574 was 650,000 dalers with expenditures of 1,008,000 dalers; for 1582 these numbers were 772,000 dalers and 1,120,000 dalers. The deficits Johan managed to handle by debasing the currency, not paying bills for imported luxuries, and requisitioning commodities from his subjects and then not paying for them. He increased compulsory labor service, sold warships, and neglected to pay foreign troops and even Swedish soldiers. He imposed a royal monopoly on the lucrative copper production and sale, and had new taxes on farm products and the booming fur trade. In spite of everything, the crown debt, by 1583, was over a million dalers.

Even more disturbing to the aristocracy was Johan's raising of the sons of lower nobility and even gentry in high government offices. He had increased the number of secretaries to eighteen and filled the positions with men from decidedly lower castes. No longer was it necessary to import civil servants from outside the country as merchants and lesser nobles could send their sons to universities in Germany and elsewhere, then get them into government office. The high aristocracy was finding itself excluded from these high paying and influential positions. The nobility began to demand more representation in the crown's administration.

And so the three-way struggle teetered back and forth with each side playing off one against another. The Riksdag was called upon to referee when one of the opponents felt it had an advantage with the Estates. Finally, the factions coalesced. The Råd became so worried about the country's financial straits it developed and proposed to the king a comprehensive plan for economic reform. An accounting system was instituted for the crown and standard wages for royal attendants and government workers established. Royal servants and outlays for banquets would be reduced. The royal mint would be supervised by two nobles.

Johan acquiesced and gained the Råd's support. In 1586 Ture Bielke was appointed royal treasurer and the Råd gained some control over the country's finances, carrying out some economic reforms.

For its part, the Råd published, in 1586, a treatise vigorously supporting the crown's rights in its contest with the duchy. The Pro Lege Rege et Grege, written by one of its members, Erik Sparre, was based on the Magnus Eriksson Land Law, but also drew on Roman law and English common law. Above all it was designed for 16th century Swedish conditions and was remarkable in its evenhandedness in handling class interests. Sparre attempted to take into consideration the common welfare of all Sweden. He has become known as the father of Swedish constitutional law. He would remain at the center of the political stage for the next fourteen years.

Sparre argued that the dukes could exercise independent rights only insofar as those rights did not contradict, interfere with or curtail crown rule. A duke did not have sovereign authority, but was subject to the king — great for Johan. Sparre, however, went on to say that the law was supreme even over the crown, that it was Swedish tradition (common law) that kings were created by vote of the Estates (the people) and could be removed by the same. The Succession Pact of 1544 was itself a law passed by the Riksdag in no way superior to other statutes and, in fact, subservient to common law. Laws, he went on to say, were enacted by the Estates and all were subject to those laws whether represented or not, born or unborn. The Riksdag was, in effect, a national legislature and the supreme law of the land. These were pronouncements ahead of their time.

With the Råd on his side Johan now forced Karl to negotiate by threatening to bring him before the Riksdag. On February 13, 1587, an agreement between the brothers was concluded. Karl capitulated on nearly every point, with lagmän to be appointed by the king, and duchy court decisions could be appealed to the crown court. Taxation and customs dues were to be in line with the rest of the kingdom and he could no longer negotiate special favors with nobility or peasants. Karl could not mint coinage and all troops in the duchy were obliged to swear an oath to the king. Only in the matters of the liturgy and his family inheritance was Karl able to hold his own. And so the triangular struggle for domination subsided for the moment only to be kicked up again by a completely different catalyst.

9. A Swedish Prince on the Polish Throne and the Second Northern War

Once again Sweden's internal matters were about to be affected by events outside the country, this time by the death of eastern rulers. In Russia the long reign of Ivan IV (the Terrible) finally came to an end in March 1584. In terms of territorial expansion, his rule (1547–1584) had been very successful.

In 1552 Ivan had led 100,000 Russian troops against the khanate of Kazan. At the junction of the two rivers, the Kama and the Volga, he laid siege to the fortress of Kazan, garrisoned by 30,000 Tartars, the remnants of the once powerful Mongol Empire in Russia. Employing 150 cannon and German engineers, he took the stronghold after a long and bloody siege. Its fall gave the tsar all the territory east to the Urals and access to western Siberia, an area even the Mongols hadn't conquered. The next year the Astrakhan Tartars submitted and by 1566 this territory was fully annexed extending Russian jurisdiction to the Caspian Sea. With the subjugation of these Tartars, many of the Cossacks west of the Don River switched their allegiance from Lithuania to the tsar securing Southern Russia. He had broken the back of Tartar domination that had plagued Muscovy for so long and acquired large areas extending Russian territory far to the east and south.

With Ivan's death begins what is known in Russian history as the "Time of Troubles." After several strong rulers and constant territorial expansion, the Muscovite state would see a series of power struggles. The constant expansion temporarily subsided and at times there was chaos in the country itself. Foreign nations intervened in Russia's internal affairs, Sweden among them.

Like Russia, Poland was going through the aftermath of the death of a strong ruler and the end of a long, expansionist dynasty. Sigismund II Augustus died in 1573, the last of the Jagiellonica kings, the dynasty that had ruled the country for 200 years. His reign had seen the final incorporation of Lithuania into the Polish Empire. Lithuania, which had had its own great empire during the Middle Ages, was now much reduced and caught between an aggressive Poland and an expanding Russia. From time to time Poland and Lithuania had had kings who were relatives and sometimes even the same king, but had remained separate countries in part because of religious differences, Poland being Roman Catholic and Lithuania Orthodox Catholic. The Reformation, with a substantial conversion to Protestantism particularly among the nobility, helped to break down this barrier. With Russian pressure increasing, the two states united under the Union of Lublin in 1569. Thus Sigismund II Augustus greatly expanded his realm, but much of the power was transferred to a united parliament (the *Sejm*) representing the nobles of both countries.

According to the agreement there was to be a sharing of all things between the two countries. In fact Poland quickly came to dominate. Polish settlers rapidly moved into Lithuanian territory. Government offices were filled by Poles and the Lithuanian gentry became thoroughly Polandized. Orthodox Lithuanians were severely persecuted and many either fled to Russia or converted. Ancient Lithuania disappeared as a nation. At the same time, the aristocracy became all powerful. Through the parliament, or Sejm, the nobles ground the peasants into serfdom and controlled the crown by holding the purse strings and the ability to determine the monarch.

With the death of Sigismund II Augustus the united Sejm was responsible for electing a new king. Henry of Anjou was selected after much delay. The newly elected king found the parliamentary-monarchy untenable and after only three years escaped back to Anjou. Later he would become king of France as Henry III. The Polish nobles next chose Stephen Bathory of Transylvania, a capable general. He personally took the field against the tsar and expanded Polish territory at Russian expense.

Bathory died in 1586 and once again the Sejm was looking for a king. Candidates included Tsar Feodor I of Russia (supported by Lithuanian Orthodox nobles), Cardinal Andreas Bathory, Maximilian (archbishop of Austria), Johan himself, and Johan's son Sigismund, heir to the Swedish throne and a descendant of the Jagiellonica line through his mother.

The Roman Catholic majority of the Sejm rejected Feodor on grounds of religion and fear of a Russian takeover. The good cardinal had too many enemies among the anti–Bathory faction. The contest came down to Maximilian, supported by the old Bathory opposition, and Sigismund. The Swedish prince had the support of the Polish chancellor Zamoyski, leader of the Bathory party, and the imperialists who wanted to continue the conquest of Russia to create a great Slavic state. Sweden would give them additional troops, ports in the Gulf of Finland and most importantly the most powerful navy in the Baltic. Sigismund was also backed by Bathory's widow, Queen Ann, his mother's older sister who had already made him heir to her estates. Plus he was Roman Catholic and spoke Polish.

It seemed a perfect selection, but Johan had reservations. He had a genuine fondness for his son and did not want to have him move away, nor did he trust the Polish aristocratic parliament. Three delegations from Poland came to Stockholm to plead for Sigismund's candidacy. In the end, however, the advantages in stymieing Russia won Johan over. He could not afford even the chance of a united Poland and Russia, and his son on the Polish throne would give him a powerful ally in his Livonian war.

On August 19, 1587, a majority of the Sejm elected Sigismund king, but three days later a minority selected Maximilian and backed his military operation to gain the throne. Chancellor Zamayski moved quickly to attack this insurrection and within four months had defeated the minority forces and taken Maximilian prisoner. Sigismund's Polish throne was secure.

No sooner had Sigismund departed for Warsaw than Johan began to regret his decision. He loved his son and wanted nothing so much as to have him back in Sweden. Sigismund, for his part was finding, as Henry of Anjou had discovered, that ruling Poland with the Sejm treating the crown with such contempt, was impossible and he began to look for an exit strategy.

Johan came up with a plan to solve several problems with one move. He called for a summit of the two nations at Reval. He would take a large army and meet Sigismund there with his large Polish army. The combined Swedish-Polish force would be enough to convince

Boris Godunov, the Russian ruler, to establish a long term peace with Sweden. At the conference, outside Polish control, Sigismund would abdicate and go home with his father. It was a grand plan, but fraught with complications.

Johan arranged the conference then began raising the troops to accompany him. Since the Swedish army was already in Estonia, he had to appeal to the nobility who were loath to support the project. What's more, the Råd interfered, insisting Johan take several of their members with him. He landed at Reval on August 5, 1589, with eight nobles including Erik Sparre and a small military escort. Three weeks later Sigismund arrived with several Polish Sejm members and a similarly small Polish military contingent. Father and son's plans had been thwarted by their respective aristocracies. The Polish and Swedish nobles, staff and military did not get along and at times brawled openly in the streets of Reval.

However, they did co-operate enough to frustrate their sovereigns' plans. The Polish nobles had no intention of losing a king and be forced to go through another election so soon, and both parties thought they could still extract some advantage out of the union that would come with Johan's death. Even local Swedish troops in Estonia and their commanders sided with the Råd believing the Poles would help in the war effort. Finally, at the end of September, Sigismund left to return to Warsaw, pushed by his nobles to organize a defense against a Tartar invasion of Podolia.

A bitter and vengeful Johan returned to Stockholm never to see his son again. The Råd had defeated his plan to recover his son and this he would never forgive. Upon his return he began forging an alliance with Karl against the Råd. His brother was only too willing to cooperate in the hope of regaining some of his ducal privileges. The two worked to first isolate those eight members who had blocked Johan's plans in Reval and then cut the power of the Råd itself. They waged a propaganda war and were so successful that the eight offending nobles were purged from the Råd and even spent some time in prison though in the long run they all recovered their positions.

To deal with the Råd itself, the royal brothers called a meeting of the Estates in the spring of 1590. At the Riksdag Johan and Karl accused the council of bringing about the failure of the Reval meeting to gain a peace treaty with Russia by not supplying the necessary troops as requested by the king. Further, the great magnates, as represented by the Råd, had interfered in the prosecution of the war by offering to cede Estonia to the Poles—this was clear duplicity as it was Johan who had offered Estonia in exchange for Sigismund's release—and that they had fomented strife between supporters of Johan and Karl.

The Estates listened to the charges, but were cautious in pronouncing any grand judgments. Minor nobles were able to gain some concessions in getting the same share of fines, levied in their territory, as the counts and barons (the great magnates) received. The royal brothers pushed through a new succession pact recognizing Sigismund's rights to the throne, but also recognizing Karl and his new son, Johan, by Gunilla Bielke. Johan had won some of his revenge, but he was now spent. In reality, Karl had been running the government for some time as Johan's health declined. One of Johan's last actions was to recall Karl Henriksson Horn from Estonia and have him tried.

Horn, one of Sweden's most successful and long suffering generals, was accused of treason for the surrender of Ivangorod. He had actually made the concession to save Narva, a much more important prize. Horn was convicted and condemned to die, though he was only to serve a short period in prison. Johan pardoned him just before his death in 1590.

For all of Johan's defeats in religious matters, his frustrations in politics, and loss of a beloved son, one area of endeavor was very nearly an unqualified success. That was in his foreign policy and that meant the issue of Estonia. At the beginning of his reign Johan was left with the disastrous outcome of the Northern Seven Years War. In Estonia, Sweden had come away with only Reval and Weissenstein, and even these were to be fiefs retained for and at the pleasure of the holy Roman emperor. All the rest of Erik's hard won Livionian territory was stripped away and turned over to Denmark.

The other elements of the Stettin treaty were just as odious to Johan: the ransom of Älvsborg, indemnity and free trade status to Lübeck, and Russian Narva to be a free and open port. Sweden got only Frederick's recognition of Sweden's independence, a point seven years of war had already confirmed, and the emperor's promise to pay for Sweden's expenses in keeping most of Estonia out of Ivan's hands.

Johan did pay the first installment for Älvsborg on time — he needed Sweden's only western port — and eventually handed over the rest of the money, though always tardy, and he was driven to sell some of his warships and debase the country's currency to do it. Lübeck on the other hand was another matter. The once powerful city no longer had the military strength to coerce the new Baltic power and Johan simply ignored the city council's entreaties for the money. The special trade privileges were granted, but became ineffective when Johan extended the same privileges to Stralsund, the German port city in western Pomerania, which had stuck by Sweden the entire war. What's more, Johan made no attempt to rein in Swedish privateers that savaged Lübeck's shipping throughout the Baltic. Repeated complaints lodged by the city were ignored by Johan. Though Sweden had gained little from the war, Lübeck was the combatant that lost the most. The impotency of the once powerful Hanseatic League was exposed and Lübeck's position as a second rate power confirmed. Maritime nation-states and land empires were coming to dominate the region.

As for Narva, Johan ignored the terms of the Stettin peace treaty. Within months of the accord, Johan had his navy back in the Gulf of Finland harassing merchantmen trading with the Russian port. The Dutch and the Danes complained and in the interest of trying to keep the peace with Frederick, Johan would, from time to time, exempt Danish ships, but Swedish privateers made no such concessions. Occasionally, Frederick would even acquiesce to Johan's demands to suspend trade with Narva. So there was some give and take between the two former enemies.

With Lübeck, however, it was all take. The city's captured crews were treated severely. Ships and cargoes were impounded. In 1574 an entire fleet of sixteen merchantmen was captured and taken to a Swedish port. Profits from these ships and the booty helped pay for the war in Livonia which Johan was prosecuting as best he could with his limited resources.

Maximilian II was never able to pay Sweden the promised reimbursement for the wars with Russia so the emperor became a non-player in the struggle for the Baltic region and Sweden kept her hard won territory in Estonia. Again the contest for the northern part of Livonia settled into a four way struggle between Russia, Sweden, Denmark and Poland. The stage was set for the Second Northern War. With Johan's connections to the Polish court, there should have been a Swedish-Polish alliance, a formidable partnership with Poland's resources in manpower complimenting Sweden's navy. Although both countries tried to negotiate from time to time no formal treaty was ever established; competing interests in Livonia-Estonia were the main reason.

Ivan, however, greatly feared such an alliance. He had his hands full trying to handle a power struggle in Moscow with the clergy and boyars (the Russian great magnates). Though preoccupied, he did his best to look out for Russian interests in the Baltics. He declared the Danish Magnus king of Livonia, giving him Oberpahlen as a capital and sending him what

Russian troops as he could spare. Magnus, now acting as Ivan's surrogate, laid siege to Reval in August 1570. The city burghers sponsored a stout defense and Johan gave what assistance he could, supplying the city by sea. The siege dragged on for eight months ending in failure, but as usual in these Baltic conflicts, the surrounding countryside was pillaged and burned.

So Magnus and his Muscovite troops abandoned the siege in 1571, the same year Johan and Sigismund II Augustus made a real try at developing some kind of alliance. Johan sent a permanent legate to Krakow and discussions were opened in a search for points of agreement. Unfortunately, Sigismund died the next year, in July 1572, before real progress could be made.

For several years Ivan had been preoccupied with internal matters. In his struggle with the clergy and the *boyars*, he had experimented with alternative forms of administration, creating chaos in the country until the weakened state of affairs was exposed through a raid carried out by the Tartars of Crimea that reached all the way to Moscow where they looted and burned the city. As many as 800,000 Russians may have died and 130,000 taken captive to be sold as slaves. This 1571 disaster galvanized Ivan into action. He dumped his political maneuvers, centralized political control in the Kremlin again and sent the army out to push back the borders on all fronts.

In Finland Muscovite troops raided all the way to Helsingfors, but no permanent border changes occurred. In 1575 a two year truce quieted this frontier. In September 1572 the Russians pushed into Estonia and marched on Weissenstein, taking it in January 1573. After capturing the city they proceeded to roast alive the Swedish commander and some of his staff, another indication of the barbarous nature of this war. Sweden retaliated by besieging Wesenburg, but failed to take it. Faced with this new Russian aggression, Johan had to find new ways to fight this war. Thus begins the tragic story of a company of soldiers who left their highland homes to die on foreign soil in a war a continent away.

At the end of 1572 King Johan III contracted with a Scottish nobleman, Archibald Ruthven, for the services of 3,000 Scottish mercenaries for the war in Estonia. They were to be mostly infantry needed for the siege work typical of the war in Livonia. Although Ruthven received a government license for only 1,600 men, he was able to more than fill his commission with some 3,000 infantry and 760 cavalry. In June and July these forces were transported from Scotland to Älvsborg where they began the overland march to the Östergötland ports of Söderköping and Norrköping where they were to embark for Estonia. The trek did not go well.

The overland march was accomplished piecemeal, breaking the army up into groups of a few hundred men each. After slowing their march and doing some pillaging, to get wages from Johan, the Scots did get to port, most in Östergötland, but a few made it up to Stockholm. Joined by another 300 Scottish cavalry recruited from troops already in Sweden, the Ruthven army eventually arrived at Reval. Here they joined Swedish and Finnish troops and German mercenaries, mostly cavalry and artillery crewmen. They were under the overall command of Marshal Klas Åkesson Tott, but the field commander was Pontus de la Gardie, "Colonel of troops in Livland."

De la Gardie moved his combined army out of Reval and laid siege to the Russian stronghold of Wesenberg in January 1573. The infantry dug in, the artillery was brought to bear and the cavalry scouted the perimeter to cut off any relief effort.

Two attempts to storm the walls in January failed. An attempt in early March to attack through a breach in the walls was repulsed with over 1,000 men lost. An attempt to tunnel under the wall was foiled by the defenders and an incendiary attack intended to set fire to the town inside the walls came to nothing. By mid–March morale was low, supplies were running out and hostilities between the army factions were boiling over.

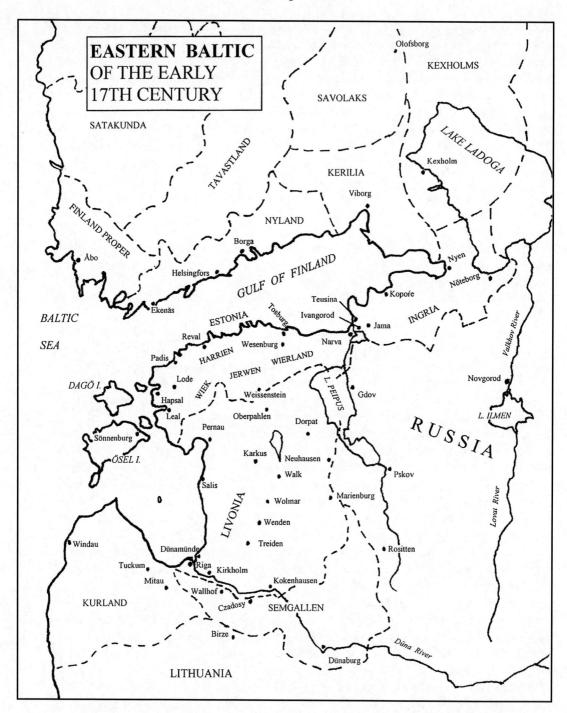

EASTERN BALTIC
OF THE EARLY
17TH CENTURY

On March 17, insults led to a brawl and the brawl turned into a battle. The Scottish infantry wrested the artillery from the German gunners and turned them on the German cavalry. The German horse retaliated, charging the Scots. Neither the German or Swedish infantry intervened, so the Scots got off one round at most before the German cavalry was among them. Thirty Germans were killed, but over 1,500 Scottish infantry were cut down. The slaughter ended Johan's 1573 campaign in dismal failure.

The effects of the disaster were far reaching. Never again would Johan rely so heavily on mercenaries. Tott was removed as overall eastern commander and replaced with de la Gardie. The siege was lifted by the end of March and the army returned to Reval where recriminations, investigations, and even a few trials crippled Johan's efforts to take the offense for over a year.

At the same time the German mercenaries were threatening Johan for lack of back pay. In early 1573 the situation was so bad that it produced an outright mutiny. Johan offered three fortresses, Hapsal, Leal and Lode in the Wiek, as collateral against full payment by midsummer on condition they not be turned over to Ivan or his puppet, Magnus. When payment was not made, the mercenaries promptly turned over the castles to Frederick, effectively giving control of eastern Estonia to the Danes. Johan's situation in Swedish Livonia had reached low ebb. He controlled only Reval and its environs. Even here he was again threatened by a Muscovite force in 1575. Fortunately this army moved off to the south and captured Pernau from the Poles in July. Even the Reval burghers began scouting for a new champion when Russian forces again laid siege in January 1577. The siege was lifted in March before a full fledged revolt took place.

Ivan now demanded that Frederick turn over the three fortresses acquired from Sweden to Magnus in his behalf. The Danish king refused and the tsar himself led a 30,000 man invasion force that first took Polish Dünaburg, then devastated Danish Livonia, including the island of Ösel. Hapsal, Lode and Leal were surrendered without contest as the German mercenaries were getting no more pay from Frederick than they had from Johan. Kokenhausen, on the Düna, tried a ploy to avoid Russian attack by surrendering to Magnus. Ivan sent a force anyway and captured the fortress, executing the commander.

Some of Ivan's success can be attributed to a new dimension introduced by him into the Livonian war: numbers of troops. Whereas, a good sized army in the Baltic region had previously been a few thousand men, Ivan brought a force of tens of thousands including the feared Tartar and Cossack cavalries. Instead of the usual highly trained, professional mercenaries, Ivan used mostly native troops in armies of a larger size.

By late August, Ivan had pushed on to Wenden, the very heart of Livonia, the old capital of the Brothers of the Sword and symbol of the country itself. Here Magnus, who was conducting an ineffective siege, was arrested. Ivan quickly took the city, but the castle managed to hold out for some time. Finally, with Russian troops isolating the fortress and closing in, the remaining three hundred men, women and children assembled in the main tower and blew themselves up with four tons of gunpowder. Irregardless of the Stettin peace treaty, Ivan now controlled all of Livonia-Estonia except Reval, held by Johan III; Riga, still under Polish control; and Ösel Island, Frederick's last outpost. Magnus, terrified for his own safety, escaped and fled to Kurland where he died five years later.

Frederick negotiated with Sweden, renouncing Danish claims to Estonia granted under the Stettin peace treaty in exchange for Johan giving up claim to Ösel. He accepted payment from Poland for Livonian lands they occupied, but were claimed by Magnus at the time of his abdication. Thus Frederick II withdrew from the Livonian war, leaving it to the other three belligerents.

As Johan's fortunes in Estonia deteriorated, he cast about for an ally. He was approached by William the Silent of the rebellious Netherlands, but Johan had little interest in helping a struggling revolution involving the troublesome Calvinists and competing Dutch merchants. Their oppressor, the Spanish, however, was another matter.

Philip II had gold from the New World pouring into his treasury and Johan had ships and guns to trade, commodities that Philip could use in the Americas, in his war with the revolting Dutch, and in his intermittent wars with Elizabeth I. Spain also wanted to gain control of the Sound to shut off Dutch and English trade to the Baltic in hopes of crippling their economies. Taking the Sound away from Denmark was in Johan's interests, of course, but for different reasons. He wanted to end the toll on Swedish ships and gain unimpeded access to the west. A great coalition began to take shape. Philip II sent an embassy to Stockholm where the two countries worked out a plan that would include Poland in a three nation, anti–Danish alliance. According to the plan Helsingør and Helsingborg would be captured with Spanish troops carried and backed by the Swedish navy. The Sound would be in the hands of the triple alliance. A treaty draft was approved by Johan and forwarded to Philip, but there it died. Perhaps such an adventure was just too far afield for the Spanish monarch. Johan did not push the issue, being reluctant to take action that would certainly precipitate a new war with Frederick.

The two Scandinavian kings were being careful to avoid conflict and even cooperating in patrolling the Baltic for pirates. West of the Sound, Huguenot and Netherlands rebel privateers were harassing merchantmen. Frederick sent ships to patrol these waters, but with only limited effectiveness. East of the Sound, however, where Danish and Swedish navies dominated, the seas were made safe for commerce. Russia and Poland, having no navies of their own, offered privateer licenses to any ship owners willing to risk attacking ships in Baltic waters. Russia was after Swedish commerce and Poland hoped to cut off Prussia and Danzig from resupply by sea. But Denmark, with Sweden's cooperation, worked to clear the seas, treating any privateers caught as common pirates. So effective were their efforts that the Baltic became one of the safest maritime areas in the world. Scandinavian, Dutch and English ships could sail these waters with small crews and no armament, increasing profits, encouraging investment and further rendering the Hanseatic League obsolete. The Hansa was dead, Baltic trade boomed and the Scandinavian navies dominated.

To the west Johan's foreign policy was stymied, but in the east there was new hope. Following Sigismund II Augustus' death and Henry's abdication, the Polish Sejm elected a skilled and courageous military leader as king, Stephen Bathory of Transylvania. After his coronation, Bathory was occupied with an insubordinate Danzig. When this was settled, by the end of 1577, he was able to turn his attention to the Russian incursions. The capture of Wenden had been a huge symbolic and strategic victory for Ivan and here the Swedes and Poles collaborated in an attack. The allies struck in early 1578. It was the first serious defeat for Ivan's offensive conquest of Livonia and marked the turning point of the Second Northern War.

Ivan had left 22,000 Russian troops to garrison the castles of his newly won territory, but it wasn't enough. Lithuanian forces captured Dünaburg with a combination of force and subterfuge. Swedish and Polish armies combined in an attack on Wenden and captured both city and fortress.

Ivan was not about to see his hard won gains taken without a fight. In September 1578 he sent an 18,000 man army back into Livonia to reestablish control. The Muscovites captured Oberpahlen from the Swedes, then marched onto Wenden and laid siege. A relief effort was improvised by the allies. An army of 5,500 Polish, German and Swedish troops was rushed to the city. The small army was able to defeat the Russian cavalry in the field and drive them off, leaving the besieging infantry unprotected in their trenches. The would-be attackers were slaughtered. Many Russian boyars were taken prisoner. Twenty guns and thousands of horses were taken, so many that the entire Swedish infantry rode back to Reval on horseback. The Russian hold on Livonia had been broken.

This open field battle at Wenden was unusual for the Second Northern War. There were few pitched battles between armies in the Livonian wars. As an invading army approached, there might be some skirmishing at the border, but the defenders would quickly pull back into their fortresses leaving the countryside to the invaders who would promptly pillage, rape and burn the surrounding area as they lay siege to the fortifications. Huge siege guns were moved into position and the bombardment would begin. High trajectory mortars lobbing explosives or incendiary shells over the walls caused much death and destruction inside the fortifications, particularly if the defensive position was a walled city.

The Russians had gigantic guns called *kartouven* that fired a fifty-two-pound iron ball eight inches in diameter. The gun weighed eight thousand pounds and required at least twenty horses or oxen to move it. Cannon firing five- to twenty-five-pound balls were common. In artillery, however, the Swedes had the advantage.

Johan purchased foreign cannon, mostly iron, but his own domestically produced pieces were superior. As in its naval artillery, Sweden's royal foundries manufactured brass guns using native copper. These coppers could be built lighter and stronger than iron cannon. Bigger powder charges could be used, increasing the effectiveness against defensive walls and the coppers cooled faster than iron pieces allowing an increased rate of fire. The most powerful cannons used in the war were the Swedish double and half kartouven that hurled a twenty-four-pound ball at a high velocity. These weapons were about to be put to good use as Sweden took the offense.

The two temporary allies were not able to combine forces again for such an effective attack as the one on Wenden, but each began an aggressive offense spreading Ivan's defensive forces thin and in this sense they did act for their mutual benefit. Bathory's goal, besides recovering Livonia and eastern Lithuania, was Pskov and Novgorod. Johan had always kept his eye on Narva.

In 1579 Bathory took Polock and the next year Velike Luki and Kholm. By 1581 he was at the gates of Pskov laying siege to the city.

Henrik Klassan Horn, a Finnish commander, meanwhile attacked Narva, deep in Russian territory, but was repulsed. Johan now placed Pontus de la Gardie as overall commander of Estonian-Finnish armies. He was the mercenary who entered Swedish service at the fall of Varberg. De la Gardie turned out to be an excellent general. The Swedes took Kexholm on the Finnish frontier in 1580 giving Sweden a port on Lake Ladoga. Johan claimed the whole province and a strip of land from there to the Arctic Sea. The same year de la Gardie took Padis in the Wiek giving Reval some breathing room. He then split the army and the next year pushed east with one division capturing Tosburg and Wesenburg. This established a good sized Swedish enclave in Estonia by summer. Meanwhile, Horn, with the western division, continued the conquest of the Wiek recovering Lode, Hapsal and Leal that same summer.

By the end of that fall, de la Gardie had reached Narva, with a solid supply line to back him, not just sea communication. The Swedish doubles and half kartouven cannon pulverized the one hundred and sixty foot thick walls in two days. Narva was taken and de la Gardie put to the sword every man, woman and child, over 7,000 people in the city.

Before year's end de la Gardie had taken Ivangorod, Jama and Kopoŕe expanding Swedish territory to include almost all of Ingia at the eastern end of the Gulf of Finland and threatening Novgorod. Horn, to the west, took Weissenstein, completing the conquest of Estonia. Johan now controlled all the area around the Gulf of Finland.

Bathory, meanwhile, was bogged down in a five month siege of Pskov, which he was unable to win. But the pressure from both Sweden and Poland brought Ivan to the negotiating table.

NORTHERN EUROPEAN ARTILLERY

Late Medieval Bombard constructed
with iron staves banded with hoops
similar to a barrel

Swedish heavy siege gun
late 16th century

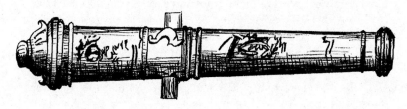

Ornate cannon
17th century

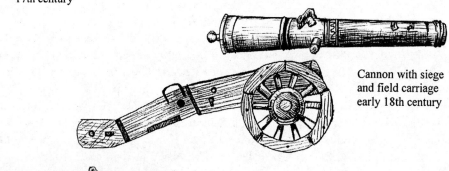

Cannon with siege
and field carriage
early 18th century

Cannon with garrison and ship carriage
early 18th century

Illustrations by Amanda Peterson

In 1582 Ivan settled with Bathory at Iam Zapolskii giving up all claims of Livonia to Poland, but he saved Pskov which would have given Bathory a straight shot at Novgorod. Bathory also received Dorpat in Livonia in trade for Velike Luki deep in Novgorod territory. This ten year truce agreement released both parties for action against Sweden.

First, Bathory threatened Johan in an effort to get the remainder of Livonia, Estonia, and particularly Narva turned over to him. But Johan was as belligerent as ever, telling Bathory to come ahead and give it a try. Pressured by the Sejm and Queen Ann, and with an empty treasury, he finally acquiesced and a Swedish-Polish war was averted.

Matters between Johan and Ivan were also settled in a truce concluded in 1583 to last for three years and which was extended another three years until 1589. During the negotiations Johan demanded territory in addition to the areas actually conquered from Russia, namely Novgorod, Pskov, Gdov, Ladoga, Porchov and Nöteborg. In short he was asking for control of all of Ingria and western Novgorod, a preposterous pretension. None of this was granted, of course, but it did set a precedent for future Swedish ambitions, aspirations that would be acted upon by future Swedish kings.

What Johan coveted was complete control of Russia's trade with the west. The conquest of Narva had proved something of a hollow victory. As a second rate port it had been important because it provided direct access to Russian interior trade centers. Now in Swedish hands it lost its value. Of course, de la Gardie's liquidation of the population probably didn't help the city's commercial value.

English, Dutch and other merchants shifted trade to ports with better harbors. Two of the ports were Viborg and Reval, which was agreeable to Johan, but much of the Russian trade went through Dorpat to Riga and Pernau, both in Polish hands. Also, merchants were avoiding the Baltic altogether by passing around the North Cape to the White Sea where a new port, Archangel, had replaced the old St. Nicolas. Besides providing direct access to Russia, the route avoided the Danish Sound and its costly toll. For his part, Frederick claimed the same toll right on ships passing between Iceland and Norway, both in Danish hands. Even though he had the Faeroe and Shetland islands to operate from, there was just too much sea to enforce an effective toll collection. However, in 1583, Queen Elizabeth, needing Danish concessions, signed the treaty of Haderslev, by which England was granted the right to pass through the waterway in return for 100 *rose nobles* per year. France agreed to the same terms legitimizing the toll and the route formally. Johan's only recourse was to try to close the route at the opposite end.

Since the Middle Ages Swedish traders and trappers had worked the Scandinavian Arctic, collecting furs and trading with the Lapps that inhabited the region. These *birkarlar* operated much like American mountain men of the eighteenth and nineteenth centuries, spending long winters running trap lines and augmenting their catch with pelts purchased from native people. By the fifteenth century, Swedish colonists began to move into the more accessible arctic coastlands and were followed by the king's bailiffs who collected taxes not only on the settlers and birkarlar, but the Lapps as well. Gustav Vasa had sent soldiers to protect his subject colonists from Russian raids and to see that his bailiffs were unmolested. As the value of skins increased during the 1500s, Lapp families found themselves at the mercy of three countries, Sweden, Denmark-Norway and Russia. All three collected taxes in this region though none of them could maintain control. Gradually Sweden tried to gain jurisdiction over the area. In 1570, at the Stettin Peace Conference, Sweden had tried to lay claim to sovereignty over the region. With the capture of Kexholm, Johan demanded the land from Lake Ladoga to the Arctic Ocean. In 1582 he advanced his claim to all taxes from Lapps in the strip of land. Finally, in 1591, and again in 1592, Johan sent expeditions into the Kola Peninsula in an attempt to annex this area, gain control of the White Sea, and close the port of Archangel. Both attempts failed and western European ships continued to round the North Cape to Russia.

Ivan IV died in March 1584 and was succeeded by his son Feodor, but Boris Godunov was maneuvering to gather the reins of power in his own hands and so he arranged for the three year extension of the truce with Sweden to 1590. Stephen Bathory died in 1586 and the crown went to Johan's son and heir to the Swedish throne, Sigismund III.

With the Swedish-Russian truce expiring in 1590, Johan and Sigismund tried the maneuver at Reval that proved a disappointment. Sensing Swedish weakness, Russia renewed hostilities and invaded Ingria. Surprised Swedish forces under Karl Henricksson Horn — Pontus de la Gardie had drowned in an accident in 1585 — mounted a stout defense, but Horn was able to save Narva only by surrendering Ivangorad and Kopoŕe. This was the action that prompted his recall to Stockholm and imprisonment for a time. But he was pardoned by Johan just before the king died. Godunov, still consolidating his power, signed a twelve year peace with Poland and a two year truce with Sweden during which a formal peace treaty was to be negotiated. The treaty of Teusina was signed May 18, 1595, bringing the Second Northern War to an end after thirty-seven years of devastating warfare in the area once ruled with an iron fist by German warrior-monks.

By the terms of the treaty Estonia would be part of the Swedish realm and Poland would acquire Livonia. In Estonia, Swedish law and administration replaced the tyranny of the German lords. A peasantry, ground under the heel of the Livonian Knights and impoverished from years of pillaging by armies from four nations, found relief under their new masters.

An ignorant and downtrodden clergy was invigorated by a crown supported church ready to educate, reform and rebuild. Land grants were handed out to Swedish aristocrats and for the first time the nobility took an interest in this imperialism which could be of benefit to them.

Ingria and Kexholm were ceded back to Russia, but Sweden did get a new eastern Finnish border, farther east than the old one and extending to the Arctic Ocean. Russia, at last, recognized Swedish sovereignty from Malanger Fjord across the North Cape to Varanger Fjord.

Given his many disappointments in domestic affairs, Johan III's foreign policy must be considered his one area of real success. He secured the north for Sweden and made the Gulf of Finland a Swedish waterway. He had seen his son placed on the Polish throne, though he gained neither pleasure nor political advantage from this. Now that son was in line to be king of Sweden as well. A united Sweden and Poland was to be feared by all the nations of the north.

10. Sigismund III and Wars in the North

King Johan III was dead. His body lay in state in the great courtyard of Stockholm Castle. The anti-liturgists, anti-imperialists and clergy must have pondered their future. They had just lost a king who had striven for reconciliation with Rome. Now they were about to inherit a monarch who was a devout Roman Catholic. Would Catholicism be reinstated in Sweden as Queen Mary had attempted in England? And there were political issues. Would the union of the Swedish and Polish crowns mean a strong, single front against Denmark, Russia and the Germans, or would Poland merely strip Sweden of her hard won eastern Baltic possessions and make her a province of the Commonwealth?

Even these questions were overshadowed by the immediate problem of the succession itself. Sigismund was still in Warsaw negotiating with the Sejm for permission to go to Sweden and claim his throne. The nobles wanted two things: assurance Sigismund would not simply take the Swedish crown and abdicate his Polish throne, and they wanted Estonia, particularly Narva, which Sigismund could now give them.

Meanwhile, in Sweden the old power struggle was receiving new vigor. It was still king versus Råd, versus duke, only Johan had been replaced by Sigismund. The antagonism flared quickly with Count Axel Leijonhufvud trying to gain a following in Västergötland by claiming Duke Karl was agitating for the overthrow of the monarchy. Karl sent a troop of his ducal cavalry to arrest the count, who fled across the border into Denmark. Next, the duke made overtures to members of the Råd for a reconciliation, particularly with Erik Sparre, the old constitutionalist. He argued cooperation was necessary to maintaining a viable government in the absence of the king. By January 8, 1593, these two factions were able to come to an agreement. Karl was recognized as "leading personage" of the realm and would carry on the government in partnership with the Råd. Besides the need to provide a government for the country, this cooperation was driven by their mutual interest in seeing Sweden not become a province of Poland ruled from Warsaw. Neither Karl nor the aristocracy had any intention of having Poland replace Denmark as their master or being absorbed and dominated by Poland as Lithuania had been.

Sigismund sent a letter notifying the Råd that it would be several months before he would be able to depart for Sweden. He signaled that he approved of their arrangement for an interim government until his arrival.

Though Sigismund does not seem to have understood it, two legs of the power structure had united leaving him alone as the third. Karl, in particular, was in a position of strength. He was the recognized leader of the county, temporarily at least, with a substantial power base. His duchy made him the richest man in the country and provided him with his own army and navy. Karl may have seen himself as the regent in the style of the Stures, the *de facto* ruler of Sweden for an absent king.

Had Sigismund moved quickly, he might have secured his Swedish throne with little problem; he was the legal heir and had the whole of Poland-Lithuania to back him up. But he tended to vacillate before taking decisive action. He was the most affable of the Vasas, even tempered, not given to rages or periods of depression. He was a gifted painter, a talent he would exercise to be by himself, which he often preferred. He would probably be seen as a good man by modern standards, not driven by overambition as was characteristic of the Vasa clan. In many ways he was the least like his royal family, an introvert without the gift of oratory or the common touch typical of his grandfather. Above all he was sincere in his religion. He would do his duty as best he could here on earth, but his real goal was to attain the kingdom of Heaven in the next life.

Though slow to excite, Sigismund was becoming more and more worried by his uncle's position of power in Sweden. These suspicions were fed by Axel Leijonhufvud who moved on to Poland after his escape to Denmark. He reinforced Sigismund's concerns with wild tales of Karl's usurpation of monarchal rights. As evidence to substantiate his stories he could point to the church council being called in Sweden and the formation of the interim government without consulting the heir to the throne.

The struggle between Karl and Sigismund has often been glossed over as merely a confrontation based on religion. Religion was certainly a factor, but so was the Swedish fear of a Polish takeover. The real basis of the conflict, however, was the ambitions of the two Vasas, the foreign heir and the native prince. Still the Reformation and Counter-Reformation were powerful forces in Europe at this time. They could be used to whip up emotions and deliver allies. So it was probably for more than one reason that Karl and the Råd saw fit to call together an assembly to meet at Uppsala in March 1593. In attendance were over 300 clergy, a few representatives of the other Estates and nine members of the Råd giving it more authority than a simple church gathering. Karl did not sit in on the deliberations, but his shadow loomed large in the background. He kept close tabs on the proceedings and was even consulted by emissaries from the assembly on particularly important matters.

The object of the meeting was to settle differences within the church so that a united front would be presented against any attempt by Sigismund to reinstate Catholicism. How real was this threat? Swedes had only to look at the Huguenot Wars raging in France and the Dutch war for independence. The defeat of the Spanish Armada in 1588 was still fresh in their minds. Even though Poland had guaranteed religious rights to the Protestants of that country, the fear of papal imposition in Sweden was real. To mitigate this fear, Sigismund had sent an open letter to his Swedish subjects in January 1593 guaranteeing his protection of the prevailing faith in the country.

In spite of Sigismund's reassurances to the Swedes, the church in Rome had not given up on its wayward northern flock. Pope Clement VIII was elected in 1592 and saw an opportunity with a Catholic prince on the Swedish throne. He appointed Germanico Masapina nuncio to Poland and gave him the specific assignment to bring about the reconversion of Sweden. At Johan's death he appointed a special council of six cardinals on Swedish affairs. The events in Rome were unknown to Sigismund's subjects in Sweden. They were, nevertheless, fearful enough that the council moved effectively on several of the church's most divisive matters: the liturgy controversy and the adoption of a confesio.

The liturgy question was dispensed with easily. The anti-liturgist wing of the church had grown rapidly during the last few years of Johan's reign, becoming an overwhelming majority within the church. The liturgists lost out. Johan's *Red Book* was denounced as heretical, giving it one last and final rejection. Exorcism was retained. Rituals and ceremonies were set as outlined in the Church Ordinance of 1571.

As to a confession of faith, the *Augustana Invariata* was adopted. The Swedish church had now come together with a unified base of beliefs: the Bible, the Church Ordinance of 1571 and the *Augustana Invariata*. But the assembly went further. It voted to condemn all papists. It sent notice to the government it wanted the removal of all Catholic priests from the country and the suppression of the nunnery of Vadstena. What's more, the assembly called for the persecution of anyone raising a voice against the church and the condemnation of heretics. This last was to include Calvinists and Zwinglians, a question that nearly split the meeting open. The issue became so divisive it was referred to Karl who, though personally opposed to its inclusion, sided with the majority in the interests of unity. A resolution was adopted by the end of March. It was eventually endorsed by 7 bishops and 1,556 clergy. Karl signed it along with 14 members of the Råd and 218 other nobles. The burgher masters and councils of 36 towns, the provinces, and the representatives of 197 counties also signed. The Uppsala Resolution was the declaration of Swedish Lutheranism.

The Protestant Church in Sweden had come a long way, from a fight to gain the right to practice its faith, to full acceptance. Now its beliefs were agreed upon and any dissention was to be stifled. Henceforth, opposing views would not be tolerated. Ecclesiastic Sweden had moved from intolerance to accommodation, back to intolerance.

In addition, the Uppsala Assembly declared Abraham Augermannus archbishop, authorized a recoinage and reopened the University of Uppsala, all intrusions on regal authority. An *ad hoc* provisional government was developing. Sigismund had to get to Sweden before all his power was usurped. He did have one powerful ally among his Swedish subjects and that was Klas Fleming, governor and military commander of Finland, *lagman* of Uppsala and member of the Råd.

At the end of the Second Northern War, Fleming had not disbanded his troops. Instead, he maintained them as a private army, forcing Finnish peasants to quarter them without compensation. This meant he was one of only three men in Sweden with a significant fighting force, the other two being Karl and Sigismund. He was also completely loyal to Sigismund.

The heir apparent could delay no longer. By August 1, 1593, Sigismund was in Danzig. In order to leave Poland he had to promise the Sejm that once crowned he would cede Estonia to Poland. While in Danzig, waiting for a fleet provided by Fleming to take him to Stockholm, Sigismund received an emissary from Clement VIII bearing 20,000 scudi and instructions not to grant Sweden any guarantee of religious freedom. But he had already done this in his letter in January. Still, the message was clear, the pope had high expectations for the new sovereign. And for insurance he had Malaspina in the royal entourage.

Finally, on September 30, Fleming's fleet was able to transport Sigismund to Stockholm. At the capital he was confronted by Karl and the Råd demanding he accept the Uppsala Resolution and confirm Augermannus as archbishop or there would be no coronation.

Presented with this ultimatum, Sigismund stalled. He understood that the apparent united front was only superficial, that underneath there were deep divisions between Karl and the nobles. The council, led by Erik Sparre, the old constitutionalist, wanted to see the monarchy subject to the law and restrained from totalitarianism. Karl, on the other hand, was more interested in maintaining his ducal authority and gaining a position of dominance in the Swedish government. Sigismund's efforts to drive a wedge between the two were impeded by the antics of his Jesuit confessors and Malaspina. Their belligerent attitude antagonized the Swedish clergy, who were quick to spread their distrust throughout the church and subsequently to the parishioners. In a short time the king was cast as a threat to Swedish Lutheranism by the clergy and seen as such by the peasants.

Sigismund tried to find a crack in the alliance facing him. He first appealed to the Råd, offering concessions particularly to the nobles condemned at Reval, but Erik Sparres was able to keep the aristocracy in line. He next turned to his uncle with hints of guarantees for his duchy and maybe rights of succession, only to be rebuffed. At last he tried the peasants, reissuing his letter of religious guarantees and sending spokesmen to the markets proclaiming his position. But the gentry and peasants were already convinced of this Polish-Catholic's true intentions and would not listen. Sigismund was beaten. He might as well have been in a foreign land, quite alone and without allies except for Fleming, who was himself an outcast.

The Estates met on February 1, 1594, for the internment of Johan III's body in the great cathedral of Uppsala. Even here the lines were drawn. Klas Fleming, though marshal and admiral, was not allowed to wear these badges of office. Malaspina was not even allowed to attend and Abraham Angermannus gave the funeral oration. It was a demonstration of Sigismund's impotence.

Following the internment, the Riksdag met to consider the matter of the coronation. Sigismund fought for a compromise, but found no chink in the front facing him and finally had to concede on all counts as the peasants threatened to depart if matters were not quickly settled. On the morning of February 18, Angermannus was consecrated as the new archbishop and that afternoon he preached the sermon at the coronation of Sigismund I, king of Sweden.

The coronation oath was taken directly from the old Land Law and contained nothing extraordinary. However, prior to the ceremony, the new king was forced to sign an accession charter, something new in Swedish politics, but a document that would be required of all succeeding monarchs through Karl XI in 1672.

The charter set down the terms agreed to at the Uppsala Riksdag of 1594. As for religion, Sigismund promised to maintain the Lutheran faith in Sweden as defined by the *Augustina Invariata* and the Uppsala Resolution. Non-Lutherans could not be appointed to office or participate in the education system. Key government offices were reserved for members of the aristocracy. He promised to maintain good relations between Sweden and Poland. He would rule Sweden with the advice and consent of Duke Karl and the Råd, not make war without the consent of the Estates, nor raise taxes without consulting the taxed. In his absence Karl and the Råd would act in his behalf. Erik Sparres had gotten his constitutional monarchy. If Karl and the Råd could work together they could effectively rule Sweden. Sigismund was left constrained in Sweden as much as he was in Poland.

Though outmaneuvered and humiliated to this point, the new king wasn't finished. First, he ordered in a Polish fleet to secure his retreat to Warsaw. It arrived in June with 1,500 soldiers on board. With some military backing, he was able to take the initiative. He appointed his own commanders of the great castles of Sweden and made them responsible directly to him. Next, he created the office of regional governor (*ståthållare*). Each would rule one or more provinces. Klas Fleming would be ståthållare of Finland. Östergötland and Västergötland would be ruled by Arvid and Erik Gustavsson Stenbock respectively. Both served notice they would not prevent the practice of Catholicism in their territories. Erik Brahe, an openly practicing Roman Catholic, was appointed ståthållare of Stockholm, Uppland and Norroland, in direct defiance of the charter Sigismund had been obliged to sign. Finally, just before sailing on August 4, he issued a writ forbidding Karl or the Råd from calling a Riksdag without his express permission. Thus, Sigismund countered the alliance arrayed against him and made certain the three way power struggle would continue.

With their monarch again absent, the Råd searched for a way to govern the country. They needed some method of managing the newly appointed ståthållare before they had time to test the extent of their power. They turned to Karl as the only individual with adequate clout, calling him to Stockholm for a meeting. By September 1594 they had come to an agreement. Karl was named "head of government." Karl and the Råd signed mutual pledges of support. A letter was immediately sent to Sigismund explaining the actions taken and the need for a government to run the country. The king replied in a letter six months later refusing to sanction the elevation of Karl to any such office.

Checked once again by his nephew, the duke called for a meeting of all the Estates. The Råd complained, but finally consented. A Riksdag was called to assemble September 29, 1595. Karl drew up an agenda which was forwarded to Sigismund for comment. After weeks of no reply from the absent monarch, the Estates met with the duke who pushed for recognition as head of government and the title of *riksföreståndare* with the right to appoint all officials in the country. The peasant estate backed Karl, but the nobility, headed by Erik Sparres, and the clergy under Archbishop Angermannus, held out for a more limited authority for Karl. In the end, the coalition won. Karl was given the title of *riksföreståndare*, but was to rule with not just the Råd's advise, but its consent and according to the law of the land (Sparre's constitutionalisms). Thus, the Resolution of Söderköping, October 22, 1594, seemed to legitimize Karl's position as the de facto head of state within limits. Though disappointed in the final statement from the Estates meeting, it did have a clause that was to benefit him; it was that persons who did not subscribe to the resolution would be considered "lopped off"[1] and if officeholders, could be removed, a direct threat to the ståthållares. Further, if such backsliders actively resisted the resolution, Karl had the authority to "resist and pursue"[2] them.

The resolution was widely circulated. Meetings were held throughout the provinces explaining how and why Karl and the Råd were to rule in the king's absence. Karl wasted no time. The lopping off process started with declaring Arvid Stenbock deprived of office. The nunnery at Vadstena was closed. On November 4 a letter from Sigismund arrived forbidding the holding of the Riksdag and if it had been held, its proceedings were to be considered illegal and all agreements null and void. The nobility and particularly the Råd were trapped. Their acts were insubordination at least if not outright treason. Their necks could very well be on the line.

The same was true of Duke Karl, of course, but he was in the game for all the chips and was not the least bit squeamish. Stenbock and the nunnery were just the prelude to the real test which was Fleming, the duke's only real rival under the king.

Klas Fleming had forbidden any of his subjects from attending the Riksdag and had severely punished those few nobles who had. His billeting of troops with the peasants was becoming intolerable. Fleming was using the butter revenue to pay his soldiers, but this was insufficient. The discontented troops were only to happy to deal mercilessly with any rebellious peasants and not above a little pillaging when given half an excuse.

There were, in effect, two rulers in Sweden: Karl in Sweden proper and Fleming in Finland. This, the Duke Karl would not tolerate. He pushed the Råd to grant him troops to attack Fleming, but an emissary sent by Sigismund in the summer of 1596 killed this drive. It relayed the message that any attack on Fleming would be considered an attack on the king. Sigismund also sent a commission to Fleming giving him the authority to resist any move against him even by force if necessary, and the Finn had 5,000 ready soldiers with which to comply.

Karl's situation became even more untenable with the arrival of a second emissary from Sigismund in the late summer of 1596 ordering Karl to resign as riksföreståndare or cut back his authority in accordance with the Ordinance of Government. In Finland, the oppressed peasants of Österbotten appealed to Karl for relief, but the duke had none to give. He could only advise them to take matters into their own hands. The peasants did just that in what is known as the Club War.

In November 1596, the peasants of Österbotten rose up, killing what soldiers they could lay their hands on and burning the estates of Fleming's supporters, generally the nobles. The revolt spread to southern Finland where the peasants received some support from the clergy, but they had no organized army. Fleming brought his troops together, faced the mob at St. Michel in January 1597, and slaughtered the rebels. A final battle was fought at Santavuoriwc on February 24 and organized resistance was ended. The Club War was over. Some 3,000 peasants died. Fleming had put down the revolt, but Karl won the propaganda war.

The duke railed at the injustices done by Fleming and cited this as an example of what can happen when the ståthållares were left to exercise unbridled authority. He called for an assembly of the Estates to meet and decide these issues of a divided country and an undefined government.

On February 18, 1597, a Riksdag assembled at Arboga with heavy representation on the part of the peasants and burghers, but the nobility stayed away. Only the aristocracy from the Karl's duchy and the weasely Axel Leijonhufvud attended. Leijonhufvud had return to Sweden and managed to ingratiate himself to the duke.

At the assembly Karl pushed for dictatorial powers, but this the Estates would not grant. They did defy the king in offering Karl the office of riksföreståndare, but reaffirmed the Söderköping Resolution. He must rule with the consent of the Råd. Karl asked for a levy of troops for an attack on Finland and again was refused. He was given only the authority to send an emissary. Karl was still in power, but frustrated in not gaining the tools to consolidate his authority. He would have to resort to force to get what he wanted.

Meanwhile, the nobility's organization was disintegrating. Several members, including Erik Sparre and Erik Stenbock, slipped across the Danish border and headed for Poland to entreat the king to return and counter Karl's growing power. Eric Stenbock's departure left Älvsborg Castle without a commander. Karl quickly took advantage, sending his own captain to assume command. Next Karl led a fleet against Kalmar, still held by Karl Stenbock who capitulated in June. Arvid Stenbock, the last of the ståthållares, then fled to Poland. Karl now controlled Sweden militarily, but Finland still offered a back door to his adversaries.

Klas Fleming died April 13, 1597, leaving Arvid Eriksson Stålarm in charge. Though more of a gentleman, Stålarm was not about to accede to Karl's demands. In September 1597, Karl sailed for Finland with an army. He took Åbo by the end of the month and had the Finnish Estates recognize him as riksföreståndare, but did not have sufficient forces to conquer the entire country. In October he had to return to Stockholm and Stålarm quickly retook Åbo. Karl had gained little in Finland; still his position in Sweden was sound. If Sigismund was to retain his Swedish throne he would have to act soon.

What followed was a flurry of activity on both sides of the Baltic. In February 1598, Karl called another Riksdag to consolidate his power and forge ties with the nobility. He followed this with a special assembly of the Estates in the south at Vadstena in June and one in the north at Stockholm in July.

For his part Sigismund dispatched Samuel Laski to Sweden to reconnoiter, disrupt the Riksdag, and ask a declaration of loyalty from Archbishop Angermannus. Angermannus pledged his fealty to the king, counteracting Karl's proposition that this was a struggle to preserve the Swedish Lutheran Church. Erik Sparre was sent to Pomerania and Mecklenburg to get their promise of neutrality in any upcoming hostilities. He also went on to Denmark to solicit assistance from Christian IV, but was only partially successful. The Danish king would cooperate, but not actively participate in any possible war. Danzig, Lübeck and Rostok were pressured to break off trade relations with Sweden. Polish privateers attacked Swedish merchantmen in German harbors and on the open sea.

The Sejm was now alarmed. Sweden might separate itself from the not so tight union, breaking up even the appearance of a coalition against their common enemy Russia. The Polish Council authorized money and troops for an intervention in Sweden to restore Sigismund's authority.

On July 23, 1598, Sigismund left Danzig with 80 transports, a few warships, about 4,500 troops, the exiled members of the Råd, and a few Polish senators. Eight days later the fleet put in at Kalmar and confronted the fortress, which surrendered without a fight. In spite of Karl's best efforts, his nephew and sovereign was back in Sweden. A showdown was now inevitable.

The opponents were about evenly matched. Sigismund had his inferior fleet, and 5,000 Polish cavalry at his immediate command. The Råd, except for the undependable Axel Leijonhufvud, were with him as were a majority of the nobility in Sweden. Archbishop Angermannus and the city of Stockholm remained loyal along with a good share of the Swedish army, especially the Uppland cavalry. Småland and Västergötland strongly supported their king, but Östergötland was about evenly divided. Stålarm kept Finland in the king's camp although the peasants favored Karl and might be rallied to his cause if given a chance. Estonia would stay with the king.

At the core of Karl's support was Dalarna and his own duchy with its small army and significant fleet. It was the Swedish peasantry that provided the duke his strength in numbers. Except for the three southern provinces they were solidly behind him.

Sigismund's plan called for a two part campaign. He would land in the south and Stålarm, with his Finnish army, was to land in the north joining up with the Uppland Cavalry. Coordination proved to be a problem, however, and Stålarm landed prematurely at Uppland while Sigismund was still in Danzig. Stålarm was forced to withdraw. The false start drew Karl's fleet into the northern Baltic where it lay sidelined in the Åland Islands waiting for a north wind to bring it back into action. Thus Sigismund was able to make his unopposed crossing and easy landing at Kalmar.

The king advanced his fleet and most of his troops up the coast to Stegeborg where his sister Anna was living. He took the castle without opposition. A few of his ships got separated and wound up in the Stockholm Skerries. On one of these vessels was Laski, who had many contacts in the capital. He sailed on into the harbor and Stockholm came over to his side. He and Archbishop Angermannus then proceeded to secure the city and surrounding countryside for their king.

Karl, meanwhile, had assembled his army, consisting of his ducal troops and a large peasant militia, at Linköping. Sigismund, at Stegeborg, waited for the return of Stålarm in the north to push the two pronged attack. Karl had to move before the Finnish army arrived. On September 8 he advanced against Stegeborg, but the attack was poorly executed and the king's Polish troops proved their mettle. The attack was beaten back with heavy losses. Had

Sigismund followed up the defeat, he might have annihilated Karl's army, but the Råd intervened and persuaded the king that a slaughter of Swedish men by foreign troops might provoke a general uprising in Karl's behalf. The opportunity for victory was squandered; Karl
and his army escaped back to Linköping where he reorganized and rebuilt his forces.

At the same time the winds finally changed at sea and Karl's fleet was able to sail south.
By September 20 it lay off Stegeborg. Sigismund's fleet of mostly transports was no match for
the Swedish war fleet so the king found himself cut off at sea facing a numerically superior
force on land.

Sigismund was still confident of victory. He felt his experienced troops and commanders, though heavily outnumbered, were more than a match for Karl's peasant militia. On September 21 he broke out of Stegesborg and marched toward Linköping, catching Karl by
surprise. Karl rushed to set up a defensive position along the Stånge River near Stångebro.

The two armies closed and skirmishes broke out between opposing forces along the
stream, threatening to develop into a full scale battle. Karl called for a truce which Sigismund
accepted, pulling the main body of his troops back from the river. Karl, however, made no
such move to disengage, but sent men forward to take the two bridges between the armies.
One of these was captured, breaking Sigismund's forward line. Stretched thin, his men were
thrown into confusion as they pulled back and tried to regroup into a second defensive line.

Sigismund's situation was now desperate. To his rear Karl's fleet had forced the Polish
transports and the few warships to surrender. His baggage and wounded, left behind at Stegesborg at the breakout, were lost. He was in a poor defensive position facing a much larger
army. Sigismund now called for a truce which Karl accepted on condition the king turn over
to him the members of the Råd in his camp. Sigismund had no choice but to comply, sending to Karl the nobles who represented the king's Swedish support, among them, Erik Sparre.
Next Karl forced Sigismund to sign the Treaty of Linköping on September 28 calling for the
king to abide by his charter and that all appointments Karl had made would stand. A Riksdag was to be called within five months to decide all issues.

Three days later Stålarm arrived in Stockholm with his Finnish army, but it was too late.
The civil war was over so he returned to Finland.

Sigismund moved to Kalmar where he was joined by his sister Anna. From there he was
expected to sail to Stockholm where the Riksdag would meet to decide the government. He
still held the moral high ground. Even Karl had not called for an abdication, wanting only to
rule in the king's absence. On September 22 Sigismund and Anna set sail, but instead of going
to Stockholm, they crossed the Baltic and landed at Danzig. Sigismund left behind a strong
garrison at Kalmar Castle and some army units in the city, but otherwise he was evacuating
Sweden. He would never see his native country again.

The nation was stunned. With the Råd members as Karl's prisoners, royalist support
among the aristocracy collapsed. Burghers, clergy and army units loyal to the king were left
disorganized and demoralized. The Linköping Treaty was swept away by the king's flight and
no official government remained.

What prompted the sudden change in plans? Historians have not determined the answer.
There was an incursion by Cossacks into southern Lithuania and perhaps the Sejm sent an
urgent demand that he return to put down the insurrection. Possibly, he had learned of some
threat to kill or imprison him upon his arrival at Stockholm. In any case, the course of history was certainly altered by his flight and de facto abdication.

Karl was quick to take advantage of the unexpected situation and moved to consolidate
his power. The Uppland Cavalry, left dangling, turned to Karl for direction. By November

Älvsborg had submitted, followed by Stockholm. Karl led his troops to Småland and attacked Kalmar. On the first of May he stormed the city. Within two weeks the castle surrendered, closing Sigismund's last door to return.

With the country under military control, Karl took the fleet and army, and crossed over to Finland. He captured Äbo, Helsingfors and Viborg in September and October. By the end of 1599, he had control of all Finland. He then proceeded to purge the nobility for atrocities they had committed during the Club War. It was an excuse to curry favor with the peasants and eliminate potential future problems. The young son of Klas Fleming was one of those executed. Arvid Stålarm was sent to Stockholm for trial.

In Estonia partisans loyal to Karl seized power in Narva in October 1599 fearing Sigismund might try to turn the country over to Poland. Most of the army followed their lead and began taking control of outposts and forts across the country. In March 1600 Reval was taken, securing the country for the duke. Militarily Karl now controlled all of Sweden and its positions, but political and legal issues were far from settled.

In July 1599, the Estates assembled to decide how to respond to Sigismund's desertion. They voted unanimously to renounce their allegiance to him and declared him deposed. They then considered possible replacements. There were three candidates: Wladyslav (Sigismund's four year old son), the young son of Johan III, and Karl. The Riksdag was not willing to risk authority being passed to an untested child and pressed Karl to accept the crown, but Karl refused. He needed to maintain some semblance of a proper succession in order to secure the throne for his young son Gustav Adolf. He proposed sending a letter to Sigismund advising him that if Wladyslav was returned to Sweden within 12 months to be raised as a Lutheran, he would inherit the throne. Meanwhile, Karl would rule as regent. The Estates were unhappy with the year's postponement, but had little choice and agreed.

Early March 1600, the Estates again met, this time at Linköping. Over 800 members were in attendance for this was to be a momentous event. Before the Riksdag were two questions, the formation of a new government and the disposition of the position held by Karl.

Again the Riksdag called for the coronation of Karl and again he held them off. The twelve months were not yet up. Sigismund might still agree to send his son to take the throne. In the meantime, Karl was given the title of riksföreståndare for life in behalf of the absent monarch. It would be another four years before Karl would formally be crowned king of Sweden.

As for the prisoners, a 155 member court was empanelled with two alternating presidents, the unscrupulous Alex Leijonhufvud and the respected Erik Brahe, a Roman Catholic and former ståthållåre. The prosecutor would be Karl himself. The accused were the five members of the Råd turned over to Karl at Stångeboro including Erik Sparre, five other nobles, and the two Finns, one of them being Arvid Stålarm.

They were accused of not recognizing Karl as riksföreståndare and promoting the overthrow of Protestantism in Sweden. Actually, there was some truth to this last charge as Sigismund was supposed to have promised Malaspina that if he had to take Sweden by force he would reinstate Catholicism in the county.

All the accused were convicted, five receiving the death penalty. On March 20, 1600, the executions were carried out in the Linköping marketplace. Among those beheaded was Erik Sparre. The old constitutionalist who had been at the center of Swedish politics for three decades was finally removed from the scene. Karl was the ruler of Sweden and king apparent.

11. Karl IX and the Second Polish War

Karl would rule Sweden for eleven years though he didn't officially accept the throne until 1604 and was not actually crowned until 1607. This last would secure the monarchical succession for his oldest son, Gustav Adolf. Like his father, Karl had a good business sense and his duchy had prospered under his administration, but he had many of the Vasas' disagreeable traits: an evil temper, paranoia, unbounded ambition and savage ruthlessness. He was personally brave and did not blanch at leading his troops in the field from the front. He was a warrior king in every way. But he seems to have lacked his father's good sense and ability to judge situations. This would cause him problems in domestic politics, and would prove to be disastrous in foreign affairs.

Karl began his reign by trying to win over the aristocracy with leniency. But the discovery of a Bonde-Posse plot against him among the aristocracy of Vöstergötland changed his approach. After that he rode roughshod over his opponents in the nobility. There were other conspiracies, some at home and some at the Polish court where a few members of each of the great magnate families resided. In connection with one of these episodes, Archbishop Angermannus was imprisoned and died. In the end Karl managed to alienate nearly all of the nobility.

The Råd had ceased to exist with the trial of Linköping as most of the members were either executed or exiled. However, tensions increased with Denmark and Karl found he needed the council. The 1570 Treaty of Stettin called for disputes between the two countries be discussed at the border by their councils. Karl had to reconstitute the Råd. He called upon the Riksdag to nominate the members, but limited the membership to twelve as prescribed in the old Land Law (though the number of member had grown over the years — prior to Karl's decimating purge). He also asked that six members be added from Estonia, signifying the incorporation of this Baltic province into Sweden. He got the twelve he needed, but the Estates would not recognize the additional six. The new Råd did counsel the king and run the government when he was away at the Livonian Wars.

In church matters Karl tried to meddle much as Johan had done except in the opposite direction. Where his brother leaned toward Catholicism, Karl tried to influence the Swedish church to move away from what he saw as reminders of Rome's influence. He was not a Calvinist for he rejected some of their basic tenets, but he did admire the austere simplicity of their religion. When the church rewrote the handbook on services and the Mass, Karl submitted his own version. When the clergy wrote a revised catechism, Karl stepped in with his rendition. In both instances, church officials made no decision and tactfully waited for the king's passing, then adopted their own version. Karl was no more successful than Johan had been at influencing the Swedish Lutheran Church to his liking.

It was in foreign policy that Karl would have the most detrimental effect on his country leaving his son and heir, Gustav Adolf, a military nightmare. In 1600 Karl's situation looked promising. Peace, if not assured, did appear quite possible though Sweden's old adversaries Denmark, Poland and Russia would bear watching. Karl scouted around for allies. Overtures were made to England, the Netherlands and France. Queen Elizabeth was having her own problems with Poland, but was characteristically wary of any unnecessary entanglements. The Dutch were unhappy with Swedish privateers harassing their Baltic merchantmen and Henry IV of France leaned toward support for Sigismund's return. Most of the German princes could not afford the enmity of Poland. Only the elector of Palatinate (Karl's first wife's brother) and Maurice of Hess (first cousin to Karl's second wife) showed any inclination to back the new ruler and their support was tepid at best.

Meanwhile Sigismund had revived an old project of Stephen Bathory's: unite Poland and Russia into one great Slavic nation. He initiated negotiations which produced a twenty year truce between the two countries beginning in 1601.

Given these circumstances, no meaningful allies and a possible Polish-Russian coalition, one would expect Karl to sit tight and use the time to strengthen his forces. He did not. In August of 1600 he plunged into Polish Livonia with his army from Estonia. Why did Karl initiate this unprovoked war? Maybe he saw it as an extension of the Swedish civil war or as his duty to protect Protestant Livonia from Catholic Poland. Perhaps he just wanted the rich trading city of Riga. Maybe it was all of these plus opportunity. The Polish army was in the south fighting Cossacks and local insurrections. There were but 2,000 troops in Livonia as opposed to 17,000 Swedish soldiers in Estonia.

The invasion proceeded at a rapid pace. By the end of October 1600 Karl had taken Pernau and Dorpat. In the spring of 1601 he advanced to the Düna and by May his fleet was completing a blockade of Riga. He laid siege to Kokenhausen but became bogged down, not able to quickly take the fortress.

By the summer of 1601 Sigismund was finally able to free up a small army from the southern campaigns and begin his march north. He defeated the Kokenhousen besiegers and broke the investment. Karl left garrisons at fortified points in Livonia, but withdrew the main body of his army back into Estonia. His soldiers were no match for the Polish troops even though far superior in numbers. The efficient, effective army of Erik XIV and Johan III no longer existed. It was a casualty of the civil war, neglect and poor training. The Swedish soldiers discarded their cumbersome pikes and heavy body armor on the march. Disciplined linear formations and regimental organization had disappeared. The old arquebuses had not been replaced by modern matchlock and wheel-lock muskets now common in most European armies. These deficiencies were even more apparent because of the enemy they faced.

In most of the continent, the pike, backed by improved shoulder guns, had made the heavy cavalry charge a bloody proposition. The nobility, which constituted much of the heavy mounted troops, needed a new approach. A new tactic was developed in which the cavalry charged up to the enemy line, discharged their pistols or carbines, then wheeled and retreated. The next line of cavalry repeated the maneuver to allowing the first line to reload. This was supposed to weaken the line until they could charge through. In reality this caracole tactic rendered the cavalry much less effective.

But Polish warfare against mounted Cossacks and Tartars had only served to strengthen their cavalry arm. As much as 60 percent to 75 percent of a Polish-Lithuanian army was cavalry. Polish horse included light cavalry, mostly Cossack and Tartar horsemen, medium cavalry of German mercenaries and the mail-armored Pancerni (Panzers). But the elite of the cavalry, about one-third in number, were the Winged Hussars. These were drawn from the nobility, which in Poland-Lithuania constituted about 10 percent of the population versus 2 percent to 3 percent in Western Europe. The Hussars outfitted themselves and spared no expense on armor or arms. Their horses were large, sixteen to eighteen hands, and bred for war. They carried an 18 foot lance, cavalry saber, and short bow and arrows of the Mongolian type, replaced later by carbines and pistols. They often carried one or two extra pistols in their boots or in saddle holsters. On their saddles they kept another sword called a *pallasz*. This heavy sword was four to six feet long with a blade that had a square cross-section. The pallasz was used to stab and penetrate armor once the lance was lost or broken.

A hussar's armor was three-quarter plate of the Venetian type with an eastern style *Szyszak* helmet. Over one shoulder he wore an animal skin of wolf, leopard or tiger. Under his armor was a scarlet tunic which showed through the silver armor plate. Most distinctive, however, was the hussar's wings. One or two wood frames were mounted on the back plate armor. Rising up the back they curved forward to just over the helmet. Each wing was embossed in gold and decorated with expensive fabric. A row of eagle or raven feathers trailed along the back edge. At a full gallop these feathers made a whirling sound further intimidating the target of their overpowering attack. Only a hedge of pikes protecting squadrons of musketeers could break up a Polish close order charge, none of which Karl's troops possessed.

Karl was, however, about to get some help from an unexpected source. At this time Philip III of Spain bestowed on Sigismund the Order of the Golden Fleece. This was seen by the German princes as an indication that Spain was about to ally itself with Poland. Panic spread through Germany prompting Maurice of Hess to send one of Germany's ablest commanders, John of Nassau, to Karl. John was well versed in the Dutch system of warfare which had been successful against the vaunted Spanish formations. He stayed in Estonia for several months training Swedish troops, but the effect was negated by their lack of modern weapons and the all important pike. Swedish forays into Livonia were easily beaten back. By the summer of 1602 only Dorpat and Pernua remained in Swedish hands and they were effectively isolated.

The Polish army under Zólkiewicz invaded Estonia and by July 1602 had taken Weissenstein. John of Nassau threw up his hands in despair and left for Germany. Karl, in desperation, turned to his old enemy Arvid Stålarm, appointing him commander of Estonian-Livonian troops, but things went no better. In 1603 Zólkiewicz recaptured Dorpat and continued to devastate Estonia at will. Swedish control was reduced to the areas around Reval and Narva.

Karl, meanwhile, had determined to completely reform the army. He meant to create a core of professionals, partially replacing his Swedish conscripts. At the Riksdag of Norrköping (1604), he badgered the Estates into agreeing to a special three year tax (the contribution) in order to hire 9,000 mercenaries. While he was building this professional army he ordered Stålarm to take defensive positions and try to hold his ground, but then criticized him for inactivity. Finally, Stålarm took the field and met Zólkiewski in the open near Weissenstein. The Poles carved up the Swedes in a near disaster.

Stålarm was removed and Karl personally took command once more. He landed in Estonia with a plan to win the war in one blow. He marched to Riga with an army of 11,000 men hoping to force the Poles to battle. He would crush them with his superior numbers. The first part of the plan worked and the opposing forces faced each other for an open field pitched

POLISH CAVALRY OF THE 17TH CENTURY

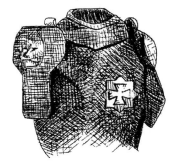

Pancerni [Panzar]
(Medium to Heavy Cavalry)

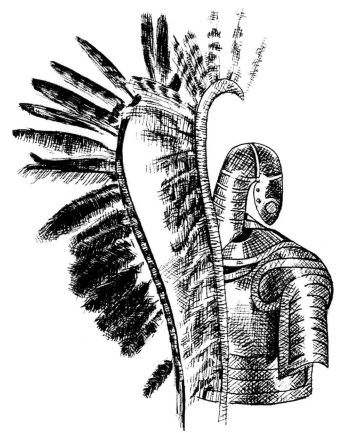

Winged Hussars (Heavy Cavalry)

Cossack
(Light Cavalry)

Illustrations by Amanda Peterson

battle near Kirkholm in September 1605. Zólkiewski had only 3,400 men for this pivotal battle. The fighting opened with the engagement of the two cavalry forces. The Swedish horse
was quickly routed, leaving the foot exposed. Again the lack of pikemen left the infantry at
the mercy of the Polish cavalry and they were cut to pieces. The Polish infantry then moved
in to complete the route. Over 7,600 Swedes were killed against less than 900 of the enemy.
Karl barely escaped with his life. It was the worst defeat the Swedish army would ever suffer.

Sigismund was ecstatic. Reval was saved, Livonia rescued and Estonia on the verge of
capture including the much coveted Narva. He even had dreams of regaining his Swedish
throne if the victory could be followed up properly. But just when so many possibilities seemed
within his grasp, events intervened to void the accomplishment.

In Poland the Rokosz of Zebrzydowski erupted into a full scale insurrection and Sigismund had no chance to take advantage of his Baltic victory. Swedish Estonia was saved and
the war would drag on for two more decades.

By 1604-05 relations with Denmark were becoming increasingly strained. Christian IV
still had the Sound toll and the tradition of being the dominant power in the Baltic, but Erik's
victories at sea and Johan's advances in Estonia challenged this mystique of supremacy. Karl
already had Viborg, Narva and Reval, and was blockading Riga. Domination of the Russian
trade was within his reach if he could take the key trade centers of Livonia.

In the north Karl was challenging Danish (Norwegian) rights to collect taxes in Lapland. He had sent settlers to establish colonies at Lycksele, Arvidshaur, Jokkmokk and Kare-
suacdo. Travel facilities to and through Lapland were improved. Blockhouses were built to
guard the colonies and churches built to minister to Swedes and Lapps alike. At his coronation in 1607 he accepted the title of "King of the Lapps of Northland" and he appointed a
ståthållare for Lappmark with orders to build a fort at Vadsø for 100 men.

All these provocations incensed King Christian IV. He applied to the Danish Council
for a declaration of war against Sweden. The council refused. The best Christian could do
was order his officials in the north to burn the Swedish blockhouses and churches. He would
appeal to the council for war again and again for the rest of the decade.

Karl's foreign affairs problems were beginning to stack up like cordwood. First it was war
with Poland, then he antagonized Christian, depending on the Danish council to keep him in
check. Finally, there was Russia. Here Godunov had been careful to avoid conflict with Sweden, but on April 13, 1605, Boris Godunov died and his son Feodor ascended to the throne.

The new tsar was immediately challenged for his right to the crown by a ghost. Prince
Dmitry had been the last son and heir of Ivan IV (the Terrible) and was murdered in his apart-
ment in Uglick by a band of hooligans. The town rose up and killed the murderers. So the
instigators of the crime were never discovered. Later a Russian claiming to be the murdered
Dmitry surfaced in Poland. He was treated well by some of the Polish nobility, introduced
to King Sigismund and given assistance. He converted to Roman Catholicism and married a
Polish nobleman's daughter. Malcontents from Russia flocked to his service until, in 1604,
"Dmitry" invaded Russia with his gathering. He made good progress until he reached Novgorod, where he was defeated. He seems to have led a charmed life for next he shows up at
Putivl backed by 40,000 Cossacks. It is at this point that Godunov died and his son Feodor
was installed as tsar. Much of the Russian army, however, accepted the pretender as the real
Dmitry. Feodor was dethroned and murdered and Dmitry was made tsar. This was the pattern of the Time of Troubles. It is a period in which no ruler lasted long; government and
society were in chaos. The Russian Orthodox Church was one of the few stabilizing forces
holding the county together.

Dmitry, with all his Polish connections, looked like a real threat to Karl, but in less than a year he had been murdered and replaced by Vasilij Shuiskij. Shuiskij was selected by the boyars. He was hated in the provinces and by the civil service because he was thought to have been the real agent behind the murder of the actual Dmitry in Uglich in 1591.

In July 1607 a second false Dmitry emerged. Also known as "The Bandit," he was backed by the Volga Cossacks, various provincial factions, and many in the government. The Cossacks of the Don supported him as did the Poles who had supported the first Dmitry pretender. He was also supported by remnants of the Zebrzydowski Rokosz, which Sigismund had by this time completely crushed.

Shuiskij turned to Poland for help negotiating a four year truce in 1608, but no military commitment. By the fall of 1608, The Bandit controlled Ivangorod, Pskov, Nöteburg, Kexholm and 22 other towns. Finally, Shuiskij was forced to turn to Sweden for help before he was completely cut off from the Baltic.

At the local level a relative of Shuiskij had concluded an agreement with the Swedish commander in Livonia. This agreement was later formalized as the Treaty of Viborg on February 28, 1609. For the first time a treaty between Sweden and Russia was signed by the tsar himself. The treaty reaffirmed the Peace of Teusina. The tsar relinquished all claim to Estonia and Livonia. A permanent alliance against Poland was created and Kexholm was to be handed over to Sweden. This was a doubly good deal for Shuiskij as Kexholm refused to submit and Swedish forces had to lay siege to the city to take position. In exchange Karl would supply 5,000 Swedish troops under Jakob de la Gardie, son of Johan's successful general Pontus. The Swedish forces contained a large number of the mercenaries that Karl had been incorporating into his army, thanks to the contribution tax.

The Swedish army crossed into Russian territory and started fighting its way toward Moscow. The Swedes took towns, forts and roadways as they pushed southeast toward the capital. Twice The Bandit organized armies in defensive positions to block the Swedish advance and twice he was defeated. Roads were captured and reopened so supplies could get through. On March 12, 1610, the Swedish army entered Moscow in triumph.

At the same time a second army loyal to the tsar approached from the east. Tsar Shuiskij's regime was rescued. The Bandit's support evaporated and he fled to Kaluga.

The old rivalry between Karl and Sigismund resurfaced to be played out one more time. The Swedish prince on the Polish throne had been bested in his native country, but had met Karl a second time in Livonia where he had triumphed only to see the fruits of victory snatched away by the Rokosz. The rebellion had been quelled, freeing Sigismund to once again challenge his nephew. At first Zólkiewski, Sigismund's brilliant general, had attacked Swedish positions in Livonia, taking Pernau in 1609, but now all attention was turned toward Muscovy.

Besides the Swedish dynastic struggle, Sigismund saw the Treaty of Viborg as a violation of his truce with the tsar, giving him the excuse to attack. In September 1609 Zolkiewski crossed the Polish-Russian frontier and laid siege to Smoleńsk. The Swedish dynastic rivalry was about to be played out on a continental stage, in the very heart of the vast Russian Empire.

Karl had an army in Moscow and had extracted territorial concessions from the tsar in exchange for troops. Sigismund had an army across the border in Russia attacking Smoleńsk with every prospect of expanding Polish territory. At the same time both kings were angling to have one of their heirs on the Russian throne. Karl was promoting his youngest son, Karl Filip, and Sigismund had in mind his son Wladyslav. If either were to succeed, it would create a powerful alliance and place the other in a desperate situation.

Karl took the first step by sending more troops to aid Tsar Shuiskij. An additional 4,000 men joined the army already at Moscow in exchange for the promise of more territorial concessions by the tsar — Karl was pressing for Nöteborg and territory in the Kola Peninsula. The Swedish commanders Christoph Horn and Jakob de la Gardie, both of whom had studied tactics under Maurice of Nassau, now had an army of about 7,000 men. Besides a small contingent of Swedish and Finnish troops, most of these were French, German and British mercenaries, a small but capable force.

The pendulum which had swung in Karl's favor for a few months was about to swing back the other way. In February 1610 the Russian factions, who had just lost The Bandit as their candidate for tsar, cast about for a new champion and settled on Wladyslav as their alternative to Shuiskij. Sigismund now sent Zólkiewski's army deep into Russia in an attempt to secure the throne for his son.

The Swedish army backed by Russian troops camped at Klushino to block his advance. The Muscovite contingent numbered some 30,000 men. Half were peasant conscripts with little or no experience or training. The 15,000 more dependable troops consisted of regular infantry which Horn and de la Gardie had tried to train in modern tactics, but had just not had enough time. The rest were Russian cavalry and mounted arquebusiers.

Against this huge army Zólkiewski brought a Polish force of less than 7,000. But it was an experienced army of mostly cavalry, 5,600 Hussars, 700 mounted Cossacks, 300 Lithuanian cavalry, 200 infantry and 2 small field guns. Zólkiewski took his army on a forced march through forests to reach the Swedish-Russian encampment just before dawn for a surprise attack.

Surprise, however, was lost as Zólkiewski encountered a town and a palisade between himself and the enemy camp. His troops burned the town and smashed gaps in the palisade, giving the Swedish and Russian army time to assemble. The Swedish infantry manned the palisade supported by the cavalry. To the left and right were the masses of Muscovite cavalry to prevent any flanking by the fast moving enemy horse.

Zólkiewski sent a regiment of his Hussars against the Russian cavalry on his right. His mounted troops charged again and again, smashing or losing their lances until they were reduced to fighting with sabers. Another regiment attacked the Swedish infantry, but was impeded by the palisade and pike men, then picked apart by musket fire.

Finally, the Russian horse on the left began to give way under the repeated attacks of the determined Polish cavalry. Tsar Shuiskij called for Swedish reinforcements and de la Gardie obliged, sending in his mercenary horse which used the caracole style tactics of firing their carbines, then retiring to reload as the next file came forward to fire. The Poles simply waited for the first rank to fire then charged with sabers before the next rank was in line. The mercenary cavalry broke and with it the last of the Russian horse, exposing the left flank of the Swedish infantry.

While the engaged Polish Hussars and Cossacks drove the Russian and Swedish horse from the field, along with Horn and de la Gardie, Zólkiewski sent a fresh regiment of cavalry, his infantry and two guns against the center. Without cavalry protection and with their commanders absent, individuals and then whole units of mercenaries began to desert to the Polish side. Horn and de la Gardie recovered and made their way back to the front, but it was too late. A truce was called and terms negotiated. De la Gardie led less than 400 Swedish and Finnish troops back to Novgorod and thence to Estonia.

Zólkiewski pushed on to Moscow while the boyars rose up and deposed Shuiskij. On August 17, they chose Wladyslav to be tsar. A delegation was sent to Sigismund's camp at the siege of Smoleńsk to propose the offer.

De la Gardie tried to salvage something from the defeat. First he made overtures to The Bandit, but the second Dmitry pretender was murdered in December 1610. Next he allied himself with a party developing to oppose Wladyslav called the National Rising. The new party endorsed Karl Filip for tsar in June 1611. Again it was Swede against Swedish-Pole in this Russian drama. However, the leader of the National Rising party was killed by some of his own Cossacks and the party disintegrated.

There was nothing left but to take what territory they could before Russia recovered. In March 1611 Kexholm finally fell to Swedish forces and on July 15 de la Gardie captured Novgorod. Sweden had taken some significant scraps, but Sigismund had the big prize, a grand united Slavic state, if he could consolidate his power.

Sigismund had an army in Moscow and the only organized party in the country had endorsed his son as tsar. And the Polish king was about to take Smoleńsk, the crown jewel of western Russia. It certainly looked like the Vasa progeny had won everywhere but in his native country.

Karl had won in Sweden, but had been bested in all other contests by his nephew. He had wars in Livonia and Russia, and in April 1611 he received a herald from Christian IV that Denmark was declaring war on Sweden. The Danish king had finally prevailed on his council to go to war. In the spring Danish forces crossed the border into Småland and attacked Kalmar. The town fell in May and the castle surrendered two months later before Karl could get there with an army. When he did arrive it was with too little and it was altogether too late. All he could do was try to prevent further loss of territory. With both armies going into winter quarters, Karl left the front for Stockholm, but fell ill before he could make it home. His health was failing rapidly.

In August of 1609 he had suffered a stroke which incapacitated him for several months and permanently affected his speech and hearing. He had taken Halley's Comet in 1607 as an omen of his approaching end. At the Riksdag of 1610, he spoke with difficulty in broken sentences. Though he fought hard to retain his grip on the government, many individuals were shifting their allegiance to the Råd.

The council had become reinvigorated. The leadership which had lapsed with the death of Erik Sparre had refocused on Axel Oxenstierna when he became a member in 1609. Even Karl's wife, Kristina of Holstein, made alliances with the new Råd leader and other members of the nobility while still queen.

On October 30, 1611, at Nyköping, on his way back from the war front in Småland, Karl died. He left to his son and heir, not yet seventeen years of age, a country deep in war with fronts in Russia, Livonia and now in Sweden itself. A Danish army was in control of a good share of Småland, including Kalmar, the strongest fortress in the country. The new king faced a possible family coalition of Sigismund and his son on the two Slavic thrones. This powerful combination could overwhelm Sweden and allow Sigismund to regain his Swedish throne.

Gustav Adolf was inheriting a country in mortal peril. Karl had worked hard with the characteristic Vasa stubbornness, paranoia and zeal. Without his father's intuitive abilities, however, he had badly miscalculated in foreign affairs while making enemies of just about all classes in Sweden. Karl looked upon his son with great expectations. He saw in him the savior of the nation, a youth of uncommon abilities and potential. Karl hoped Gustav would succeed where he had failed and rescue the Swedish nation. The young Vasa would do all of that and much more. Indeed, Sweden was about to burst onto the world stage as a major European power.

12. Gustav Adolf's Rise to Power

On October 30, 1611, at Nyköping, Södermanland, Karl IX of Sweden passed from this life. At his bedside, fittingly, were the two men destined to shape the future of the emerging young nation and propel it to a position of pre-eminence among European powers. The one, Gustav Adolf, not much more than a boy of 16 years, had already led troops in the field of battle. The other, Axel Oxenstierna, only 28, had established himself as leader of the Råd and the strength behind the aristocracy's push to regain power in the Swedish government usurped by Karl's secretaries.

Count Axel Oxenstierna came from one of the great magnate families of Sweden having extensive land holdings in Södermanland and Uppland. The family name, combining the words for ox and forehead, can be traced back to the middle 14th century. The young count's ancestors had long played a major role in Swedish politics, dominating the government, along with the Vasas, in the mid–15th century. Among these power brokers were Jöns Bengtsson Oxenstierna, archbishop of Sweden, who with Kettil Karlsson Vasa, martial bishop of Linköping, controlled the throne, making and breaking kings at will. There was Sten Kristiernsson Oxenstiena, involved in the Gustav Trolle affair of 1516 and Gustav Oxenstierna, Råd member and supporter of Erik Sparre against Duke Karl.

Axel was born in Fånö, Uppland, and like so many other young noblemen of his time was sent to Germany for an education, to Rostock, Jena and Wittenberg. Upon his return to Sweden in 1603 his family arranged his appointment as *kammarjunker* (assistant to the king) to Karl IX. As part of his duties he served a diplomatic mission to Mecklenburg. During his absence he was appointed to the Råd and upon his return quickly became the recognized leader of the nobility's movement to regain political power. It was he that Kristina, the queen, turned to when Karl IX's health and grasp on power began to fail. By the time of the king's death Axel had already become one of the most powerful men in Sweden.

In habit Oxenstierna was austere, using pomp and ostentatiousness only when required to impress foreign courts or visiting dignitaries. By inclination he was a constitutionalist, a disciple of Erik Sparre believing in a limited monarchy constrained by a sagacious, benevolent aristocracy. Here his views would collide with an equally strong personality in King Gustav, who would demand unfettered power. Likewise, in international affairs the two would conflict. Gustav held bold visions of a league of northern Lutheran nations and a union of Protestant German states where Axel's allegiance was to Sweden alone. He would work tirelessly for his country, putting her interests first. In politics and economics he was brilliant, perhaps a genius. The French cardinal Richelieu would say of him, he was "an inexhaustible source of well-matured counsels."[1] Few times in history have countries been blessed with such a statesman.

The other notable at the king's bedside as Karl's life ebbed away was his eldest son and heir apparent to the throne. Only in his mid-teens, Gustav Adolf had already shown signs of his ability as a warrior and leader of men.

Gustav was a soldier's general. At a little over six feet, he was tall for his time, a big man, powerfully built. He had a formidable reputation as a hand-to-hand combatant. He led his troops from the front. Like Alexander of Macedon he was often in the very thick of the heaviest fighting. And like the ancient warrior king he would receive his share of battle wounds. He carried Stonewall Jackson's belief that God would protect him until it was his time to die. Riding into the teeth of cannon and musket fire or trundling through the streets of Stockholm in a carriage, it was all the same to him. As with the great Civil War general, this attitude would cut short an essential commander's career before the war was won.

Gustav was born December 9, 1594. At the time Karl, then forty-four, was duke of Södermanland. By chance the family had been visiting the national capital instead of residing at the duchy seat of Nyköping when he was born. Gustav's mother, Kristina of Holstein, was Karl's second wife. Only a daughter, Katarina, survived from Karl's first union; all other children had died at birth or in early childhood.

It is ironic that Gustav's godfather was Erik Sparre, then chancellor, leader of the Råd and an adherent supporter of Karl at that time. Within months Sparre would change allegiance to Sigismund and eventually be imprisoned, then executed by Karl.

Gustav's mother also had ties to Sigismund. As a girl the young Swedish prince had courted her, sending her gifts as tokens of his troth. When Sigismund took the throne of Poland in 1587 (Kristina was then fourteen), the match was favored by Sigismund's sister Princess Anna and by his aunt Elizabeth of Mecklenburg. However, there were religious and political problems.

Kristina was a devout Lutheran and her country, Holstein, an active Protestant state. Her mother, also named Kristina, was from Hesse, an even more belligerent leader of German Protestantism leaning toward Calvinism. Sigismund, trying hard to consolidate power in his new country, could ill afford a marriage with a reform minded princess from a state quarreling with the emperor. He needed alliances with the Hapsburgs, not conflict. After years of dallying, Sigismund settled on the Archduchess Anna of Austria, whom he married in 1592. Kristina and Karl were married later the same year. Six months after Gustav's birth in Stockholm, Wladyslav, a Swedish-Polish prince, was born in Krakow.

There can be little doubt that some animosity resulting from the broken relationship between Sigismund and Kristina was passed on to Gustav from his mother. She would also have provided him with a thorough knowledge of political events in northern Germany and her view of the German Reformation. These connections with Germany would play an important role in Gustav's life and, therefore, in the history of Sweden.

In fact, the first correspondence of record from Gustav was to Friedrich, count of Palatinate, in 1602. The young Gustav writes to the German aristocrat, about his own age, that he has heard of his intellectual talents and princely virtues. He proposes a pledge of good relations as has existed between their fathers. The count, who later became famous in history as the Winter King (Friedrich V of Bohemia), replied in kind. The paths of these two historical figures would cross and re-cross until even their deaths would nearly coincide.

Gustav made his first foreign visit in 1600, accompanying his family to Estonia where Karl took personal command of the army fighting his nephew and Poland. The royal family stayed in Reval and even Weissenstein before it was captured by the enemy. Gustav would certainly have had close contact with soldiers and civilians involved in the war, providing an early introduction to military matters and the soldering arts.

On their trip home the Vasa family nearly met with disaster. They were part of a large fleet that left Reval in the autumn of 1601 which ran into packice in the Gulf of Finland barring their way. Several ships were sunk. The family did make landfall in Finland and spent Christmas at Åbo Castle. The royal party finally made it to Stockholm in March 1602, traveling by sleigh around the Gulf of Bothnia in the winter months. This trip would give Gustav first hand experience of severe winter conditions in the remote northern parts of the realm.

Like his grandfather, stories are told about Gustav's youth, though they have a little less the aura of legend about them. Three anecdotes recorded by Gyllenhielm, Gustav's half-brother, are among those familiar to Swedish schoolchildren. On one occasion Duke Karl is on an outing with young Gustav and some friends. Gustav's companions warn him not to enter a particular patch of bushes as "there were adders there."[2] The royal prince replies, "Give me a stick; I'll kill them!"[3] His proud father quipped, "Did you think he would be frightened?"[4]

Another time Gustav is at Kalmar port where the Swedish war fleet is docked. The young prince is asked which ship he likes the best. Gustav points to the Black Knight. When asked why, he replies, "Because it has the most guns."[5]

On another occasion a peasant from Öland brought Gustav a pony of the type bred on that island. The little prince thanked the man, then said, "I shall pay you for the horse, for I imagine you could do with some money."[6] Gustav paid the delighted peasant on the spot. These stories were meant to portray the young prince as generous, courageous, and of high moral standards even as a child.

Gustav's early education was from his mother. He learned to speak German almost as early as Swedish and could read and write in his mother's tongue before he was proficient in his own.

At the age of eight, shortly after the family's return to Stockholm from Finland, Gustav received a formal instructor, one Johan Skytte. Though the son of a peasant, he was considered, at 25, one of Sweden's leading intellectuals. Two years into his calling as royal tutor he produced Sweden's first printed treatises on teaching entitled *A Brief Instruction in Such Arts and Virtues as a Prince Shall Practice and Use Who Would Anon Rule Land and People Prosperously.* It provided guidance such as, God gives power to the ruler whose duty it is to protect and care for the people. But understand that people are ever changing and often disloyal. A prince must know the military arts and lead in battle (the warrior king). Always maintain patience and control while dealing with your council and don't trust advisors who are yes men.

Part of the education, of course, was religious and in this Skytte was generally orthodox Lutheran. Later Skytte was assisted in his princely instruction duties by an older and somewhat eccentric talent named Johan Bure. This often brooding individual had an original and inquiring mind that stimulated Gustav's curiosity and admiration. He was the greatest runic expert of his day and reveled in the ancient sagas which appealed to the young prince's taste for old Swedish history. Bure would become one of Gustav's confidants and as king Gustav would seek his advice in later years.

Gustav's education extended to practical statesmanship, history and law. Particular emphasis was placed on languages. According to Oxenstierna the young prince had "a thorough knowledge and perfect command of many foreign tongues, so that he spoke Latin, German, Dutch, French and Italian like a native, understood Spanish, English and Scottish and had besides some notion of Polish and Russian."[7] He was still studying Greek in 1627. Latin was important as the international language of diplomacy and much of the day's military theory was written in Spanish.

As for politics, his education was along practical lines. From age ten on he attended council meetings and the Assemblies of the Estates with his father. When given an opportunity the prince always sided with the king. Until his father's death Gustav's support for Karl was unwavering.

In temperament Gustav seems to have had some of the Vasa traits of violent temper and mood swings, but in Gustav these troublesome characteristics were kept in check by well developed habits of self-control. The prince also exhibited a sense of humor and cheerful disposition lacking in others of his line. He did, however, have the Vasa strong will and hot-blooded temperament.

At fifteen years of age he announced he would no longer be "controlled." He slacked off in his studies and turned to card playing, hunting, military exercises and female court society. He became known as a marksman and good horseman. Peasants of the Mälar district spoke of his generosity when he stayed with them on his hunting trips.

Gustav's interest in some of the ladies of the Swedish court was countered with an all out attempt by his family to find him a bride of suitable stature. The houses of Brandenburg, Saxony and Württemberg were considered, but the focus of the search soon settled on the court of James I of England whose daughter Elizabeth was available. Johan Skytte and Gustav Stenbock, the Swedish embassy to the English court, encouraged such an arrangement though they had no authority to make a formal proposal.

The English king favored the match as there were few eligible Protestant princes of marriageable age at the time. James abhorred the suggestion of his queen that their daughter should marry the very Catholic Spanish prince. Shortly after the Swedish embassy left England, James announced to his brother-in-law, the Danish king, that Karl IX had proposed marriage between Gustav and his daughter.

Christian IV, seething with animosity toward Karl and his northern policy, quickly passed word to his sister, Queen Ann. James's wife did all she could to discourage any prospects of carrying through such a marriage. Her efforts were aided by the outbreak of open hostilities between Denmark and Sweden in the Kalmar War which, indeed, put an end to the marriage negotiations. While Gustav was leading troops in one battle after another, other suitors were found for the English princess. Elizabeth and Gustav's stars were to cross again though the two were destined never to meet.

As Gustav plunged more and more into war and affairs of state, Elizabeth found a match in the young Friedrich, count of Palatinate, the same Friedrich Gustav had written to as a child. The count appeared to be a prospect for the throne of Bohemia. Indeed, the English court was not disappointed as the Bohemians did name Friedrich V king following their revolt against the Hapsburgs in 1619. However, the Winter King's reign was cut short by the Battle of White Mountain and soon after even the Palatine was taken from him.

In 1632, in the midst of the Thirty Years' War while the exiled royal pair was in The Hague, Elizabeth gave birth to their second son, who she insisted be named Gustav Adolf. Friedrich was visiting Gustav's headquarters deep in Germany at the time making plans for recovery of his lost domains. These prospects died at the Battle of Lützen and within days the former count and once king followed his prospective benefactor to the grave. Little Gustav Adolf survived for only nine years; his mother, Elizabeth, lived another thirty.

Of overriding importance to Karl IX was his son's education in the military arts. In this

Skytte saw to it that Gustav had a thorough background including Caesar, Vegetius, Aelian and Frontinus. In terms of modern warfare his tutor steered the prince toward the Dutch tactical methods used successfully against Spain and the Dutch style of fortifications perfected by Simon Stevin. Prince Maurice of Orange served as his model general. Gustav had met Count John of Nassau when the famous general had led Swedish forces in Estonia and conferred again with him years later while on his German campaign. The young prince never missed an opportunity to listen to and converse with visiting military experts and his father's generals. Of special use was instruction received from Jakob de la Gardie upon his return after serving several years under Prince Maurice.

The youthful prince's impulsive phase seems to have been short lived. His interest in parties, cards and girls began to include, then center on, hunting and soldiering. More and more he turned to military affairs and even to politics.

At his father's coronation in 1607, Gustav was named duke of Finland, Estonia and Livonia. Young Karl Filip, his brother, received Södermanland and Johan (Johan III's son with Gunilla Bielke, his second wife) was invested with Östergötland. Though the heir apparent to the throne did not receive any administrative rights to go along with his titles, at the beginning of his Russian campaign in 1609 de la Gardie was commissioned Duke Gustav Adolf's lieutenant-general for all Finland. Shortly after, Gustav was also given Västermanland and parts of Dalarna. With these titles, he received administrative privileges and royal revenues derived from the lands.

As Karl IX's health declined Gustav assumed more and more of the royal burden. At the Stockholm Riksdag of 1609 he addressed the Estates for the first time in place of his father. During Karl's last Riksdag, that of Örebro in 1610, the old king, still recovering from his stroke of the previous year, could only welcome the Estates. The rest of the oral communication was handled by Gustav. The young prince was called upon to counter the rising influence of the nobility. Led by their new champion, Alex Oxenstierna, the aristocracy was taking full advantage of the king's weakened condition to appropriate the power of Karl's secretaries.

It was at this meeting of the Estates that Gustav was declared to have "so far arrived at man's estate as to be able to bear armor and weapons."[8] This was surely a moment the royal prince had been waiting for with much anticipation. He had begged his father to be allowed to participate in the Russian campaign, requests that were continually denied. But now the realities of war were much closer to home with Danish forces invading the homeland.

Once again a Danish king was entertaining visions of the old Kalmar Union though this time Christian IV seems to have had more limited immediate objectives. Primarily, he was incensed by Karl's aggressive program in the far north threatening Danish-Norwegian arctic holdings and possibly her free and open maritime access to Russia via Archangel. His other concern was Sweden's possible threat to Danish dominance of the Baltic. This naval superiority, won at great cost from the Hanseatic League, had been successfully challenged by Karl's older brother Erik and Sweden still possessed the larger force, though the country's 24,000 tons of warships had been allowed to deteriorate since King Erik and Commander Horn's heady days of naval victories over the Danish. Most of the ships were in home ports in disrepair. The active warships were in the Gulf of Finland or being used in Karl's blockade of Riga.

Christian considered this blockade an infringement on Danish *dominium Maris Baltici* (rule over the Baltic Sea). Though his navy totaled only 15,000 tons in warships, he had kept it in good repair and fitted with up to date armament. In 1610 he dispatched a fleet to the eastern Baltic and broke the Riga blockade. The next year he finally convinced the Danish

Council to agree to war with his northern antagonist and immediately built an army of mercenaries, this time mostly Scottish.

In a swift move Christian led his army and fleet in an attack on Öland, the long narrow island beside Småland. With his ships blockading Borgholm, the main fortress on the island, he landed his expeditionary force. Surrounded and cut off, the stronghold surrendered.

Now fully alarmed, Karl sent Gustav to Östergotland to raise troops while he set about scraping together such conscripts and foreign mercenaries as he could find around Stockholm. With most of the Swedish army in Russia occupying Novgorod and the rest in Estonia-Livonia, the king was left with few resources.

Leaving a garrison on Öland, Christian next turned his attention to Kalmar, blockading the port and leading his army in an attack on the town. Old reports say the town was taken after three tries and the loss of 1,500 men. The fortress was now isolated by land and by sea. Karl IX finally arrived, but with a small force and his mostly conscript army was no match for Christian's professionals. Kalmar Castle fell to the Danes and over 7,000 tons of Swedish warships in the harbor had to be scuttled to prevent Danish seizure.

Christian's contemplated campaign north to capture Stockholm was abandoned for lack of sufficient resources. The Danish king boarded most of his army and sailed home, leaving a substantial garrison at Kalmar.

Karl could do little more than harass stragglers. So, after pummeling an enemy detachment caught in the open, he left for Nyköping and the Estates meeting. Gustav, however, was not about to pass up his first chance at some heroism.

In Östergotland the young warrior was able to put together a couple of companies of cavalry. In midsummer 1611 he led these troops on a raid across Småland into Blekinge where he surprised and captured the town of Kristianopel. Stories are told about this first military exploit of the future Swedish monarch.

One tale relates how Gustav intercepted a letter from a town official asking King Christian for soldiers to stop the border raids devastating the county. The warrior prince then disguised his troops as partisan militia and was able to enter the fortified town and take it. Modern historians cast doubt on the authenticity of this story, but seem to agree on the validity of a second anecdote from this campaign. According to this account Gustav did capture the town in a surprise attack and as he was surveying the marketplace with one of his companies — the other was busy looting the town — he was approached by the town pastor begging for safe passage out of the village for himself and his family. The sixteen year old royal commander grabbed the priest and held him fast for some time berating him for all the rumors and falsehoods being circulated by the Danes against his father. The cleric must surely have thought his time had come, but in the end Gustav freed him and allowed his family to escape before he burned the town. Such were the cruelties of the border wars.

Gathering more troops the warrior prince crossed over to Öland in October and captured the stronghold of Borgholm, repatriating the island. He granted clemency to the Danish garrison, an act uncharacteristically lenient for the time. This was his last exploit before he received word of his father's critical illness. The warrior prince was about to become a warrior king.

13. Gustav Builds His Army

Karl IX was dead, leaving his nation and the Råd with an army overseas and an enemy deep inside the country. The council gathered to meet with Queen Kristina (Karl's widow), Gustav and Johan, duke of Östergötland. Oxenstierna, though maintaining a low profile, pulled the strings in the negotiations leading up to the Assembly of the Estates scheduled for December. His overriding purpose was the preservation of the nation though secondarily he wanted to see a constitutional monarchy in place of the unrestrained kingship of Karl IX. The Råd wanted to reinstate control of the government by the aristocracy and eliminate the hated secretariat. Both appeared to have the upper hand in dealing with an heir apparent of only seventeen, but this advantage was tempered by outside conditions.

There was Sigismund, Gustav's first cousin, who still maintained his title of king of Sweden and refused to open any correspondence not so addressed. Furthermore, his claim was recognized by the Catholic powers of Europe, particularly the Hapsburgs of Austria and Spain. Throughout his reign Gustav would be referred to in these courts as the duke of Södermanland or duke of Finland. With a large share of the old Swedish nobility still at the Polish court there was always the danger that some coalition might try to reconquer the upstart monarchy.

This rivalry extended into Eastern Europe with the struggle for Livonia-Estonia still smoldering between Sweden and Poland. In Russia, deep in its Time of Troubles, a faction in Moscow advocated the Polish prince Wladyslav as the new tsar. This claim was backed up by a Polish force of occupation in the Russian capital. While in Novgorod, recently conquered by Jakob de la Gardie, the king of Sweden was proclaimed the Russian protector. According to the treaty of capitulation this province would support a Swedish prince as tsar (Gustav or Karl Filip his brother). Finally, there was Christian IV's invasion of Småland and his capture of Kalmar Castle. The Danish king hoped to expand his territory at the least and perhaps conquer the whole country.

Oxenstierna and the Råd had on their hands an heir who, according to the Succession Agreement of 1604, could not even share the government with the regents for another year (at eighteen) and could not be king outright until he was twenty-four. Still they recognized that in Gustav they had a youth of unusual abilities and when Queen Kristina and Duke Johan refused to accept the position of regents, the council moved to press for recognition of Gustav as head of state.

The Riksdag of Nyköping met in December and by year's end had voted to entrust the government to Gustav under certain provisions. He would be bound by the rule of law and the First Estate (the nobility) was to be granted considerable extension of its rights in the government. Duke Johan of Östergötland would share in any decisions in changes of the law and questions of foreign policy. The Råd and Kristina as regent for Karl Filip were also to be consulted. The charter Gustav was forced to sign to gain power recognized these conditions. There was also a clause dictating that all council members, and important civil and military offices were reserved for noblemen of Swedish birth. The rule of the secretaries would be ended.

One of Gustav's first acts as the new king was to appoint Axel Oxenstierna chancellor. Thus began one of the truly remarkable symbiotic relationships in governmental history. It was a partnership that would last all of Gustav's life. The young king's dynamic, sometimes impetuous, exuberance was almost perfectly balanced by the chancellor's imperturbability, tireless and calming control of affairs. His grasp of situations and administrative abilities provided the means for turning Gustav's ideas into practical reality. A letter written by the king in 1630 illustrates the interdependency and affection the two men had for each other: "I know that I may rely upon you to take care of my memory, and to look after the welfare of my family as you would that God should look after you and yours."[1] Gustav expresses his trust in his chancellor and friend. He continues, "Natural affection forces these lines from my pen in order to prepare you as an instrument sent to me from God to light me through many a dark place."[2] Gustav seems resigned to an early death: "My life and soul and everything that God has given me, I commend into His keeping; hoping always the best in this world, and after this life peace, and joy, and felicity. And the same I wish for you when your hour shall come."[3] Then he closes with, "I remain, for as long as I live, ever your gracious and affectionate Gustav Adolf."[4]

But Gustav was not above tweaking his chancellor's beard occasionally just to keep things in balance. In 1617 the king had Johan Skytte, his old tutor and the son of a commoner who was also associated with the repugnant (to the nobility) reign of Karl IX, admitted to the Råd. Though Oxenstierna and Skytte kept their mutual hostility cloaked by stiff courtesy as long as Gustav was alive, after his death the two would open a breach in Swedish politics that would last for years.

In assuming the reins of government, Gustav took the title "Elected King and Hereditary Prince of the Swedes, Goths and Wends." Noticeably absent was the title, "King of the Lapps of Northland," insisted upon by his father. It was this label and the aggressive policy that went with it that Christian had used to finally get his council's approval to attack Sweden. With this obvious gesture to defuse the tension between the two Scandinavian nations, Gustav turned his attention to prosecuting the war.

Unable to pull reinforcements from either Livonia or Russia for fear of engendering a Polish takeover, the new king tried to import mercenaries to bolster his poorly trained Swedish conscripts. The Norwegian provinces of Jämtland and Härjedalen were easily overrun being on the east side of the mountainous peninsula divide and hard to reach from the west. But in 1612 Christian dealt the young monarch and his nation a severe blow. In May the Danish fleet blockaded then attacked Älvsborg, Sweden's window to the west. The fortress fell and Sweden's western fleet had to be destroyed to prevent its capture. The loss also blocked Gustav's avenue for obtaining the mercenaries he was importing from Scotland. An attempt was made to bring troops in through Norway, but the independent minded Norwegians objected.

Up to this point support in this subjugated nation for Christian's war had been miniscule. An 8,000 man army of Norwegian peasants called for by the king only partially materialized and then evaporated through desertions before it could be put into action. But the invasion of the homeland by a thousand Scots, even if they were just passing through, could not be tolerated. At Kringen in the Gudbrandsdal Valley a Norwegian peasant army met the invaders, defeated them and drove them back into the sea. The young Swedish king would not get his mercenaries from the west.

The war had come to a stalemate. Christian had taken two key Swedish fortresses, but had lost two provinces. He dominated the sea, but did not have the resources to build an army big enough to invade the whole country or even take the capital. Gustav could ambush and harass any Danish forces caught outside their fortifications, but could not muster an army capable of driving them out or retake the castles. By the end of 1612 both sides were looking for a way out and this was provided when King James I of England, Christian's brother-in-law, offered to mediate a peace.

The Peace of Knäred, signed January 21, 1613, gave both sides much of what they wanted, but had one stipulation particularly favoring Christian. Sweden promised not to levy tolls on shipping to Riga unless actually blockading the port. Denmark won permission to use the three crowns insignia on her coat of arms. Sweden relinquished all rights to the arctic northern coastline and the inhabiting Lapps. Denmark gave up all claim to the Swedish throne and Swedish shipping would be exempt from the Sound toll. All captured territory was returned with the one exception. Älvsborg, Göta and several surrounding counties would be retained by Denmark until a one million *riksdaler* indemnity was paid.

The ransom was to be paid in four yearly installments beginning in 1616. Once again the nation was subjected to a crushing debt. Christian felt his northern neighbor was incapable of raising so large a sum. A bankrupt nation with a starving population would be ripe for takeover. He calculated that after a missed payment he could keep the Swedish port, then strangle the country by shutting off shipping through the Sound. He might gain in peace what he had not won by war.

Besides the ransom, there were the ordinary costs of government to be maintained and all this with the most productive agricultural provinces in the south of Sweden devastated by the war. Gustav had to resort to borrowing money from some of the great magnate families, particularly Jakob de la Gardie and even the queen mother, to keep the state afloat. To pay the indemnity the Riksdag voted to levy a special four year tax, later extended an additional two years. Every adult Swede was to pay according to his ability. Gustav and Duke Johan were assessed 32 percent of all their revenues. Riksdalers, not a Swedish currency, had to be purchased on the open market using Swedish trade goods.

Given the lead time Sweden was able to pay the first installment in 1616. The second was achieved by borrowing 150,000 riksdalers from the Dutch to augment the meager one year's receipts from the special tax. A large consignment of copper from the Berkslag sold in Amsterdam was used to meet the third. Much of the fourth installment was again borrowed from the Dutch putting the country in debt to the Netherlands by nearly a quarter of a million riksdalers.

The nation recovered her window to the west. Christian got his million riksdalers, but lost his best chance of gaining Sweden. Never again would the nation be seriously threatened by a Danish takeover.

Meanwhile Gustav had to deal with the Polish crisis in Russia. By the time Gustav had secured the throne the tide had turned against Sigismund and his son Wladyslav. True, the Polish prince was still supported by a large faction including much of the aristocracy and a Polish army held Moscow to reinforce his claim, but sentiments were beginning to stir, particularly among the peasants and Cossacks, for a native prince. Even some of the nobility were tiring of the incessant political instability and general disorder throughout the country. This rising nationalistic spirit was fed by word from Smoleńsk, under siege by Sigismund with the other Polish army on Russian soil, that the Orthodox population there had been persecuted by the invaders.

The Don Cossacks began a march toward Moscow and peasants from southwest Russia started to assemble and move toward the capital. The patriarch of the Russian Orthodox Church in Moscow, Hermogén, issued a proclamation saying, "If the prince [Wladyslav] will not come to Moscow sovereignty, be baptized into the Orthodox Christian faith, and take the Lithuanians [and Poles] out of the Moscow state, then I give my blessing to all who will come to Moscow and die for the Orthodox faith."[5]

The Poles reacted by arresting and imprisoning the patriarch in Moscow and his representatives in Smoleńsk. Then they issued an order that no Russian in the capital could bear arms.

On March 18, 1611, a large crowd assembled in the middle of Moscow to protest the Polish occupation. German auxiliaries with the Polish garrison charged the mob, slaughtering some 7,000 unarmed people.

Word of the brutal massacre by foreigners spread. Muscovites in the outer parts of the city took up arms and moved against the city's occupiers, forcing them to retreat into the Kremlin and the city center. Parts of the capital were set afire and burned to the ground. Within days the Cossacks, peasants, even boyars and nobles from the south, east and west had encamped outside the city. Over 100,000 Russians besieged the foreign army in the center of the capital.

On June 3 Sigismund finally took Smoleńsk by storm. The Polish king sent his general Zólkiewski on to Moscow with a relief force, but he could not get through and was finally turned back.

Meanwhile, dissention erupted in the encampment outside the city. Arguments between the various factions grew until the Cossacks decided to take charge by force, attacking several of the gentry leaders. Much of the camp broke up and returned to their homes. The desperate Polish army in the Kremlin thought they saw in this an opportunity and brought Patriarch Hermogén to Red Square to address the citizens. He was ordered to persuade the people not to resist the Polish occupation. But when allowed to speak Hermogén declared: "Blessed be those who come to save the Moscow sovereignty; and you , traitors, be accursed."[6] The patriarch was quickly pulled from the podium and returned to prison where he died a few months later of starvation.

In late 1611 a second nationalistic movement began, this time in the north. In Novgorod gentry and nobles made large donations to sustain a growing army. Swedish forces made no attempt to interfere with this assemblage advancing from its quarter toward Moscow. At the outskirts of the city they met with what was left of the previous host now dominated by the Cossacks. At about the same time Zólkiewski arrived with an army in a second attempt to relieve the Polish garrison trapped in the Kremlin.

Dissention between the two Russian groups allowed Zólkiewski to penetrate all the way to the western gate of Moscow by the end of August. In early September, however, the Cossacks were persuaded into joining the new nationalist host and Zólkiewski was driven off for a second time. In October the Cossacks stormed the inner city and in November the Polish garrison surrendered. The Kremlin was back in Russian hands after a year and a half of Polish occupation. Many clergy, gentry and boyar leaders were set free, including a young nobleman named Michael Romanov. Early the next year letters were sent to all the towns across Russia inviting them to send representatives from the clergy, trades, artisans and peasants to elect a tsar. The assembly gathered at Moscow in January 1613. After all the hostilities with the Poles, Wladislav was no longer acceptable and the assembly turned to Karl Filip, backed by the Novgorod delegation. It looked like de la Gardie's efforts were about to be brought to fruition. On February 7 the delegates agreed to offer Karl Filip the throne. But now there was delay at the Swedish court. The royal family and the council were reluctant to send the Swedish prince into this maelstrom of Russian politics. Finally, Karl Filip left Stockholm and arrived at Viborg ready to present himself to the assembly, but by then it was too late.

On February 21, 1613, the Russian Assembly selected Michael Romanov as tsar. His candidacy had been proposed by a faction of the gentry and was acceptable to the Cossacks who opposed any foreign name, Pole or Swede. He was relatively unknown, not tainted by the Time of Troubles intrigues. Above all he had been blessed by the honored patriarch of Moscow (now dead) and he was a relative by marriage of the last great tsar, Ivan IV. Thus, Michael was connected to the ancient dynasty of Rurik (the Varangian princes) which the Russian people always turn to in their hour of need.

With the election of Michael, the Russian Time of Troubles came to an end. There was, for the most part, a united country behind the new tsar. The nation had chosen a native prince behind whom nearly all factions could unite. Some of the disgruntled Cossacks returned to the steppes of southern Russia to foment rebellion. If the new tsar's internal problems were somewhat decreased, his border troubles were almost overwhelming.

To the north Sweden held the provinces of Novgorod and Ingria and to the west Poland occupied Smoleńsk with an army ready to enforce Sigismund's still active aspirations for his son. In the southwest Turkey was threatening. Only in the east was there unremitting good news.

Here Russian colonizers were steadily advancing eastward across Siberia led by the enterprising Cossacks. These marvelously adaptable pathfinders pushed on through tundra and dense forests on foot or on more traditional horseback. When they encountered river and stream networks common to parts of Siberia these horsemen became boatmen, adopting and inventing methods and craft allowing them to swiftly subdue this frontier. By the 1620s they had reached the halfway point, founding the town of Eniseisk. In the forties settlers were locating along the Lena River and by 1643 they had reached the Pacific. Resistance was scattered and only on a local level. Tribes and villages were overcome individually with no established nation or organized armies to defeat. The conquest of Siberia was, in some respects, analogous to America's winning of the West. Both would supply their conquerors with untold wealth in natural resources, but Siberia was not as hospitable as western North America and never saw the mass migrations responsible for welding the vast American frontier to its progenitor.

Besides the invading armies, the new tsar had to deal with a battered economy. Large areas of the country had been devastated by the wars; in some areas whole sections of peasant populations had picked up and left the land. Michael, who turned out to be a weak personality and came to be dominated by courtiers, had to extract his country from these wars and the devastation. Of the antagonists Sweden seemed to be the most likely to be willing to deal. Gustav was being pressed by the Råd to conclude hostilities with Russia before Poland did, freeing his cousin to turn on Livonia.

A peace conference met at Viborg in 1613 where Gustav laid out his demands. Sweden was to be given the provinces of Ingria, Kexholm and Novgorod, and the towns of Gdov, Pskov and Archangel in exchange for a peace treaty. His idea was to create a buffer area around Finland and gain control of all of Russia's trade to the west. Like the demands of Johan III in 1583 these conditions were outrageous. Negotiations dragged on for several months and then collapsed.

Gustav left for the Muscovy front and in so doing left behind a romance that had titillated the courts of Europe. One of the beauties at the Swedish court had caught the young monarch's eye. This was a lady-in-waiting to the queen mother, Countess Ebba von Brahe. She was from one of the great magnate families of Sweden and entirely eligible to be the king's wife. In spite of this she seems to have had doubts about the intentions of the young monarch. These misgivings were overcome and Gustav made some efforts to arrange an engagement, but was blocked and outmaneuvered by his mother. Kristina felt her son needed a match that would strengthen the throne or build an alliance.

When Gustav arrived in Ingria in June 1614, he found the fortresses of the province firmly in Swedish hands. He combined his reinforcements with de la Gardie's army, then advanced on Gdov, which fell later that year. Pskov was attacked next, but resisted stoutly. The siege continued through 1615 when both countries, fearing Polish adventurism, again began looking for a way out. Talks were begun that year at Diderina with the Dutch and English mediating.

Negotiations dragged on into the new year because Gustav was holding tough on his demands. When the Peace of Stolbova was finally signed on February 27, 1617, the Swedish king obtained much of what he wanted. He gave up Novgorod and Pskov and renounced Karl Filip's pretensions to the Russian throne, but he retained the provinces of Kexholm and Ingria with their strong fortifications of Kexholm, Nöteborg, Jama, Ivangorod and Kopoŕe. Finland and Estonia were now protected by buffer provinces and Russia was cut off from the Baltic. Indeed, a man could now ride from Stockholm to Reval entirely in Swedish territory.

The treaty came none to soon for Russia as later that year Poland mounted a campaign led by Wladyslav and supported by the Dnieper Cossacks that carried all the way to the gates of Moscow. A truce followed and also an exchange of prisoners which freed the tsar's father. Once out of confinement, Philaret took charge in Moscow, removing the court favorites who had gained control of the government. The Russian state was gradually righting itself.

Not all of Gustav's time was taken up with events of war. For the first few months he was in Russia, the young king wrote often to Ebba Brahe, but gradually the letters became more infrequent. The queen mother had won as Gustav's attentions wandered elsewhere. At the siege of Pskov the king had an affair with the wife of one of his Dutch sapper officers who would die in the fighting. Margareta Slots would bear Gustav a son, move to Sweden where she was provided with a comfortable living, and later marry an engineer in the Swedish army. Ebba married Gustav's famous eastern front general, Jakob de la Gardie, whom the king elevated to count. He bestowed on the couple an earldom in Sweden, the only such estate he ever created inside the country.

Freed from two of the three wars his father had bequeathed him, Gustav could turn his attentions to Sigismund, his cousin, and the Polish threat. First, he and Oxenstierna searched for allies, support previous Swedish kings had done little to cultivate. Gustav I had not wanted to entangle his country with reciprocal agreements that could draw her into the affairs, and especially the wars, of his southern neighbors. His sons seem to have been almost reckless in their disregard for help they might have received from such alliances. But the new king was less concerned about foreign entanglements and more worried about conflicts draining scarce national resources. Commitments with other countries might encourage potential adversaries to think twice before attacking. Also, Gustav had a wider vision than his predecessors. Sweden was already a power around the north Baltic. He saw his country dominating the entire sea. Friendly nations would be needed to facilitate this kind of aggression. In this the Swedish monarch was unwittingly assisted by his old enemy Denmark.

During the Kalmar War Christian had menaced English and Dutch merchant shipping he felt was aiding Sweden. The Peace of Knäred was further proof to them that Danish *dominium Maris Baltici* was a potential. As a counterbalance, the United Provinces arranged a treaty with Lübeck in 1613 and before the year was out a treaty was also concluded with Sweden. Christian also aided Sweden's cause by meddling through plots in Lower Saxony, trying to obtain counties for his son to rule. The northern German states became concerned and Maurice of Hesse-Kassel sent an embassy to Stockholm in 1613. Friedrich of Palatine's representatives arrived the next year. Both urged Gustav to join the German Protestant Union. While Gustav maintained good relations with both old friends of Sweden and he was sympathetic with their causes, he refused too close a relationship. He could see, as everyone else could see, that the Catholic League and the Protestant states of Germany were headed for a showdown and he had no intention of becoming entangled in the conflict. He would help by pursuing objectives against Poland. Any campaign in Livonia would keep Sigismund occupied, preventing him from assisting the emperor and the Catholic cause. He might, however, make a different kind of alliance with one of the German states.

Gustav's marriage ambitions had been twice frustrated by queens. Queen Ann of England had meddled all she could to prevent his marrying her daughter Elizabeth, now the wife of Friedrich V, and his own queen mother had blocked his advances toward Ebba Brahe, now wed to his general de la Gardie. This time he would conduct his own marriage project and he would look for a match providing political advantage.

His choice was Maria Eleonora, sister of George William, elector of Brandenburg. After Saxony, it was considered the most important Lutheran state in Germany. While the lady seemed willing her brother was appalled at the prospect which would jeopardize his own political schemes.

William came from the house of Hohenzollern. A branch of this line had ruled the duchy of East Prussia since 1525, but had died out in 1618. The duchy should have passed to the Hohenzollern existing family, but the duchy of East Prussia was subject to Poland and William needed Sigismund's approval to obtain his title. To ensure success he had been carefully promoting the match of his sister to Sigismund's son Wladyslav. However, there was a faction in Berlin that preferred the close ties to Protestant Sweden that a marriage to Gustav would provide.

Encouraged by this party, the Swedish monarch journeyed to Berlin in 1620. After pursuing his goal for a few months, he departed and made a tour of the other Protestant German courts. His purpose was twofold: to apply some pressure to attain his marriage goal and to see for himself the political and military situation in the Holy Roman Empire. He carried away a dismal picture of the Protestant position. The leaders of the Protestant party, he concluded, were feeble, militarily incompetent, self-serving and poorly organized. This view would not be enhanced by his experiences in the future.

Gustav returned to Berlin and with the assistance of the strong-willed electress-dowager secured the hand of Maria. They were married November 25, 1620. Though the Swedish monarch prevailed, the trophy proved to be less than he had hoped. True, the achievement was a poke in the eye of Sigismund, but the hoped for political advantages never materialized. Furthermore, Maria turned out to have a weak personality of little use at court or in the government. What is more, she would provide Gustav with no male heir.

On August 26, 1617, the Estates gathered in Stockholm for Gustav's coronation. He was twenty-three years old, had extracted the country from the Kalmar War and had engineered the Peace of Stolbova ending the Russian War under favorable conditions. As part of his welcoming speech he pointed out the strategic and economic advantages this peace would bring Sweden, but he also addressed internal problems the country faced: lawlessness, corruption, political favoritism, abuses in the judicial system, inconsistent taxation and moral decline. It is remarkable that a new monarch of such a young age would recognize these kinds of problems. With the help of Alex Oxenstiena and others he was about to revolutionize his country's political system, judiciary and taxation.

There was a foundation to work from and suggestions for improvements had been made. The government had, from long held custom, five great offices of state: the high steward, marshal, admiral, treasurer and the chancellor. Of these only the treasurer had specific duties and a real political existence that carried over from one king to the next. The other offices might be important and carry political weight depending on the whims of the current monarch. The crown did have civil servants drawn from the gentry, but they had no fixed duties or regular salaries. The highest level of these offices was the secretaries which ran the government under the last Vasa monarchs. In addition the king had his bailiffs spread out across the country to collect taxes and look after his interests. There was no central court system. Each county and province had its own judiciary with the only appeal going directly to the king.

This whole system worked reasonably well under Gustav I who had the energy and business sense to run the nation as he would a manor. It worked less well under kings like Johan III who had neither the ability nor interest to manage the government in detail. Because of Johan's inept management, the nobility had concluded it needed to be more directly involved in governing. This movement was given impetus by the rule of the secretaries.

Erik Sparre had developed a plan to reorganize the government as early as 1594. He proposed the creation of five departments, each headed by one of the officers of state, much like the U.S. presidential cabinet and its departments. The idea did not die with Sparre. It was given new life with the Charter of 1611 that Gustav was forced to sign. It called for central and local government offices to be filled with members of the Swedish nobility with fixed salaries. Gustav's absence due to the Russian war further emphasized the need for a government that could run the country efficiently on its own. It would be left to Oxenstierna to take all these deficiencies and ideas and develop a sound administration capable of supporting a great European power.

Gustav Adolf was altogether as energetic, capable and thorough as his grandfather. He could and did run the country well when at home. But he was overseas much of his reign. Fortunately, he had a talent lacking in the first Gustav, that of selecting and then trusting good subordinates. Government administration was becoming too big and complicated for men of even Gustav and Oxenstierna's abilities to control singlehandedly and both men would be out of the country for extended periods of time. Not only the nobility, but educated men from the lower classes would be required to operate this government of a great nation.

Gustav's reforms began with the appointment of Axel Oxenstierna as chancellor on January 6, 1612, less than a week after his own assumption of power. Oxenstierna started with the judiciary, creating Sweden's first supreme court. By the Judiciary Ordinances of 1614 and 1615, the high steward was made head of this court with four members of the council and nine assessors to assist him. Five of the assessors were to be from the nobility and expert in the law. Four were to be commoners. They were to hold court five months of the year in Stockholm and would be the final say in the law, although the king could still be petitioned to hear a specific case. The court would keep its own records providing an archive of case law. Precise rules of evidence emerged and the legal profession developed. Fairness and equitable treatment for all citizens throughout the nation became a reality.

Even more important for a country about to become a great European power was the reform of the treasury which Oxenstierna initiated in 1618. He established a board headed by the state treasurer to oversee the country's finances. The treasurer was given a staff to keep precise records and for the first time financial planning for the nation became possible. In 1624 the board hired a Dutchman, Abraham Cabeljan, as auditor-general and he introduced the system of double-entry bookkeeping to the Swedish financial world. Without a solid financial organization the country would never have been able to support the far ranging wars and the taxation systems necessary to support them.

The state office of admiral was given a department to supervise which included executive and judicial authority as it would run its own courts-martial. The Department of the Army was added, rounding out the military offices as conceived by Eric Sparre.

Finally, there was Oxenstierna's own department of the Chancellery, a sort of super state department. Foreign policy was entirely within its purview. But it also delved into local government, state infrastructure, religion, education, law enforcement and any other area not specifically delegated to another department. This was Oxenstierna's kingdom and he ran it in an authoritarian manner at first. However, with his removal to Elbing in 1626, he was forced to delegate much of this authority. By the Chancellery Ordinance of 1626, he established an executive staff of two chancery-counselors and a deputy to run things in his absence. He delegated day-to-day business to these men, but always kept the office of counselor and first advisor to the king for himself and this was heartily approved of by Gustav.

When both king and chancellor were absent from the country, the functional head of government devolved to the Råd, which was given its own staff and directed to remain in Stockholm unless called to an outside location on an errand. By the Ordinance of the House of Nobility of 1626, which fixed the procedures and membership of the First Estate, no Råd member could hold a seat in the Nobility House. The council (Råd) became a government institution of civil servants viewed by the Estates as part of the establishment. The aristocracy was firmly entrenched in the national government, but with their position they acquired the associated responsibilities. Erick Sparre's ideas had been fully implemented. This transformation was laid out in the Form of Government issued in 1634.

Thus, an administration was developed that freed the king to pursue his overseas adventures, supply him with the materials of war and even allow the chancellor to be absent without missing a beat. Other European nations were impressed and Peter the Great would use it as his model in his governmental reforms.

One of the outgrowths of these reforms was that Stockholm became one of the true capitals alongside the other centers of European government. With a permanent national administrative body in residence, with associated foreign embassies and supporting industries the town grew into a real city with a mix of merchants, tradesmen, even clerks, lawyers and bankers, along with the government officials.

As important as the new central government reforms were, improvements in local institutions were vital if the king was to be able to rely on the taxpaying commoner for support. The free peasant must be made to feel he was being dealt with fairly by his king. Corruption and inequities had to be stamped out. Gustav Vasa had personally supervised his bailiffs, checking their accounts himself. This was no longer possible.

Gustav Adolf defined the major governing areas, the provinces, as to their exact geographical boundaries, 23 in all. The office of ståthållare (governor) already existed, but it was ill-defined. Ståthållares sometime ruled a province and sometimes a castle or area in a province under another ståthållare. This office was changed to *landshövding* by the Instruction of

1635 and the holder was put in charge of a province. He was to be the king's representative in all matters except judicial. Bailiffs, henceforth, would report and pass taxes to the landshövding where accounts would be audited before being sent to the national treasury at Stockholm.

Below the province, the county (*härader*) remained with a sheriff (*häradshöving*), county court (häradsting) and standing county jury (*häradsnämnd*). Within the counties the parish council and vestry still fought for the rights of the parishioners. So government below the province changed little, but here, at the very local level, it always had to be much more responsive to the people.

All this expansion of government offices and the civil service raised the need for men educated in secular fields. Schools and particularly the University of Uppsala had always concentrated on ecclesiastic studies. Skytte, in charge of the accounting and auditing division of the treasury, complained he could not handle all the work alone and could find no one qualified to help him. In 1623 Oxenstierna was frustrated because he could find no Swedish diplomat fluent enough in Latin to conduct negotiations with the Poles. The king and chancellor went about remedying this by creating a new type of school. This was the gymnasium, first founded at Västernås in 1623. By 1632 six more were established and four more by 1643. These were secondary education institutions designed to teach promising youngsters in the fields of geography, history, mathematics, science and law.

The University of Uppsala was also reorganized. The number of colleges was raised from four to thirteen in 1620. Two years later there were eighteen including law, medicine, mathematics, history and political science. The university was endowed with 317 manors from Vasa family estates to be held free of taxes, all revenues for the school. Scholarships were provided for poor boys of special talent. In 1632 the University of Dorpat was founded in Livonia to educate administrators for the Swedish Baltic provinces. Here languages were emphasized including French, Lettish, Estonian and Ingrian. Eventually this improved education system would produce more qualified administrators than were needed. Government officials could select the very best and education became an avenue for upward social mobility.

Finally, there was the Riksdag, that unruly, transient, unpredictable body of three, four or five estates representing the people. They had a long history in Swedish government, but were defined only by custom as to number and membership. The Ordinance of 1617 set the number of estates at four: nobility, clergy, burghers and peasantry.

Once only an extension of the Råd, the estate of the nobles, under Gustav, became important in looking after the interests of the aristocracy. As the Råd was more and more absorbed into the government, its outlook shifted in favor of the crown and the nation as a whole rather than for the benefit of the upper class. The estate of nobles was left to fend for the upper class.

The clergy was probably the next most powerful estate for it not only represented the national church, but was in close contact with the commoners through the parish priests and tended to act as their voice. Also, it was the best organized of the estates because of the church hierarchical structure. The king, chancellor and Råd could negotiate with the clergy and reach an agreement that would endure and also carry weight with the people. Thus, the clergy often assumed the key role in settling political decisions.

The burghers, representing the business community, trades and merchants, was the least considered of the estates. Though growing rapidly, they still represented a small segment of the population and the wealth of the nation. At the same time a good share of the civil servants came from this class so their influence in the government was felt in other ways.

Finally, there was the peasant estate, representing the largest segment of the population by far and the main taxpayers, but the hardest to organize and assemble. The farmers and herdsmen could not afford, nor could they take the time to make the long journeys to the Riksdags. Yet the clout they wielded was enormous and often used by Gustav's predecessors to cow the nobility.

As the need for more and higher taxes developed through Gustav's reign, as well as increased troop conscriptions, frequent Riksdags were required. To facilitate this need representatives from the Estates began to meet in the 1620s instead of the entire Riksdag. The beginnings of a representative democracy were being established.

By 1627 Gustav had also created a secret committee of representatives from the three upper Estates to meet with him on foreign policy. These were matters considered too sensitive to communicate to the general population through the Riksdag. Control of finances was excluded from this group. Over the next century this committee would grow to have great importance.

All these changes produced a government capable of mobilizing the resources of a relatively small (in population and industry) nation, allowing it to become a world power. Still, an efficient government and industrious population does not necessarily translate to victory on the battlefield. To win wars, an effective and efficient war machine is needed and here Gustav Adolf was to prove his genius.

He first dealt with his navy. Gustav was the only Swedish king to have commanded a ship at sea. The Kalmar War had not only demonstrated the poor condition of the Swedish marine force, but many of the ships had been scuttled at Kalmar and again at Älvsborg. The young king began to rebuild the fleet immediately, but his ships would be bigger, stronger and better armed than his father's. Above all, his seamen, recruited from the coastal towns of the country, were trained, then practiced and drilled until they became a superior fighting force.

A true admiralty was developed under Klas Fleming, the appointed vice-admiral under Karl Karlsson Gyllenhielm. Though not originally a seaman, he learned fast and quickly became an expert in naval affairs. He organized the fleet's command structure and communication system. Discipline and dependability were ingrained in the service. Probably the greatest demonstration of his effective administration was the 1630 expedition to Germany. Gustav's main army of 15,000 men was loaded onto a hundred transports at Stockholm. Covered by a fleet of warships, the troop-carriers rendezvoused with seven other contingents sailing from ports all over the Baltic. The enormous fleet crossed the sea and discharged its troops at Peenemünde, a feat of unprecedented skill and coordination. The Swedish navy became the dominant force in the Baltic.

And this was entirely necessary for the Swedish Empire was, first of all, a maritime empire. As the Carthaginians tried to control the Mediterranean and the Spanish tried to control first the North Sea (Caribbean) and then the South Sea (Pacific), Gustav needed the command of the Baltic. In a time before aircraft he could swoop down on a port or coast and deposit an irresistible force. Communication, supply, and reinforcement avenues had to be kept open. Blockades, tolls at Baltic ports and tariffs had to be enforced. The free flow of merchantmen between the empire's ports had to be maintained. All this the navy accomplished without ever engaging in a major sea battle during Gustav's reign. The Danish navy patrolled the Sound and forced the division of the Swedish fleets, but did not challenge Gustav in the open sea.

As efficient as the Swedish government had become and as effective as its naval arm was made to be, the battles of this age were land battles. It was the army that had to win the victories. Here again Gustav applied his talents and developed an army superior to any other fighting force of his time.

He learned from the Kalmar War that the Swedish militia and conscripts could not stand against the Danish mercenary professionals. In Livonia Karl IX's commanders had tried to introduce the Dutch style of warfare, but discipline and time to complete the training were lacking. Swedish troops had thrown away their heavy body armor and cumbersome pikes, opening themselves up to the devastating Polish cavalry charge. On the Russian front Jakob de la Gardie's Swedish-Finnish troops with German mercenaries and Russian auxiliaries had fared better against other, poorly trained Russians, but were beaten when contending with Sigismund's experienced Polish army.

When Gustav took command of the troops in Novgorod he leaned heavily on mercenaries. Without time to create an army of his own design he did the best he could with what his father had left him and de la Gardie had maintained, but after the Peace of Stolbovo, the king began to building his own army.

The problem of recruitment was the first order of business. Traditionally Sweden had relied on volunteer militia for its infantry, supplemented by conscripts. Military literature of the time derided this approach and the Kalmar War, pitting Sweden's amateurs against Danish professional mercenaries, seemed to prove the point. Heavy cavalry was also a problem. Again tradition called for the nobility to provide horsemen in exchange for tax exception. But Karl IX had received only twenty armed horsemen in response to his call to arms for the Danish war. Making matters worse, there was no permanent corps of troops or cache of officers and non-commissioned officers (NCOs) ready to train and lead recruited or conscripted troops in the field. Mercenaries had been used to a greater degree in Livonia and Russia, but they required large sums of money to maintain and were notoriously fickle, shifting from one side to the other for the promise of higher wages or more booty. As to generals, the country had finally developed a few. Jakob de la Gardie and Gustav Horn were professionals who had officered under Maurice of Orange, but these were exceptions. Gustav's general corps was small and for the most part poorly trained. All this Gustav contemplated after the Russian war was concluded and gradually his vision began to emerge.

Defying conventional military wisdom of his day, Gustav decided on a national conscript army as the mainstay of his forces. Conscripts were less expensive than mercenaries and would make a relatively large standing army possible. Patriotism and loyalty to their king could be used as motivators. They could be trained in the tactics and weapons Gustav wanted them to use, not those they preferred or brought from somewhere else. The peasant farm boys were quiet, reliant and used to hardship. Gustav said of them, "They never complained, they were used to heat, cold, hunger and lack of sleep, but not to luxury and pleasure. They were satisfied with little. Obedient, strong and disciplined, they would defy all death and evil if properly led."[7] Finally, if trained, they would obey orders and do it promptly instead of dragging their feet or refusing orders altogether as professionals sometimes did.

But the process of conscription would have to be fair and seen as such by the peasants who would bear the brunt of the conscription burden. To this end Gustav drew up the Ordinance for Military Personnel which defined exactly the conscription process. All males over 15 years of age in each parish were grouped into files of twenty men (ten men in cities), a sort of draft registration. The king would issue a call for some number of recruits to be selected from each file. The actual selection was made by the conscription commission made up of a military officer, the local sheriff, the county court jury and the parish priest. In this way the crown got the troops it needed, but decisions as to who would serve were made at the local level where hardship cases, volunteers, etc., could be taken into consideration.

Having solved the problem of obtaining foot, Gustav turned to the even more difficult question of raising horse. The knight-service system had broken down, especially with the advent of taxes on the nobility first employed to raise money for the Älvsborg ransom, but used later as more money was needed for foreign wars. Gustav was never able to raise even 400 cavalrymen in this way. His final solution was to offer inducements to volunteers. The granting of land in conquered territory and the possibility of command positions in the military or government office helped to fill the ranks of his cavalry. Often these volunteers came from classes other than the high aristocracy and brought common farm steeds instead of the large chargers bred for war used by the old heavily armored knights and men-at-arms. But with the new lighter, more mobile troop units, this was not a serious problem (cavalry body armor was reduced to harness and helmet). The warrior king welded them into superb fighting units.

Through these devices the government established a reliable supply of manpower, but it had to be organized in an efficient manner. This was done through Oxenstierna's creation of the provincial regiments. Provincial regiments were administrative units at the province level which levied the requirements on the counties and parishes, then moved those troops on to field army units. Each provisional regiment was to supply three field regiments. Thus a field regiment would be made up of men from the same area, an advantage in creating *esprit de corps*. This same organizational process was eventually applied to cavalry and artillery regiments as well.

So the king and his chancellor built a reliable recruiting system capable of drafting the soldiers needed and getting them to the field, but it was the molding of those resources into a disciplined, superbly equipped and trained, highly maneuverable army that was to provide Sweden with the most powerful military in Europe. In this Gustav was the architect and builder.

The young king applied his talents to battlefield theory at a time when there were two competing tactical styles. Through most of the sixteenth century the Spanish tercio dominated European battlefields. The tercio was a mass of some 3,000 infantry armed with pikes and halberds. This formation, an improvement over the Swiss dense mass of pikemen, was designed by Gonzalvo di Cordoba about 1494 and came to dominate the battlefield for the next hundred years. His smallest unit was a squad of 25 men. Ten squads made up a company and 10 companies formed a regiment. The creation of units allowed for some maneuverability, but in the heat of battle the formation usually collapsed into a mob. Around the perimeter of this formation bristling with sharp points were stationed musketeers who could fire at the enemy, but withdraw behind the pikes if threatened by cavalry. The tercio put an end to the heavy cavalry charge of the Middle Ages as the sixteen foot pike easily outranged the horseman's lance. Cavalry units adopted the caracole tact of charging to the edge of the tercio, discharging their pistols or carbines, then wheeling and retreating as a second squadron advances. Against this solid block of really long spears the cavalry became almost totally ineffective except in Poland where the advantage of the shear mass of horse and rider armed with lance and saber was maintained.

The big disadvantage of the tercio was its immobility and difficulty in maneuvering. It was, in effect, a defensive formation. In an effort to create some offense, the number of soldiers in a tercio was reduced to 1,600 with more officers and NCOs. Maneuverability was improved. The tercio could advance in a lumbering fashion crushing a lighter armed or less numerous force in front of it.

ARMY OF GUSTAV ADOLF

Infantry Pike (9-11 feet)

Matchlock Musket

Wheel lock Musket

Regimental or Leather Gun (3 pounder) developed by Gustav

Swedish Musketeer

Sword

ARMY OF KARL XII

Flintlock Musket

Infantry Pike (7-9 feet)

Karl's Sword

Light Field Gun (4 pounder)

Swedish Dragoon

Illustrations by Amanda Peterson

Another problem with the tercio was that only firearms on the side facing the enemy could be used. Musketeers on the other three sides were left out of the fight. In the last quarter of the century Maurice of Orange invented tactics designed to overcome the tercio's inadequacies. Instead of great blocks of troops he arranged his forces in battalions of 550 men each. Within the battalion, soldiers were arranged in lines with each man in the second file located between the two in front of him. Thus, muskets could be fired from both front ranks and pikes could be leveled by both. Maurice also recognized the value of training and drill. With an increased number of officers and NCOs, due to the smaller units, the Dutch were able to move battalions from one point on the field to another, giving the commander some control over shaping the battle. Both schools had their adherents, but neither tactic made full use of the power of the projectile firing shoulder arms available or the potential for maneuverability with smaller units of better trained troops. Gustav would learn from both schools, then develop his own tactics superior to anything on the continent.

Gustav's basic infantry unit was the company composed of 51 soldiers. Eight companies formed a squadron and this was Gustav's primary tactical unit. A cavalry squadron contained 175 men instead of the 408 for infantry. Two squadrons made up a field regiment which was the unit used to maneuver troops in the field. Regiments were often combined into brigades both for movement in battle and for marches.

Infantrymen were armed with either a pike or a musket. The pike was made lighter and reduced from 18 feet to 9. Body armor was lightened from breastplate, shield, arm and leg armor to a harness and helmet. The matchlock was of the best quality, lighter and less prone to misfire than others used in Europe. Musket weight was reduced from 14 pounds to 10. The Swedish musketeers did not have to use the fork to support their weapons. Some units were armed with the more advanced wheel locks. With the improved weapons and drill, the rate of fire in battle was increased to four times per hour, three times that of the enemy. The warrior king arranged his soldiers in platoons according to weapon and these were deployed in lines after the Dutch fashion, but not so deep. Whereas a Dutch battle order might be ten ranks with battalions stacked one behind the other, Gustav kept his to no more than six. He wanted a maximum number of troops to be engaged in the battle, not two or three files at the rear contributing nothing. He also used the pike not only as a defensive weapon, but as an offensive device to exploit an opening in the enemy line. To create the hole, Gustav used his musketeers.

Where Maurice's intention was to produce a continuous rolling fire, Gustav wanted a shattering single volley, a blast that would blow the opening for his pikemen to exploit. To this end he placed his platoons of musketeers together and had them fire as a unit. While they were reloading, the pikemen charged, covering their reloading and possibly carrying the battle. But if they were repelled the musketeers would be ready to fire another volley.

These new weapons and new tactics required first class discipline to be successful and in this Gustav spared no effort. The use of these weapons and maneuvering in the field were practiced incessantly. The standards of discipline were codified in the Articles of War of 1621 written by Gustav himself and revised by Oxenstierna. The Swedish army was perhaps the best trained army in the world at that time.

Likewise, the cavalry underwent extensive and continual training. And here again Gustav had his own tactics; the emasculated horse maneuvers of the day were discarded. The king had learned from his cousin's Polish mounted troops. Swedish cavalry was still armed with pistol or carbine, but also with the sword. They would not merely approach the enemy, fire and retire. No, they would charge using the sword and weight of the horse to effect. Like the pikemen Gustav expected his horse to attack through an opening in the enemy line and to create this hole he attached musketeers to the cavalry. The shoulder arms firing a single salvo would create a gap and the cavalry would charge, covering the musketeers' reload. Again training and discipline were essential.

Artillery certainly did not escape the king's attention for he was himself an excellent gunner. Gradually he standardized the size of guns and shot by weight of the projectile fired: twenty-four pounder, twelve and six. He was aided in this as Sweden had the iron and copper to manufacture its own armaments and do so less expensively than buying them abroad. Sweden was probably alone among European states in this ability.

Mounted guns of the early seventeenth century were used mostly in siege work. If used on an open battlefield, they were placed where they were expected to do the most good in the fighting, but relocation was generally not an option. Often the battle would move out of their range or they might just as likely be overrun.

After much experimenting under Gustav's direct supervision, the Swedes came up with the regimental piece. This was a three pounder, light enough to be pulled by one horse or moved by two men. With this mobility it could be used right at the front, adding immeasurably to the musketeer's firepower. They had a higher rate of fire than the musket and with the introduction of canister ball and grapeshot for close range, these pieces became decisive on many a battlefield. Regimental pieces were assigned to both infantry and cavalry units. For his German campaign Gustav took with him one piece for every 100 men, a weapon unavailable to the enemy.

Finally, king and chancellor had to provide for quartering this new standing army when not on campaign. Soldiers were placed with farmers. The soldiers were expected to work as farmhands in return for their board and keep. The farmer also got to deduct the soldier's pay from his obligations to the crown. Officers were given farms of their own and the taxes were subtracted from the owner's pay. Thus, a national standing army was ready for the king's call.

As Gustav moved from campaign to campaign, his army would grow far beyond what could be supplied from Sweden's 1.5 million population. Mercenaries had to be used to make up the difference. However, the Swedish conscript regiments would always remain the central core of his army. They were well trained and dependable. There was a trust and bond between these troops and their commander acquired only by leaders who share their soldiers' circumstances, their hardships and dangers, commanders who lead from the front. In order to bring mercenaries up to something approaching this standard, hired professionals were required to submit to the same articles of war and the same extensive training. They were led by Swedish officers and NCOs.

Drawing on all his talents and multiple skills, Gustav Adolf, with the help of his brilliant chancellor, had created the strongest, most efficient army his country had ever possessed. Its capabilities and his were about to be tested.

14. Gustav Extends Swedish Power in Livonia and Prussia

On August 17, 1621, Gustav Adolf disembarked from his rebuilt navy at Pernau, Livonia, with an army of his own design. It had been 16 years since his father's expedition that ended in the disastrous Battle of Kirkholm. Had Oxenstierna's and his king's reforms made a difference? The new Swedish army was about to receive its baptism of fire.

Put on the back burner by both Sweden and Poland while they were occupied in Russia, the conflict in Livonia had smoldered for a decade. It had become increasingly active as the countries withdrew from the eastern conflict. Sigismund, while still tied down in Muscovy, tried to destabilize Sweden's position in the Baltics through propaganda and intrigues. Having extracted himself from conflicts with Denmark and Russia, Gustav wanted nothing more than peace in the region and tried to negotiate with his cousin, but to no avail.

Meanwhile, there was unrest among the nobility of the Duchy of Kurland deep in Polish Baltic territory. Problems grew until Duke William was forced to flee the country. He took refuge in Sweden. At the same time one of the nobles, Wohmar von Farensbach, proposed turning over the island fort of Dünamünde to Gustav if he would send a force of occupation. The fort guarded the mouth of the Düna River and was across from Riga. An expeditionary army was sent to the fort which was duly surrendered to the Swedish general Nils Stiensköld. He was in an excellent position to also take Riga. He did move on Pernau and captured that important port, but there his ambitions died. By the end of 1618 the Truce of Tolsburg was signed with Poland calling for a stabilized situation until November 1620. Gustav pushed for a longer cessation of the conflict even offering to return Pernau, but was rebuffed. Sigismund's schemes and intrigues continued.

At the time of the expiration of the truce, the Polish king was grappling with Turkey in a war for Christendom. A Polish army had been crushed at the Battle of Cecora in Moldavia where the king's brilliant general Zódlkiewski was killed. Now he had 45,000 Poles, Lithuanians and Ukrainian Cossacks defending a five square mile fortified camp at Chocim against a force of Turks twice that size. With his cousin thus occupied, Gustav took the opportunity to increase his bargaining position.

In July 1621 he landed a force at Dünamünde, then disembarked his main army at Pernau in early August. His force consisted of 14,700 foot and 3,150 horse arriving on 106 transports covered by 25 galleons, 3 pinnaces, 7 galleys and 7 light warships. By August 29 the army was outside Riga to begin the attack. With Gustav were his brother Karl Filip, Jackob de la Gardie and Gustav Horn. Though not a pitched battle, this would be the first test of his new army.

Riga had been the target of Swedish aggression before, but this time the threat seemed ominous though the taking of such a city would not be a trivial matter. Riga was one of the old Hanseatic League trade centers and was still independent though it recognized Sigismund as protector.

Gustav reconnoitered the city himself on August 11 and was fired on from one of the towers. He found Riga to be well defended. The city was built on a peninsula, surrounded by an 18 foot thick medieval wall with some twenty towers. A water filled moat ran around the sides not protected by the Düna River. Supplies of food and ammunition were plentiful. The garrison was made up of 300 Polish regulars and a 3,700 man citizen army. On the 12th Gustav sent a letter to the city council offering to negotiate a settlement. The council replied that they would not consider any terms without Sigismund's permission. And if attacked they would defend themselves with all means available. So the line was drawn and a siege inevitable.

Gustav's army began entrenchments on the 13th under fire. Riga sent infantry and cavalry units to attack the besiegers, but the Swedes drove them back. By the 16th heavy artillery was in place and the bombardment of the city begun. The Swedish *kartoger* (42 pounders) and half *kartoger* (24 pounders) threw their heavy projectiles against the walls and towers. Mortars tossed incendiary shells over the walls into the city itself. Fires raged, but the city fought back valiantly conducting repairs to the towers and walls by night.

By the 18th Ebbenholm and Riga's other defenses across the river were taken and the following day her flotilla was cleared from the Düna. On the 20th trench works on the land side of the city were completed and Riga was cut off from the outside world. Duke Johan took Riedricksholm across the river and on the 23rd Dahlen Castle on an island in the Düna fell, completing the city's isolation.

Gustav now turned his guns against the main towers of the city, the Jakobbastion, Sandtower and Nyportbastion on the land side, and fired at the Marstallbastion and Redtower on the river side from Ebbenholm across the Düna. Riga returned fire with cannon mounted on the walls and in the city. Musket fire was exchanged between the walls and the entrenchments producing heavy casualties on both sides. In Riga the city council building was destroyed by fire. Gradually despair began to spread within the city walls.

By the 29th artillery in the Jakobbastion had been neutralized and the gate at the Sandtower destroyed. The Swedes tried a surprise night attack on the Marstallbastion from across the river, but it failed with heavy losses. Some of the Swedish guns had cracked and blown up due to the heavy firing, killing men of the gun crews. Attempts to attack from the land side by filling in the moat and using small boats also failed.

On August 30 Field Hetman Krzyszto II Radziwill arrived with 1,500 Lithuanian troops and three guns. He joined the small partisan force outside the city that had been harassing the Swedes. New hope sprung inside the city. The combined army attacked, but could make no headway against the Swedish trench works and guns. Gustav was prepared. Like Julias Caesar at Alesia, he had built a defensive perimeter of trenches facing outward ringing the siege trenches.

Radziwill pulled back and camped that night. On the 31st Swedish gunfire was leveled on Radziwill's camp and he withdrew, leaving the city to fend for itself. The high hopes and jubilation inside the city were dashed.

On September 1 the Swedes were able to drain the moat. Now, trenches, tunnels and breastworks could be built right to the wall. The defenders dug tunnels to intercept the besieger's tunnels and planted mines under their trenches just as the Swedes were planting mines in their tunnels under the city's walls and towers. Some of these tunnels intersected and miners fought with shovels and picks beneath the earth.

Herman Wrangel took his Mansfeldt Regiment across the moat and seized the first city fortifications to be taken by the Swedes, but a well placed mine caused heavy casualties. Over the next several days artillery fire was concentrated on Jakobbastion, Nyportbastion and Sandtower followed by repeated attempts to storm the fortifications. Though none were successful and heavy casualties were suffered, the defenses were wearing down.

Gustav had several mines placed under the city walls and many assault bridges readied for deployment. On the 12th he sent a last letter urging the defenders to negotiate before the final attack. The city accepted the invitation and on September 15, 1621, Riga surrendered to Sweden. Gustav's new army had passed its first test.

Gustav led his victorious troops into Kurland where he took the capital of Mitau before Radziwill could reinforce it. By year's end Gustav had taken Wolmar. Radziwill remained just clear of the Swedish armies, waiting for Sigismund to send reinforcements.

Riga was a port city of 30,000 people, three times the size of Stockholm. It was prosperous, the main trade center for goods flowing west out of Russia and Lithuania. It would become the greatest city in the Swedish Empire.

By the terms of the surrender, the city was to send representatives to the Riksdag and its citizens had the right of appeal to the Swedish Supreme Court. Still, in peace negotiations with Sigismund, Gustav offered to give up all his Livonian positions in exchange for a long term truce (50 to 60 years) or a permanent peace treaty. But Sigismund harbored ambitions of obtaining the Swedish throne and now he had Livonian territory to recover from his cousin as well. What's more, the Swedish army suffered terribly during the winter of 1622, losing half its number to disease and starvation. Finally, in October 1622 Gustav accepted a two year truce leaving Riga and Pernau in his hands. Gustav had returned to Stockholm leaving Karl Filip in Livonia to oversee the new Swedish territories. Karl Filip would die there of typhus the next year along with half his army.

Just as things were quieting in Livonia, Denmark began agitating for better treatment from Sweden. Christian IV complained the provisions of the Peace of Knäred were not being adhered to by the Swedes. In particular, Sweden was extending the free trade provision and exemption of the Sound Toll to its new ports of Riga and Pernau. At the same time, Sweden had imposed a sales tax on some commodities being exported to Denmark.

In May 1624 the parties met at Sjöaryd for two months of tough negotiations. Christian more than met his match in Alex Oxenstierna and his king backed by the Swedish navy. The Danish fleet was in a state of disrepair and Christian did not have the money to hire the usual mercenary army. He was forced to back down on all points. The Agreement of Sjöaryd was a humiliating defeat for Christian. It, in effect, recognized Sweden's equality with Denmark as a naval and military power. It marked the shift of Baltic sea supremacy from Denmark to Sweden.

As the truce of 1622 with Poland neared expiration Oxenstierna met with Polish envoys at Daler to work out an extension. Sigismund's terms were unreasonable, negotiations were broken off and both countries readied for war.

In 1624 rumors circulated that Sigismund was about to try to recover his Swedish throne. A mercenary army was rumored to be gathering at Danzig to board a new Polish fleet being constructed there. Poland was to attack Estonia and Finland while the Swedes at the Polish court would return and spark a revolt in Sweden itself. Gustav began a mobilization effort in Sweden then sent a fleet to Danzig to investigate. All the rumors proved to be false except for the new fleet that Sigismund was building, but the scare was serious enough to convince Gustav he needed to settle things with his cousin once and for all.

In June 1625 Johan Banér landed in Livonia with 12,000 troops and marched on Kokenhúsen. The town surrendered, but not the fort. Banér laid siege. In July Gustav arrived at the mouth of the Düna with another 8,000 men and marched to join Banér. Kokenhausen Fortress surrendered on the 15th. The Swedes advanced through Livonia taking towns and castles. Dorpar fell to Jakob de la Gardie and Gustav Horn. Birze surrendered to Svante Banér following a six day siege. During the summer Marienburg and Neuhausen were conquered.

Radziwill could respond only by raiding Czadosy and other border towns. He captured a couple of Swedish emissaries, Johan Adler and Arvid Horn, which only caused more problems for Sigismund. With all of Livonia under Swedish control, the army went into winter quarters. The campaign season had been very successful although Gustav Horn had been wounded. The Swedish army was better prepared for winter than in previous Livonian campaigns and would have been quite comfortable except for harassment by Polish Cossack patrols.

However, on Christmas 1625 disease broke out in the Swedish camp. Gustav wrote Oxenstierna that the soldiers were dying off like dogs. Gustav, watching his army disappear right from under him, decided to do something while he still had soldiers to fight. The only Polish army in the vicinity that could threaten him come spring was a 6,000 man force under Johan Stanislaus at Wallhof fifty miles away, south of the Düna.

The Swedish king, now 31 years old, assembled 1,000 musketeers, 6 guns and 2,100 cavalrymen, and set out for Wallhof. Most of the horse were Finnish dragoons called Hakkapällites from their battle cry, "Hakka pälle" meaning "strike to the head." In a forced march over difficult winter terrain, the small army covered the fifty miles in 36 hours, arriving the morning of January 17, 1626.

The Poles had encamped between two wooded areas. Gustav surprised the predominantly Lithuanian army with a dawn attack. The woods prevented the Polish hetman, Sapieha, from using his usual tactic of outflanking the enemy with his excellent cavalry of 2,500 men including the Winged Hussars, some of whom had been at Kirkholm. Instead, Gustav sent companies of musketeers into the woods to enfield the camp and any formations advancing on the Swedes. He placed the bulk of his infantry squarely in front of the camp and butchered the Hussars as they charged into the well ordered ranks of pikemen, cutting them down with musket fire on three sides. The Polish-Lithuanian army was annihilated, 1,500 killed, three guns and 150 men captured along with the camp, wagon train and baggage. The Battle of Kirkholm had been avenged and Livonia secured as a Swedish province.

Gustav had led in his first pitched battle. He had tactical command without any of his generals present and again his army had performed magnificently. His new tactics, arms and formations had proven flexible and effective in an open field battle. All Europe began to take notice of Sweden's young king and his remarkable new army.

While Gustav was securing Livonia, the situation of the Protestant princes of Germany was deteriorating. Imperial and Catholic League armies were steadily conquering the wayward states one by one. James I of England and George William of Brandenburg were so alarmed they both approached Gustav in 1624 proposing he head a league of Protestant states to oppose the emperor's advance. Gustav replied that he would consider the proposal under certain conditions. First, the Dutch must be part of any coalition and an Anglo-Dutch fleet of at least 48 ships be assembled and made available to protect his Baltic and North Sea lines of communication. An army of 32,000 men would be provided and paid. A German harbor in the North Sea and the Baltic would be supplied and Danzig's neutrality guaranteed. Bethlen Gabor, prince of Transylvania, would be part of the alliance and, finally, Gustav would be supreme commander of all coalition forces.

These conditions went beyond anything either ruler was prepared to deliver. So the Protestant cause turned elsewhere to look for a champion and found it in Christian IV of Denmark. Still smarting from his defeat at the conference of Sjöaryd and anxious to recoup his prestige, he made an agreement with James I in February 1625 to lead an army into Germany on condition England provide 7,000 men to add to his 5,000 and subsidize the expedition to the tune of £180,000 per year. It seemed a win for both parties. James got his campaign against the emperor in Germany and Christian trumped Gustav as leader of Protestant Europe.

A congress in The Hague was called for November 1625 to organize the proposed Protestant League. Christian's project was taking shape. However, in September England and the Dutch signed the Treaty of Southampton agreeing to make war, not in Germany, but against Spain. Buckingham's expedition against Cadiz ended in disaster, discouraging the English Parliament from providing funds for more of the king's misadventures. The Hague Congress was poorly attended by even the German princes and the Great Protestant League died before it was even born. Christian was left to face the Imperial armies almost alone. Gustav must have watched all this with some satisfaction. His old nemesis had been seduced into the German quagmire and left badly exposed.

For Gustav, these events provided opportunity. Christian would be occupied in Germany. The Imperial advance might be slowed and Gustav was free to try to bring Sigismund to terms. He counseled with Oxenstierna on what the next move should be. His cousin was still not willing to concede his claim to the Swedish throne or enter a long term peace agreement even for the return of Livonia. More pressure must be applied. The choice of Prussia was obvious. Gustav would move the scene of operations from the Düna to the Vistula River, the life artery of Poland. Krakow, Warsaw and Thorn were all situated along this great river that connected them to the Baltic and the markets for their grain. If Gustav could cut this commercial avenue strangling the hinterland, the Polish parliament would force Sigismund to negotiate. Besides, Polish Prussia was prosperous. It had not suffered the decades of devastating warfare that Livonia had. There was an abundance of grain and cattle to feed his army. And Gustav would be doing his part to help the Protestant cause in Germany, keeping Sigismund occupied and, perhaps, forcing the emperor to divert resources.

As soon as the winter of 1626 broke, the Swedish king appeared off the East Prussian port of Pillau with 150 ships and 25,000 men. The town was located in territory belonging to Gustav's brother-in-law George William of Brandenburg, from whom he expected assistance. George William, having earlier solicited the Swedish monarch's help, now found himself caught between the hammer and anvil of the two cousins. His East Prussian duchy was completely surrounded by Polish territory, yet he had a Swedish army on his doorstep. He withheld active support, but did not hinder Gustav's landing and advance into Polish Prussia, thus gaining the animosity of both monarchs.

Gustav marched around and then along the southern shore of the Frisches Haff heading for the Vistula River. Just inside Polish territory he came to Braunsberg, which pledged allegiance to the Swedish king. Further on, Elbing did the same. By the first of July he had taken possession of all Royal Polish Prussia except Danzig, Mewe and Dirschau. Elbing, Marienburg, and the Danziger Haupt would form his power base in Prussia, remaining in his camp for the rest of the war. Gustav sent for Alex Oxenstierna to cross the Baltic and organize a government for the new Swedish territory. He became chancellor-in-the-field and governor of Swedish Prussia with headquarters at Elbing.

The ease of conquest was because Prussia had, not so long ago, been under control of the Teutonic Knights and had become Protestant. It was with relief that the nobles and burghers traded a Catholic ruler for a Protestant protector.

By July 12 Gustav had crossed the Vistula and stormed Mewe. Dirschau was next to surrender. The Swedish king then turned his attention to Danzig, offering to leave the port a free city requiring only her pledge of neutrality and the expulsion of Sigismund's embryonic war fleet. Danzig was a strong and prosperous city, one of the old Hanseatic League trading centers. Still, the city burghers had no desire go to war with the king who had reduced Riga. A neutrality might have been worked out but for Gustav's impatience. As negotiations dragged on, the Swedish monarch became less and less accommodating, making increasingly undiplomatic demands. Danzig finally broke off talks, turning from a potential neutral to an enemy. As Gustav began preparations for a siege he received word that Sigismund was finally bringing up a major army to contest the Swedish invasion.

The Polish king had settled matters with the Ottoman Turks and could now bring his army north. Missing would be 3,000 Hussars under Field Hetman Stanislaw Koniecpolski that were drawn off to the Ukraine to handle a Tartar threat. Sigismund advanced through Poland with the major part of his army including infantry, guns and some 30,000 Hussars, Cossacks and *Pancerna*. As he reached the Vistula between Mewe and Dirschau, he sent a detachment to take Mewe garrisoned by a small Swedish force. Gustav turned from Danzig and hastened up the Vistula to rescue his troops at Mewe. He found the Polish army blocking his way. Sigismund had arranged his veteran troops on high ground anchoring one flank on the river and the other on a wooded area. On September 22 Gustav sent one of his generals, Heinrich von Thurn, to attack the wooded area while he deployed the rest of his troops opposite Sigismund's position.

Thurn's troops took the woods for a time, but were eventually driven out. Meanwhile, Sigismund sent his Hussars against the Swedish left. They quickly swept through Gustav's cavalry, but were battered and driven back by his dug-in infantry. Both sides maneuvered for seven days, Gustav trying to get a relief force to Mewe and Sigismund blocking his movements. On the 29th the Poles made two general attacks using combined forces. All three mounted sections, Hussars, *Pancerna* and Cossacks, fought furiously. Again the Swedish cavalry was scattered, but the infantry held with the musketeers and regimental guns inflicting terrible losses. The Hussars were completely demoralized and it was only with difficulty that Sigismund was able to get them to charge the Swedish infantry on October 1.

Again the battle was joined on an open plain with the Swedes advancing and being driven back. The Hussars charged carrying the first line of Swedish foot, but then were pummeled by a salvo from the second line and withdrew in disorder. Finally, a Swedish infantry unit gained a section of the high ground dominated, until then, by Polish forces. They immediately dug in and were able to hold their position until nightfall. By morning artillery had been moved to a position able to hit the Polish encampment. Sigismund lifted the siege of Mewe and withdrew. Prince Sladislov covered the retreat.

This battle must have been a shock to the Poles. For the first time since the days of Karl IX a major Polish army had been beaten by the Swedes. Sigismund had brought a large army, chosen the site of battle, and initiated most of the encounters. Yet, he lost. The cousins had much to consider as they settled into winter quarters. Sigismund returned to Warsaw leaving Field Hetman Koniecpoliski, who had joined him from the Ukraine campaign, in charge. Gustav returned to Stockholm in time for the birth of his daughter, Christina, who would be his only living heir. He left the army entrenched around Danzig and his navy maintaining a tight blockade. During the winter Koniecpoliski received a contingent of Imperial troops

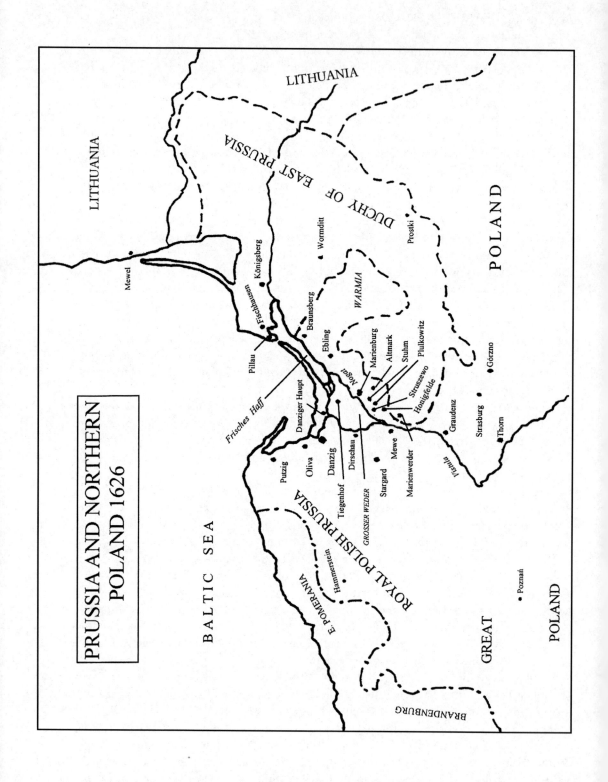

PRUSSIA AND NORTHERN POLAND 1626

BALTIC SEA

LITHUANIA

LITHUANIA

DUCHY OF EAST PRUSSIA

POLAND

GREAT

POLAND

ROYAL POLISH PRUSSIA

E. POMERANIA

WARMIA

GROSSER WEDER

Frisches Haff

Mewel

Königsberg

Fischhausen

Braunsberg

Wormditt

Prostki

Pillau

Ebling

Nogat

Marienburg

Altmark

Stuhm

Plulkowitz

Struszewo

Honigfelde

Górzno

Danziger Haupt

Putzig

Oliva

Danzig

Dirschau

Tiegenhof

Stargard

Mewe

Marienwerder

Graudenz

Strasburg

Thorn

Vistula

Hammerstein

Poznań

BRANDENBURG

detached from Wallenstein's armies pushing north toward the Baltic coast and into Danish Jutland. Like it or not Gustav was being drawn more and more directly into the German religious war.

Even before the spring thaw the Polish general began the 1627 campaign by attacking Putzig, a small town, part of the cordon around Danzig. Among the garrison captured were Commandant Nicholas Horn and 400 Swedish regulars. Koniecpoliski also intercepted 8,000 German mercenaries on their way to take service with the Swedish king. They were turned back promising not to join Gustav's army for at least two years.

The Swedish king, meanwhile, was held up from his return by contrary winds. He arrived at Pillau again with 6,000 new recruits only to find that George William had fitted out 4,000 Prussian bluecoats and had them entrenched at Pillau in support of Sigismund. Completely exasperated with his brother-in-law, Gustav immediately attacked the works, captured the Prussians and made them part of his army. Arriving at Dirschau he found he now had 35,000 men under him including Swedes, mercenary Scots and Germans, and local recruits.

His first order of business was the siege of Danzig. While conducting inspections the king was hit in the hip by a musket ball. During his recuperation, Sigismund pushed into Livonia with a Polish army pressing de la Gardie enough so that Gustav was obliged to send Gustav Horn with reinforcements. Koniecpoliski maneuvered to within six miles of the Danzig siege works. As soon as Gustav had recovered sufficiently to sit a horse, he led his army into the field against the Polish hetman.

Again the Poles had the advantage of choosing the battle site near Dirschau. On August 17, 1627, the Swedes deployed on their front and as usual dug in. Koniecpoliski was a more canny general than his monarch and made no attempt to charge the Swedish earthworks. Instead he sent his cavalry forward to try to draw the Swedes into the open, but Gustav did not bite and after two hours the hetman recalled his horse.

This was the opportunity Gustav had been waiting for. As the retiring cavalry passed over a narrow causeway through marshy ground on the way back to their camp, the Swedish king launched his cavalry. The Polish Hussars turned to defend themselves, but were limited in their ability to maneuver because of the bog. The rear guard was cut down and the rest tried to flee as best they could through the marsh. Nearly 100 cavalrymen were killed or drowned in the swamp. Casualties would have been much higher except for the intervention of the Polish foot and horse which rushed to the site to cover the retreat. This was indeed a humiliating defeat for the Polish cavalry, to be driven from the field by Swedish horse.

On the second day of the battle Gustav, having numeric superiority, advanced on the Polish camp with his foot. The Polish cavalry was put to rout and the Swedish infantry was closing on the encampment when Gustav was hit in the shoulder close to the neck by a musket ball. The advance stopped while the army rallied around their general then pulled back carrying their king from the field. The deep wound put him in bed for three months, effectively ending the Swedish summer offensive.

At the same time Koniecpolski was contemplating a change in tactics. Dirschau was further proof to him that the Swedes were not going to be driven out by a major pitched battle. Indeed, the Poles had been bested in the open field battles with Gustav so far. It was obvious that Swedish infantry could more than hold its own against the vaunted Polish cavalry, which had even been beaten by the rapidly improving Swedish horse. Still the Polish hetman had the advantage in mobility. Polish cavalry overall was still superior to Swedish. Koniecpolski had at his disposal the highly mobile Cossack light cavalry, the dependable Panzers (*Pancerna*) and the excellent Hussar heavy cavalry. In numbers, his horse was far superior to Gustav's.

Sweden had the bigger army in Prussia, but most of it was tied down in garrison duty around the country and particularly in the siege of Danzig. The Polish general would avoid any open field battles and let his horse range across the countryside destroying crops, driving off stock and attacking small isolated towns and forts where he could quickly concentrate his cavalry in overwhelming numbers. He would starve and harass Gustav into leaving the country.

With the coming of the winter of 1626–27, the Swedish king returned to Stockholm to raise more troops. Danzig purchased 5,000 German mercenary infantry which they used to recover several Vistula river crossings between Marienburg and Dirschau, effectively cutting off Putzig by land.

Koniecpolski pulled his main army back to Graudenz where he built a strong encampment. When the Vistula and Nogat rivers had frozen over, he sent his Cossacks raiding through the countryside, burning grain stocks and driving off livestock. These tough, hardy and ruthless men were ideally suited for this kind of work. By the end of that winter hardly a village in the Grosser Werder had not been sacked by these pillaging marauders.

The Polish hetman besieged Putzig. Cut off by land and not able to get regular supplies by sea because of stormy weather, it fell in April opening a gap in the Danzig siege line. Also in that month the Poles caught 2,500 German mercenaries from Pomerania on their way to Hammerstein to join the Swedish army. Some were induced to join the Poles, the rest were turned back, then massacred by peasants in retaliation for savagery they had inflicted on the population earlier on their march in.

Both sides suffered much from disease and desertions. The Swedes lost 13 percent of their infantry and 20 percent of their cavalry. The Polish army was reduced similarly and had the additional problem of not being able to pay its mercenaries.

Gustav returned in May 1627 with 7,000 infantry and in June 1,700 cavalry arrived from Sweden. These troops were used in reinforcing the various garrisons and trying to waylay the Polish raiding parties.

Koniecpolski's Flavian tactics were working. In July he was able to take Mewe, forcing Gustav to march south to recover this important stronghold and river crossing. In October he captured Wormditt, but otherwise he had little to show for the summer campaign season. Koniecpolski continued to avoid open battle; instead he raided and burned the Swedish supply bases.

On November 28 a fleet of ten Polish warships slipped out of Danzig Harbor and surprised the Swedish blockade vessels. The Swedish flagship was captured and another warship sunk. The Polish navy had its first victory, albeit a minor one and at the cost of almost 500 sailors.

The campaign season of 1628 was little different except it was a summer of heavy rains making army movement difficult and unpleasant. Gustav added more cavalry to try to suppress the Polish raids. He now had 8,870 foot and 6,100 horse, but the situation remained a stalemate. In Livonia Gustav Horn was holding his own against Sigismund. There, the war had been reduced to a conflict of attrition with no breakthroughs on either side.

The real action that summer was at the seaport of Stralsund, an old Hanseatic League city and traditional ally of the Swedish Vasas. The Hapsburg-Catholic League armies had, by the spring of 1628, crushed Christian IV's Danish forces and driven to the Baltic coast taking the port of Wismar. The Imperial general Wallenstein was given the title of High Admiral of the Baltic by the emperor. He called for Spanish ships from Dunkirk to come north to join the corps of his Baltic navy. Though he was able to take several more Baltic ports he recognized Stralsund was the key to Baltic domination. It was an excellent harbor and well positioned to threaten both Sweden and the Danish islands.

In February 1628 Wallenstein sent his chief lieutenant, Hans George von Arnim, to attack the city. He was able to take the island of Dänholm, which commanded the harbor. In April Wallenstein laid siege to the city. Gustav offered support to the city burghers, but the city council hoped to get help from other Hansa cities with whom they had treaties. The power of the old Hanseatic League, however, had long since been broken. Reval and Riga were now in Swedish hands. Lübeck, Settin and Rostack were still independent but feared less they should provoke Wallenstein. Wismar was already controlled by Imperial forces and Danzig was fighting for her life against Sweden.

Gustav had left behind a strong force in Sweden to man homeland defenses and come to the aid of Denmark or Stralsund if either seemed at the point of collapse. By May the port city knew she would receive no assistance from the other Hansa cities and was nearing defeat. The Swedish king sent word to Sweden to rush troops to the imperiled city, but it was Christian who arrived first.

Between May 25th and 28th detachments of Danish troops arrived, bolstering the spirits of the defenders. In early July a larger contingent of Christian's soldiers landed. The crisis was past by the time the advance guard of Swedish troops arrived in late June. The main body landed in July, securing the city. Wallenstein raised his siege and retreated having lost some 12,000 men in his futile attempt to take the city.

By participating in rescuing the city, Gustav had fought not just imperial troops as he had already done in East Prussia, but had faced an Imperial general. Though still technically neutral in the German religions wars, the Swedish king had taken another step toward involvement.

The relief of Stralsund left the two Scandinavian monarchs with a problem. Danish and Swedish soldiers, mutual enemies for decades, were occupying the same city. The situation was untenable and Gustav offered to withdraw if the city would prefer to retain the Danish troops as defenders. The city council, however, voted to accept Swedish protection and Christian began a measured evacuation.

If Gustav was to supply the defense for the city, he wanted some guarantee of loyalty and the burghers militia was obliged to swear allegiance to the Swedish king. Gradually Gustav reinforced his garrison until the Swedish commander became the effective city commandant. Within a year the city had a Swedish governor and was an integral part of Sweden's Baltic empire.

Meanwhile, the war in East Prussia chugged along. In spite of the numbing cold rains and floods, Gustav tried a drive south along the Vistula. He reached all the way to Graudenz and Koniecpolski's fortified encampment. He demonstrated outside the earthworks for a few days, but the hetman would not be drawn out and the works were too strong for the Swedish army to storm so Gustav retired, accomplishing little.

In spite of the free roaming Polish cavalry, the Swedes were extending their territory south and east. The summer of 1627 they had taken Wormditt and in October 1628 Gustav captured Strasburg though he lost nearly 5,000 men in the campaign. Marienburg had become the main Swedish fort facing Polish Grandenz.

Still, Koniecpolski's burn and plunder guerilla tactics were having an effect. The Grosser Werder, once the breadbasket of north central Europe, had become a net importer of grain. The Swedes had shut down the Polish lifeline to the Baltic, stifling trade from Poland. The once rich and prosperous Polish Prussia was becoming a wasteland.

By the beginning of 1629 Swedish forces had shifted even further toward cavalry with 15,400 infantry, mostly on garrison duty or involved in the Danzig siege, and 7,650 horse.

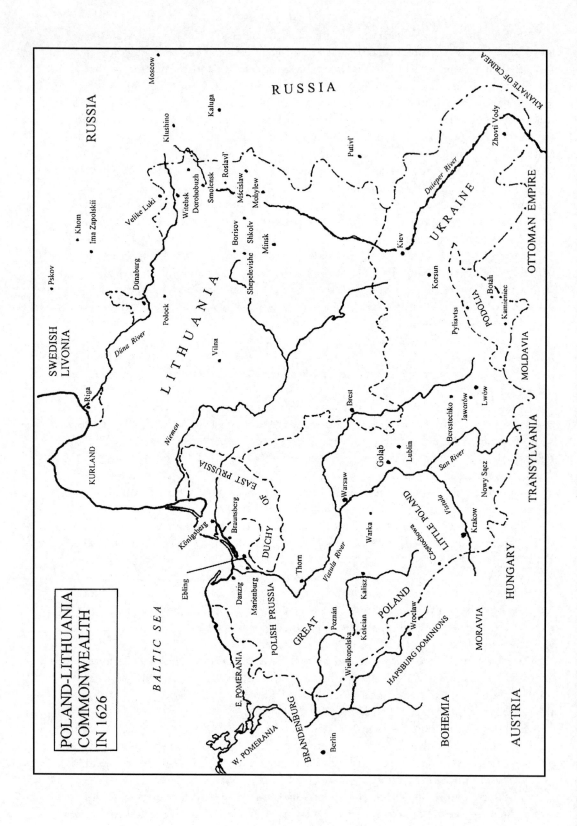

POLAND-LITHUANIA
COMMONWEALTH
IN 1626

BALTIC SEA

RUSSIA

RUSSIA

SWEDISH
LIVONIA

KURLAND

LITHUANIA

Moscow

Kaluga

Klushino

Khom

Ima Zapolskii

Velike Luki

Pskov

Dünaburg

Düna River

Riga

Polock

Vilna

Witebsk
Dorohobuzh
Smolensk
Roslavl'
Mścislaw
Mohylew

Borisov
Shkolv
Shepelevishc
Minsk

Putivl'

Dnieper River

Kiev

UKRAINE

Korsun

Pyliavtsi

PODOLIA

Botah
Kamieniec

MOLDAVIA

OTTOMAN EMPIRE

KHANATE OF CRIMEA

Zhovti Vody

TRANSYLVANIA

HUNGARY

Niemen

EAST PRUSSIA

Königsberg

Ebling

Braunsberg

Danzig
Marienburg

POLISH PRUSSIA

W. POMERANIA

E. POMERANIA

BRANDENBURG

Berlin

GREAT

Poznań

Wielkopolska

Kościan

Kalisz

DUCHY

OF

Thorn

Vistula River

Warsaw

Brest

Golab
Lublin

Berestechko
Jaworów
Lwów

San River

Nowy Sącz

Warka

LITTLE POLAND

Częstochowa

Krakow

Wrocław

POLAND

HAPSBURG DOMINIONS

MORAVIA

BOHEMIA

AUSTRIA

Early in the year General Stanislaw Potocki undertook the blockade of the isolated garrison at Strasburg. In February Wrangel organized a relief effort and drove toward the imperiled town. Over half his army was cavalry, some 3,400 men. He met Potocki at Górzno.

Potocki drew up his forces and waited for the attack. Wrangel deployed his infantry in front of the Polish line, then sent his cavalry on a flanking attack, a maneuver typical of Polish forces. The Swedish cavalry scattered Potocki's mounted troops, then turned to roll up the line. The Poles had been beaten at their own game. Polish defenses collapsed. Potocki lost nearly half his army, almost 2,000 casualties. Strasburg was relieved and Wrangel turned toward Thorn on the Vistula. He threatened the city, but without any heavy guns or siege equipment he could do little and retired northward, avoiding Graudenz.

When the spring campaign season of 1629 began Gustav had 23,000 troops to Koniecpolski's 19,000, but, as before, the Swedes were stretched across a wide territory in many, sometimes small, garrisons. In June Gustav received word that Wallenstein was sending 5,000 Imperial troops under Hans Georg von Arnim to reinforce the Poles. The Swedish king set out immediately with 5,450 horse and 1,900 foot to intercept the German forces before they could reach Graudenz, but he was too late. Arnim arrived on June 25.

Gustav, now at Marienburg, was heavily outnumbered and decided to withdraw. He sent his infantry north towards Stuhm and used his cavalry to cover the retreat. Arnim wanted to assemble the entire Polish and Imperial army for an attack on the retreating Swedes. Koniecpolski was afraid they would slip away and ordered an immediate advance. On June 17, a unit of dragoons caught up with the Swedish rear guard, some 2,000 horse and a few musketeers under Johan Wilhelm at a river crossing on the Leibe near Honigfelde.

Wilhelm formed up on the crest of a hill above the river. Koniecpolski placed Arnim's cavalry in the center of his line and put the Cossacks to the left. Wilhelm tried to flank the Cossacks, but was instead flanked himself by Koniecpolski leading his Hussars through a valley hidden from Wilhelm's view. The Swedish horse was scattered, but regrouped at Struszewo, where they were reinforced. Here they met the Cossacks head on and drove them back until the Hussars caught up with the battle. Then, outnumbered, the Swedes retreated to Pulkowitz where Gustav met them with the main body of his cavalry.

A full scale cavalry battle took place with both Polish and Imperial horse engaged. Twice Gustav was almost killed or captured. At nightfall the Swedes were able to slip away to join their infantry at Stuhm. The Swedish king had successfully covered his retreat, but at a cost of nearly a thousand casualties. The Swedish cavalry had performed admirably, standing up to the best horse of both Poland and the emperor. In the end they had left the field to the enemy and the effect was to restore, to some extent, Polish morale.

Gustav withdrew into his extensive defensive works at Marienburg. Koniecpolski and Arnim concentrated their forces outside these works and spent the summer besieging and attacking the Swedes in their defensive position. As the Polish offense continued, peace negotiations were begun to end the stalemate.

The French cardinal Richelieu sent his chief envoy, Hercule de Charnacé, to try to end the war so the Swedes might be free to enter the German war. Richelieu had already made an alliance with the Dutch and was at war with the Hapsburgs in Italy. Imperial successes in northern Germany and Denmark threatened Dutch trade in the Baltic, a main source of their revenue. France could not afford to have her old enemy, the Hapsburgs, take over the Baltic and outflank them.

Charnacé was joined by George William as mediators and through the summer of 1629 they worked at hammering out a treaty Sigismund could live with. The Polish king was also under considerable pressure to end the long conflict with Sweden. The Sejm was tired of the huge tax burden required to maintain armies in both Livonia and Prussia. They had little to show for all their sacrifices. Livonia and especially Riga had been lost, their part of the Prussia was now in Swedish hands and the Vistula trade to the Baltic blocked. The Polish Baltic fleet Sigismund had been building was bottled up in Danzig Harbor. The Polish nobles had had enough of their king's Vasa feud.

Gustav was little better off. Simultaneous wars in Livonia and Prussia had stretched his country to the breaking point in both manpower and money. Financing the war through crown income only was not sufficient. New taxes were created and passed by the Riksdag: the Stock and Land Tax of 1620, the Little Toll of 1622 on all goods brought to market (a sales tax) and the Mill Toll of 1625 on all grain brought to mills for grinding. By the late 1620s the financial burden on Sweden was being alleviated somewhat by tolls on trade at Prussian ports and the taxing of the conquered territories.

The Truce of Altmark, September 1629, gave Gustav what he had been striving for, a guaranteed six year cessation in the conflict with Poland. In addition, Gustav kept Livonia north of the Düna and Elbing in East Prussia including the surrounding area and the duties collected from the ports. Marienburg, Danziger Haupt and the Grosser Werder were turned over to George William to administer for the duration of the truce. Then they would go to Sweden if no permanent peace was agreed to. As insurance, Sweden was allowed to occupy and collect tolls on George William's cities of Pillau, Fischhausen, Lochstädt and Memel.

On February 18, 1630, the Treaty of Tiegenhaft was concluded with Danzig by which Sweden received the lion's share of the 5.5 percent toll on the rich Danzig trade. All these revenue sources helped relieve the financial strain on the homeland and made possible Gustav's German expedition. Sweden now controlled most of the major ports in the eastern Baltic. The eastern part of the sea had indeed become a Swedish lake. Sigismund removed his warships from Danzig to Wismar where they joined Wallenstein's Imperial fleet.

The long Swedish-Polish war had ended, the struggle between the Vasa princes finally concluded. It had been a conflict stretching from Moscow to the Vistula. In the end it turned Sweden into a major European power. Sweden's theater of war had been Eastern Europe so far. But soon Central and Western Europe would learn first hand of this new rising military force.

15. Gustav Enters Germany and the Thirty Years' War

On May 19, 1630, Gustav stood before an Assembly of the Råd and the three upper Estates. He addressed those present, the Peasant Estate (not represented) and all Swedish citizens. The speech is considered a masterpiece. He celebrated the union of the king and his subjects. It was a farewell address in which he prophesied his own end:

> As it is bound to occur, according to His word, that the jar carries water on the farm until at last it is broken: so be it with me ultimately. How often I have been in the midst of blood and danger in the cause of our Swedish Kingdom and yet through God's mercy, even though injured, have been allowed to return. Now I must shed blood one last time. So before I leave you I commend you, my Swedish subjects, to the protection of Almighty God and desire that we will meet again in His heavenly Kingdom.[1]

He urged the nobility to remember their ancestors, the ancient Goths and to follow their example in courage and steadfastness. To the Burghers he wished "that your little cabins may become great houses of stone, your little boats great ships and merchantmen, and that the oil in your cruse fail not."[2]

For the peasants, "My wish for them is that their meadows may be green with grass, their fields bear an hundred fold, so that their barns may be full; and that they may so increase and multiply in all plenteousness that they may gladly and without sighing perform the duties and obligations that lie upon them."[3]

The clergy were admonished to remember that they had the power to "turn and twist the hearts of men,"[4] and were warned to be good examples following church precepts and guard against the sin of pride. Thus the great Vasa king bid farewell to his countrymen and for the last time departed Sweden for a campaign on foreign soil.

On June 17 the great fleet left Älvsnabben and on July 26, 1630, it arrived off the German coast. Gustav waded ashore and fell to his knees imploring God for mercy in the battles to come. The Lion of the North had come to Germany for his final and greatest campaign. The events that had precipitated this endeavor were both religious and political with roots imbedded in the Catholic Counter-Reformation.

The Reformation is generally considered to have begun with Martin Luther's posting of the 95 theses on the Wittenberg Castle in 1517. Lutheranism spread in Germany and to Sweden where it became the state religion. This form of Protestantism also became established in Denmark, Iceland, Norway, Finland and in the northern Baltic states. Other forms, notably Calvinism, spread in Switzerland, France, the Netherlands and even to the Americas. Under Henry VIII and his daughter Elizabeth, England had severed its church from Rome. This reform from outside the Church of Rome also migrated eastward into Poland, Lithuania, Hungary, and Austria. But reform from inside the Catholic Church was also taking place.

The term Counter-Revolution is a bit of a misnomer. Although the Protestant movement did provide impetus, parties inside the Roman Church had been agitating for changes for some time. As early as the late fourteenth century, reformers such as John Hess, John Wycliffe and St. Catherine of Siena were pushing for changes. St. Bridget of Sweden had fought corruption in the church in both Sweden and in Rome in the mid–1300s. Gradually, a small but growing reform party began to take shape within the church. The Oratory of Divine Love, a society of both priests and laymen, became the focus of this movement.

Founded in Genoa as a group dedicated to charitable works, it expanded into the spiritual arena and then into the church hierarchy in Rome. Prestige was lent to the movement from abroad by such men as Thomas More, Desiderius Erasmus of Rotterdam, John Fisher and Cardinal Jiménez. From this group came St. Cajetan and Cardinal Carafa, who would later be Pope Paul IV. The reform party viewed the church as having become badly corrupted; they called for revamping of certain practices of the church, of the ecclesiastic administration, and reform of the clergy.

During the Middle Ages much of the Roman Catholic Church became thoroughly integrated into the feudal political system. Many monasteries were operated like fiefs. Some bishops took on the appendages of barons, even having their own standing military force; witness the Bishop's Cavalry in Sweden. The papal state fought to extend its territory like any other feudal principality.

With the coming of the Renaissance many of the bishops, cardinals and even some popes assumed the ostentatious trappings of the central and southern European courts of the period. Great harm to church prestige was done by the well publicized scandals of some of the fifteenth century's immoral papal courts.

The French Captivity (1309–1377), and the Great Schism (1378–1417) further eroded the authority of the pope. His position was weakened to the point where he could not be of help to moderate reformers like Girolamo Savonarola and Nicholas of Cusa.

The worldliness of the church peaked under Alexander IV (1492–1503) and Leo X (1513–1522). Leo X raised funds to rebuild St. Peter's Basilica using the high-pressure sale of indulgences in the German states. This was one of the excesses which prompted Martin Luther to post his ninety-five theses.

At the lowest levels of the church the main problem was education. While most priests and monks were sincere and hard working, and seminary educated clergy were well prepared to serve, many parish priests were poorly trained and self-indulgent. Consequently, immorality, drunkenness, slovenliness and poor officiating of the sacraments was rampant. The high ideals of the early church had eroded to a point that disgusted the reformers.

Following Leo X, the reform party was able to bring about a conference to review these issues, the Fifth Lateran Council, and get a like minded pope elected, Adrian VI. However, the council accomplished little and Adrian died before he could accomplish anything.

Under his successor, Clement VII (1523–34), the reform party began to make real progress. Threatened by an expanding Lutheranism, they founded the Theatines (1524) and the Capuchins (1525), religious orders dedicated to evangelizing common people. They were assisted by the influence of the Holy Roman emperor, Charles V, who was battling Lutheranism in his domain. Also, the sack of Rome in 1527 by a renegade army of German, Italian and Spanish mercenaries doused the last embers of territorial expansionist ambitions of the papal court. The stage was set for the Catholic Reformation.

In 1534 Paul III, from the reform party, became pope. That same year St. Ignatius of Loyola founded the Society of Jesus. Loyola was a Spanish nobleman and soldier who narrowly escaped death from a severe battle wound. Upon recovery, he vowed that he would serve only Almighty God and the pope of Rome, God's representative on earth. The Jesuits constructed their order like a military organization with the head of the order carrying the title of general. Members were carefully screened, then subjected to intense training. Their vows of chastity, obedience and poverty were rigidly enforced. There was autocratic rule and iron discipline in this new order where the excesses and rich living of the Renaissance church had no place. Jesuits were pious, dedicated, tough, aggressive and fearless. They became the most effective instrument in stopping, then rolling back, the Protestant movement.

The society's evangelism also spread to Asia and the Americas. An example of their effectiveness is found in South America where they brought the church to native Americans, establishing self-sufficient mission-haciendas on the Colombian Llanos, an environment so hostile even the conquistadors only traveled through it. To these tropical plains, sparsely populated to this day, stretching across eastern Colombia and western Venezuela, they brought civilization. In the Amazon Basin they fought the Spanish and Portuguese slave traders and in Uruguay they built an ecclesiastic empire complete with a native militia. Yet when Rome ordered their removal in 1767, the obedient fathers packed up and left the continent, abandoning all they had built.

In Europe, the Jesuits and Capuchins were instrumental in the Catholic offensive against Protestantism winning back Austria, Poland, southern Netherlands, France and parts of Germany, Hungary, and Bohemia. In Spain the religious reforms of the Carmelites of St. Theresa of Avila and St. John of the Cross along with the effectiveness of the Spanish Inquisition prevented Protestantism from even gaining a foothold. Here as in Ireland and Italy the church was never seriously threatened.

In 1545 Pope Paul II convened the First Council of Trent to deal with reforms. The council met in three sessions in 1545–47, 1551–52 and 1562–63. It rejected any compromise with Protestantism, reaffirming the basic tenets of Catholicism. The seven sacraments were upheld including transubstantiation of the consecrated bread and wine. Salvation by faith and, in contrast to Lutheranism, by works was preserved. Other aspects, rejected by the liberal reformers, were reaffirmed: indulgences, though excesses were curbed, pilgrimages, emphasis of saints and relics, and worship of the Virgin. The basic structure of the church was retained, but more emphasis was placed on the education of parish priests through diocese seminary schools. Manuals and handbooks were produced describing the conduct and expectations of a good priest and confessor.

Paul III was followed by Pope Paul IV (1555–59) who began a determined campaign to eliminate Protestantism. His primary tools in this effort were the Inquisition and censorship of prohibited books. Perhaps his biggest contribution, however, was the reform of the papal court. Paul IV stripped the Vatican of its Renaissance worldliness giving it the dignified, almost monastic atmosphere it retains to this day.

Julius III and Pius IV continued the Council of Trent meetings and pressed the work of reform and combating Protestantism. With the end of the councils in 1563 emphasis shifted to implementing the councils recommendations. The papacy of Pius V (1566–72) was right for the time. He came from humble beginnings; poor, possibly an orphan, he joined the Dominican order as a young man. The Dominican Brothers taught him humility and to engage in a life of service to the destitute and diseased. They instilled in him a regard for the less fortunate. As pontiff he carried on these practices, donating liberally to charities and hospitals. Even as pope he lived his monastic vows of poverty and kept a simple life style. He did his best to extend this philosophy throughout the church. He combated Protestantism by encouraging the Inquisition and was an advocate of Jesuit evangelism in Europe and missionary work in the Americas.

Pius V was followed by Gregory XIII and then Sixtus V (1585–90) who changed the direction of the Catholic Reformation from an approach of compelling attendance through threats and fear to attracting adherence. He was aided in this by the new early Baroque era that emphasized order and balance.

It was a period of revolution in the arts and sciences. Copernicus and others had already challenged the very tenets of science as prescribed by Ptolemy and Aristotle, concepts that had ruled for over a thousand years. Now Descartes, Galileo and Kepler were breaking new ground, challenging the Aristotelian methods of science, expanding human knowledge in diverse fields of science and geography. The new movement extended to architecture where the dark and dreary interiors of the Middle Age churches and castles were being replaced by decorated, lighted interiors, pleasing to the senses and spiritually uplifting. Sixtus fostered a great rebuilding of churches and cathedrals in Rome and throughout the church. Congregations were enticed to remain faithful rather than coerced. In less than a hundred years the Church of Rome had carried out these reforms and turned from defense to offense in the quest for souls.

Gustav Vasa was about to be pulled into this religious conflict very directly, a world quite foreign to him. His view of this world would change with experience. At the Öregro Riksdag of 1617 he expressed his outlook, the sentiments of a young man and an inexperienced king:

> This religion, if I may call it that, is not only in itself idolatry, the invention and fancy of men — clearly contrary to the word of God in the Holy Scriptures wherein standeth written our way to salvation, but it embraces one principle which is especially damning: with heretics, as they call us, shall no man keep faith. And King Sigismund has made it clear enough in all his actions that he has well learned to apply this popish maxim, as well against us as against others. What can we expect of King Sigismund, who is not only wicked himself, but allows himself to be ruled by those Devil's minions, the Jesuits, who have been the instigators of the fearful tyrannies practiced in Spain, France and elsewhere? These Jesuits and their Inquisition have spared neither high nor low, man or woman.[5]

These are fiery words from a youth just returned from a war involving his Catholic cousin and with the Spanish Armada's attack on England in 1588 still fresh in everyone's minds. He had, no doubt, heard stories of Jesuit triumphs in Poland, Hungary and Austria. But that same year his religious world of "us against them" got more complicated.

The Treaty of Stolbova in that year gave Sweden the provinces of Kexholms and Ingria. A large part of the populations were Finns of the Greek Orthodox faith. Gustav worked hard at incorporating these people into his realm. Great pains were taken to keep good relations with the Greek church. He tried to change the perception, common among Swedes of the time, that Russians were not Christians, a notion useful up to then in inciting Swedes and Finns to war against this traditional foe. A conference was even held at the Uppsala University on the subject in 1620. The king pointed out that Protestants and Orthodox Christians had a common enemy in the Church of Rome. In the main, Gustav won this battle for the hearts of the people in the newly acquired districts. There was no religious war or open hatred toward the newly acquired territories and their people.

The following year at the fall of Riga, the king had the members of the Jesuit College located there brought before him. Among the men was the Norwegian Laurentius Nicolai, the infamous *Klasterlasse* of King Johan III's time. Upon recognizing him Gustav burst out, "You old limb of Satan!"[6] The king demanded to know what he was going to do in the after-life when he had to pay for following false doctrines in this life. The priest, now an old man, drew himself up proudly and retorted that it was not he who would pay, but those who followed the Lutheran practices. There was much debate as to the disposition of the heretics, but in the end Father Laurentius and the Jesuits were all escorted safely to Polish territory.

The Swedish monarch moved from the Livonian War to the Prussian campaign, then to the invasion of Germany. The north German states were Protestant, but as he progressed further south, he encountered cities and territories primarily Catholic. By this time one of his chief allies was France, a Catholic nation led, for all practical purposes, by Cardinal Richelieu, a Catholic clergyman. In fact a section of the alliance agreement required Gustav to not interfere with German Catholics' practice of their faith. The Swedish king made good on this promise. Where militarily possible, he avoided molesting Catholic churches and monasteries. When monks and priests were displaced by war, he sheltered and protected them. Because of Gustav's policy and the discipline maintained in his army, the Jesuits of Mainz later said, "We suffered no interference in the exercises of our religion."[7] In Munich the king even engaged the Jesuits in debate and conversation. The Capuchin Fathers were particularly taken with the heretical conqueror, urging him to return to the fold. Gustav seems to have taken this as a compliment, a far cry from his outburst at Riga eleven years earlier.

At Augsburg he personally assured the town council that all Catholics would be protected saying, "Since the judgment belongs to God alone, each man must answer to Him for his faith."[8]

After a year in Germany, Gustav's purpose was not to convert the country by the sword, but to restore the religious freedom that had existed earlier, allowing each state to practice the form of Christianity it believed. Ultimately, he had respect for those "who sought to serve the Lord according to their understanding and after the fashion of their fathers."[9]

Gustav dropped to his knees on the shores of the Baltic at Peenemünde and prayed for his army and the cause upon which they were embarking. Yet the Protestant cause was not the only or even the primary reason for his intervention in this German civil war. He empathized with the Lutheran princes who had been overrun by the emperor's and League of Catholic States' forces, but he neither counted on nor did he trust these Protestant rulers. He knew that politics were as important as religion in this war. Protestant princes would fight for power and territory just as readily as for religion. Likewise the Catholic League princes would join the emperor in his war until they felt their own independence was threatened. Motivations in this war were many and complex, often conflicting.

So it was with the king of Sweden. The final impetus for entering this conflict was the safety of his country. Certainly the argument that won his countrymen's support was the danger Hapsburg occupation of the Baltic seaports represented to the people. Swedes had been watching the progress of the war with great interest as any substantial change in the political situation would affect them directly.

Europe had been expecting the war between Spain and the Netherlands to be renewed upon the expiration of the Truce of 1621. Germany would be involved as Spain needed part of its territory to use as an overland route to convey troops from its provinces in Italy to the Netherlands war. Their sea route had been effectively blocked by Dutch warships. Before this eventuality occurred, a religious war erupted in the Holy Roman Empire.

By the terms of the Peace of Augsburg in 1555, Lutheranism was given official recognition in the empire. Lands taken from the Church of Rome were to remain in the hands of

Protestant and secular factions. Each prince could decide whether his state would be Catholic or Lutheran. This peace worked for a time, but by the early 17th century it was falling apart.

The slide toward a military resolution became more and more evident as states, particularly in Protestant northern Germany, appropriated additional church property. Some rulers had become Calvinists, a form of Protestantism not covered by the peace agreement. At the same time the government of the empire was controlled by the Catholic princes creating opposition in the north. Alliances were formed to protect the rights of their members, the Catholic League headed by Maximilian of Bavaria and the Protestant Union under Friedrich of the Palatine Electorate. Add to this the aggressive surge of the Counter-Reformation and all of the elements for a bloody conflict were in place. Only a spark was needed.

The igniting incendiary was the election of the new emperor, Ferdinand II (1619–37). Charles V had been fought to a standstill by the Protestant princes and had agreed to the Augsburg Peace. His rule was followed by Ferdinand I (1556–64) and Maximilian II (1564–76) who devoted their energies to fighting the Ottoman Turks encroaching through the Balkans. Rudolf II (1576–1612) preferred to play with astrology and search for the philosopher's stone, an item he hoped would turn base metals into gold. In Ferdinand II, however, the empire would have a Hapsburg ruler ready to push the Counter-Reformation in all of Germany. As Duke of Styria he had already stamped out Protestantism in his home state. A foreboding was felt nowhere more strongly than in Bohemia.

Bohemia, today's Czech Republic, was a rich country, providing almost half the revenues of the emperor. A majority of its inhabitants were Lutheran, Calvinist or members of one of the Hessite sects. The Catholic minority was, however, growing in strength thanks to the Counter-Reformation, the Jesuits, and support of the Hapsburgs. Not only did the Bohemian Protestant nobles fear Ferdinand's religious interference, but loss of political independence as well. They had been pressured to accept Ferdinand as their future king as well as emperor. While Ferdinand was in Frankfort for his election and coronation as emperor, the Bohemian nobles struck.

The rebels seized control of the country, formed an alliance with Bethlen Gabor, prince of Transylvania, and Friedrich, elector of Palatine. Once in control, the Bohemian nobles elected Friedrich king, then marched on Vienna. Queen Ann of England, wife of James I, seemed to have made a good choice. Her daughter, Elizabeth, was married to the ruler of the Upper and Lower Palatinate and now he was king of Bohemia instead of Gustav, that "illegitimate" king of Sweden.

But Ferdinand was not about to lose the riches of his most productive state. He immediately turned to his Hapsburg relatives, the king of Spain and Maximilian of Bavaria, who supplied him with troops and money. He was also supported by the Protestant elector of Saxony. With these resources he went after the rebel king.

First he threatened the other princes of the Protestant Union and the organization disintegrated leaving the Palatinate elector and new Bohemian king to fight on his own. Adding Austrian troops to his army, the emperor advanced into Bohemia and brought Friedrich to heel at the Battle of White Mountain near Prague (1620) where he obtained a decisive victory. The Winter King and Elizabeth escaped to the Netherlands and exile.

The formerly elective monarchy of Bohemia was made a permanent hereditary Hapsburg kingdom. The Lower Palatinate was turned over to Spain, giving that country its avenue to bring troops from Italy to the Netherlands war. The Upper Palatinate and the office of elector were given to Maximilian of Bavaria, who set about recovering the country for the Church of Rome. The first phase of the Thirty Years' War had been won by the emperor though he still had the war with Transylvania which would smolder until 1626.

With the emperor having gained a stunning triumph, England and the Netherlands began casting around for a champion to lead the Protestant cause in Germany and they first approached Gustav. But his demands were too high and they finally settled on King Christian IV of Denmark, who was part of the empire as count of Holstein. France was also worried it might be encircled by Spain if that country should be successful in conquering the Netherlands. Christian raised an army of 30,000 troops and advanced into Germany on December 9, 1625, as the commander of Protestant forces. The second phase of the Thirty Years' War had begun.

To oppose this new threat Ferdinand placed the army of the Catholic League under the command of the very capable Bavarian general Jan Tserclaes Tilly, who had already distinguished himself in the Bohemian war. But this army, by itself, was not sufficient and the rest of his forces, so successful in Bohemia, were committed in Transylvania. Ferdinand needed a new imperial army and his answer came from a Bohemian nobleman, Albrecht von Wallenstein. Born a Lutheran, he had converted to Catholicism and married a wealthy widow who conveniently died soon afterward. He had parlayed this small fortune into a very large one. Wallenstein was so wealthy that he could offer Ferdinand a 50,000 man army raised at his expense. The emperor need only pay wages once the troops were in the field. Frederick accepted his offer on April 7, 1625, and now the emperor had two armies in the field in Northern Germany.

Wallenstein defeated Protestant forces on April 25 at Dessau on the Elbe River and again at Kosel on July 9. Meanwhile, Tilly routed Christian at the Battle of Lutter on the Barenberg. During the winter of 1626–27 Christian equipped a new army only to be defeated by Tilly again and driven from Germany. League forces pushed on into Jutland relegating Christian to his island possessions protected by his navy. The champion of the Protestant cause had been crushed.

Wallenstein, meanwhile, had driven to the Baltic coast taking most of the seaport cites. Only Stettin, Stralsund, Rostock and Lübeck retained a precarious independence. His lieutenant, Hans George von Arnim, had occupied the large island of Rügen and then attacked Stralsund in 1628, but was repulsed due to the intervention of Denmark and Sweden. In February Wallenstein was installed as duke of Mecklenburg, the rightful dukes having been driven from the territory. In April Ferdinand gave him the title of general of the Oceanic and Baltic seas. He was already assembling an Imperial navy at Wismar while Sigismund was doing the same at Danzig. Ferdinand invited Spain to send ships to create a Hapsburg Baltic fleet, an intrusion neither Denmark nor Sweden could afford. Besides the threat of Hapsburg-Polish domination of the Baltic, Imperial control of the northern German Baltic ports provided access to Sweden by either the Hapsburgs or Sigismund or worse, a combination. It was this threat that finally compelled Gustav to act, and convinced the nobles and peasants to support his intervention in the German war.

In March 1629 Ferdinand issued the Edict of Restitution demanding all properties taken from the Church of Rome since the Treaty of Passau (1552) be returned. On March 22 the Peace of Lübeck was signed, restoring conquered Danish territory to Christian in exchange for his removal from the war. Frederick's power had reached its zenith. Only Magdeburg, which had resisted Wallenstein's siege, and a few scattered principalities and coastal cities remained unconquered. Not since the days of Charles V had the holy Roman emperor so completely dominated his domain. Still he had some problems and one of those was Wallenstein, who had just helped him achieve this supremacy.

Wallenstein's huge army, now almost 70,000 men, was divided and quartered in various

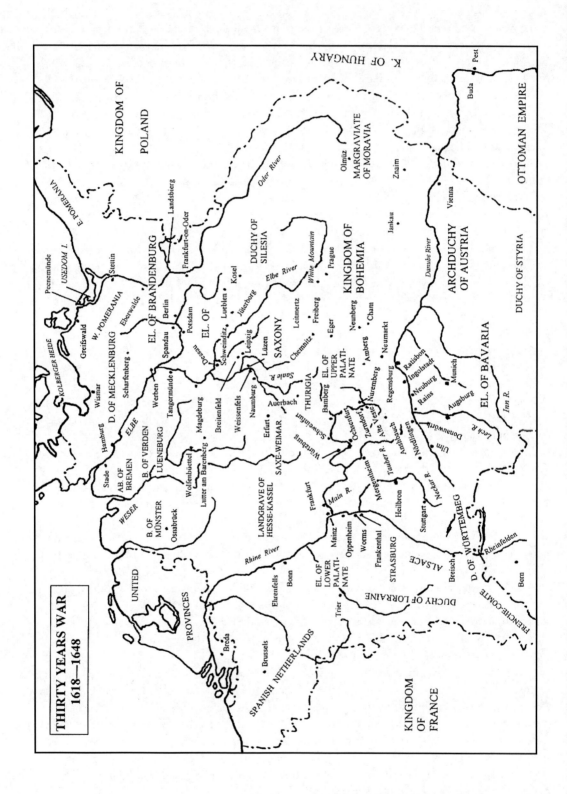

THIRTY YEARS WAR
1618—1648

parts of the empire. The German princes complained loudly about the burden of supporting these mercenaries on their lands. Also they feared Wallenstein's increasing power. Maximilian particularly eyed the ambitious general with suspicion. Finally, the conquered princes and city burghers protested the ill treatment they received at the hands of Wallenstein's soldiers. Unrestrained looting, pillaging and raping had been the order of the day as the army had invaded northern Germany, they claimed.

Bowing to this pressure, Ferdinand twice reduced the size of the Imperial army after 1628. On August 30, 1630, he removed Wallenstein altogether as commander of the Imperial army. The first two phases of the Thirty Years' War were over and the part dominated by Gustav Adolf was about to begin.

On June 17, 1630, Gustav left Älvsnabben with 15,000 soldiers on a hundred transports covered by a fleet of warships. Under Admiral Karl Karlsson Gyllenheilm and his chief assistant, Klas Fleming, seven other contingents sailed from points all around the Baltic loaded with troops. On June 26 Gustav reached landfall at Peenemünde on the island of Usedom in Pomerania and by July 26 he had his advance party ashore. Swedes and mercenaries continued to arrive so that by November he had 42,100 soldiers in his expeditionary force. For the Protestant nobles and commoners the Lion of the North had arrived to push back the tide of Catholicism which had engulfed northern Germany. Wallenstein dismissed this new intruder as the Snow King who would quickly melt away as he moved south. To the northern German princes he was an invader, though a Protestant. The question was would he fold as Christian had? Remembering Friedrich, the Winter King, they could not risk alienating the emperor further. Gustav would be on his own.

The Swedish king led a small force to reconnoiter the Island of Usedom, expelling several Imperial garrisons as he advanced, then he crossed to the island of Wollin where Imperial detachments fled before him. None of the Protestant princes came to his aid. He was quite alone with his Swedish army in a foreign land. The only exception was Stralsund which declared for him with its 5,000 troops. The city's allegiance also gave him the island of Rügen.

Gustav now brought his ships around the islands, then secured, and into the Stettiner Haff. He swiftly advanced with a force of 9,000 men on 51 ships through the inland sea to its head and by July 18 was at the city of Stettin, capital of Pomerania. He landed his troops below the city and met with Bogislaw XIV, duke of Pomerania, and the townspeople. Overawed by the Swedish force Bogislaw capitulated, signing a treaty giving a cash contribution of 200,000 riksdalers and the Pomeranian army to Gustav. The 5,000 troops were taken into the Swedish army as the White Brigade, which would distinguish itself in Gustav's service. The monetary arrangements of the treaty set the pattern for the rest of the campaign. The occupation would pay for itself and not require Sweden's total support. Bogislaw was elderly and childless. The probable beneficiary of this situation was Gustav's father-in-law, George William of Brandenburg. So the king also inserted in the treaty a provision requiring the next duke, upon Bogislaw's death, ratify this treaty or Sweden would hold the country as protectorate until expenses for the war were reimbursed and the treaty ratified. Pomerania would stay friendly to Sweden one way or the other.

While the Swedish king had not been seriously threatened so far, he was still confined to the coastal area of Pomerania and Imperial forces were concentrating around him. To the west the count of Savelli commanded at Anklam, bringing reinforcements down the Tollense Valley. Torquato Conti was thoroughly entrenched a few miles up the Oder in Gartz and Greifenhagen on either side of the river. And to the east of Wollin Island, Colberg was held by Imperial forces. A chain of garrisons stretched between these strong points ringing Gustavo in on the coast.

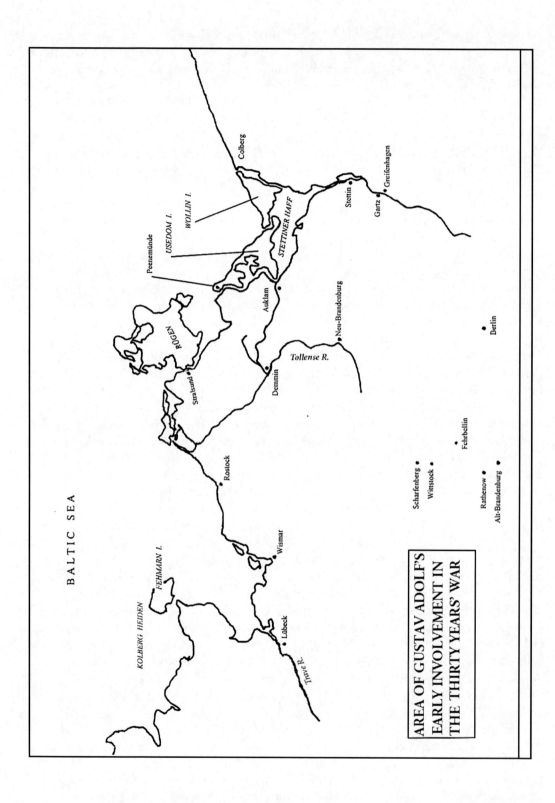

BALTIC SEA

KOLBERG/ HEIDEN

FEHMARN I.

Lübeck

Trave R.

Wismar

Rostock

Stralsund

RÜGEN

Demmin

Tollense R.

Auklam

Peenemünde

USEDOM I.

WOLLIN I.

STETTINER HAFF

Colberg

Stettin

Gartz

Greifenhagen

Neu-Brandenburg

Berlin

Fehrbellin

Scharfenberg

Wittstock

Rathenow

Alt-Brandenburg

AREA OF GUSTAV ADOLF'S
EARLY INVOLVEMENT IN
THE THIRTY YEARS' WAR

In late summer the king received his second important voluntary ally in this German country. On August 1, 1630, Sweden concluded a treaty with the great city of Magdenburg, strategically located on the Elbe River. The city had already survived a siege by Wallenstein in 1629 and was now ready to throw its lot in with Gustav. The alliance was a real morale boaster and cost the king nothing, at least for the time being. The Imperial siege had not been very effective and the city was able to maintain good supplies of food and war materials via the river.

At the end of the month Wallenstein was relieved of his command. Tilly took control of the Imperial troops in addition to the Catholic League army he had commanded during the Danish War.

Before winter set in there was some activity on both sides. Gustav sailed with a portion of his army to Stralsund, leaving Horn in command at Stettin. Conti attacked the town in the king's absence, but Horn drove him back with heavy losses.

Gustav, meanwhile, laid siege to the fortified town of Demmin that contained the bridge crossing the Tollense, part of the road to Auklam. The importance of Demmin was typical of the situation in northern Germany. Bridges on the main roads, crossing important rivers, were all guarded by fortified towns or cities. Thus military movement and supplies required the capture or cooperation of these strategic points throughout the country.

Savelli made an attempt to raise the siege, bringing 3,000 troops. The Italian arranged his soldiers in a long line in an attempt to outflank and envelop Gustav's smaller force. The disciplined Swedes, who were concentrated in the center, split the middle of Savelli's line then turned right and left and rolled up the Imperial line. Demmin fell to the Swedes and Savelli was forced out of Auklam giving Gustav control of the coast from Stettin to Stralsund.

With winter approaching Gustav moved a detachment of his Swedish troops used to winter warfare up the Oder and invested Gartz and Greifenhagen. They surrendered in January of the new year. Also in January 1631, Gustav concluded the Treaty of Bärwalde with France. Richelieu and Gustav agreed to an alliance to last five years. During that time France would pay Sweden 400,000 riksdalers per year to keep 30,000 foot and 6,000 horse in Germany. Gustav was to be tolerant of Roman Catholics in territories occupied by his army and treat Bavaria and the League as neutrals as long as they acted the same. This last was to be of short duration for Tilly was at the time investing Magdeburg and was mixing Imperial, League and Bavarian troops at will. Richelieu, who was trying to drive a wedge between the emperor and Maximilian turning Bavaria into a client state, would only see his plans frustrated.

By March Gustav had cleared Mecklenburg and Pomerania of Imperial garrisons. In that month Tilly pounced on a weak Swedish position at Neu-Brandenburg and put to the sword not only all the Swedes and Scots in the garrison, but every man woman and child in the town. He then turned his full attention to Magdeburg and by the end of the month had taken several of the outer works.

In an effort to divert Tilly's attention Gustav marched on Frankfurt-on-Oder. The tactic worked and Tilly started for the city, taking a large portion of his besieging army to relieve Frankfurt. However, on Palm Sunday (April 3), the king called upon Banér's Blue Brigade and Hepbar's Yellow to storm the walls. At the same time a Scottish regiment blew the main gate and, after taking some casualties from cannon at the entrance, poured into the city streets. A second gate was opened from the inside and Bauditzen's cavalry charged through into a garden area of the city. In street fighting an Irish regiment under Colonel Walter Butler resisted bravely and died to a man. The Imperialists asked for a truce, but were met with the cry "Neu-Brandenburg Quarter." Uncharacteristically, the usually well disciplined troops committed scandalous excesses upon the Protestant population. The whole operation had ended so quickly that Tilly had no time to intervene. He returned to Magdeburg and intensified his siege.

Gustav's only alternative was to aid his ally by direct intervention, but the route to the city lay through the territories of George William of Brandenburg and John George of Saxony. At the beginning of May Gustav marched on Berlin and his father-in-law allowed Gustav to place a Swedish garrison at Spandau to guard his supply line. Gustav proceeded to Potsdam and was negotiating with the elector of Saxony for permission to cross his territory when he received news that Magdeburg had fallen on May 10. But there was more.

During the sacking that followed, a great fire swept through the city destroying nearly all of it; 20,000 persons were killed or died in the flames. Though the fire deprived Tilly of an important base of operations it was a propaganda disaster for the Swedish king. An open ally that Gustav had pledged to help and protect had been defeated and destroyed.

In the end Gustav was able to work out an agreement with John George. The elector allowed his domain to be divided into 10 quartering areas, each to contribute 30,000 riksdalers per month to the Swedish war effort.

Turning his attention to Mecklenburg, Gustav finally took Greifswald and reinstated the dukes ousted by Wallenstein to their rightful rule. Swedish general Todt was left in command of troops in the country with orders to clear the duchy of Imperial forces.

During the winter months the Protestant princes held a congress at Leipzig to try to come to terms with developments in Germany. If they could revive the old Protestant Union, they might induce Gustav to retire from Germany or at least stop further adventurism. At the same time they would be unified against the emperor and in a position to protect their rights. The congress failed, however, and the only result was to encourage a revolt against the emperor in southern Germany. In Württemberg, Prince Wilhelm von Baden and a group of the princes were arming themselves. Nearby, William V of Hesse-Kassel was preparing for war. Tilly now turned south to deal with these upstarts leaving a military vacuum in northern Germany. Gustav wasted little time in filling it.

He left Brandenburg and on July 2 took the bridge, town and fortification of Tangermünde giving him access to the west side of the Elbe and a new area for supplies. He was followed by Tilly's lieutenant, Pappenheim, who could do little, being badly outnumbered.

On the tenth of July Gustav moved down river to a big bend at Werben where he built a fortified camp. As usual the Swedish sappers did an excellent job of constructing field works. Pappenheim was completely powerless to take any action and sent messages to Tilly to return with the main body of the Imperial Army.

Meanwhile, Tilly had crushed the rebellious princes in the south with more than the usual pillaging, massacres and destruction. However, when he turned to the Landgrave of Hesse he found an adversary of some mattle. While the Hessians did not have sufficient forces to meet the old general in open battle, they did fall back from his approach skillfully, destroying supplies and ambushing isolated units. Because of these Fabian tactics and Pappenheim's pleas Tilly finally broke off his pursuit of the Landgrave and returned to northern Germany and his primary concern, the Swedish king.

Tilly arrived with 27,000 men against Gustav's 16,000 entrenched troops. The king was not about to be drawn out into a pitched battle. But he did lead 4,000 men on a cavalry attack on detachments of Imperial horse guarding three towns. Tilly's troops were severely mauled, irritating the old general even more.

Tilly advanced on Gustav's works on August 6 with 15,000 foot, 7,000 horse and 16 heavy guns. He bombarded the earthworks then on the 7th assaulted the encampment. The Swedish works had suffered little damage from the heavy barrage and the attack was easily thrown back. In addition Baudetzen led a cavalry attack that outflanked Tilly and added to his losses. Then word came that Horn was on his way with another 9,000 soldiers.

Tilly pulled out to lick his wounds, having lost some 6,000 men. It was the first time in his life the 72-year-old general had lost an engagement he was personally commanding. In the Lion of the North Tilly had met a worthy adversary.

Shortly after the successful defense Gustav received a contingent of English troops as a result of a previously concluded agreement with Charles I. So 6,000 men under the earl of Hamilton landed at Peenemünde and began to make their way to Gustav's headquarters. Additional troops and money would trickle in but never reach the promised level. The English king had his own problems with his Parliament, leading eventually to civil war.

Even with this setback at Werben, the emperor felt he was in a strong position. The rebellion in the south had been crushed. Hesse was on the defensive and the war in Italy had been concluded. Veterans of that campaign now joined Tilley's army bringing it to over 40,000 men. Ferdinand ordered Tilly to settle with Saxony, the only other rebellious prince of any military consequence. John George had 16,000 men under arms commanded by the capable Hans Georg von Arnim. The emperor ordered the Saxon elector to turn this force over to Tilly and when he was refused ordered the old general to march on Leipzig. Ravaging the countryside as he went Tilly advanced on the city.

John George was finally forced to commit and he turned to the Swedish king for help. On September 2 the Saxon prince, "concluded an alliance with Gustav, 'for as long as the danger from the enemy shall continue.'"[10] John George would keep his own army and generals. It was a contract forced by necessity upon both parties fully agreeable to neither.

All forces now converged on Leipzig with Tilly getting there first. The burghers resisted stoutly, burning the suburbs outside the walls and closing the gates. Tilly commenced his attack on September 4, opening with his heavy batteries. As he learned of the advance of the allies he offered reasonable terms to the city and the gates were opened. The old general now turned to greet his adversaries in an open-field pitched battle, exactly the situation for which he had hoped.

On September 7, 1631, the two armies drew up their forces near the small town of Breitenfeld not far from Leipzig. The allies had the numerical advantage with 24,000 Swedish troops and 18,000 Saxons. Tilly fielded 35,000 men.

The Imperial and League forces were deployed in the Spanish fashion with the massed tercios in the center, seventeen battalia, fifty files, ten deep. On the left flank was Pappenheim with his heavy cavalry, the famous Black Cuirassiers. Covering the right flank was Furstemberg with his veteran heavy cavalry just arrived from Italy. Light Croatian cavalry was scattered in front and between the wings. Tilly arranged his troops on a ridge with his heavy guns commanding the field down the slope where his enemy would have to cross a marshy area then attack up the incline. He encouraged his troops, riding before the ranks to the shouts of "Father Tilly."

The allies crossed the marshy area then formed up half a mile away. The Swedish right wing was commanded by Marshal Banér. Here five brigades of cavalry under Todt formed the first line. Four more formed the second. In the center of the line was the infantry, four Swedish brigades under Winkel, Cur Hall, Teuffel and Aken Oxenstierna. A cavalry regiment and two Scottish regiments of foot were in ready reserve. The second line was composed of one Scottish and two German brigades of foot under Hepburn, Vitzhum and Thurn respectively. Behind this second line were two more regiments of cavalry in reserve.

The left cavalry wing was commanded by Marshal Horn. Three brigades of cavalry formed the first line. A second line was composed of two regiments of horse. As usual detachments of musketeers were deployed with the cavalry units. Regimental guns were arranged in front of their units and the army's heavy guns were deployed to the left of center under Torstensson. To the left of Horn, but separated by the Leipzig-Düben road, was the Saxon army under Arnim drawn up in a single line, Spanish style. Again infantry and guns were concentrated in the middle with cavalry on the wings. This army looked magnificent with gleaming armor and bright embroidery as contrasted with the Swedes' worn and battlefield look. But the main difference was in training and experience, and the Saxons had neither. Gustav was careful that there was separation between the two as he wanted to make sure his Swedes had room to maneuver without becoming entangled with the Saxon mass. The great pitched battle for which Tilly had yearned and Gustav had seen as inevitable was underway.

The engagement opened with the two armies' artillery pounding each other for two hours. Pappenheim then launched an attack on the Swedish right. He led his Black Cavalry in an oblique charge to the front of Banér's right, smashing the line and outflanking him at the same time. The Imperial heavy cavalry was trained in the caracole tactic. This pitted pistol against Swedish muskets, a fight the shoulder weapons were going to win. The combined use of the light regimental guns and muskets shattered Pappenheim's attack. Seven times the Bohemian general advanced and seven times he was thrown back with heavy losses.

Tilly sent a regiment of Holstein foot in to save the situation, but it was destroyed by the Swedish pikemen. Pappenheim's flanking movement was outflanked by a regiment of Swedish reserves and crushed. Horn then went on the offense sending his Gotland and Finnish horse in a saber charge into the ranks of the Imperial cavalry. Not only did he clear Pappenheim from his front, but he drove him from the field.

It was a different story, however, on the left of the allied line. Here Furstemberg had also charged forward with his veteran heavy cavalry straight at the Saxon body of troops. The inexperienced Saxons in all their finery stood for only a moment then began to yield. John George and his bodyguard tried to hold the line and encourage the troops, but as the mass of horse thundered into their ranks, unit after unit turned and fled. The elector was swept from the field by his retreating army. The whole Saxon line disintegrated, the proud and shiny troops broke and ran. Almost half the allied forces had been routed and the left flank completely exposed.

Tilly quickly took advantage of the situation. He set his tercios in motion forward and to the right. As his mass of infantry passed the allied line and moved into the space previously occupied by the Saxons, he wheeled them to the left ready to roll up the Swedish flank, a classic prescription for victory. But the maneuvering of such a large body of troops had taken some time and Gustav was able to react with his smaller, well disciplined units. Horn wheeled his left flank to a position behind the Düben road using the ditches to provide rough ground to his front. The king reinforced him with two brigades from the center. By the time Furstenberg had returned from driving the Saxons from the field, rejoining Tilly's massed infantry in attack, it was against a well formed front line. The Swedish army not only held, but inflicted dreadful casualties.

Once Gustav could see his new line was in good order and holding, he hurried back to the center, sending more troops to the left, into the line. Then with four regiments of Swedish cavalry he led a charge up the hill directly at the Imperial artillery on the crest. His fast moving light cavalry swept through the batteries sabering the gunners until the gun crews abandoned their weapons and fled the field. The king's men now turned the heavy pieces on Tilly's massed infantry pressing against Horn's Düben Road line. Torslensen wheeled the Swedish artillery into line to join the onslaught.

Rushing back down the slope the king took command again of the center, wheeling it in line with Horn and the Düben Road so that the whole front was now 90 degrees to the original front orientation. Furstenberg's horsemen had become dispersed. Tilly's infantry was an inert mass stacked up against the Swedish pikemen. Raked by musket fire, pounded by their own heavy artillery and the Swedish lighter guns, it was unable to even disengage in any kind of orderly manner. Command control no longer existed among the Imperial forces and finally, near sunset, men began to stream away. By dusk the withdrawal had turned into a stampede and the Imperial mass of infantry melted before the Swedes.

The retreat was covered by Count Cronenburg's cuirassiers, the only unbroken Imperial unit left. But the Swedish army was too exhausted to maintain any kind of hot pursuit. Tilly, twice wounded, collected his forces as best he could and withdrew to Halberstad, then to Weser.

The great battle that was to put an end to the Lion of the North was over. Imperial losses were 7,000 killed with 6,000 wounded or captured. Swedish losses were 2,100 killed or wounded. Gustav's victory at Breitenfeld was cheered by his supporters, Louis of France, Charles I of England and the Dutch Republic. It catapulted Sweden to the level of a great European power and caused military experts to reevaluate contemporary tactics. The Snow King, it seems, was made more of iron than of ice.

16. Gustav's Court on the Rhine and the Battle of Lützen

Between September 14 and 16 Gustav and John George met to discuss strategy. The elector was very apologetic for the performance of his army, but Gustav would not make it an issue and instead insisted on discussing the future. It was decided the two would spilt up, Saxons advancing up the Oder into Silesia and the Swedes into Thurigia toward the Rhine.

By September 22, Gustav had taken Erfurt and made it his supply depot and command center in central Germany. On October 4 he took Würzburg, storming the castle of Marienburg which produced a rich haul of booty and a store of books that he sent to the Uppsala University library. At Würzburg, however, he found himself in immediate danger.

Tilly had taken his beaten army into western Germany where he joined forces with Charles of Lorraine and built his army back to strength. By mid–October he was outside Ochsenfurt with 40,000 men only a day's march from Gustav. Fortunately for the king and his badly outnumbered army Tilly had been ordered by the emperor to move on south and not engage the Swedes. Tilly headed south and Gustav proceeded on down the Main River entering Frankfurt on November 17. He marched cross-country to Oppenheim where he ran into a Spanish garrison. Taking the town, he crossed the Rhine, then moved upriver to take Worms on December 7, which had been abandoned by a Lorraine garrison. He turned about and marched downriver, forcing the elector to flee Mainz, arriving there five days later. The Spanish detachments in the area except for Don Philip gathered at Frankenthal, above Worms, which the Swedes blockaded. The landgrave of Hesse, now free of Tilly's threat, moved down the Rhine seizing Ehrenfells. Gustav placed his artillery outside Mainz, but Philip, gauging the hopelessness of the situation, capitulated. Gustav had defeated Spanish forces and taken Spanish posts. He had tweaked the nose of one more European power. Gustav celebrated Christmas in Mainz with all north-central and a good share of western Germany in his hands.

During the winter of 1631–32 the Swedish king established his court in Mainz. Oxenstierna and the queen joined him there. Envoys from the German states and ambassadors from the courts of Europe arrived. At this moment in history Gustav Adolf was the most powerful man in Europe. Though Sweden would remain one of the greatest military powers on the continent for another thirty years, never again would a Swedish monarch be in this exalted position. Here he treated with an embassy from George Rákóczy, the new ruler of Transylvania. He exchanged missions with the khan of the Crimean Tartars, exploring the idea of opening a second front against the Hapsburgs. The plan never bore fruit, but it did establish a line of communication that would last for almost a century and be useful to Karl X and Karl XII. Likewise, Gustav made little progress in convincing the Swiss cantons to join him.

With Russia, however, he had better success. Sweden's Truce of Altmark with Russia was good until 1635, but Russia's peace with Poland was due to expire in 1632 and the tsar was preparing for a renewed conflict with the hope of recovering Smoleńsk. Russian agents were given permission to recruit mercenaries in Swedish occupied Germany. In March 1631 a permanent Swedish embassy was established in Moscow.

In April 1632 Sigismund III died, opening the election process for his successor. Gustav put his name forward, but only half seriously. Wladyslav, Sigismund's son, won the crown easily which raised the question of how he would handle relations with Sweden along the Vistula and the Düna.

Christian IV of Denmark was also arousing concern. Confined to his own territory and in no position to be a military threat, he was busy plotting with the German states on his border. In June 1632 Gustav concluded an alliance with Frederick III of Holstein-Gottorp, Christian's dynastic rival, which formalized an alliance that would stand for the next three generations.

On the Rhine, Gustav had placed himself in direct contact with both Spain and France. He had attacked and taken Spanish garrisons. Philip IV considered the wisdom of a retaliatory strike or even an open war with Sweden. Spain decided, however, she could not afford another enemy and both sides moved to down play the confrontation.

Richelieu, on the other hand, was in a real quandary. He was still pursuing his dream of dividing Maximilian from the emperor and making Bavaria his protectorate, but there had been no progress in this direction. What's more his Swedish ally had not behaved in the fashion he had choreographed. True, Gustav had decisively defeated the emperor's forces, but now he was in the Rhineland, an area the French wanted to dominate. Lorraine was key to French ambitions. The elector of Trier was a French client. Richelieu had planned on contending with Spain for control of the area, not Sweden. Though the French-Swedish alliance would survive this strain, any hopes for a close friendship had been set back.

To Charles I, Gustav was the Dragoon King, the monarch who led his troops in person, champion of the Protestant cause in Germany and as such, responsible to restore Friedrich V to his rightful place as elector of the Palatinate. The Winter King hastened to Gustav's Winter Court to plead his case and would trail after his armies for the next several months, leaving his wife and the Swedish king's namesake in The Hague. Gustav treated Friedrich with all the courtesies due a royal personage, but was not about to turn over key territories to a weak and undependable ruler. This would have to come later when the war was won.

With Oxenstierna's arrival, the king and his chancellor began organizing a central government for Swedish Germany. There was a chancery, a standing council, exchequer and judicial authority. A system of taxation, tolls and customs was implemented. A "Church Ordinance for Lutheran Germany" was issued declaring the protection of Lutherans and Catholics in Calvinist areas. Swedish generals and German princes were installed as administrators of conquered territories with ultimate sovereignty reserved to the Swedish crown. By the spring of 1632 a Swedish empire in Germany had been created.

As winter turned to spring Gustav prepared for the summer campaign. He seems to have had in mind a sweep of southern Germany, up the Rhine, over to the Danube, through Bavaria all the way to Vienna, the Imperial capital. The intention was to conquer southern Germany in the same way he had taken the north. In the process he would bring the emperor's army to battle and finally destroy Hapsburg power, a lofty ambition, something France and the Turks had so far been unable to accomplish. To carry out this ambitious campaign he would need additional forces and during the winter the king was busy recruiting.

His Army of the Rhine, under his immediate command, was being increased from 19,000 to 46,000. The Franconian Army under Marshal Horn would be raised from 8,500 to 30,000. The Army of Lower Saxony under Actatius Todt was to be increased from 7,800 men to 21,000. Banér's Magdenberg Army would go from 12,000 troops to 39,000. The Mecklenburg Corps was to be raised from 3,900 to 11,000. The Weimar Corps under Duke William, almost entirely horse, had 4,000 and was to become 8,500. Forces under the landgrave of Hesse were to be raised from 8,000 to 18,400. Garrison troops spread over a hundred German towns and cities numbered about 12,500 and would increase to 18,000. In addition, 7,200 cavalry and 1,500 more infantry were arriving from Sweden and Finland. Total forces to be ready for the summer campaign were to be 153,000 foot and 43,500 horse, more troops than Germany had ever seen under one commander.

Gustav's ally John George and his general Arnim with 20,000 Saxons were wintering in Prague. The Swedish king watched his ally nervously. True, Arnim was taking measures to train his troops, but the Saxon elector's independence meant he could not be counted on to cooperate with the king's strategy and might even require rescuing. While pushing deep into Silesia, he had not secured the country from the Oder to the Elbe. A thrust by Imperial forces could cut him off, requiring Gustav to act. And the emperor was not sitting idle these winter months.

Tilly had taken up position at Nördlingen with Imperial and League forces to block just such a move as Gustav was contemplating. Ferdinand had recalled Wallenstein from his retirement of mystical and astrological studies in Znaim where he had moved from Prague when the Saxons arrived. Wallenstein agreed to raise and train another army in Bohemia. The king of Spain sent 300,000 *ducats* for the project and Hungary offered 300,000 riksdalers to add to the Emperor's coffers.

Wallenstein, once he had his army organized and trained, would be in a position to threaten the Saxon army. Also, Gustav was wary of possible communication between Wallwnstein and Arnim, his former lieutenant. The whole situation in eastern Germany was very unsettling.

Finally, there was trouble in northwestern Germany. At the end of 1631, Pappenheim had been sent to Hameln to organize resistance in the area under Swedish control. He raised only about 8,000 men, but was able to stay active and keep occupied some 30,000 troops in four Swedish armies trying to catch him. The danger was a breakout to the southeast into the Thuringian area or into Saxony, cutting Gustav's lifeline to Mecklenberg and Pomerania.

By March 1632 these threats had become too serious to ignore and Gustav could wait no longer. Before his various armies had reached their full projected strength the king left Mainz under Oxenstierna's command and started for the Danube. The immediate cause for action was a confrontation between Tilly and Horn that was precipitated by the bishop of Bamberg. The good bishop had double-crossed the Swedes, with whom he had a treaty of neutrality, by asking Tilly for assistance and protection. Gustav sent Horn and his army of Franconia to reduce the double-dealer. Horn marched up the Neckar River to Heilbron, then on to Mergentheim on the Tauber, clearing Imperial garrisons as he went. By February 1 he was at Bamberg. The city was not well fortified and the bishop evacuated with the League troops stationed there. Still Horn had to put down a minor insurrection before the city could be called entirely quelled.

Tilly was ordered to assist the good bishop and set out immediately for the north. He marched to Amberg, where he met the bishop, then went on to Nuremberg via Neumarkt. Leaving a garrison there he started for Bamberg with 20,000 men.

Horn was dealing with several problems. He had just lost his young wife, the daughter of Oxenstierna, and two children to disease; and the troops under his command had not been thoroughly trained. Also, Bamberg was not a very defensible town even though Horn had made some real improvements during his time there. As Tilly approached one of his dragoon units collided with a regiment of Horn's cavalry and drove it back into a newly recruited infantry battalion. The inexperienced battalion of foot broke, spreading panic in the trenches guarding the city. Tilly took advantage of the opening and fed more troops into the assault. Horn counterattacked with a regiment of horse and a battalion of foot, stalling the assault long enough to blow the bridges and saving his artillery and baggage train.

Horn abandoned Bamberg, crossed the Main, and headed down the right bank to Hassfurt, then to Schweinfurt. Leaving a garrison at Schweinfurt, he fell back to Geldesheim. Tilly, pursuing Horn, stopped at Schweinfurt to besiege the three corps left there.

In early March Gustav launched his campaign, moving up the Main with 25,000 men, well fed and well trained. At Kitzingen he picked up Horn on March 14. He also ordered Banér from the Elbe and Duke William of Weimar to join him. Their combined force would give him over 45,000 men.

Tilly abandoned the Schweinfurt siege in the face of a larger army and moved further east. He passed Bamberg and was ordered by Maximilian to retreat into the Upper Palatinate in the hope Gustav would follow, sparing Bavaria. But the Swedish king would not cooperate and when he found out there was no army between him and Bavaria he headed straight for the Danube.

After a short visit to Nuremberg, a city that had twice defied Tilly when Imperial forces had appeared before it, he marched for Donauwörth. At Donauwörth and ten miles away at Hochstadt the Swedes secured points of crossing, taking both towns after sharp engagements.

Tilly, finding Gustav had not trailed him, was forced to try to intercept him. He crossed the Danube and deployed at the junction of the great river with the Lech River. Tilly's right flank rested on the Danube and his left on the town of Rain. He built earthworks off the river, which passed through a marshy area just before entering the Danube. To attack him, the Swedes would have to cross a marsh, a swift running river, more marsh and finally a slope right into entrenched troops and heavy guns. The Imperialists believed any attack along this line would be suicide. But Gustav, reconnoitering himself, found a bend in the river which would allow him to set up converging fire of musket and cannon, making an attack possible.

To screen his intentions the king had bonfires built along the river, then fed them with green and wet brush. Dense smoke filled the valley. Under this cover the Swedes moved seventy-two cannon to the bend of the river. They opened fire on April 4. On the 5th 300 Finnish volunteers crossed the river to establish a bridgehead. A trestle type bridge that had been built in the nearby town was brought up to span the river. Gustav led reinforcements across to back up the Finns as he sent a cavalry detachment upriver to see if they could find a crossing. By afternoon Gustav had enough infantry and light artillery across to attack, but Tilly beat him to it.

In spite of the heavy smoke the old general had discovered the point of crossing and sent his own infantry to attack the position. Wrangel's musketeers, posted along the opposite side of the river, delivered heavy fire, driving the Imperialists back with heavy losses.

On the 6th more Swedish infantry and artillery crossed and began fighting their way through the marshy area. Meanwhile, the cavalry detachment had found a ford and led the whole Swedish horse across to threaten Tilly's left. Though still secure in his entrenchment, the old general was now threatened from both his front and left. It was time to smash the exposed troops on his front and drive them back into the marshes. He personally led the next mass infantry charge, but he was hit by a three-pound ball that shattered his thigh. Tilly was carried from the field.

His second-in-command was struck in the temple by a bullet and was also carried from the field. Command now devolved to Maximilian, not experienced as a front line officer. The counterattack was broken off. The next morning Maximilian and his Bavarian troops, who had seen little action, were on the road to Neuburg. Imperial and League soldiers, who had done the fighting, left their works and, bearing their wounded general, moved to Ingolstadt where Tilly died two weeks later. Imperial losses at the battle were estimated at 2,000 to 4,000 with Swedish casualties at half that.

The way to Bavaria now lay open to Gustav. His army took Rain and then Augsburg, considered the cradle of Protestantism. Here he was received in state and the city officials took an oath of allegiance to the Swedish king.

Passing through Neuburg, Maximilian encamped at Ingolstadt. Gustav, after a few days rest at Augsburg, marched to Ingolstadt where his first assault was repulsed with some losses. On May 2 Maximilian withdrew from the city to Ratisbon, forty miles downriver, leaving a considerable garrison of Imperial, League and Austrian troops. Ratisbon was a free Protestant city which resisted Maximilian's entrance. The Bavarians reduced it then committed awful atrocities upon the population. Ingolstadt was one of the few cities in this part of Germany with modern fortifications. Most German forts and castles had defense systems left over from the Middle Ages, but Ingolstadt had the thick walls running at sharp angles to each other, arranged so that gunfire from one could rake the attackers of another. These new fortresses were common in Flanders and the Netherlands where constant warfare had necessitated these improvements. In most of Germany they were rare, Inglstadt being an exception.

While Gustav was having his way in Bavaria, Wallenstein began to move on the Saxons. His new army of Bohemian, Spanish, German, Turk and Croatian mercenaries was well equipped thanks to his own and Spanish money. He collected his forces at Znaim, where he could guard Vienna, and started for Prague.

At this critical time, John George managed to be away hunting. Arnim moved his army to Leitmertz, at the junction of the Elbe and Eger rivers, leaving a substantial garrison at Prague which Wallenstein now attacked. The Saxons fought bravely and repulsed two assaults following a terrible cannonade. At night, however, traitors within the city admitted a contingent of Imperial troops who surprised the Saxon garrison and all was lost. Arnim retreated back into Saxony. Wallenstein captured Eger and the remaining towns in Bohemia.

While keeping an eye on Wallenstein's movements and investing Ingolstadt, Gustav allowed himself a side trip to Munich, capital of Bavaria. He arrived May 10, Ascension Day, entered the city, which did not resist, and proceeded to the Electorate Palace where Swedish prayers were read. He then attended a Catholic service after which he had a discussion with Jesuits and Capuchins. Strict discipline was maintained by his army and there was no looting or burning. Leaving a garrison at the capital the king left Munich and marched to Donauwörth where he could track the movements of Maximilian and Wallenstein.

His two adversaries had united at Eger, giving them an army of 48,000 men in a position to threaten Nuremberg. On June 4 Gustav marched to the city's defense with only 18,500 troops and 70 guns, leaving a large contingent in Bavaria under Banér. At Nuremberg the king constructed a large earthen defense system around the city, outside its walls. Wallenstein, with all Imperial, League and Bavarian troops under his command built an entrenched encampment at Zirudorf where he could watch the Swedish king's movements, raid his supply lines and pounce on any forces caught out in the open. Meanwhile Gustav, though badly outnumbered, was doing the same.

Gustav needed reinforcements and he set Oxenstierna to work arranging the logistics. Horn with his 5,500 man army of the Rhine met the call. William V in Lower Saxony also responded. Two other generals were engaged in hot pursuit of Pappenheim and failed to come. William of Weirmar, who had already started an invasion of Saxony, was diverted by the call and turned to aid Gustav with his 5,000 troops. John George sent two regiments of Saxons. By August 17, 1632, the various contingents had joined the king. But now both sides began to have health problems in their huge camps where sanitation was anything but adequate by modern standards. Wallenstein had pillaged and burned his way to the Main, which meant he had no stores to draw from in the surrounding countryside. While Nuremberg had originally been well stocked, an army of this size could depreciate even a huge store in short order. Time was running out and Gustav looked for an opening.

The weakest point in Wallenstein's line seemed to be an old castle ruin on a hill above the river called Alte Veste on the Imperial left. The bluff was just outside Wallenstein's perimeter, but had an Imperial detachment guarding it. If the king could gain the hilltop he would have a commanding position from which to attack the duke's lines. On the night of August 21 Gustav brought his army to the town of Fürth, which he captured. He crossed the river and built a fortified camp close to the old castle ruins. On the night of the 22nd a rumor passed through the camp that Wallenstein was withdrawing. Acting on this bad information Gustav attacked Alte Veste the morning of the 24th. Wallenstein rushed six of his best regiments to Alte Veste, then followed with the rest of his army. A hundred Imperial cannon poured shot and shell into the attacking Swedes. Gustav's guns from the river answered, but could not be brought forward because of the steep, slippery slope. For twelve hours the battle raged, but the king could not gain the hillcrest. By evening it was raining and the king halted the attack.

Early the next morning Gustav renewed his efforts, but Wallenstein had brought up fresh troops and with these he counterattacked, driving the Swedes back to the river and their earthworks at Fürth. The first battle between the two great generals had gone to the Bohemian duke. Gustav had suffered 2,400 casualties including 1000 dead. Wallenstein lost just 600 men. The legend of Swedish invincibility had suffered a severe blow.

His nose bloodied, the king pulled his troops back into the encampment at Fürth. The crowded conditions quickly led to an outbreak of disease followed by desertions. Within twenty days he had lost a third of his army. On September 8 he broke camp. Leaving Oxenstierna with 6,000 men to garrison Nuremberg, he headed south. He was also leaving John George to his own devices, but the Saxon regiments lent him for the Alte Veste battle had acquitted themselves well and with Wallenstein tied up, Arnim had cleared most of Saxony of Imperial forces.

Gustav crossed the Danube and threatened western Bavaria. When this brought no response from Wallenstein, he turned and threatened Ingolstadt. This did at least bring Maximilian and his Bavarian contingent rushing south to take up position at Regensburg. The other Swedish armies were doing well. Horn was completing the mopping up operation on the Rhine and the landgrave was reducing Alsace. Todt was busy chasing Pappenheim in Lower Saxony.

Then Gustav received word that Wallenstein had ordered Pappenheim to the south-east to join him for an invasion of Saxony. Their combined force could overwhelm John George.

Gustav broke off his operations in Bavaria and headed north. He reached Nördlinger on

October 10 where he learned that the two Imperialists had not yet joined up. A week later he was back at Nuremberg to pick up Oxenstierna and his Swedish forces. In the next 17 days his troops marched 400 miles, reaching the Thuringian Passes with the intention of heading off Pappenheim. He would have been too late, except for Bernard of Weimar who moved his army into the passes ahead of Pappenheim and held them until the king's arrival. Gustav pushed his men harder than ever to get to Naumberg and prevent Wallenstein from crossing the Saale. Here the Swedish king built a fortified camp and gathered his forces. Wallenstein interpreted this move as Gustav going into winter quarters. He had drawn the wrong conclusion. Based on this misconception, the Bohemian duke spread his army out to cut off Swedish supply lines, calculating that by spring the invaders would be sick, starved and ready for annihilation. He was still convinced of his original assessment that this "little enemy" was indeed the "Snow King" and would simply melt away given some pressure.

Gustav, of course, had no intention of ending the 1632 campaign season and was just waiting for an opportunity. On November 4 he received the astonishing news that Wallenstein was dispersing his forces, apparently going into winter quarters. He is said to have exclaimed, "Now in very truth I believe God has delivered him into my hands."[1] In fact Wallenstein had removed fifteen regiments to quarters in other parts of the country, including nine under Pappenheim stationed thirty-five miles away. Gustav had a slight advantage in numbers, 20,000 to Wallenstein's 18,000, but his cavalry was weak, 6,200 compared to the Imperial 8,600. And he did not have any of his best generals with him. Horn, Banér, and Todt were away at other fronts. The advantage of surprise, he felt, would more than make up for these weaknesses.

Very early on November 5, 1632, the Swedish king rolled his troops out for the march to the area planned for the attack. The king hoped for a complete surprise, but at the Rippach River crossing a detachment of Imperial troops blundered into the advancing army. Now it was the Swedes who were surprised. They wasted several hours in forming up and sweeping the enemy from their path. It was time that might have made the difference.

Wallenstein was immediately warned of Gustav's threat and sent couriers to Pappenheim, the only sizable force close enough to help. Riders arrived at Pappenheim's camp at midnight and he immediately dispatched his cavalry. The infantry did not start for another six hours.

Meanwhile, the Swedish army did not reach Wallenstein's front until late evening and Gustav held up the attack until dawn. At 5:00 am on November 6, 1632, reveille sounded. After a quick meal, prayers and hymns were sung. The Swedish army fell in line and was ready for battle by 8:00 in the morning, but fog obscured the field. Gustav waited until after 10:00 when the mist had thinned. The attack did not commence until nearly 11:00 a.m.

Wallenstein had organized his position carefully. His right was anchored by the town of Lützen, whose windmills provided excellent cover for musketeers. His front was protected by a ditch and the elevated road running from Lützen to Leipzig. But Wallenstein's left was unsecured. This was the gap that Pappenheim was to fill.

Gustav deployed his troops with Nicholas Brahe, count of Weissemberg, front and center, commanding the famous Yellow Brigade. The second line in the center was commanded by the dependable old Klaphausen backed up by a reserve of horse under Colonel Ohm. The left consisted of columns of cavalry interspersed with detachments of musketeers and was commanded by Duke Bernard. The right wing of horse and musketeers was commanded by the king with Stalhauske, captain of the Finnish horse, second.

Gustav opened with his artillery then ordered his center forward across the ditch and road into the Imperial tercios. The Swedish right enveloped Wallenstein's unsupported left.

But at that moment Pappenheim appeared with his cavalry and charged into the left of the line. Before he could affect the battle, he was hit by a cannonball and his regiments refused to fight, leaving the scene of battle. At the same time the Swedish center was driving the Imperialists back, capturing several guns which they turned on the enemy.

Suddenly, the fog returned, obscuring the situation on the battlefield. Gustav could not see just how close to victory the Swedish army was. The right and center were gaining ground steadily. Only on the left front was progress impeded and here Gustav brought up his Småland cavalry regiment. He led the charge meant to drive the enemy back, but was immediately hit by a musket ball, losing control of his horse which carried him away from his escort into the thick of the fray. An Imperial horseman shot him in the back with a pistol and he fell from his saddle. A final shot to the head ended his life.

Bernard of Weimar took command and renewed the general attack all along the line. The right stumbled for now they ran into Piccolomini and his Black Cuirassiers who charged the Swedish line furiously again and again. But the center made steady progress capturing more guns and driving the Imperialists back. On the left, the death of their king had only spurred his soldiers on until they took the windmills, unhinging Wallenstein's right flank. At sunset Pappenheim's infantry finally arrived, but it was too late. The Battle of Lützen had been decided. Gustav had beaten his wily adversary, Wallenstein, but it had cost him his life.

Gustav Adolf Vasa, ruler of an empire stretching from the Arctic to the Danube, from Kexholms to Alseas, was dead. He left a Swedish Empire encompassing much of northern and central Europe. Gustav had reinvigorated the Protestant cause in Germany; there was to be a congress in Ulm to form a new Protestant League. Emperor Frederick's conquest of all of Germany, which had been so close in 1630, had been smashed.

17. Oxenstierna Takes Control and Prosecutes the War in Germany

The 39-year-old King Gustav lay among the dead on the Lüzen battlefield. His nearly stripped body was recovered by his soldiers, who mourned their loss. An officer in a Scottish regiment is quoted to have lamented, "He was, 'the captain of kings and king of captains.'"[1] He was a soldier's general, suffering their campaigns with them and leading from the front. He died in battle as he thought he would and, perhaps, as he would have preferred.

Maria Eleanora came to Weissenfels to claim her husband's body and take the king home. The slow procession through Germany was punctuated by many interruptions to allow the body to lie in state. After two years the royal procession reached Stockholm, where Gustav Adolf Vasa was laid to rest at the Ridderholm Church in the capital.

At her father's death, six-year-old Christina Augusta became Queen of the Swedes, Goths, and Vandals, Great Princess of Finland, Duchess of Estonia and Karelia, and Lady of Ingria. The country rallied around her as the symbol of Swedish unity and accord at a time of national insecurity that comes with the loss of a strong national leader. During a series of meetings and ceremonies the child was able to get only snatches of sleep and later wrote of the period in her life, "that I knew neither my misfortune nor my fortune. I remember, however, that I was enchanted to see all these people at my feet, kissing my hand."[2]

After months of separation the newly minted queen met her mother and the funeral procession at Nyköping where the queen mother showed uncharacteristic motherly emotion toward her daughter. After the funeral Maria took complete control of her eight-year-old daughter's life and at the same time entered a period of intense mourning, filling her rooms with black draperies and minimizing communication with the outside world. Still ten years away from maturity Christina was queen in name only. The real head of state was the chancellor, Alex Oxenstierna, still in Germany trying to cope with the burdens of ruling this Swedish empire bequeathed to him upon the death of his close friend and king.

It was an empire like that of Alexander or Attila in that it was held together by the personality, will and force of one man. When that uniting spirit was removed these empires began to disintegrate. But for a time pure momentum would carry the empire forward.

The Battle of Lützen had broken Wallenstein's army. He had lost perhaps 12,000 men, all his artillery and Pappenheim, his best general and cavalry commander. He was forced from the field of battle and withdrew into Bohemia to reconstitute his forces.

Though the Swedish held the field and the battle restored Sweden's reputation of arms, their casualties were crippling. The Swedes lost five to seven thousand dead and wounded. Gustav's army settled into winter quarters concerned about the future without their king and commander.

The congress of Protestant princes at Ulm took place as planned and resulted in the formation of a political organization that would become the League of Heilbronn on April 13, 1633, with Oxenstierna as president. One of the league's primary functions was to provide monetary support for the Swedish forces in Germany, but the money was slow in coming. The political machinery was so cumbersome that Oxenstierna could do little to make the organization really effective. Two of the most important German states never joined. George William of Brandenburg, unhappy with Sweden's insistence on retaining control of Pomerania, remained aloof as did John George of Saxony. Other allies were also uncooperative. Adolf Frederick of Mecklenburg, William of Weimar, Frederick Ulric of Wolfenbüttel and others whom Gustav had slighted or bullied at one time or another lent only half-hearted support to the Swedish cause. They saw in the treatment of Friedrich of the Palatinate (pushed aside) the prime example of the former king's priority of military necessity over what was right. Oxenstierna had these malcontents to deal with along with his other obligations.

The aging chancellor was saddled with running the administrative apparatus organized in Germany after the Swedish conquests. He had to run the postal system, fix tolls on river crossings, regulate trade, arrange a new ecclesiastical system, organize the educational system, and arrange a tax system on households, tradesmen, farmers and stock-growers. To accomplish all this he had a whole new civil service of mostly German personnel untrained in the Swedish governmental system.

Added to this were his responsibilities as head of the Swedish government. Executive operations in Stockholm were in the hands of the regents. Oxenstierna, as chancellor, was the head of this group with his brother Baron Gabriel Oxenstierna; Baron Gylldenhielm, a natural son of Karl IX and half brother of Gustav Adolf; Gabrial Bengtsson, a cousin of the chancellor as treasurer; and Count Jacob de la Gardie, high marshal of the Army. A steady flow of correspondence ran between the chancellor and the other four regents, but mail was slow, a month in summer, two or three times that in winter. Orders and descriptions of situations might change in days, complicating the governing process immensely.

The chancellor also had to contend with an anti–Oxenstierna faction at the capital headed by Karl Karlsson Gyllenhielm, Per Banér and Oxenstierna's old enemy Johan Skytte. This group plotted to recall the chancellor. Their objective was the withdrawal of all Swedish forces from Germany and they saw Oxenstierna as the main obstruction to achieving this end.

The chancellor was performing all the labors he had previously plus those the king had been doing. Among the latter and the area Oxenstierna was least qualified in was conducting military operations. Besides trying to figure out how to supply and pay for the five field armies, he had to direct their movement and deployment, often overriding generals who were sure they knew better than he what should be done. Tactics and military strategy had been the king's sole purview. Now Oxenstierna had to delve into this sphere as well.

Sweden still had the strongest military machine in Germany. Logistically, Oxenstierna made some changes that even improved the situation. He began to gradually shift native Swedish units to northern Germany where he felt national interests were vital. This also allowed him to rotate regiments back to Sweden, replacing them with home guard units. The chancellor covered these troop movements by shifting mercenary regiments to the south, keeping the five field armies intact. The overall troop strengths remained the same, but the strategy had changed completely.

Where Gustav had conducted an offensive war, Oxenstierna shifted to a defensive strategy. Peace or at least the turning of the war over to the Protestant princes and cities was his objective with Sweden retaining the all important Baltic coastal areas. Fortunately for the chancellor, 1633 was a year of relative military inactivity.

After Lützen, Wallenstein had pulled back into Bohemia and by spring had built his army back to strength. He seemed ready for a strike at Saxony, but Arnim kept him at bay through negotiations, arranging truce after truce with his old commander. Oxenstierna appointed von Thurn army commander in Silesia in the hopes of keeping Wallenstein penned in, but Thurn proved to be incompetent and the Bohemian general moved north into Silesia with little problem and was poised to strike at Pomerania. Oxenstierna ordered Duke Bernard of Saxe-Weimar, who had retained command of Gustav's army of the Main-Danube and added a few contingents from the Heilbronn League, to advance east up the Danube. Maximilian's Bavarian troops were occupied with a revolt of the Bavarian peasants. Bernard lay siege to and eventually took Regensburg. He might have carried the campaign on into Austria, but here he stopped, claiming jurisdiction over the whole area. The attack did have the intended effect; Wallenstein was ordered to break off his strike to the north and prepare for a defense of the emperor and Vienna if that became necessary.

By the end of the year Maximilian had put down the revolt. Bavaria was again able to concentrate its forces against the Swedes and Austria was out of danger. Wallenstein, meanwhile, continued to agitate problems with his communications to Arnim and even schemed with France. His ambition was feared by both the emperor and Maximilian. Ferdinand finally declared him guilty of treason. Wallenstein was murdered by a renegade unit of his own troops February 25, 1634, in Eger. His death removed the last really aggressive element within Germany. More and more the Thirty Years' War would be influenced by countries outside the empire.

In 1634 France increased its hold on Lorraine, forcing the duke to flee, and crept steadily toward Alsace. Spain sent reinforcements to its garrisons in western Germany and in support of Ferdinand. The emperor placed Imperial forces under the command of his son Ferdinand of Hungary. Maximilian appointed the duke of Lorraine commander of the Bavarian Army. With Wallenstein gone, Arnim drove into Bavaria and tried to retake Prague, but was driven back.

Imperial and Bavarian forces moved west retaking Regensburg and laying siege to Nördlingen by the first of September. The Imperial thrust had to be stopped and Oxenstierna ordered Horn's Army of the Rhine and Barnard's League army forward to relieve the siege. These combined armies numbered 25,000 men and looked sufficient to take on the Imperial-Bavarian Army. But on September 2, a Spanish army arrived, bringing the Imperial forces to over 33,000 men.

The Swedish operation went wrong from the start. A surprise night attack was planned, but the baggage train and heavy artillery got ahead of the infantry advance and warned the Imperial army of the movement. The battle opened on September 6, 1634, with Swedish cavalry charges being thrown back. Scottish infantry gained a footing in the Imperial works, but were eventually driven out by a counterattack of Spanish infantry. Horn's infantry made some progress, even outflanking the Imperialists, but was eventually stopped and reversed. A strong counterattack against Bernard's wing pushed the Germans back into Horn's retreating troops and the Swedish retreat became a rout. A considerable portion of the Swedish army was captured, including Field Marshal Horn. The battle to relieve Nördlingen was a disaster. All of the Danube was lost. Oxenstierna fell back to the Main and reorganized his forces. In March 1635, Duke Bernard was put in command of all Swedish and League troops in central Germany. John Banér retained his independent command in the northern part of the country.

The Heilbronn League, which had never lived up to its promise, now began to disintegrate. As early as April 1634 at the Frankfurt convention of the league, a divisive rift was opened between Sweden and George William of Brandenburg, who was actually not a member. After Nördlingen the league looked for support outside Sweden. It turned to France and concluded the Treaty of Löffler-Streiff which transferred French support in the form of money from Sweden to the league, but no monies were ever paid. Oxenstierna refused to sign the treaty and in March 1635 the last meeting of the league under Swedish auspices was held. Attendance was miserable. If the league was to continue it would be as a French client. Oxenstierna wished Richelieu good luck for he was divorcing himself from the organization. But the French were no more successful than the Swedes had been with the Heilbronn League and it finally dissolved.

In southern Germany all was lost and now the north began to turn against the Swedes as well. In June 16, 1634, John George had opened peace negotiations with the emperor. On November 14 they issued the Preliminaries of Pirna outlining the conditions for a permanent peace between the two parties. The emperor was gradually reasserting his hold over Germany and was now readily accepting Spanish troops into his domain. France had made gains in western Germany, Alsace and Lorraine, but had given up on any alliance with Bavaria and was losing influence with the Protestant princes. Intensifying the situation, Spain and France declared open war on one another in mid–1635.

Oxenstierna and Richelieu, both searching for support in the German war, agreed to meet. In March 1635 the Swedish chancellor left southern Germany to confer with the cardinal at Compiégue. The treaty signed there bound neither party to any hard and fast commitments. It was, rather, a recognition of common interests and a promise of mutual, but unspecified, support in the German conflict.

Oxenstierna returned to Germany at Stade in June of 1635 to find the situation had deteriorated still further. On May 20 the emperor and John George had signed the Peace of Prague. Forfeiting their freedoms, concerned only with the desire for peace and in a rush of nationalism, the princes and independent cities of Germany quickly followed Saxony's example and settled with Ferdinand. Within a few months only William V of Hesse-Kassel and Bernard of Saxe-Weimar remained loyal to the Swedish cause. Swedish military forces in Germany were reduced to only Banér's small army in Pomerania and Mecklenburg, which had not been paid for some time. Upon his return Oxenstierna was taken and literally held as a hostage by the officers in their camp in Mecklenburg demanding back pay or they would cross to Sweden and march on Stockholm to collect.

At this absolute low point in the chancellor's affairs in Germany, he received word of the Truce of Stuhmsdorf, September 2, 1635. The government in Stockholm had for some time been conducting negotiations with Poland to make a final settlement concerning Swedish holdings in Prussia. The inexperienced and divided negotiators had allowed themselves to be manipulated by the French, who were mediating. The outcome was an accord that relinquished all territorial rights in Prussia along with the rights to the port tolls and taxes vital to financing Sweden's overseas war machine. Oxenstierna was outraged that he was not informed of these conditions until two months after the conclusion of the treaty. First southern Germany and now Prussia were lost to him. The only consolation was that he was able to transfer the 9,700 troops in Prussia to Pomerania along with their commander, Lennart Torstensson. This force became very useful for on October 6, 1635, John George declared war on Sweden, followed by George William on January 6, 1636. With the reinforcements Banér was able to defeat Saxon attempts to drive the Swedes out of the country. A series of victories in limited engagements brought matters to a stalemate. It was under these conditions Oxenstierna took leave of Germany in July 1636 to return to Sweden. He was forced to detour through France and Holland, landing at Dalarö, outside Stockholm, July 16, 1636, not knowing what kind of reception to expect.

Four days later Oxenstierna gave his report to the Råd and was surprised to find overwhelming support for him as the head of the government. On July 22 the Estates passed a resolution recognizing the chancellor as such. For all the wrangling between the home government and the absent chancellor, there was now peace and accord between them.

Meanwhile, Spanish and Imperial forces had made progress against the French in Alsace and Lorraine, but were eventually stopped. Two French and Dutch armies attempted an invasion of the Spanish Netherlands, but this campaign also ground to a halt accomplishing little. In the fall of 1636, with Oxenstierna's departure, Ferdinand turned his Imperial army against the Swedes.

The combined Imperial-Saxon army forced its way into Brandenburg, driving the smaller Swedish army back. Banér gave ground looking for an opportunity for a decisive battle that might save the Swedish cause. His chance came on September 24, 1636, when Imperial-Saxon forces were drawn up near the town of Scharfenberg on a ridge facing a marshy lowland. The coalition had reinforced their earthworks by placing a string of wagons along the front to use as cover and to break up any cavalry charge. Heavy artillery was arranged along the line to blast the Swedes coming out of the marshy low ground. It was a prescription for annihilation, but Banér proved a wily opponent.

Instead of attacking head on, the 40-year-old general brought his troops through a wooded area south of the town of Wittstock on the German left flank. The battle line, with the center under Banér, the left commanded by Leslie and the right by Torstensson, threatened to roll up the Imperial-Saxon line. The Germans were forced to pull their troops out of their prepared works and shift them to the left, developing a whole new front. Banér's assault was halted as the superior numbers of the repositioning German troops began to build. The combat was intense and bloody with both sides heavily engaged. This battle saw some of the heaviest and bloodiest cavalry engagements of the war.

In addition to his surprise flank attack, Banér had sent a column under Lieutenant-General King around to the left to attack the area the Germans had originally intended to be the scene of the battle, but was now vacated. King's men had been delayed in getting through a woods and then the marshy lowland, but by late afternoon they had found their way back to the battlefield just as the Swedish main attack was stalling out and on the verge of collapse due to the numerical superiority of the Germans.

King had outflanked the Germans' right and now attacked rolling up the line. The Imperial-Saxon army was forced to shift once again to meet this new threat, which relieved the pressure against Banér's main front. The battle might have turned into a rout, but darkness intervened and both sides pulled back for the night.

The next morning, the Swedes advanced to renew the fight but found no one in front of them. During the night the Germans had fled their positions, abandoning their artillery. Banér held the field and stopped this latest thrust to drive Sweden from northern Germany. He had defeated Gallas, the general who had engineered the defeat of the Swedes at Nördlingen. Swedish military prestige was revived.

Banér sent his cavalry after the fleeing Imperialists and Saxons who left a trail of dead, wounded, arms and wagons. The Swedish horse caught up with the remnants of the German army and completed the annihilation. Sweden's position, for the moment at least, was secure.

During the winter of 1636–37 Banér rebuilt his army. He received new troops from Sweden and Finland, but these recruits, though loyal, were not well trained and the Swedish field marshal used them mostly for garrison duty. For his field army he preferred German mercenaries who could withstand the diseases rampant in the military camps. He had a good share of Scots, Irish and English as well. The old disciplined army of Swedes and Finns of Gustav's day no longer existed. Banér and his mercenaries were not squeamish about living off the countryside they passed though. In fact Banér amassed a fortune from looting conquered territories, cities and towns.

By spring he had 14,000 men in the field and he began a campaign to bring George William to heel, leaving Wrangel in Pomerania with a small force to guard the back door. He invaded Saxony and laid siege to the capital, Leipzig. In early June a final storming was prepared. Ladders, short pikes, hand grenades and axes were ready. Two large mines were used to blow the Grimmagate and a thirty foot wide breach was made in the wall by cannon fire. As the sun rose, the defenders braced for the onslaught, but the attack never came. Banér's attention had been diverted by a large Imperial army approaching his entrenchments.

Gallas had assembled an army of 47,000 Saxons, Brandenburgers, Hessians, Lueneburgers and Imperialists, and was advancing to relieve the siege. The first units were being thrown around Banér's works. The Swedish commander had to act quickly or face certain catastrophe.

On June 18 he pulled out of his works and headed north. Everything that could not be carried at a rapid rate was burned. Gallas sent his fast moving cavalry to try to block the retreat while bringing his infantry and guns along as fast as possible. It was a race for survival.

At Lueblen Croat light cavalry got ahead of Banér's troops and had to be attacked. At Jueterbog Banér's rearguard was overtaken and cut down; 600 men were killed and another 400 taken prisoner. At Liebrose the Swedish army was forced to battle and in a counterattack drove some of their pursuers into a swamp where a number were drowned. Finally, on June 27 Banér's flight was brought to a halt. At the Warthe River Gallas pushed ahead of the Swedish army. Banér found a three mile long battle line drawn up at Landsberg blocking his path. It looked like the race between Gallas and the Swedish general was over.

There was one possible avenue of escape. Poland lay only 35 miles away to the east. Banér sent his wife along with several high ranking officers to the border to arrange entry and provide for some kind of security. Gallas, however, discovered the preparations and shifted his army to the east. On June 30 Banér broke camp and marched out, not to the east, however, but to the west. The whole exercise in preparing for an escape to Poland had been a ruse.

Banér led the vanguard that cut its way through the lightly held positions to the west and the army escaped. They crossed the Oder and by July 4 had joined Wrangel's forces at Eberwalde. The escape was an incredible feat performed by a canny general who once more bested his German adversary.

However, Banér and Wrangel together had only 11,000 men. Banér had lost most of his equipment. The countryside was devastated, not able to support even this small army, and the Swedes did not have the money to pay their mercenaries. Gallas moved into Pomerania taking garrisons, cities, towns and even the ports. Desertions and disease reduced the Swedish army to only 7,000 men as Gallas closed in.

But just when the situation seemed completely hopeless, Banér received word that the Germans were pulling back. The ports and towns of Pomerania were being abandoned by the Imperial army and Gallas was evacuating the province. It was not the Swedish army that had defeated Gallas, but logistics. As hard as it was to feed Banér's small army in the devastated countryside, it was impossible to sustain the huge German army. Gallas pulled back to the Elbe where supplies were available and went into winter quarters.

With Sweden's situation in Germany in a sorry state at the beginning of 1638, a new emperor was breathing easier. Nearly all the German princes had returned to his fold. With Spain's help France was being held at bay. In December 1636, Ferdinand's son was elected emperor of the Holy Roman Empire and on February 15, 1637, Ferdinand III succeeded his father on the Imperial throne.

The Spanish war in the Netherlands had ground to a stalemate with the only significant action being the Dutch retaking of Breda which had been lost in 1626.

Over the winter Banér received 180,000 riksdalers from the Swedish government and was able to rebuild his army. In addition, 9,000 Swedish and 5,000 Finnish recruits arrived strengthening the army to 21,000 men. Pomerania had been totally devastated. The cities and countryside had been destroyed by starvation and disease. Cites overflowed with refugees displaced from farms and small towns ravaged by the invading armies. Social systems failed and the judiciary collapsed. The educational and religious organizations were in chaos. The country was near anarchy. Under these conditions it became necessary for Sweden to annex the province. Banér was appointed governor-general of a barren land, devastated population and shattered economy. He did what he could to organize a government and get the country on its feet. All of which slowed down his campaign the next season.

However, it was logistics as much as his preoccupation with local government that was the reason for Banér's immobility. He could feed his army by sea from across the Baltic as long as he stayed close to the coast. But Gallas on the Pomeranian border was rapidly depleting his supply base with no readily available new source. Disease and desertions were taking their toll on the German army while Banér procrastinated. Finally, in September the Swedish army started south.

Gallas departed his death camp ahead of the Swedes and retreated southward leaving a trail of dead and dying. The way was strewn with baggage, wagons and a devastated countryside.

Banér, as usual, moved quickly, but before he could catch up with the German army the effects of the denuded land began to take its toll on his army. His 650 man Västergötland cavalry was reduced to 300 while the Östergötland horse counted only 40 troopers fit for service. Not only the men, but also the animals died. An attempt was made to stem the wave of disease by selecting a few accused witches from among the camp followers and executing them. When this didn't help and with much of his cavalry now afoot, Banér was forced to abandon his pursuit and return north to revitalize his poor army.

Meanwhile, in southern Germany, Bernard of Saxe-Weimar and his Army of the Rhine were taken into French service, giving Richelieu a credible force within Germany.

By the end of the year Banér was once more resupplied and ready to advance on the Imperial forces. In January 1639 he crossed the Elbe and wrote to Bernard to move up the Rhine into central Germany where the two could unite. Bernard, leading an army paid by France, had crossed the Rhine in 1638 and defeated an Imperial army at Rheinfelden. He then laid siege to Breisch forcing the city into starvation. After being reduced to eating rats, cats and finally humans, including seven Swedish war prisoners, the city surrendered. However, content with this victory Bernard refused to move further in spite of the proddings by both Richelieu and Banér.

The Swedes, meanwhile, advanced on Erfurt to relieve a Swedish garrison being invested by Imperial forces. Driving away the Germans, Banér moved into southern Saxony. By February he had seized Zwickan and Chemnitz, outposts guarding the passes into Bohemia. Next he attacked the old medieval city of Freiberg. Though the walls were not up to modern standards, Banér lacked the heavy guns needed to breach them and had to settle, once again, for a protracted siege. The garrison, backed by the townspeople, put up a stout defense. Banér received word that an Imperial army was approaching to raise the siege. The Swedish field marshal decided to try a final assault on the walls. Though carried out bravely, the attack failed with the loss of over 500 men. Banér was now forced to turn and meet the new threat. He lifted the siege and by forced march met the Imperial army at Chemnitz on April 4. In spite of their exhausted state, Banér's troops defeated the Germans, capturing cannon and baggage train.

Banér marched into Bohemia and by May 20, 1639, stood at the walls of Prague. This country had been untouched by war for five years so supplies were plentiful. Again the Swedish army lacked the heavy artillery necessary to take the city. He, nevertheless, surrounded Prague and pounded it with his light field pieces which did little damage.

A Hungarian army showed up intending to raise the siege. It attacked in the old Polish style with lance and saber. Banér's hardened veterans cut them down with musket and pike. Banér was growing impatient. He could defeat the armies sent against him, but didn't have the guns to take the fortified positions and without these he could not conquer Bohemia.

In frustration he decided if he couldn't conquer the country no one was going to have it. He unleashed his cavalry regiments and infantry brigades to crisscross Bohemia looting, burning and pillaging. Contemporary sources claim over 1,000 castles were destroyed. Hardly a city, town or farmstead was spared. Starvation and disease followed the wanton destruction so that half of the population died. Rural areas were left deserted as peasants either died or fled to the cities for protection. Three quarters of the once flourishing towns and villages ceased to exist. For years afterward the Bohemian word for Swede was synonymous with bandit, thief and murderer. This period of devastation became known as "the time of the Swedes."

The new emperor, Ferdinand III, was not the stern, iron-willed ruler that his father had been and he agonized over this destruction and suffering in his realm. He sent a raiding party into Livonia led by an English colonel, Booth, in the hopes of diverting Banér from his rampage, but the Swedish field marshal made no effort to follow. The emperor tried to negotiate, but was rebuffed. Finally, Ferdinand threw all of his remaining resources into raising another army. He mustered 30,000 men which were sent into Bohemia to drive the Swedish forces out. Gallas, who had proven no match for Banér, was replaced with an Italian veteran, Piccolomini. The new general maneuvered cautiously as he entered Czech territory.

Banér was not intimidated and left only in late winter 1640 when all logistical supplies had been destroyed. Having been ill for some time, his fever worsened again as he left Bohemia in search of fresh supply sources. North, then west he moved with Piccolomini dogging his trail, but not closing for battle.

Banér sent letter after letter to Bernard and Richelieu encouraging a joint action. He would move south and the French would move east to squeeze the emperor into submission. But Duke Bernard would not be provoked. Finally, in that winter of 1639–40 Bernard died at 35 years of age. His army of 10,000 hardened veterans known as the Bernardines was enlisted by the French and placed under the command of General Guébriant.

The Spanish had been the counterbalance to the rising power of France and had for a long time been the source of money for the emperor. But now Spain had developed its own deep-seated problems. The Dutch recapture of the fortress Breda and Bernard's conquest of Breisch had closed off the land route the Spanish were using to get troops from Italy to the

Netherlands war. An attempt to supply Spanish forces by sea was stopped when a Dutch fleet intercepted the Spanish fleet in the English Channel off Dover and delivered a crushing defeat. Dutch colonists had taken a large section of eastern coastal Brazil in the 1630s. A new Spanish armada sent to recapture the area was destroyed in a four day battle off Recife. The Portuguese revolted and proclaimed their independence under the duke of Briganza in December 1640. First Barcelona, on the other side of the Iberian Peninsula, then all of Catalonia revolted in June 1640. The once mighty Spain, the largest empire in the world, was rapidly sinking to second class status.

Guébriant proved to be a more aggressive commander than Bernard. With Spain out of the equation, at least temporarily, he led a French army, including the Bernadines, east into the heart of Germany in the winter of 1640. As he advanced Count Georg of Lueneburg and the landgravine of Hesse (Amelia Elisabeth) broke the pledge of neutrality to the emperor, joining the French-Swedish alliance. Banér immediately wheeled his army around and marched south. The allies rendezvoused at Erfurt on May 7, 1640, making a combined army of 32,000 men. Piccolomini's Imperial army had shrunk to 10,000 soldiers. For the first time in six years the empire's forces were badly outnumbered. It was the allies' chance to decide the issue in one decisive stroke. However, problems cropped up immediately crippling the initiative.

Here in the middle of Germany was a huge army of Swedes, French, Lueneburgers, Hessians and the unpredictable Bernardines, each with different objectives. Banér wanted supreme command and to move southeast, going after the heart of the empire. The Hessians and French wanted to split off and go after the Spanish in the Netherlands. The French also had to be careful to maintain their supply line through the Rhineland. They had secretly concluded a treaty with Bavaria and didn't want to violate it by entering that country. The Lueneburgers were afraid of any move that would take this ravaging mass anywhere near their territory and the Bernardines just wanted high pay, good quarters and any advance that would provide an opportunity for plunder, preferably without having to fight.

Banér was an excellent military strategist and tactical commander, but his impatience and bad temper made him a poor diplomat, so little progress was made. The allied generals discussed, wrangled and quarreled while the countryside was denuded. Piccolomini received reinforcements from Bavaria, but was still lacked enough troops to attack. No major battles were fought, but there were minor skirmishes. At Chemnitz a Västergötland cavalry detachment of 300 men was attacked by 8,000 troops under the duke of Braganza. The Swedes, commanded by Johan Printz, fought for five days, but in the end capitulated. Printz and his men were allowed to retreat north to Pomerania, thence to Sweden where he was discharged. He would surface again, however, as the dynamic governor of the Swedish colony in America.

The summer campaign season was wasted by disagreement, inactivity and indecision. The weather turned wet and cold. The fall was even more miserable. Both armies suffered from disease and desertions as the resources of the surrounding countryside diminished. Finally, a sad, tired and discouraged Banér pulled out and headed north to winter quarters. The great chance to end the war in one overwhelming campaign had been squandered.

Financial help arrived from Sweden and after a short rest Banér was contemplating a winter campaign. Late fall had turned unusually cold, freezing the rivers and lakes. The Swedish field marshal reasoned that he could move quickly under such conditions, not having to worry about who controlled what particular bridge. He brought his army back to Erfurt where the wrangling continued, but then he received word that the emperor had called an Imperial *reichstag* at Regensburg on the Danube. Ferdinand III had summoned all the German princes, electors and free city representatives to an assembly. Regensburg was only 175 miles away and the Imperial army was dispersed in winter quarters. Banér might capture all the league princes and even the emperor himself. He could end the war with one stroke.

By the end of December Banér had his army moving. On January 3 he reached Auerbach. Here 500 Imperial musketeers were captured. They told the Swedes that the emperor knew about their movements and was assembling an army at Amberg to intercept and ambush them.

Banér moved more cautiously. He sent cavalry units ahead to check on the story. One detachment came across an enemy wagon train loaded with clothing. They had no idea there was a Swedish presence in the area. A second unit captured a large depot of supplies at Hasbrouck. Nowhere was there a sign that the Swedish army had been detected. Banér had lost six precious days. Now he had to move fast. He sent three regiments of horse in a headlong dash to get to Regensburg before word of their advance reached the meeting.

Then the weather changed, thawing the river ice. Banér's cavalry crossed the Danube and reached the outskirts of the city, even capturing a royal hunting party, but no emperor. Then they had to recross the river before the ice broke up. The opportunity to get the rest of the army across the ice was lost. The attempt to kidnap the emperor and league princes failed. Banér turned around, marching his army to Cham on the Bavarian-Bohemian boarder, where he went into winter quarters. The French pulled back to the Rhineland.

On March 7, 1641, Banér received word that the Imperial army had been reconstituted and was marching to cut him off once again. Piccolomini had gathered his forces for an early spring campaign in the hopes of surprising the Swedes. He had taken several Swedish garrisons on the way, but at Neunberg he ran into a stubborn Irik Slang, a one armed Swedish colonel commanding the garrison. It took two days for the Germans to breach the old medieval walls and force the Swedes to surrender, 90 officers, 180 musketeers and 1600 cavalrymen.

The stout defense gave Banér time to evacuate and head north. His rearguard and Piccolomini's advanced corps were constantly engaged. On March 17 Banér's army crossed the Eger on a temporary bridge, making it to the mountain passes between Bohemian and Saxony. The Swedish field marshal had slipped away once again, but he had suffered heavy losses and now he succumbed to disease. He died at Merseburg Castle, Bohemia, in 1641. His death was mourned by his soldiers, but celebrated in Bohemia — "the old arsonist" was dead.

With Oxenstierna's return to Sweden, Johan Banér had been the head of the Swedish presence in Germany and in the Thirty Years' War. He had kept the coastal area in Swedish hands, the primary concern, and had expanded Sweden's territorial claims over much of eastern Germany and Bohemia. The see-saw war had been conducted with a mostly mercenary army using the same scorched earth tactics as his enemies. He was a cunning and ruthless old fox who kept Sweden in the war for as long as he lived.

Clearly, Swedish emphasis had shifted from western Germany where the French were active to eastern Germany so the emperor was forced to conduct a two-front war. All sides were becoming exhausted by the grueling contest. At least Sweden was fighting on foreign soil and the country was spared the devastation wrought in Germany. And the Baltic coast remained in Swedish or allied hands keeping the all important commercial waterways open. Still the drain on resources was significant and some decisive event or campaign was yearned for, even anticipated.

18. War with Denmark as the Thirty Years' War Winds Down

As the summer campaign season of 1641 opened, the Swedish army in Germany numbered only 13,000 troops. A mere 500 were Swedes and Finns, and most of these were employed in garrison duty or were in Stålhaudské's corps in Silisia.

With Banér's death, Wrangel was left in command of the main Swedish army in Germany and he had a rebellion on his hands. Payrolls for this largely mercenary army had become undependable with back pay sometimes building up for months. As the troops became more and more restless, the colonels, as regimental commanders, banded together to support one another. They agreed that if soldiers of one regiment revolted the other colonels would put it down. Quickly the colonels learned their ad hoc organization had power that could be directed not only downward to their troops, but upward toward the generals. This "conspiracy" began making demands on the army general staff. They demanded from the generals and the Swedish government back pay and two months' future wages. The group of colonels also wanted to participate in major army decisions. By this time, Piccolomini had rebuilt the Imperial army and once again was moving north — the Swedish command had no choice but to give in to the regimental commanders. Back pay was forthcoming along with reinforcements.

After the breakup of the allied army at Erfurt, the Lueneburgian corps had returned home and invested the Imperial occupied town of Wolfenbüettel. Piccolomini with 21,000 troops was moving to relieve the siege. The Swedes, with 20,000 men, pushed to arrive first. The race to the site ended in a tie. The Swedish army had just started to dig in when the Imperialists attacked.

On June 19, 1641, Piccolomini led a cavalry charge against the Swedish right flank. This wing had had time to dig in and throw up timber works. Piccolomini's troops were caught by artillery fire at close range from entrenchments hidden by dense foliage. The Germans were thrown back. On the right flank, however, Imperial horse met Swedish cavalry which was not dug in, and these they drove back in disorder. A counterattack by two regiments of Bernardines forced Piccolomini's troops to retreat, keeping the Swedish line intact. Both wings had held, but it was in the center of the line where the bloodiest fighting occurred.

The Swedish line ran through a woods with open areas on either side. Swedish artillery was concentrated on either side of the woods providing a clear field of fire. In the wooded area Banér's veteran Blue Regiment of infantry was well entrenched. The German command meant to attack all along this line in hopes of overrunning the cannon placed at the edges of the woods and apply pressure in the woods at the same time. But the charging infantry veered away from the left and right into the wooded center to avoid the heavy artillery fire. Amongst the trees, the German formations broke up. Officers quickly lost control. The attack became a disorganized mass of men. Artillery to the right and left of the woods were turned on this mob along with the muskets. The Germans in the woods were enfiladed with grape, solid shot and musket fire from both sides and the front. Nevertheless, by sheer weight of numbers they were able to push into the trenches and drive the Blue Regiment back. A Swedish reserve brigade was brought up and counterattacked, regaining the trenches. The Imperial army had now been forced back on all fronts. Piccolomini called off the attack and retreated, leaving the siege in allied hands. Wolfenbüettel fell to the allies within a few weeks. Both sides pulled back to lick their wounds and neither army made any decisive moves the rest of the summer.

In December 1640 George William, the elector of Brandenburg, died and was succeeded by his son Frederick William, who would become known as the Great Elector. In July 1641 he issued a proclamation of neutrality and signed a two year truce with Sweden. Many of the lesser Protestant princes followed suit, distancing themselves from the emperor.

At the death of John Banér, Oxenstierna appointed Lennart Torstensson commander of Swedish forces in Germany and governor-general of Pomerania. He was raised to the rank of field marshal. In November 1641 Torstensson arrived in Germany with 7,000 fresh Swedish recruits. He spent the winter restoring discipline to the army, stiffening mercenary units with loyal Swedish and Finnish conscripts. He had trimmed away all the baggage train that was not absolutely necessary and cut back the usual huge body of camp followers that dogged all armies of that time. Thus he was able to move long distances with greater speed.

He created the field artillery as a separate arm of the army, distinct from the infantry and cavalry, with its own functions and command structure. These innovations would prove critical in the campaigns and battles to come. The Swedish army began to resemble once again the old army of Gustav Adolf in spirit and discipline. By spring 1642 he was ready to move.

He marched first into Saxony. Arnim had died a year earlier and with no inspired leadership the elector's forces were easily defeated at the Battle of Schweidnitz. In June 1642 he marched into Moravia and took the capitol, Olmüz (Omoluoc). Here he constructed extensive fortifications, making it the stronghold of Swedish occupied east Germany for the rest of the war. From Olmüz it was an easy march to Vienna which alarmed the emperor sufficiently so that he hurriedly raised a large army of German mercenaries which was combined with Austrian troops.

The German-Austrian army under Piccolomini and Archduke Leopold of Austria marched north into Bohemia threatening to cut the Swedes off. Torstensson fell back though Silesia into Saxony where he met some resistance. He invested Leipzig, which allowed the Imperial army time to close on him. Badly outnumbered, Torstensson did not want to get caught in a static position so he retreated to Breitenfeld and deployed for battle. On October 23, 1642, the Imperial army reached the field and began to fall into line. Not waiting for the German-Austrian attack and before Piccolomini could get his ranks fully assembled Torstensson led a charge against the enemy left flank. They were met by a deadly cannonade of grapeshot and solid shell, but were able to break through the Imperial line, taking the artillery positions. The Swedes turned the captured guns to enfilade the Germans, then Torstensson wheeled his troops and rolled up the German line. Piccolomini and Leopold lost half their army in the rout. The Imperial force was broken and could only retire into Bohemia. Leipzig fell to the Swedes a month later.

On December 4, 1641, Armand-Jean du Plessis, Cardinal Richelieu, died. The real political power in France and the architect of the rise of the Bourbon supremacy over the Haps-

burgs of Spain and Germany was removed from the scene. Louis XIII appointed as his successor Sicilian Ginlio Mazarini.

The French, with a better trained army and commanders that were gaining experience,
were performing favorably against the Spanish and Germans. By June 1642 they had retaken
the Piedmont of Northern Italy and were making steady progress against the Hapsburgs in
southern Germany. On all fronts the emperor was losing ground.

As the campaign season of 1643 opened, Torstensson again invaded Moravia, but was
stopped short by Oxenstierna's orders to attack Denmark. A new threat had emerged; the
back door to Swedish Germany and the homeland itself needed to be closed and sealed.

Antagonism had been building between Sweden and Denmark for some time. The old
jealousies and rivalries were exacerbated by Denmark's handling of the Sound Toll. Sweden
was supposed to be exempt by the provisions of the Peace of Knäred (1613), but Christian IV
kept imposing exemptions, particularly when shipments of arms were involved. He also raised
the toll generally to obtain financing to rebuild his military. Both the Dutch and the Swedes
were becoming increasingly weary of these Danish actions. Christian was also corresponding,
and it was assumed plotting, with the Hapsburgs which threatened both the Netherlands and
Sweden. Oxenstierna determined to put a stop to all this before the Danish military grew too
strong. The eventual excuse for war was provided by one of those side issues that makes history read more like a novel.

Maria Eleanora, Gustav Adolf's widow and the queen mother, had been deprived of any
presence in the Swedish government, even excluded from direct authority over her own daughter, Christina, the child queen. After a long period of mourning, when she would only sulk
and scheme in her castle at Gripsholm, her dislike for her adopted country turned to hate
and she began to look for a way out. Instead of openly declaring a visit to another country,
she secretly plotted with the Danish king to make an escape. In the dead of night she and a
trusted lady-in-waiting crept from her castle to a waiting carriage for an incognito journey
to Nyköping. At the port the two conspirators boarded a sloop that conveyed them to a Danish warship sent by Christian. The ship took the queen mother to Gotland Island where Christian was waiting for her with great anticipation, or at least that is what the gossip mills of the
European courts reported. Maria Eleanora, at 44, was reputed to be a handsome woman and
Christian, though now 63, was still quite vigorous as he was soon to prove in battle. The
whole "affair" became a delicious scandal that titillated the courts of Europe for months.
When the Swedish government finally determined that the queen mother had indeed taken
up residence in Denmark, it was proffered as the main reason for war. Though not quite a
Helen of Troy episode, it was still a plausible excuse to begin hostilities.

Torstensson moved his forces from eastern Germany to the base of the Jutland Peninsula where he attacked Holstein, which fell quickly. By the end of the year his army of hardened veterans was advancing through Jutland, sweeping all before it. Meanwhile, Gustav
Horn, who had returned to Sweden after eight years in German captivity, led the Swedish
home army into Skåne. By February Horn had subdued the province except for Malmö.
Swedish forces also overran Jämtland and Härjedalen as was usually the case in a Danish war.

Christian escaped to his islands and was aided by an unusually mild winter so the sea
between those islands remained unfrozen, preventing Torstensson and Horn from linking up
as planned. Christian now threw all his energy and resources into bolstering his navy as that
was all that stood between him and annihilation.

In May 1644 the Dutch sent a fleet of 21 armed merchantmen to support Torstensson in
an island hopping operation. These ships had held their own against Spanish and Portuguese

men-o-war. After defeating the Portuguese in the Indian Ocean they had been hired by Venice and performed well in action in the Mediterranean and Atlantic.

As this fleet approached Lister Dyb on the west coast of Jutland to rendezvous with the Swedes, it was intercepted by a Danish squadron of equal size commanded by Christian himself. The engagement was a draw with no great damage done to either side.

A second battle in which the merchantmen had numerical superiority was more decisive. The Dutch fleet was badly damaged and saved only because of the Dutch crews' excellent seamanship. Following this second confrontation the merchantmen withdrew and returned to the Netherlands. Apparently the larger guns and heavier hulled warships of the Scandinavian navies were too much for the merchantmen. The double hulled Danish and Swedish war ships were now superior to the men-o-war of southern European nations. The defeat of the Dutch left Torstensson and Horn stranded on either side of the Danish islands where Christian was holed up. As long as his fleet controlled the sea around those islands he was safe.

In June 1644 the Swedish fleet put to sea, sailing for the south Baltic. On July 1 it met the Danish fleet off Kolberger Heide between Germany and the Danish Islands. The Danes had thirty ships of 300 to 1,300 tons and the Swedes thirty-four of 300 to 1,700. The Swedish fleet had the windward position and attacked four times but failed to close, resulting in an indecisive battle with few casualties. However, the Danish admiral was killed, and the king wounded, receiving shrapnel and losing an eye. But Christian didn't need a big victory. All he required was to prevent the Dutch or Swedish ships from transporting Swedish troops onto his islands and that he had accomplished.

With a stalemate existing between the Danish and Swedish land forces, Torstensson turned over command of the Jutland front to Wrangle and headed south again for the heart of Germany. In August the Swedish navy returned to Stockholm and Christian, thinking the crisis had passed, decommissioned most of his navy to concentrate resources on his army to recover Skåne.

However, in August a few Dutch hired merchantmen succeeded in getting through the Sound and reached Kalmar. They were finally able to rendezvous with the Swedish fleet in the Baltic. The Swedes could sail the southern Baltic in winter because of their ports in Germany. On October 13 this combined fleet of 14 Swedish ships and 19 Dutch met a Danish squadron of 15 warships. The Danes thought this was an invasion force that had to be stopped. So they gave battle in spite of their numerical disadvantage.

Again the Dutch armed merchantmen fared badly. One ship was sunk and several were severely damaged. But the Swedish fleet captured ten Danish warships and burned two others. The Danish navy ceased to be a factor for the rest of the war except to blockade the Sound. The Dutch sent a fleet of 49 ships to the Sound and forced the Danes to let 300 merchantmen pass without paying the toll. Christian's islands were now vulnerable to a Swedish invasion. His annihilation seemed only a matter of time, but politics intervened.

On December 8, 1644, Christina came of age and gained legal control of the government. Would she be able to rest power from the regents used to having their way? Did she have the Vasa family characteristic strong will and dominant personality? She faced a determined chancellor and restive Råd. The war weary Estates were nearly in revolt, especially the peasants, who had born the brunt of the war burden. She had the war in Germany which had gone some better since Torstensson's arrival. There was the Danish war which seemed on the verge of being won. With Sweden's sudden dominance of the sea, Christian might be crushed and Denmark-Norway absorbed as additions to the Swedish realm. The eighteen-year-old queen had much to deal with and how she conducted her reign would decide the fate of her country.

19. Queen Christina and the Athens of the North

The eighteen-year-old Christina was now queen. She ruled over a kingdom that included the old Swedish-Finnish domain, Estonia, Livonia, Ingria and Karelia. Her armies occupied German Pomerania, Mecklenburg, most of Silesia, Danish Jutland, and Skåne. These last brought with them two wars, the latest Danish war and the final stage of the Thirty Years' War. The war with Denmark had become a stalemate with Sweden unable to take the Danish islands to complete the conquest and Christian IV too weak to do anything but hold on to those islands and the cities on them, most importantly Copenhagen. It was only in the waning days of 1644 that the Swedish navy had been able to gain control of the Baltic making an invasion of the Danish islands possible.

The German war, likewise, had no clear winner. France and Sweden held strong hands, able to move their armies almost at will, but could not deliver a knockout punch to the combined strength of the Hapsburgs. The emperor and Spain held on backed by Bavaria, a strengthening Austria and a growing German nationalism which fostered a hatred for all foreigners. The war had devastated the country itself and all parties were searching for a way to end the expensive and inconclusive morass. This war was complicated by the 80 year old war in the Netherlands in which the Dutch were gaining in power against a weakening Spain. There was the civil war in England spreading fear among monarchies all over the continent. For Sweden, the new power in Europe, it was a dangerous world. For the new queen it was certainly a daunting situation, but Christina was not an ordinary woman either in talents or background.

The young monarch acquired a certain amount of prestige as daughter and heir of Gustav Adolf the Great. Her father was the blue eyed, golden maned "Lion of the North," not only in Sweden and Germany, but to all of Europe. He was the defender of Protestantism who had raised his scarcely considered nation on the very periphery of European consciousness to international prominence. Sweden was now a power to be reckoned with.

Her mother was the princess of Brandenburg, a not inconsequential state surrounding the city of Berlin. At the time, it did not compare to a Rome, Paris or even London, but its snug brick and stone houses arranged on a flat plain were more cosmopolitan than the wooden houses with sod roofs gathered around the Stockholm Castle and business district.

Maria Eleanora was pretty, feminine and emotional to the point of being neurotic. She loved the arts and followed the fashion of the time even to including buffoons and dwarfs in her court. She was fluent in French, the language of the European courts, but never learned to write German correctly or even bothered to become conversant in Swedish. She brought with her German ladies-in-waiting to attend her.

By all accounts she loved Gustav deeply and could hardly be consoled at his absences. They shared a love of music, architecture and art. Gustav, though not a composer like his uncle Eric XIV, did play the lute well. They brought German musicians to the court where orchestral music and dances became the rage. But while this interest in the arts was a large part of Maria Eleanora's life, they could only be diversions for a king constantly at the battle front. These long separations along with the queen's delicate health also made the bearing of an heir problematic.

A year after their wedding Maria Eleanora miscarried and was seriously ill. In 1623 a daughter, Christina Augusta, was born, but died within a year. In May 1624 the queen, again pregnant, was in good spirits with Gustav home. She insisted upon accompanying him on a review of the navy when a storm struck, almost capsizing their boat. The queen was rushed to the castle, but a short time later a son was born dead.

The need for an heir was, by now, a matter of concern for the government with the only surviving Vasa with a claim to the throne being Sigismund of Poland. Because of this Gustav allowed Maria Eleanora to join him in Livonia at Reval in January 1626. By April the royal couple was at Åbo on their way back to Stockholm and the queen was pregnant. This time no risks were taken and Christina was born in Stockholm on December 8, 1626.

At birth the princess was covered with hair, so much so that at first it was not clear as to her gender. The queen herself and the court rejoiced at the birth of a healthy heir, but then the truth was discovered and the mood changed to despair. Gustav's reaction was characteristically optimistic when his sister, Katarina the Countess of Palatinate, brought the baby to him.

"Let us thank God, my sister. I hope that this girl will be worth a son to me."[1] Realizing the difficulty in getting the child he added: "I am content. I pray to God that He will preserve her."[2] As if verbalizing a premonition, Gustav continued: "She should be clever, since she has deceived us all."[3]

Gustav had the birth celebrated as the birth of a male heir would have been celebrated and she was educated as if she were a Swedish prince. At two years of age the king took Christina to Kalmar Harbor to review the navy. When the ships fired their great guns in salute, Gustav was afraid the child would be frightened, but she showed no sign of fear, only clapping for more. Christina was four when her father gave his great speech to the Estates before his departure to Germany and again the princess accompanied him, giving a little memorized speech following his. When he left she cried inconsolably for three days. Soon her mother would depart as well, leaving her in the care of her aunt (Gustav's sister) Katarina, wife of Johann Casimir of Palatinate.

At six she received news of her father's death and experienced all the attention that went with her new status as the "Little Queen." Upon her mother's return she was subjected to the queen mother's excessive mourning. A dark and dreary apartment with humorless buffoons and dwarfs now playing the part of servants was her world. The queen mother, who had shown little interest in her daughter previously, now controlled her every moment. Any attempt by the Regency or Råd to remove the girl to a more healthy environment met with emotional outbursts to the point where the government officials gave in entirely. Thus Christina's situation stood until Oxenstierna's return from Germany.

With the chancellor's arrival Christina's life changed completely. He had her removed from the queen mother's care. Maria Eleanora left Stockholm, retiring to Gripsholm and seclusion. It was from here she would take flight to Denmark causing the great scandal. Eventually she left Christian IV's court for Brandenburg. In 1648, with her daughter then queen, Maria Eleanora returned to Sweden to live out her days. She died in 1655.

Removed from her mother's care, Christina was placed with Gustav's half sister Katarina, the only adult Vasa left in Sweden. It was Katarina and her family who Gustav had appointed to take care of his daughter in her childhood when her own royal parents were out of the country. Now Christina was only too glad to be reunited with her foster family.

Katarina was married to Johann Casimir, a count of Palatinate. In 1622 the Thirty Years' War had forced them to flee Germany. They had taken up residence at the castle in Nyköping where their eldest son was born. Karl Gustav was four years older than Christina and the two had become fast friends. Now she was back with her adopted family and children her own age. Besides Karl there were three other sons and two daughters, Eleanora and Maria Euphrosyne. The last would later become her intimate friend.

Christina's education now began in earnest. At eight years of age the child queen was already studying twelve hours a day. She had the Vasa brilliant mind driven by her own unquenchable thirst for knowledge. Before his death Gustav had appointed two governors to guide his daughter's training. One was Axel Banér, brother of the great field marshal and close friend of the king. He was expert in arms and horsemanship, but fond of wine and women. He was always completely honest with the young queen and became a trusted advisor though he would die when she was only thirteen.

The second instructor was Gustav Horn, nephew of the famous general. Unlike Banér, he spoke several languages and had traveled widely, providing Christina with insight into other lands, peoples and especially their governments. In addition she had full access to the Regency appointed to rule in her stead until her maturity.

Here were some of the most illustrious men of her time. There was the chancellor, Alex Oxenstierna, and his brother, Baron Gabriel Gust Oxenstierna, the high steward. He would die in 1641 and be replaced by Per Brahe. There was Gustav's illegitimate half brother, Baron Karl Karlson Gyllenhielm, natural son of Karl IX. Rounding out the Regency were the grand marshal, Count Jacob de la Gardie, and the grand treasurer, Gabriel Oxenstierna, Alex's cousin.

Christina's primary instructor was Johannes Matthiae, a close friend of her father's, who guided her learning in religion, letters and science. Gustav appointed him not suspecting that he had strong Calvinist leanings and an unusual tolerance for all religions. He would have considerable influence over her and gain her affection above all others. He later became bishop of Strängnäs, but would eventually lose the position due to his religious biases aided, of course, by the jealousies and bigotry of his enemies. Christina would look after him and protect him all his life.

Thus, king and chancellor saw to it the young queen received an education that was ordinarily reserved for male heirs and Christina had the ability, drive and will to take every advantage of it. She also learned to ride well, hunt and shoot superbly. A French ambassador once said of her, "she could hit a running hare quicker than any man."[4] If the child had grown into an attractive young lady these tomboy traits might have disappeared, but Christina grew up to be slovenly in dress; she hated feminine frivolity, could swear like one of her soldiers and took her pleasure in distinctly unfeminine activities, such as riding, racing, and hunting, and when these distractions were not available, she would walk for hours, exhausting those accompanying her.

In stature she was small and plump, though she would grow thin at times due to ill health, with a classic feminine neck and bosom. She had a perfect complexion though she made no attempt to take care of it and shunned any kind of make-up except on special state occasions, and then would tolerate only the very basics. Her most attractive attributes were her full, lustrous eyes that hinted at her intelligence. Her main imperfection was a shoulder that was lower than the other, a defect she blamed on being dropped as an infant. She worked at disguising this malformation. She generally dressed in mostly masculine clothing, flat shoes, plain gray jacket, velvet cavalry cap, ruffles at her wrist and hair plainly braided. Her only concession to her sex was a skirt and that was short by the day's standards. She once said, "Some people are silly enough to be slaves and martyrs to clothes and fashion and are unhappy if they do not spend their lives between the mirror and the comb. Tidiness is only for the idle."[5]

As the young queen entered her late teens there was much speculation as to a proper marriage. Candidates abounded, both domestic and foreign. Christina had, however, already made some progress in this field. Her close friendship with Karl Gustav, oldest of the Palatine children, had developed into something more. He was handsome with dark hair, a natural leader of the Palatine band of children. He must have been a dashing figure in his cavalry uniform, donned in his late teens when he entered military service. He and Christina certainly had some kind of understanding, perhaps a secret engagement. The relationship might have developed into an early marriage, something Johann Casimir was promoting, but in 1642 Karl left Sweden to join Field Marshal Lennart Torstensson's army in Germany. Endearing letters were traded between the two during this separation. Because of Karl's abilities as an officer, he quickly rose to command a cavalry regiment under Torstensson.

Changes were occurring in the Swedish government, changes that would affect Christina's position as queen. The 1634 Riksdag made law the Form of Government, a constitution written by Alex Oxenstierna. It fixed the Riksdag as the parliament or congress though it could not initiate legislation. The king proposed laws in writing to the Estates Assembly in the Hall of State. No copies were allowed to be taken out of the building and no non-member was allowed to be present except the sons of nobles. This legislative body was composed of 500 representatives from the four Estates (nobility, clergy, burghers and peasants) placed in a systematic seating arrangement. Upon receiving the proposed legislation from the king, the Estates separated to debate and returned with written replies. They were free to accept or reject the monarch's proposals, but they had to come to an agreement amongst themselves.

The king could still issue ordinances, proclamations and grant privileges which had the effect of law, but the crown could not raise or establish new taxes or tolls without the consent of the Riksdag. The king might still get around this law by negotiating directly with the provinces, but this was difficult and produced inconsistent results.

The nobility was divided into three classes, each having a vote in the Riksdag. Thus, the nobility had the same number of votes as the other three Estates combined. The highest class of nobility was limited to families with the title of count or baron, some twelve members in 1626. The second class was composed of members of the Råd or families of former members. In 1626 there were twenty-two of these families. The third class, of ninety-two families, was composed of those that claimed the position through ancient lineage or recent government service. Economically these families might be no more affluent than the higher classes of peasants.

The Form of Government of 1634 also established a military structure that would exist until the 1925 great reduction of the armed forces. The army would consist of eight regiments of cavalry and twenty-three of infantry. Five horse and thirteen foot came from Sweden proper and the rest from Finland and other Swedish controlled territories. Each regiment was drawn from a designated recruiting area, usually a province, and the regiment would be named for the area. Thus, there was the Småland Cavalry Regiment, the Östergötland Foot, etc.

Since the time that Gustav and Oxenstierna established the regionally supported regimental recruiting system, including cavalry regiments, the old definition of nobility as families who supplied men-at-arms no longer applied. Membership was through heredity, but upward mobility was available through government or military service. The old county squire type of nobility had been replaced with "gentlemen" who were the civil servants and supplied the military officer corps. Likewise, the sons of burghers or prosperous peasants who could afford an education might rise through public service. Scholarships were available for gifted students. And in the military even the uneducated, but talented, might rise in social status. If Swedish born, the ambitious might even attain the Råd. The system wasn't perfect, but it did allow many of the brightest, most talented and industrious to rise to positions where they could do the most good for the country. In the last six years of Gustav's reign the nobility expanded from 126 families to 187.

The executive function of government was performed by the Råd and it was expected to keep the machinery of government functioning. When not serving abroad, members were required to be in their offices in Stockholm. Ten members were specifically named to stay at the capitol and run the government.

With Gustav being absent almost continually, an executive cabinet was created. This was the Regency Council consisting of the grand or high chancellor, high steward, grand marshal (of the army), grand admiral and grand treasurer. It was this group that conducted the business of the government in Gustav's absence and during Christina's minority. They expected to continue to rule even after the young queen took the throne. The aristocracy had come to dominate the government and the country.

The mid–1600s saw a boom in the Swedish economy. With Sweden in control of the Baltic, her trade and shipping grew at an unprecedented rate. Capital from the Netherlands was used to reform the already lucrative mining industry. The economy gradually shifted from one of barter to one based on currency. Crown lands and overseas holdings were sold or granted to the rich, to the aristocracy, and to new members of the nobility as rewards for service. This system produced an efficient administration of the lands, and taxes from these holdings were expected to be paid in hard currency instead of in kind. The sale of land benefited the state, which needed cash to conduct the wars, but it also enriched the highest class of nobility the most. This group of counts and barons began to separate themselves from the rest of the aristocracy by building mansions in the capital and on their country estates. They ran the Regency Council and the Råd. The country appeared to be on its way to becoming a republic of the high aristocracy, a direction Alex Oxenstierna was promoting.

Christina took her oath of office before a meeting of the Riksdag on December 7, 1644. Though the nation now had a queen in fact as well as in name, little change in government operation was expected. The Regency and Råd would continue to rule as before. But Sweden now had a queen with other ideas. The first test of wills and power was soon to come.

The war with Denmark had taken a turn in favor of Sweden. The recent Swedish naval victory had opened the possibility of Danish annihilation. Other northern countries, however, did not want Sweden to become too strong, upsetting the balance of power. They applied pressure on Sweden to come to terms. The Dutch sent a fleet of forty ships to the Sound and even Poland was making noises about becoming involved. France considered it a diversion keeping her ally from devoting full attention to the German war.

On February 25, 1645, peace negotiations opened in the little town of Brömsebro on the border between Småland (Sweden) and Blekinge (Denmark) as per tradition for wars between the two countries. Cardinal Mazarini sent M. de la Thuillerie, his ambassador, to Sweden to mediate the conference with Oxenstierna representing Sweden. Chancellor Oxenstierna wanted an agreement that would give control of the three Danish provinces on the Scandinavian Peninsula to his country, but the queen and the French pushed for immediate peace and a settlement that Denmark could live with, preventing a renewal of war.

Christina sent letters to Oxenstierna urging lenient demands and citing the Råd's urgent desire for peace. In the end the queen won though the terms were certainly favorable to Sweden. By the treaty signed in August, Sweden acquired Gotland Island, Ösel Island and the provinces of Jämtland and Härjedalen. Also, Sweden would hold Halland for thirty years as a guarantee from paying the tolls at either the Sound or the Belts. Christina was pleased with the treaty and upon Oxenstierna's return to Stockholm, gave him the title of count (the count of Södermöre), a large estate, and praised his efforts before the Råd.

Following the conclusion of the treaty, Christina fell ill, exhibiting a physical weakness that was to torment her for her entire reign. She recovered only to fall sick again with the measles. She had the Vasa mind and determination, but lacked the physical strength characteristic of her lineage.

With one war ended the young queen turned her attention to ending the other major Swedish conflict, the war in Germany. Here Sweden was also in a position of strength. Torstensson, after leaving Jutland, had once again marched toward eastern Germany. He was determined to recover Bohemian and Moravian territory lost while he was attacking Denmark. He met the first Imperial army at Jüterborg on November 23, 1644, and defeated it soundly. Bohemia was again under Swedish control.

Torstensson pushed on into Austria as Ferdinand frantically scraped together another army committing the reserves from his capital, Vienna, and incorporating troops of Maximilian I. The armies met at Jankau, a day's ride from Vienna, on March 6, 1645. The Swedes were badly outnumbered but the rough terrain prevented Götz, the Imperial general, from taking full advantage of the size of his force.

Götz deployed the Imperial forces along a series of ridges. Torstensson sent his infantry through a wooded area to attack the enemy left wing. They were successful in capturing some of the high ground and immediately moved up the field artillery. The Imperialist cavalry counterattacked, but was cut down by the murderous fire of the concentrated Swedish guns.

Torstensson then launched his own horse, including the Finnish Hakkapälites, which succeeded in surrounding the Imperialist cavalry, forcing the entire corps to surrender on the battlefield. The remaining enemy forces could do nothing but try to save themselves. The battle had been decided by the Swedish field artillery and the close coordination between all three branches of the army.

Over half the Imperial army was lost. Götz was killed and the famous Imperial cavalry destroyed. Vienna lay open and Ferdinand fled the city. Torstensson did take a bridge over the Danube to provide an entrance into the city, but his army was exhausted and he lacked siege equipment and resources for a protracted battle to take the city.

Although a Swedish army now stood at the gates of the Imperial city, Torstensson's real objective had been Moravia. He turned northeast and lay siege to Brünn. The city resisted stoutly for five months. Torstensson, now seriously ill, lifted the siege and returned to Bohemia where he turned over command to Wrangel.

On the other side of Germany, French forces had defeated the emperor's troops at the battle of Nördlingen that same year. Before the end of the year Saxony decided it had had enough and concluded a peace treaty with Sweden.

Peace negotiations to end the Thirty Years' War had been initiated in 1641. The French and Dutch were meeting with Ferdinand III's representatives at Munster. In an attempt to

divide and settle things separately with his two antagonists, the emperor arranged negotia-
tion with Sweden at a different site, namely Osnabrück. The events of 1645 brought Ferdinand to the point of near total defeat. He had lost Saxony, Brandenburg and Spain as effective
allies. A Swedish army had forced him to flee his capital. Still he held out.

In 1646 the Swedish army under Wrangel joined a French army commanded by the capable Henri de la Tour Turenne, a Protestant and student of Maurice of Nassa. The combined
force occupied Bavaria. Maximilian I signed a treaty of neutrality in March 1647 with the
two enemies providing relief for his country. Internal problems required Turenne to return
to France. Wrangel pushed ahead on his own and seized Prague. But as soon as the French
were clear of Germany, Maximilian broke his neutrality treaty and attacked Wrangel at Prague,
driving him from the city.

The last campaign of the war began in March 1648 with Turenne back in Germany and
again he combined forces with Wrangel at Ansbach. The Swedish-French army then marched
back into Bavaria where they met the Imperial-Bavarian army at the battle of Zusmarhausen
near Augsburg. The German army was defeated and fell back across the Inn River leaving the
rest of Bavaria open to the allies, who decimated the countryside to an extent extreme even
by the standards of the Thirty Years' War.

Meanwhile, a detached Swedish force under Königsmarch invaded the Upper Palatine,
then Bohemia, again leaving a wide path of destruction in its wake. Finally, the Swedes
appeared at the walls of Prague. Though his army was small and lacked heavy artillery, Königsmarch was able to take a quarter of the city because of the defection of a traitorous Imperial
officer. Königsmarch was reinforced by troops under the command of Karl Gustav arriving
from Sweden. But only a little more of the city was taken before a courier arrived with news
that there was a peace settlement.

Maximilian I had finally concluded a new peace treaty with Sweden and France. Ferdinand III then signed a treaty with both countries. Later Spain and the United Provinces
signed a separate peace treaty bringing to a close 80 years of war and recognizing the Netherlands as a sovereign state.

Taken together these treaties are called the Peace of Westphalia. The Dutch gained independence. France gained Alsace and part of Strasburg, Breisach, Philipsburg and the bishoprics of Metz, Toul and Verdun. Sweden received West Pomerania, Wismar, Stettin,
Mecklenburg and the bishoprics of Verden and Bremen, which gave her control over the estu-
aries of the Elbe and Weser rivers. With her German possessions, Sweden also gained a seat
in the Holy Roman Empire Assembly. Brandenburg picked up East Pomerania and the arch-
bishoprics of Magdeburg and Halberstadt. Lower Palatinate was restored to Charles Louis,
son of Friedrich, and an eighth elector's title was created to go along with it. Saxony kept
Lusatia. Bohemia remained a hereditary domain controlled by the emperor.

The great loser in the war was Germany. Much of the countryside was devastated. Towns
were left deserted. German and Austrian populations dropped from 21 million to 13.5 million. Bohemia, that once most fertile of all the lands, was destroyed, its population reduced
from 3,000,000 to 800,000. While the various nations haggled over the spoils, the people of
Germany turned to rebuild homes, fields, towns and cities decimated by the war. It would
recover in a surprisingly short time.

Christina had pushed for the peace in opposition to the war party of the aristocracy which
wanted more territory for Sweden. Again the young queen had won and secured peace for her
country.

With Sweden's wars winding down Christina turned her attention to making her country, one of the most powerful in Europe, into one of the most intellectually glittering. Scholars and philosophers flocked to Stockholm, some invited, some not, but all were tolerated and many were handsomely rewarded. One of the first to arrive was Isaac Vossius, who organized the royal library, cataloging the books and documents sent from conquests of the empire, particularly the war booty from Prague. Others arriving included Nicholas Heinsius, Claudius Salmsius, Johannes Scheffer, Samuel Bochart and Christian Ravius. But the most illustrious visitor by far was the renowned René Descartes. Celebrated in all Europe for his genius in the fields of physics, music, mathematics and philosophy, the prodigy had moved from his native France in 1629 to Efmond, Holland, where he had added the study of animals and the cultivation of flowers to his wide ranging pursuits. Here he had isolated himself from human contact almost entirely.

Christina had corresponded with Descartes as early as 1641 and finally induced him to come to Stockholm in 1649. She sent a ship to convey him to her capital where he arrived in October of that year. The famous philosopher and the Queen of the North spent much time together. He apparently enjoyed her company and she found his knowledge and view points fascinating. Unfortunately, their meetings were during the early hours of the day. The queen's schedule was taken up with the responsibilities of state during the day, and her evenings with social events and her constant studying. But Christina's early mornings were reserved for the French philosopher and so Descartes was obliged to make his royal visits at 5 a.m. For a man used to arising at midday and never one to overexert himself this was nearly intolerable. Still he stayed on until the cold climate and cruel schedule wore him down and he fell ill with pneumonia. He died February 1, 1650. All Europe mourned his passing. Christina was blamed for his untimely demise in the solons and courts of the continent. Indeed she may have contributed to his death by her unreasonable demands on a man of frail health.

Men of learning continued to migrate to Stockholm throughout Christina's reign, along with books, precious manuscripts and documents from all parts of the world, some purchased, some gifts and some the booty of war. The young queen succeeded in making Stockholm a center of enlightenment rivaling any in Europe. Stockholm became known as the "Athens of the North."

Besides the wars and the queen's efforts to elevate the capital's social and enlightened status, there was the question of marriage of the sovereign and succession to the throne. The primary figure in this drama was the sweetheart of the queen's youth, Karl Gustav. In December 1645 he returned to Sweden from the German wars to find a changed situation. The young girl, once his romantic interest, was now the queen, preoccupied with affairs of state, and with no intention of taking a husband anytime soon. Her attitude is reminiscent of Elizabeth I of England; both appeared to appreciate being surrounded by potential suitors, but neither had any intention of sharing their thrones. Among new interests of the queen was the French ambassador Pierre Chanut, who arrived at that time. It was with Chanut that Descartes roomed while in Stockholm. The queen took a great interest in Chanut and he became a confidant during his stay.

Karl Gustav, meanwhile, found himself shunted to the side where he could only engage in the developing political division in the government. Two parties were emerging. One, led by Oxenstierna, represented those in favor of an aristocratic form of government and was pro-war. This group also wanted to see the queen married. Members included most of the Råd and the Estate of Nobles. Opposing this faction was the queen, Palatinate count Johann Casimir, Bishop Johannes Matthiae, High Admiral Karl Karlsson Gyllenhielm (Christina's uncle), and Magnus de la Gardie.

At the 1647 Riksdag the issue of marriage was raised, but not pushed to a conclusion. A Committee of the Estates expressed the opinion that the queen should marry, but that her husband would be merely a consort with Christina retaining royal power. The young queen fired back with a proclamation to the Råd that she alone would "select the time and the occasion for her marriage and would at such time give preference of consideration to Duke Karl."[6] She also let Karl know where he stood: "that were she to marry him it would not be for love."[7]

The stage was set for a struggle between the young queen and the nobility for the control of the government, and there were plenty of examples abroad of the monarchies losing. In the Netherlands the House of Orange was caught in the same struggle and would lose after the death of William II in 1650. The French monarchy was threatened by the Fronde Revolt. In Poland, Denmark and Germany the kings and emperor were dominated by the aristocracies and in England Charles I would be executed in 1649 as Oliver Cromwell and his Roundheads took power in a bloody civil war.

Christina had taken on Oxenstierna at the peace negotiations ending the Danish war and prevailed. She had pushed hard for peace during the negotiations at Osnabrück against the efforts of the war party and again carried the day. Now it was the very power of the government itself that was at stake.

By 1647 she had probably decided against marrying Karl, but also concluded that his linage should carry on as heirs to the Swedish throne. Now began a struggle to establish the dominance of the monarchy and leave it in the hands of Karl's heirs.

Christina's first move was to have Karl appointed commander in chief of the army. She got the promotion passed by the Råd in exchange for a promise to marry Karl later. In July 1648 Karl left Sweden for the German wars expressing his desire to marry the queen.

The Riksdag of 1649 opened on January 22 and on February 22 the Committee of Estates confronted the queen with a demand to make good on her promise, to marry, at the earliest opportunity. Christina countered with a proposal that the committee appoint Karl hereditary prince and successor to the throne in the event of her death. The Estates all opposed the idea of having two potential regencies. Only the Cleric Estate showed some inclination toward acceptance. She next turned to the Råd, but met the same united front of opposition. Finally, she settled on the council representing the Estates as her best avenue to success.

At first the council was as adamant as the other government bodies had been, but then Christina played her trump card. She informed the representatives, "I declare quite definitely that it is impossible for me to marry. Such is my attitude, though the reason I have no intention of disclosing."[8] This put an entirely different light on the subject. No marriage meant no heir unless one was provided by other means. The council buckled and concurred with the queen that the matter should be brought before the Estates.

A bill was now written to be presented to the Estates naming Duke Karl Gustav as her successor. The Clergy was supportive and she enlisted the burghers. She next turned to the peasant representatives and won them over. Finally, she addressed the nobility. She made good progress with the lower aristocracy and used them against the higher levels, winning enough of the mid-level to carry the vote in the House of Nobility. By mid-March Oxenstierna grudgingly signed the bill expressing the will of the committee. Christina had triumphed once again. She had exhibited a remarkable deftness as a politician and in the process had strengthened the crown's hold on the government.

Karl, away in Germany with the army, was not happy with the events at home. He had had no voice in the proceedings and now postponed his acceptance, though it was hardly a requirement.

In the spring of 1650 Christina fell ill again and there was considerable speculation she would not survive. Oxenstierna and the Råd let it be known that they would block Karl's coronation in the event of the queen's death and would move to create an aristocratic republic.

Christina recovered, but she had seen that her efforts to secure the throne for Karl and to guarantee a strong monarchy were in jeopardy. She needed to protect both further by getting a bill passed by the Riksdag and made law. As a lever the queen was able to use the current bitter dispute between the peasants and the aristocracy. In prior days the difference between crown property, nobility lands and free peasant property was clear. On crown land peasants paid rent directly to the monarch in kind. On the noble's land the peasants paid rents to the noble who then paid taxes to the crown in coin. This was a change from the Middle Ages when the nobility was exempt because they supplied mounted troops. Finally, the free peasants, who owned their land, paid taxes in kind, directly to the monarch. But the difference between crown land and free peasant land had become blurred. More and more, free peasant land was also considered crown property, which could be turned over to nobles for supervision and collection of rent allowing the monarch to collect taxes in coin. The free peasants were supposed to retain special rights, but these may or may not be recognized by any particular noble.

Gustav Adolf, the Regency, and now Christina all continued the practice of turning additional land over to the aristocracy. At every Riksdag the peasants clamored for relief from the excessive levies placed upon them by both the crown and the nobility. Now their queen began to listen. She promised a measure of relief from the tax burden and additional levies placed on the peasants. The Peasant Estate moved to her camp. She went on to promise tax relief to the burghers and to exempt the clergy from particular communal dues. Christina further advised the Commoner Estates to demand that the special exemptions granted the nobility in paying certain dues be revoked. She won over the Commoner Estates.

But the commoners wanted to go further, to a reduction, actually reversing the prevailing process and return aristocracy lands to the crown. The one area Christina agreed with Oxenstierna on was the financial system that had allowed the government to conduct its extensive wars. She was not about to upset a system that had worked so well. On this issue she could side with the nobles without a qualm. However, she could also use this issue in her campaign. Her price for condemning the reduction program was the Noble Estate's vote for the duke as hereditary prince of Sweden. On October 9, 1650, Christina's bill was passed by the Estates making Karl Gustav and his eventual male descendents hereditary princes of Sweden. They had met her demands. Christina now held the authority of the government in her hands. The monarchy stood supreme over the country.

Surprises from the 24-year-old queen were not over, however. On August 7, 1651, Christina summoned the fifteen members of the Råd to assemble in Stockholm. She was presiding over an august group led by Axel Oxenstierna, Per Brahe and Jakob de la Gardie. Younger members included Adler Salvius and Herman Fleming. After the preliminaries, the young queen spoke. "Her Majesty finds herself obliged to inform the Council of the primary reason for this."[9]

Here she was referring to the intention to call the Estates to assemble in September. Christina told them of her enjoyment in presiding over the Råd for the past eight years. She was satisfied that the country was at peace abroad and unified at home. It was time, she said, "to hand over to Duke Karl, the hereditary prince, the government of the country."[10] She concluded by declaring that she did not need the council's advice only their approval, which was necessary for her abdication.

The Råd must have been stunned as there is no indication they had any idea of her intentions until that moment. The council flatly refused her request describing her as "wise, possessing courage and more qualified than other womenfolk."[11] No argument could dissuade them. Christina had lost the first round.

But why was the queen making this almost unheard of request? What prompted her intention to give up the throne? She answered that the nation, the duke and she herself would be better served. The nation needed a king that could lead the army into battle in times of danger as she could not. The duke's succession would be secured by the changeover now and finally there was her health, her recurring illnesses. All these were probably factors, but the deciding issue was one unknown to all except a half dozen confidents. The queen had decided to convert to Catholicism.

Christina's interest in the religion anathema to her nation might be traced back to her religious instructor, Johannes Matthiae, one of the very few men, let alone clergymen, with a tolerant view of religions.

She had learned much about the Catholic faith from the French ambassador, Chanut, who was at the Swedish court from 1646 to 1651. It was he who paved the way for René Descartes' presence from 1649 until his death in 1650. From these two men she learned the tenets of the faith.

In the summer of 1650 a new Portuguese ambassador arrived at court who spoke only his native language. He brought, as his interpreter, one Father Antonio Macedo. Father Macedo was a Jesuit priest though this was not made known to the Swedish court. Christina was not slow in figuring out the interpreter's true identity and subsequently began an intermittent dialogue with him. In August 1651 she dispatched Father Macedo to Rome to the Jesuit general requesting that two Jesuit fathers be sent to Stockholm to confer with her on religious matters.

The general replied that he would send two Italian Jesuits as requested. He selected Francesco Malines, professor of theology at Turin, and Paolo Casati, professor of mathematics and theology at the Collegio Romano in Rome. These would be two clergymen not only well versed in the theology of the church, but who would have a broad range of knowledge and be on the queen's intellectual level. The two traveled to Stockholm disguised as Italian noblemen on an excursion through northern Europe.

During private meetings with the queen they held long and wide ranging discussions on all facets of religion and other topics. By mid–May 1652 Casati was on his way back to Rome with the news that the queen had decided to become a member of the Catholic Church.

Her abdication was now mandatory. By the 1604 Norrköping Hereditary Edict, no one could be sovereign of Sweden who did not abide by the Christian religion of the nation. Further, the 1617 Religious Statutes prescribed that any person converting to the papal religion would be relieved of all inheritance and other rights and outlawed throughout the realm.

In February 1654 Christina again summoned the Råd and declared her intention to renounce the throne citing, "the true reason for this would emerge fully in time, only God knows the real motive."[12] This time she was adamant and the Estates were summoned. On June 6, 1654, the 27-year-old queen relinquished her crown.

After abdicating, Christina left Sweden for the Spanish Netherlands where she established residence. On Christmas Eve 1654 she secretly embraced the Catholic faith. The former queen of Sweden reached Rome on December 19, 1655, and was received by Pope Alexander VII.

For a time Christina was content to delve into her studies and conduct scientific experiments, but in 1657 she conspired with Cardinal Mazzarini to seize Naples and become its queen. The plot was foiled when her servant exposed her scheme to the pope. She had the offender killed in her presence, causing a scandal throughout Europe and alienating the pope.

In 1660 Christina visited her estates in Sweden and studied the theories of the philosopher's stone. By 1666 she was deep in the study of astronomy with Lubenitz. A year later she returned to Sweden in an attempt to gain the throne of Poland, left vacant due to the abdication of her second cousin John II Casimir Vasa. The campaign failed and she returned to her beloved Rome.

Christina remained politically active, supporting Pope Innocent XI in his war against the Turks and writing letters and manifestos on tolerance of the French Huguenots and defending Jews in Rome. Her apartments in Rome served as one of the great salons of Europe where intellectuals and politicians gathered. She set up an observatory in her palace in Rome and continued her studies in a wide range of subjects. She was one of the founders of the first opera house in Rome and continued to be a strong patron of the arts until her death in 1689. She is buried at St. Peter's Basilica in Rome.

As queen, Christina brought peace to her country and returned power to the throne. She enlivened the capital with culture and learning. Her father had made Sweden a world power militarily, but Christina raised the Swedish royal court to be the equal of any in Europe intellectually and culturally. She added that other dimension to complete Sweden's status as a great European nation.

20. Karl X—The Swedish Empire at Its Height

Karl Gustav, a Vasa through his mother, became Karl X of Sweden on June 6, 1654, thanks to the indomitable will and political astuteness of his cousin Christina. He was an experienced soldier and general, and would make his name as one of Sweden's aggressive warrior kings in the vein of Gustav Adolf. Karl X became king of a Sweden at peace, feared militarily and envied by its neighbors for the territories the nation had acquired at their expense.

With the geographic expansion had come an increase in population. The Sweden of Gustav I numbered perhaps a million people. The kingdom of Karl X would top 2.5 million. By conquest alone the nation would increase its population by two and one half times in less than a hundred years. With more people came more and diverse products. Trade flourished due to Sweden's control of the Baltic. An expanding economy provided Christina the means to elevate Sweden culturally, importing science and the arts, but it had been achieved at a cost. The booming economy of her early reign had been depressed by the large expenditures that did not contribute to the country's financial well being.

Karl saw as Sweden's two greatest problems the crown's weak financial position and the feeble national economy. To solve the first problem he would reverse the previous two monarchs' practice of alienating crown lands by converting aristocracy territory back to ownership by the king. In tackling the second problem his solution was to fulfill Gustav II Adolf's policy of the conquest of the Baltic rim. In particular, he would retake the Prussian towns and ports making the Baltic a Swedish lake and securing the taxes and duties from these ports and municipalities to facilitate the recovery of the Swedish economy. Control of the ports would allow Swedish merchants unrestricted access to the markets of northern Europe, further strengthening the economy.

Returning lands to the crown previously passed to the nobility is termed *reduktion* in Swedish history. At the Riksdag of 1655 Karl was able to force through a limited reduktion. Indeed, he had probably arranged for this move even before gaining the throne. The process proceeded so swiftly that he must have worked out deals with Christina, Oxenstierna and key members of the Estates Committee before his coronation. This reduktion was just a first step, affecting only land the nobility had acquired from the crown since 1632, but it paved the way for the more substantial programs that would be introduced by his son Karl XI.

At the same time the king was pushing through his reduktion bill, he was lobbying for a continuation of the foreign wars. Both these issues would test his political strength. Because Christina had both the Råd and the Riksdag formally accept Karl as her heir, Karl did not have to politick to gain the crown. He was not forced into accepting a charter at his coronation that might severely limit his authority as had been the case for the last few monarchs. The charter the new king was obliged to sign simply had him promise to do his best to keep the country out of war and required him to get the consent of the Råd and Riksdag before making changes necessary for the security and welfare of the country. The terms of Karl's oath of office restricted him only vaguely on domestic matters and not at all on foreign policy except for the anti-war clause which was considered just a formality.

Karl began preparations for war immediately upon ascending the throne. In December 1655 he applied to the Råd for the backing of a military campaign across the Baltic. The council, dominated by members of the war party, consented and Karl began hiring mercenaries which would constitute most of his army. By the time the Riksdag met in March 1655, the troops were being assembled and a cancellation by the Estates would have entailed a huge financial loss for the country. The other argument the king used was that once on foreign soil the army would pay for itself and then bring economic advantage to the homeland in terms of booty, levies and tolls collected on conquered lands. The Estates acquiesced and Karl embarked with his army in March 1655. He would be out of the country continuously until his death in 1660 except for three months in the spring of 1658 when he was in Göteburg preparing for a new campaign, and the last month of his life when he was again in Göteburg to open a Riksdag.

During his absence the government, in terms of domestic affairs, was run by the Råd and the five cabinet officers. Foreign policy, however, was conducted by Karl wherever he was located. Oxenstierna died in the autumn of 1654, leaving the chancellery in the hands of his son Erik, who died two years later. Karl did not even appoint a replacement until 1660. During the last month of his life Karl finally appointed Magnus Gabriel de la Gardie. For six years there was no strong hand in the government to oppose the king's wishes, only men with the training, experience and dedication to keep the machinery of government moving in Karl's behalf.

The reduktion was carried out by the College of Reduction which was responsible directly to the king and could not be interfered with by the Råd. The administration of crown revenues was handled by the Exchequer College presided over by Herman Fleming, who acted as an agent for the king in seeing to it Karl's wishes were carried out by the Råd. He was also president of the College of Reduction and appointed high admiral. About the only member of the Råd in a position to contradict the king was Per Brahe, the high steward. But he was generally absent from Stockholm himself, directing the defense of the southern provinces against the Danes. Thus, the aristocracy's hold on the government was weak during Karl's reign in spite of his persistent absence.

Having raised his army, Karl had to decide where to use it. Would it be Denmark at his back door, or one of the old eastern enemies, where he might take advantage of an opportunity? War had again broken out between Russia and Poland-Lithuania after a time of peace for the Commonwealth.

In 1619 Michael Romanov was tsar of Russia, but was dominated by his father, Patriarch Filaret, who returned from Polish captivity that year. Filaret, who hated Poland, would effectively run the Russian state until his death in October of 1633. In 1630 he began a rebuilding and modernization of the Russian army along the lines of western European military structure, training and tactics. Gustav had encouraged the undertaking, even helping by selling Russia modern Swedish guns and cannon, and supplying instructors. The project was well advanced, but not complete when Sigismund III died in April 1632.

The death of the monarch of the Commonwealth with its ensuing election meant no central leadership for a time and this was just too much of an opportunity for the Russians to pass up. Though not fully prepared, the new Muscovite army was mobilized and on the move by late September. Its objective was the recovery of Smoleńsk. Thirty-four thousand troops led by Mikhail Borisovich Shein took Dorogobuzh and a number of smaller forts, arriving at Smoleńsk on October 28.

Shein constructed massive trenches, building extensive siege fortifications around the city, but the campaign had been mounted so hurriedly that the heavy siege artillery had been left behind. It began arriving in December with the nineteen heaviest siege guns not arriving until March 1633.

Fortunately for Poland-Lithuania, Wladyslav IV was elected and proclaimed the new king in November 1632 without a protracted contest. He immediately prepared to relieve the siege. In February at the coronation the Sejm authorized the raising of a 23,400 man army.

While he was organizing the army, Wladyslav sent 300 men with gunpowder and other supplies to Smoleńsk. They managed to slip by the Russians and enter the city, which had been reduced to desperate straits by that time.

In early September Wladyslav arrived leading 14,000 men with the rest of the army following, including 15,000 Ukrainian Cossacks. He launched his campaign on September 7 with a series of attacks and maneuvers that forced Shein's army to abandon the siege and retreat to its main camp on the south side of the Dnieper east of Smoleńsk.

Wladyslav had Shein on the defensive and penned in so Wladyslav could operate freely in the area. He surrounded the Russian camp, placing his guns on the perimeter to shell the camp at will. He severed the Russian supply line and then sent Aleksander Piaseczyński on a raid to Dorogobuzh, some sixty miles away, where he destroyed the Russian supply base. Shein was forced to surrender. He and his army, stripped of weapons, were set on the road back to Moscow in total humiliation.

As part of the Eternal Peace of Polianovka which followed, the Commonwealth obtained recognition of its right to the Deulino territory and a war indemnity in exchange for Wladislav's renouncing the Russian throne. The Russians tried and executed Shein and his second-in-command. Their families and many of the high officers were exiled.

Shein had had the advantage in men and defensive earthworks, yet he lost the campaign even though his infantry and artillery preformed well. It was the Polish cavalry that tipped the scales in Wladyslav's favor. He outmaneuvered the Russians, trapping them in their own fortifications. Using his horse he could screen the movement of his foot and guns allowing him to concentrate forces at a single point of attack. In addition the Commonwealth's king showed brilliant military abilities, a hereditary characteristic of the Vasas.

Simultaneously with Wladyslav's success defense of Smoleńsk, Koniecpolski was defending Polish territory in the south where a combined Turkish and Tartar army of 24,500 had invaded the country. The Polish hetman, leading an army of only 11,300, met the more numerous enemy force at Kamieniec in October 1633. Taking full advantage of his superior firepower in both muskets and artillery, Koniecpolski decisively defeated the Moslem force, driving them back out of Commonwealth lands.

Flush with two victories the new king now pushed for an attack on Sweden with whom the Treaty of Altmark expired that same year. In 1635 the Sejm, still smarting from the loss of Prussian territory and angered by Gustav's encouraging the Russian attack, voted money to raise a new army of 9,000 cavalry and 11,800 infantry and dragoons.

Chancellor Oxenstierna wanted to hold a hard line with the Poles and Wladyslav wanted war. But the Swedish Regency, backed by the Råd, was intimidated by the Commonwealth buildup and with one war in Germany already was willing to deal. In exchange for the Peace Treaty of Stuhmsdorf, signed in September 1635, the Swedes returned the Royal Prussian territories to the Commonwealth, losing the associated tolls and levies. This was the treaty that Oxenstierna had complained about so bitterly, a treaty negotiated while he was in Germany.

The Sejm was quite satisfied with victories against three of its enemies, and the last without firing a shot. The Commonwealth Council contrived to curb any further outbreaks of Wladyslav's warlike tendencies. Left unchecked, the young Vasa was ready to enter the German wars emulating, he hoped, his cousin Gustav Adolf's successes and at least gobble up Silesia. He also had ambitions in recovering *his* Swedish throne from a child monarch and a woman at that. The child queen turned out to be a lot tougher and smarter than anyone expected and the Sejm saw to it Wladyslav would get no army to further his military ambitions. The Commonwealth settled into ten years of relative tranquility.

Wladyslav's reign became one of peace and prosperity for the Polish-Lithuanian Commonwealth, but it was to end in violence, plunging his country into a devastating time of war for which it was not prepared. The catastrophe began in the Ukraine, but would spread to all parts of the country as Commonwealth enemies took advantage of the country's weakness. In the Ukraine all social factions were tired of Poland's tyrannical rule by Roman Catholic, Polish speaking authorities over the Orthodox population. Especially bitter were the Cossacks whose freely elected hetman chiefs had been replaced by Commonwealth *komissars.*

In early May 1648 these Cossacks with their Tartar allies attacked a small Polish army at Zhovti Vody in the Ukraine. It took two weeks, but finally the entrenched Polish force was crushed by a coalition led by Zaporozhian hetman Bohdan Khmelnytsky. Ten days later the main Polish army in the Ukraine, some 5,000 regular soldiers and twice that number in auxiliaries, was defeated by a Cossack-Tartar force at Korsun. Jarema Wiśniowiecki escaped with 2,500 troops and left a path of destruction as he retreated out of the Ukraine. With the tangible presence of Commonwealth authority removed, the country erupted in a Cossack and peasant rebellion.

During this crisis Poland-Lithuania also found itself leaderless. Wladyslav died May 20, 1648. The Sejm hurriedly raised an army and appointed three inexperienced commanders: Mikolaj Ostroróg, Dominik Zaslawski and nineteen-year-old Aleksander Koniecpolski. With 30,000 men they marched into the Ukraine and were routed at Pyliavtsi on September 23.

Khmelnytsky reached the walls of Lwów two weeks later, carrying the war into Poland proper. Behind the city, manned by only a skeleton garrison, lay all of Poland exposed. Khmelnytsky, however, did not follow up his advantage. In exchange for a ransom, he retreated back into the Ukraine to see what the Commonwealth election would bring.

The November vote placed John Casimir, brother of Wladyslav, on the throne. The new king assembled an army and in 1651 defeated Ukrainian forces at Berestechko. A year later, however, the Polish field hetman Marcin Kalinawski led the main Polish army into Moldavia to punish the rebels. At Batoh he was caught in an ambushed and cut to pieces by Khmelnytsky.

The new Russian tsar, Alexis Romanov, son of Michael, who had gained the throne in 1645, watched the Commonwealth's plight with interest. He had been reorganizing and modernizing the Russian army. He established arms factories to produce matchlocks, flintlocks, carbines and artillery. He purchased more weapons from the Dutch, Swedes and other western countries, and he recruited unemployed mercenaries left over from the Thirty Years' War as officers, troops, and instructors.

In January 1654 Alexis's agents signed a treaty with Khmelnytsky to cooperate in a war against the Commonwealth. Again Russia's first objective was the recovery of Smoleńsk, but this time the advance would be more methodical and broad based to prevent a repeat of the encirclement that Shein had suffered. This time the heavy guns were started early so as to be on station with the army. The main army of 41,000 commanded by Ia Cherkasskii struck out directly for Smoleńsk. On the left flank were 15,000 men who were to capture Roslavl, Mścislaw and Borisov. The right flank was protected by V.B. Sheremetev with another 15,000 men advancing along the Düna through Polock and Witebsk. A 7,000 man detachment was sent south to prevent any interference from the Tartars and Khmelnytsky sent 20,000 Ukrainians into Lithuania per his agreement with the tsar. Alexis himself left Moscow in May as commander of his own regiment. A new Russian military machine was on the move to take back territories lost during the Time of Troubles.

The Commonwealth had little hope of stopping the Muscovite invasion. The Calvinist Lithuanian field hetman Janusz Radziwill had less than 10,000 troops with which to defend his country. On August 12 he successfully attacked Cherkasskii at Shkolv. But twelve days later he suffered a devastating defeat at Shepelevishe after which he retreated to Minsk. The only major field army left in Poland was sent into the Ukraine to try to quell the uprising there. Smoleńsk, with only a 3,500 man garrison, was left to defend itself.

Shein's old earthworks were still serviceable and the Russians moved in for the duration. The small city garrison fought tenaciously, but was overwhelmed and surrendered on October 3. Alexis had recovered not only Smoleńsk, but also the upper Düna, and upper Dnieper.

Karl X watched the shifting circumstances of Sweden's two old enemies for threats and opportunities while building a largely mercenary army with his country's approval. The expense of the professional soldiers could not be born for long on home soil, but where to attack? Russia was now a serious threat with her aggression on the Livonian border, but Poland's impotence provided the best opportunity. In the spring of 1655 Karl and Alexis launched simultaneous campaigns against John Casimir.

Most of the Commonwealth army was in the Ukraine under Polish hetmans Stanislaw Potocki and Stanislaw Lanckoroński, some 23,000 men. They were pinned down by Khmelnytsky supported by a Russian army of 12,000 under F.V. Buturlin. Alexis began a westward move from Smoleńsk with an army similar to the one of the previous year advancing in three divisions, the strategy that had worked so well in 1654. The two Lithuanian field hetmans Radzwill and Wincenty Gosiewski, bitter political rivals now forced to cooperate, did their best to slow the Russian advance with only 11,000 men, but were pushed steadily backward. By August 8 Vilna was taken and Alexis entered the city in triumph.

Karl, meanwhile, was attacking the Commonwealth on the Baltic side. His main objective was the recovery of Royal Prussia. Instead of landing forces in Prussia directly, he planned two campaigns; one was to hold off a Russian advance in Livonia before turning south into Poland. The other was to take Polish Royal Prussia from Swedish Pomerania. On July 12 Magnus de la Gardie seized Dünaburg up the Düna from Riga on the Swedish-Livonian frontier to block the Muscovite advance from that direction. From the west Arvid Wittenberg crossed Brandenburg with 13,650 men and 72 guns, entering Polish territory on July 21. Karl followed with additional troops. Wittenberg's opposition was an army of 14,000 conscripts hurriedly assembled. Disorganized and demoralized, this force was not up to any kind of meaningful resistance. At Ujście on July 25 the districts of Poznán and Kalisz surrendered, accepting Swedish protection and swearing fealty to Karl as their sovereign. The Swedish king with 12,700 troops caught up with Wittenberg on August 24 and the heart of Poland was open to him.

For the Calvinist Lithuanian hetman Janusz Radziwill, the Swedish entry into Poland opened up some possibilities. Frustrated and humiliated at the beating he was taking from the Russians, due mainly to a lack of support from either the Sejm or Casimir, he turned to the Swedes. Radziwill believed Poland was ready to sacrifice Lithuania to save itself from the Russian invasion. On August 17 he signed the Treaty of Kiejdany which accepted Swedish protection for Lithuania. On October 20 he attempted to split the Commonwealth Union by signing a second treaty recognizing Karl as grand duke of Lithuania. Lithuania would be aligned with Sweden, not Poland.

Poland was in a panic. John Casimir tried to rally the country. With Khmelnytsky closing on Lwów, he left Warsaw and moved west to stop the Swedes, but was forced back by Karl's advance units. He retreated to Krakow.

Karl took Warsaw on September 8, 1655. He then turned south to intercept the Commonwealth's king. Karl reached Krakow and invested the ancient Polish capital. Attempts to relieve the siege by Lanckoroński and Koniecpolski were beaten back and the city surrendered on October 19. John Casimir escaped to Silesia where he lived in exile. In the meantime, de la Gardie had conquered Kurland and crossed the Niemen, advancing on Poland from the northeast.

Overwhelmed, Polish forces capitulated. Koniecpolski, Lanckoroński and Potocki surrendered with over 15,000 troops in October. The Russians and Cossacks had taken Smoleńsk, some of Lithuania, the Ukraine and Lublin, but the Swedes had grabbed most of the prize. Karl held Warsaw and Krakow and de la Gardie was moving on East Prussia. The total occupation of Poland was almost complete. Only Lwów and Danzig at opposite ends of the country held out.

Much of Poland had been quick to enlist in the Swedish cause, but they were about to discover that military occupation came at a price. Karl had an army of foreign mercenaries to feed and pay, not to mention the Polish regulars who now joined him hoping to get back pay. Karl tried to control the looting, giving strict orders against any abuse of the population and even executing a few offenders. He levied requirements on the Polish cities of Krakow (300,000 *zloties*) and Warsaw (240,000 zloties) and instituted a system of taxation to pay his troops. He might have succeeded had he not succumbed to the temptation of persecuting the Catholic Church. To the king of the country viewed as the champion of Protestantism, the wealth of the Roman church in Poland was too much to resist.

Karl ordered the churches of Krakow to turn over 300,000 zloties to his treasury. He was informed such a staggering sum was just not available. Karl responded by authorizing the churches be stripped until the sum was raised. Once the genie is out of the bottle.... The looting began in Krakow, but quickly spread to churches, monasteries and Jesuit colleges all over the Commonwealth, then to non-ecclesiastic facilities, and finally to farms and homes. Resentment and discontent began to build among people of all social classes, but particularly among the clergy.

With most of Poland-Lithuania occupied, Karl moved north to take the real prize, the Prussian ports and trade cities. He left garrisons in southern Poland, Wittenberg with 3,000 men at Krakow and 2,000 Polish regulars of questionable loyalty at other locations. Karl invaded Royal Prussia where he faced 3,600 cavalry and 600 infantry, raised by the Prussian estates, 3,500 noble levy and mercenaries paid by the cities. Danzig was invested and a Swedish fleet moved in to blockade the seaside. With the occupation of Krakow, Warsaw and Thorn, Karl controlled the Vistula and could cut off commerce from the interior to the Baltic Sea.

The Swedish king invaded East Prussia and forced Frederick William of Brandenburg as duke of Prussia and a Polish vassal to recant his loyalty to the Polish throne and pledge fealty to Karl. Karl X had accomplished what even Gustav Adolf had not, the conquest of not just Polish Prussia, but East Prussia and nearly all of Poland. Though conditions were quite different, still it was an astounding feat that alarmed the states of Europe. Control of the Baltic was one thing, but a large Swedish land empire in Central Europe would upset power calculations all over the continent.

In early 1656 the Swedish position in Poland was similar to that of Sweden in the Thirty Years' War. The Swedes could win the battles and, with their allies, control all the major cities in the country — in this case only Danzig and Lwów held out. But, as in Germany, they could not deliver the knock-out punch. Karl's position was not secure with Swedish garrisons spread out all across the country. The large cities and strong forts were relatively safe, but the small towns and unfortified cities were vulnerable. In some cases Swedish garrisons would patrol the countryside and villages during the day, but would have to withdraw into a local castle at night.

The Commonwealth's king, John Casimir, was in exile and seemed in danger of losing his crown to the Swedish king instead of the other way around. Yet the tide had already begun to turn. Discontent with the occupation seethed across the country and by the fall of 1655 small bands of mixed noble and peasant partisans began operating throughout the Commonwealth. In Lithuania Radziwill's attempt to unite the country with Sweden failed to gain traction with either the peasants or the nobility. Most of the Polish army opposed the move and formed a confederation at Wierzbolów to continue the struggle against the invaders.

In October 1655 a band of partisans attacked a small Swedish garrison at Kościan, killing Karl's brother-in-law Frederick of Hesse. Word of the incident spread rapidly, encouraging the rising resistance movement. In the uplands of Malopolska a peasant group captured Nowy Sącz. The monastery of Jasna Góra in Częstochowa was successfully defended against a poorly organized Swedish siege.

John Casimir, recognizing the shift in momentum, issued a manifesto in November 1655 calling on all Poles to rise up and drive the invaders from Polish soil. By January 1656 he was back in Poland signing the Confederation of Tyszowce along with Potocki and Lanckoroński who brought with them much of the old regular Polish army. By February 1656, even Lubomirski, Casimir's old opponent, and Stefan Czarniecki had joined the confederation. In April Casimir arrived in the still unconquered city of Lwów and there dedicated the Commonwealth to the Virgin Mary, who was proclaimed queen of Poland. This would be a holy war to drive the heretics out. He appealed to the peasants of the country promising to improve their plight after the foreigners were expelled. Quickly, Commonwealth forces strengthened to nearly 30,000 men led by Czarniecki and Lubomirski.

Without completing his conquest of Prussia, Karl was forced to turn south to meet this new resistance gathering in the heart of Poland. His army of 11,000 cavalry met Czarniecki at Gołąb where he defeated the small Polish force of 2,400. Karl moved on to Lwów, but here he found a massive, thoroughly modern fortress. Even with the 3,000 infantry and a number of guns that had caught up with him, he didn't have a large enough force to storm the works or lay siege. In fact it was now the Swedes who were outnumbered. With the king's army down to less than 10,000 men, he left Lwów retreating north. Sapieha with a Lithuanian army of horse was coming toward him on the east bank of the San. Czarniecki with a reinforced army was moving in from the south. Karl was trapped between the Vistula and San facing potential annihilation.

Margrave Frederick of Baden left Warsaw with a force of 4,500 cavalry and dragoons to rescue the king. He met Czarniecki and Lubomirski at Warka on April 7 where the rescue force was butchered, but the diversion gave Karl the opportunity to bolt. He abandoned his guns and baggage, and drove through Sapieha's Lithuanians to make good his escape to Warsaw.

Karl was now in danger of losing everything in Poland. He needed allies who could supply troops. On June 25, 1656, he signed a military alliance with Frederick William of Brandenburg at Marienburg. In return for hereditary sovereignty over Wielkopolska he would assist Sweden with troops. Reaffirmed was his position as a Swedish vassal as far as Ducal East Prussia was concerned. German Brandenburg, though, would remain his independent electorate.

In July John Casimir arrived outside Warsaw with an army of some 40,000 men, Polish regulars, Tartars and noble levy. The ratio of cavalry to infantry was about ten to one. He crossed the Vistula to the east bank and began a march north along the river to attack the Swedish camp on that side of the river. Czarniecki with 2,000 horse stayed on the left bank to block any flanking move by the Swedish-Brandenburg forces.

Before Casimir could attack, Karl took the initiative. His army, now reinforced with Brandenburg troops, still numbered only 18,000. Like the Polish army, Karl's troops were mostly cavalry, 13,000 horse and 5,000 foot. In spite of his numerical inferiority, Karl drove head on into the Polish works adjoining the river on July 28, 1656. The Polish infantry, well dug in, held the allies off in a daylong battle.

On the second day of the battle Karl ventured a daring and risky maneuver. He pulled his infantry and guns out of the line. Using his cavalry to screen the action, he moved them around the Polish right flank and wheeled them into position creating a new front ninety degrees to the old one. Cavalry and guns were brought into line on either wing forming a complete battle line before Casimir could adjust his forces.

The Poles launched Polubiński's Hussar heavy cavalry at the right and left flanks of the Swedish-Brandenburg formation which was held by allied cavalry. The Hussars smashed into the allied lines held mostly by the Uppland and Småland horse regiments. Polubiński's 800 Hussars performed admirably, breaking through the first two ranks, but were halted at the third. The Swedish cavalry bent, but did not break and in the end drove the pride of the Polish army back into their own lines. Once again the Swedes demonstrated they had learned their lessons from the Polish cavalry and a little more of the memory of the disaster at Kircholm was erased.

John Casimir gave up Warsaw for the second time and his prospects seemed dim. But the international climate was changing rapidly. First, Frederick William withdrew his 8,500 troops from Karl's army as soon as he had taken over Wielkopolska from the Swedish garrison as agreed. A combined Dutch and Danish fleet of over 40 ships anchored off Danzig in July. They broke the blockade and were able to deliver 1,300 troops to reinforce the city's defenses. Alex declared war on Sweden in May, and Russia and Poland signed a treaty in November.

Karl moved his main army into Royal Prussia, trying to hold the territory and press the siege of Danzig. De la Gardie was in Ducal Prussia with 7,000 men which left the eastern Baltic provinces vulnerable to Russian attack. The Livonian field army was only 2,600 strong with another 7,000 troops in garrisons spread over Livonia, Estonia and Ingria.

Alexis put his army in motion, though, as usual, it took half the campaign season to get organized and moving. By midsummer he was invading the Swedish Baltics. He used the three-prong strategy that had worked so successfully in Lithuania. The smallest force was the most northern wing which raided Estonia, Ingria and Kexholm, causing devastation, but accomplishing little. To the south a 15,000 man army invested Dorpat. Further south the main army of 35,000 troops advanced down the Düna. The 3,000 man Swedish field army in Livonia gave way leaving the garrisons to fend for themselves. Dünaburg fell in July and Kokenhausen in August. A month later the Russian army was at Riga.

Riga's fortifications were modern and stronger than anything the Muscovites had run into until then. Its 5,000 man garrison easily held off the Russians even though the Muscovite heavy siege guns were employed, causing a great deal of damage. The city was open to the sea and could obtain all the supplies it needed. Eventually, the Russians gave up the assault.

At Dorpat, however, the Russians were successful. Here the medieval fortifications had been allowed to crumble and the 520 man garrison could not hold out. In October 1656 the city surrendered and Russia again had a foothold in Livonia after almost a hundred years' absence.

In 1657 Alexis mounted another attack on Livonia, but on a much smaller scale and with no success. An 8,000 man army was defeated at Walk on June 18, ending the Muscovite campaign of that year. A Lithuanian army under Gosiewski also invaded, attacking Riga and Pernua, but accomplished nothing. In early 1658 the Russians and Swedes agreed to a temporary truce. Both countries had other problems to deal with. Alexis had a new Cossack revolt on his hands and Karl's Polish-Prussian campaign was deteriorating rapidly.

After the battle of Warsaw, John Casimir regrouped at Lubin. Karl again moved north into Royal Prussia. Gosiewski led a Lithuanian army of 13,000 cavalry including a large contingent of Crimean Tartars on an invasion of Ducal Prussia. This was meant to punish Frederick William for his betrayal. He purposely spread a wide path of devastation through the countryside, something at which the Tartars were particularly adept. In addition to killing, looting and burning, they took large numbers of captives from the towns and villages which compounded the fear spread by their pillaging. On October 8, 1656, Gosiewski defeated a smaller Swedish force at Prostki, killing perhaps 5,000 allied troops. But the Lithuanian hetman was then deserted by his Tartars. After the battle they took their Prussian captives back to the Crimea to be kept or sold as slaves. On October 22 Gosiewski was himself defeated by an army of 9,000 Swedes and forced to retreat back into Lithuania.

Meanwhile, John Casimir with his reconstituted army drove into Wielkopolska, taking Łęczyca on October 4, 1656. Then he moved into Royal Prussia, taking Brombergand and Konitz. Casimir's fortunes were high as he rode unmolested into Danzig on November 15, completing the destruction of the Swedish siege. Other Polish units captured Kalisz and raided Brandenburg, further payback for the elector's duplicity.

The summer of 1656 Karl was camped at Elbing trying to maintain the Swedish position in Poland and Prussia. The blockade and siege of Danzig had been broken. Warsaw had reverted to Polish control and Krakow was under siege by Lubomirski. Karl was having trouble even maintaining control of the large cities and the small garrisons scattered across the country were quite vulnerable. Sweden could win the battles, but couldn't enforce an occupation. Karl had raised 26,400 new recruits in the last couple of years, but lost that number in Polish troops defecting to Casimir at the same time. To bring this war to a conclusion he would need allies.

In the Treaty of Labiau, November 20, 1656, Karl recognized Frederick William as sovereign over Ducal Prussia in exchange for troops. A month later he signed the Treaty of Radnot promising to back Rádkóczi of Transylvania as king of Poland, grand duke of Lithuania and recognize his control of Little Poland in exchange for entering the war.

In January 1657 Rádkóczi invaded Poland with an army of 25,000 men. He broke the siege of Krakow forcing Lubomirski to retreat. Karl and Rádkóczi joined forces along with four regiments from Brandenburg. He tried to bring Czarniecki, Lubomirski and Sapieha to a decisive battle, but the hetmans evaded any situation that would bring about a major engagement. Karl did take Brest-Litovsk in May and Rádkóczi retook Warsaw in June.

John Casimir had also been looking for allies and had succeeded in getting support from Emperor Ferdinand III by the Treaty of Vienna, December 1, 1656. However, the emperor died in April 1657 before actually supplying any troops. The next emperor, Leopold, though engaged in a contentious election, was worried about Sweden's proximity and Transylvania's aggression and agreed to send 12,000 troops. By the second Treaty of Vienna, May 27, 1657, he also promised to rush Austrian forces to take over Krakow and Poznán. Just as all these new combatants began to cross the border, redefining the war, Karl received news of hostilities at the other end of the Baltic.

Frederick III of Denmark, who had been chafing at the humiliating terms of the Brömsebro Treaty, saw the Treaty of Vienna as his opportunity. In June he declared war on Sweden and signed an alliance with the Commonwealth. Danish armies marched into Bremen from Holstein and by July his forces were in Jämtland and Västergötland. Again the homeland was threatened by the old Swedish nemesis Denmark. Karl picked 12,750 of his best troops, and marched quickly across Pomerania and Mecklenburg ready to attack Danish Holstein and Jutland. He sent Gustav Wrangel with a small force to clear the Danes out of Bremen.

He had left an 8,600 man army to defend Prussia with another 4,000 scattered in garrisons across Poland. Rádkóczi, left on his own, was no match for the Polish forces. He retreated across Poland into the Ukraine where he was surrounded and forced to surrender. Much of his army was butchered by marauding Tartars. Krakow capitulated to the Polish-Austrian siege army in August. Frederick William switched sides again, acquiring Polish recognition of his sovereignty over Ducal Prussia by the Treaties of Wehlan (September 19) and Bromberg (November 9). Elbing and Marienburg stayed in Swedish hands for some time, but by July Polish and Austrian forces had invested Thorn.

Karl, meanwhile, drove through Holstein and Jutland, crushing the inexperienced and poorly organized army Frederick threw at him. By August he was at the formidable fortress of Fredricksodde in Jutland. Modernized and recently strengthened, it was Frederick III's guardian against invasion from the south, Denmark's traditional Achilles' heel.

While Karl invested Fredricksodde, he ordered the Swedish fleet to prepare for an invasion of the Danish islands. The fleet's first task was to clear the sea and in attempting this it forced a battle with the Danish fleet off Møn which was inconclusive. With winter approaching and without clear dominance, the Swedish navy put in to Wismar. The Swedes stormed Fredriksodde in November, consolidating their control of all Jutland. Swedes and Danes both appeared to settle in for the winter, but by midwinter of 1658 the Little Belt had frozen over. On the night of January 30 Karl led 12,000 men across the ice to take Fyn from a surprised Danish garrison. The king sent scouting parties out to explore the ice over the Big Belt, but the reports were not good. The ice was too thin to support an army. However, an engineer, Erik Dahlberg, reported he had found a solid trail between the southerly islands and on February 5 Karl led 5,000 troops on a daring march from Fyn across the ice to Langeland, then Lolland and Falster to Zealand. By February 15 they were in the suburbs of Copenhagen. Panicked, Frederick signed the peace of Roskilde on March 8. As bad as the Brömsebro treaty had been, Roskilde was infinitely worse. Denmark ceded to Sweden Skåne, Blekinge, Halland

(permanently), Bohuslän, Tondheim in Norway and Bornholm Island. Karl withdrew from
Zealand to Kiel in Holstien, but maintained forces in Jutland and Fyn.

Europe was shocked at the quick and decisive Swedish triumph. The whole balance of
power on the continent was shaken. A Swedish iron grip on the Baltic seemed assured and

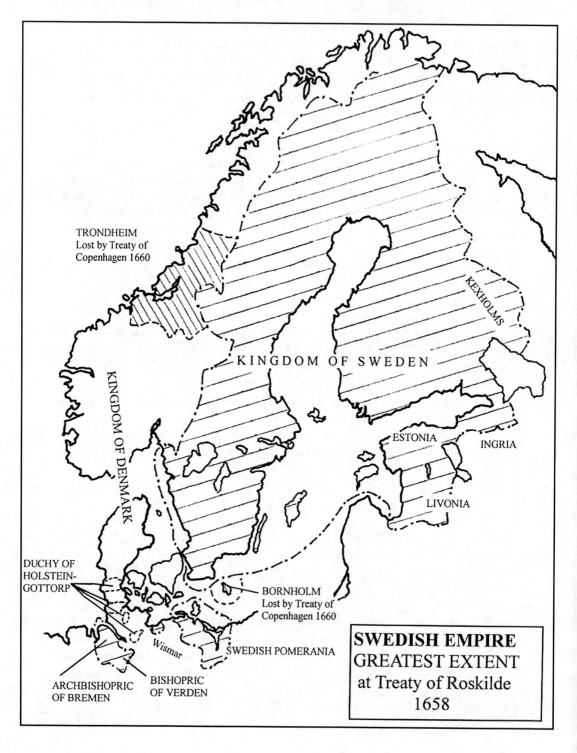

TRONDHEIM
Lost by Treaty of
Copenhagen 1660

KEXHOLMS

KINGDOM OF SWEDEN

KINGDOM OF DENMARK

ESTONIA

INGRIA

LIVONIA

DUCHY OF
HOLSTEIN-
GOTTORP

BORNHOLM
Lost by Treaty of
Copenhagen 1660

Wismar

SWEDISH POMERANIA

ARCHBISHOPRIC
OF BREMEN

BISHOPRIC
OF VERDEN

SWEDISH EMPIRE
GREATEST EXTENT
at Treaty of Roskilde
1658

her efficient, powerful armies were a threat to every country on the continent. In the hands of masterful warrior kings like Gustav Adolf or Karl X, the Swedish war machine seemed unstoppable. Karl had expanded the Swedish Empire to its greatest extent secured by treaties. True, Swedish holdings in Russia under Karl IX, in Germany at the time of Gustav Adolf and Christina, and in Poland under Karl had included more conquered lands at one time or another, but these had been lost once treaties fixed the borders.

European Sweden was now at its height in power and territorial size. Fear of Sweden's military spread throughout the continent. Only England and France were inclined to side with Sweden and even these two erstwhile allies were fickle friends.

Denmark did its best to stall on her agreement as detailed in the Treaty of Roskilde, procrastinating at every turn. Karl, in the summer of 1658, sat at Kiel with an army that could not be maintained if not used. He could plunge back into Poland-Lithuania where Sweden still held some cities and a share of Prussia or he could land in Livonia and prosecute the war against Russia. Instead, Karl decided to crush the Danes once and for all.

On August 16, 1658, he transported 10,000 men to Korsør on Zealand giving him control of both sides of the Sound. He still held Jutland and Fyn, and had ordered an army be moved into Skåne. By August 11 he was besieging Copenhagen with 5,700 troops. He had the Swedish navy blockading the city, bombarding it from the sea. On September 6 the fortress of Helsingør, 30 miles north of the capital, surrendered. Copenhagen was completely isolated and the extinction of Denmark seemed inevitable.

Europe feared the creation of a Swedish empire stretching from Ingria to Iceland, controlling not only the Baltic Sea, but much of the North Sea. Sweden would be able to control Northern and Central European maritime commerce and thereby dominate Northern Europe politically. The other European nations had to act.

England and the Netherlands had had wars in 1652–54 and 1665–67 in which both sides had built large battle fleets. The two western European countries now employed their naval might to intervene in the Baltic. Denmark had been eclipsed by Sweden as the dominant Baltic Sea power. Now Sweden was about to be challenged by the Atlantic powers. The days of Scandinavian supremacy over the Baltic were drawing to a close.

The Netherlands sent a fleet of 35 warships (some 1,800 guns), 60 cargo ships and 6 troop carriers with 3,000 soldiers to relieve the blockade of Copenhagen. On October 27, 1658, Swedish admiral Wrangel with 45 men-o-war met the Dutch in the Sound. The Swedes did not attack immediately, not sure of Dutch intentions, and thereby lost the initiative. Instead, the Dutch fleet attacked when the wind was favorable to them and a bloody six hour battle ensued. There was no clear winner of the engagement. During the battle the Dutch cargo and troop ships managed to slip past the Swedes and reach Copenhagen where they brought supplies and troops to the isolated Danish capital. The Swedish fleet withdrew to Landskrona after the battle. The Dutch had achieved their purpose. The Swedish blockade was broken.

Meanwhile, a continental army was being assembled at Hamburg to rescue Denmark from the land side. The combined force of 30,000 men included Austrians commanded by Montecuccoli, Brandenburgers under Frederick William and Poles under Czarniecki. The army marched north into Jutland. Against this onslaught Sweden was looking for support from Oliver Cromwell, with whom Karl had good relations, but the English lord protector died in early September 1658. The international army took Als Island and the fortress of Kolding. In September Swedish forces in Jutland were driven back into Fredriksodde fortress. At the end of 1658 Karl held only Fredriksodde in Jutland, which did block the allied army advance into the islands. He controlled the Danish islands except the city of Copenhagen where 10,650 Danes, reinforced by the 3,000 Dutch, held off Karl's best attempts to close out the war.

On February 10, 1659, Karl prepared to storm the city with 6,250 infantry, 2,800 horse and 1,800 sappers dressed in white camouflage. The attack failed.

On May 16, 1659, the Swedes evacuated Fredriksodden and Frederick convinced the coalition command to launch an attack against Philip of Sulzback, who was defending Fyn and Langeland. Three attempts to take the island that summer failed with heavy casualties. However, on November 24 the coalition finally defeated a Swedish cavalry army at Nyborg, forcing a Swedish evacuation of Fyn and Langeland.

Meanwhile, a Dutch-Danish fleet met the Swedish navy in a battle that could decide control of the Baltic. They were, however, interrupted by the arrival of an English fleet. The Dutch broke off the fight to defend themselves against the English, but the English had no desire to start a war and were there only to prevent further Dutch intervention. The Dutch fleet was thereby neutralized, preventing the destruction of the Swedish fleet.

In Poland Torn fell in December 1658, but the Swedes held out in Elbing and Marienburg. In Pomerania an army of 30,000 Austrians and Brandenburgers settled into a siege of Stettin. In Livonia, Mitau fell to Polubiński in January 1660.

As in Livonia and Poland, Karl was now on the defensive in Denmark. France joined England and the Netherlands in the first Concert of The Hague urging a peace based on the Treaty of Roskilde. Negotiations were begun with Karl holding out for even more concessions than Roskilde. He returned to Sweden to open a Riksdag at Göteborg.

While conducting the Estates Assembly, Karl fell ill. He died February 13, 1660, before he could conclude any of the peace treaties being negotiated. He left the Swedish Empire at its height territorially. His adventurism in Poland had been unproductive, but he had secured the southern end of the Scandinavian Peninsula for Sweden, extending the border to its present position. Though Sweden was at war with most of Northern Europe, her prestige had never been higher. Sweden was respected and feared by her neighbors, though that fear plus envy had produced a coalition Karl could not possibly defeat.

21. Sweden's Colonies and New Sweden in America

The reign of Karl X saw the far flung tentacles of Sweden's empire trimmed away. These were her overseas colonies, the possessions of New Sweden in America and Cabo Corso in Africa. Sweden's colonization efforts were aimed at developing additional markets for her iron and copper products and providing sources for other marketable commodities: furs and tobacco from America, sugar, ivory, pepper and, perhaps, slaves from Africa. The projects proved to be an overreach for a country sparse in population and still developing its own resources. Unlike Spain, Portugal, the Netherlands, England and even France, Sweden-Finland still had large areas of semi-wilderness of its own to be developed. There was little need of an outlet for an overcrowded population. Yet, in mid–seventeenth century Sweden all things seemed possible. So why should Sweden, as one of the major powers of Europe, not have her own colonial empire?

European acquisition of colonies began with Portugal's search for a route around Africa to reach the East Indies. Prince Henry the Navigator pushed his captains farther and farther along the African coast from his headquarters at Sagres where he had established his School of Navigation. First they passed Cape Bojador just south of the Canary Islands in 1433, the end of the world to Medieval Europe. Then on to Cape Verde and by 1482 the Portuguese had reached the Gold Coast, present day Ghana. Eventually, after Prince Henry's death, the Portuguese would round the tip of Africa (Dias in 1487) and reach India (Vasco de Gama in 1498) destroying Venetian domination of the spice trade. In the meantime, the Portuguese found a lucrative trade along the African coast in gold, ivory, sugar, wax, pepper, hides and slaves. Commerce was particularly profitable along the Gold Coast. Here they built a series of trading posts and forts, never penetrating far into the interior. Rather, they established trade relations with the native chiefs and kings to acquire products and slaves.

By the 17th century the Portuguese were being challenged in this African trade by the Dutch, Danes and English. Even the elector of Brandenburg would enter the fray in the late 1600s, establishing a number of trading posts along the coast of Ghana. Sweden determined not be left behind.

An African company was formed at the instigation of Louis de Geer, Sweden's main industrial developer of the age, to deal in gold, ivory and slaves. The expedition was headed by Henrik Carloff of Rostock who sailed to the Gold Coast in 1650 to plant the flag of Sweden in Africa for the Swedish African Company. Trading posts were established at Jumoree, Takoradi, Anomabu and a fortification at Accra. At Cabo Corso, Carloff purchased land from the Futu king and built his headquarters, Fort Karlsborg, in 1652. When the company did not show an immediate profit Carloff was replaced as governor. He entered Danish service and when the Danish-Swedish war erupted in 1657, he returned with a Danish force and captured the fort that same year. The Swedish African Company then sold its remaining trading posts to Denmark in 1658. In early 1660 Carloff's lieutenant, commanding the fort, sold it to the Dutch, then absconded with the money. Sweden should have retrieved the fort from Denmark at the Peace of Copenhagen in 1660, but by then it was in Dutch hands.

In December 1660 the Futu attacked Fort Karlsborg, driving out the Dutch. The Africans turned the fort over to Sweden once again. The Swedish flag flew at this African outpost until April 22, 1663, when the Dutch retook it only to lose it to the English a year later. Thus ended Sweden's bid for colonial expansion and commerce in Africa. She never had the overall commercial presence to make the enterprise profitable. Still, for some thirteen years the Swedish flag flew over the coast of Africa, one more page in the story of Sweden's Age of Greatness.

Where her colonial efforts in Africa had no permanent impact on either Sweden or Africa, New Sweden in America would have a lasting effect on both. The seeds of the New Sweden colony were planted in 1624 when a Dutch merchant and entrepreneur named Willem Usselinx came to Sweden to visit King Gustav Adolf. He was one of the founders of the Dutch West India Company but had had a falling out with its governors and was looking to establish a competitor. The two men founded the General Trading Company for Asia, Africa, America and Magellanica, also called the Old South Company. The private company raised subscriptions for money and began some initial commercial ventures. But a good share of the pledges for money were never fulfilled, including the king's 450,000 riksdaler subscription given before he left for the front, and the company foundered.

At another lull in the wars Gustav again pushed for a privately financed trading company. This time the scope was to be more limited. Voyages in European waters carrying freight for a fee would be the business. The assets and vessels of the Old South Company were transferred to this new venture. The United South Ship Company also bought an armed merchantman in 1632 named the *Kalmar Nyckel* (*Kalmar Key*) after the Kalmar Fortress. Again the company failed as did a third company called the New South Company.

With Gustav's death at Lützen, Oxenstierna picked up the quest to build Sweden's overseas commerce. He contacted a Dutch merchant living in Amsterdam for help. Samuel Blommaert was a Dutch stockholder and former director of the Dutch West India Company. Like Usselinx he was dissatisfied with the company. He was not only willing to advise a Swedish competitor, he was quite willing to invest his own money. Blummaert was particularly interested in forming a company to export Swedish copper to the African Gold Coast where it was in demand and could be traded for gold. As discussions progressed Blommaert called on an old friend for advice, Peter Minuit. The Dutchman was born in Wesel on the Rhine of French Huguenot parents. He too had been associated with the Dutch West India Company. In fact he had been director general, establishing the successful New Netherlands settlement on Manhattan Island. In 1623 he had been recalled to Amsterdam to company headquarters where he either resigned or was fired. Still filled with resentment, Minuit argued for a commercial venture in America, an area he knew intimately. These three were joined by Admiral Klas Fleming, the Finnish president of the Swedish Board of Trade and Baron Peter Spiring, a Dutchman by birth, but ennobled in Sweden. The five partners set about forming a commercial enterprise to plant a Swedish colony in "Virginia, New Netherlands and adjacent regions."[1]

In secret the Swedish government issued a charter for the New Sweden Company to be capitalized at 14,400 riksdaler. Knowledge of the enterprise had to be kept from the Dutch and English as the intended landfall would be in an area claimed by both. Half the money was subscribed by Oxenstierna, Fleming, Spiring and two other Swedes. Blommaert and five other Dutchmen came up with the remainder. The Swedish government supplied thirty muskets, a ton and a half of gunpowder, and additional money. The *Kalmar Nyckel* was signed over to the company. Company headquarters were in Stockholm, but Gothenburg was chosen as the debarkation point.

Without arousing suspicion a second smaller ship, the *Fågel Grip*, was purchased. Supplies, including spades, hoes and picks, were acquired, mostly in Amsterdam and sent to the Swedish port. Trade goods, including brightly colored cloth, wine and distilled liquors, were bought and moved to Gothenburg. A disassembled sloop was included, a boat intended to stay at the colony when the ships departed. Transportation of goods back and forth from the Netherlands to Sweden and the Baltic coast ports was so common that none of this activity raised any curiosity and so the two ships were fitted out and loaded for the voyage.

In early November 1637 the *Kalmar Nyckel* and the *Fågel Grip* set sail from Gothenburg Harbor flying the Swedish flag. Total complement of passengers and crew is not known, but were probably less than seventy. Most of the sailors were Dutch and most of the soldiers Swedes or Finns with a sprinkling of other nationalities. Two barber-surgeons were part of the company, but no women. These men were to plant crops, establish relations with the Indians and build a settlement that women and children could be brought to later.

The North America that the Swedish expedition would encounter was much different than the English Colonial America that would fight for independence a century and a half later. Russia had pushed through Siberia and reached the Pacific, but had not crossed to Alaska yet.

In New Mexico, Spain had the lonely outpost of Santa Fe marking the northernmost point of their vast American empire. The Spanish were also well ensconced in Florida with a fort at San Augustine placed there originally to prevent French incursions into their territory. France had attempted to establish a presence along the southern Atlantic coast by planting Huguenot settlements in the Carolina and northern Florida area, but the colonists had been massacred and driven out by the Spanish.

Further north the English colony of Virginia was thriving on the export of tobacco, a commodity becoming increasingly important as a trade item in Europe.

In Canada the French were well established with settlements in Acadia (Nova Scotia) and a substantial trading post at Quebec. From this outpost they could dominate the St. Lawrence Valley and trade with their friends the Algonquins and Herons, assisting them in their wars against the Iroquois.

South of New France was another English settlement, the Massachusetts Bay Colony, with offshoots already spreading to Rhode Island and Connecticut. The English were beginning to gobble up the coastline with a Virginian establishing a trading post on Kent Island in Chesapeake Bay. This outpost was reinforced in 1634 by two shiploads of English settlers landing at St. Clements Island in the Potomac River, founding the colony of Maryland. In between these English colonies was the Dutch territory of New Netherlands, the property of the Dutch West India Company. Actually, the North American enterprise was only a sideline for the Dutch commercial venture. The company's main interest was the looting of the unbelievable riches of the Spanish Main. Ships, ports, forts and settlements were fair game. Gold, silver, emeralds and pearls could be taken from the Netherlands's arch enemy in an immensely lucrative business though it was fraught with peril. The long running Dutch war of independence provided the excuse and Spanish plate fleets, ports of assembly and mining towns provided the opportunity. Precious metals and jewels were much more exciting than fish, tobacco and furs. Still, there was profit to be made even in these mundane items and New Netherlands proved to be an excellent source.

Dutch claims to the area were based on the voyage of Henry Hudson. While Canada, Florida and the Carolina coasts had been investigated early, little was known about the central coastline of Atlantic North America. Hudson, an English explorer commanding a Dutch ship, the *Half Moon*, sailed into Delaware Bay in 1609 searching for the Northwest Passage through the Americas to the Pacific and Asia beyond. On August 28 he rounded Cape Henlopen and found an expansive bay with many rivers feeding into it. It was tidal, but looked unpromising in terms of a continental passageway for the bay was full of shoals. To go further, "we must have a small *pinnasse* [a type of small boat], that must draw but foure or five foote water, to sound before him,"[2] wrote Robert Juet, Hudson's first mate. The *Half Moon* left the bay after only a one night stay at anchorage.

Hudson moved on up the coast entering New York Bay and the river that bears his name. A year after Hudson's visit, Samuel Argall, sailing for the Virginia Company, was blown off course on a trip to Bermuda. On August 17, 1610, he found shelter behind Cape Henlopen from the storm. He named the bay after his master the governor of Virginia, Thomas West, Baron de la Warr. The name stuck for the bay and the Indian tribes living along it. More information on the area was passed to the Netherlands in 1616 by Cornelis Hendricksen who explored the bay and reached the Delaware River, and by Cornelis Jacobsen May who named the cape (Cape May) on the north side of the entrance in 1620. The territory of the North River (Hudson) and the South River (Delaware) became a stopping place for Dutch fishermen and later for fur traders. Beaver hats made from the soft felt of the fur had become the fashion in Europe. The two river area was rich in beaver and the Indians were only to happy too trade for Dutch trinkets.

In 1614 the New Netherlands Company was granted a charter by the Dutch Estates General to develop the territory and give it a name. This corporation was succeeded in 1621 by the Dutch West India Company, given rights to Dutch territory in Africa and America. By 1624 they had two settlements established, a colony of Walloons (French-speaking Huguenot refugees from Spanish-controlled Netherlands) on Burlington Island upriver of present day Philadelphia, and a trading post called Fort Nassau at Gloucester across the river from today's Philadelphia. Other settlements and trading posts were established along the North River. Two of these flourished — Fort Orange at present day Albany, and New Amsterdam at the tip of Manhattan Island. The early records of these colonies have been lost, but the celebrated story of Peter Minuit buying Manhattan Island from the Indian sachems (chiefs) for trinkets worth twenty-four dollars has survived.

Minuit became director-general of New Netherlands, developing the fur trade and clearing land on Manhattan Island to plant tobacco, which he saw as a cash crop to raise money for the colony. In this he was following the successful example of the English in Virginia.

As English and French ships began to frequent the two rivers, the Dutch West India Company became worried about the vulnerability of the colony. In 1629 the Estates General of the Netherlands passed the Freedoms and Exemptions charter designed to encourage immigration. Individual settlers were granted all the land they could cultivate just for coming to the colony. This enticement was only moderately successful in inducing immigrants because of the expense of the trip. More successful was the section aimed at the company stockholders.

Any investor who settled fifty adults in America had the right to buy a sixteen mile tract along a river or eight miles on both shores. He received the hereditary title of patroon (roughly

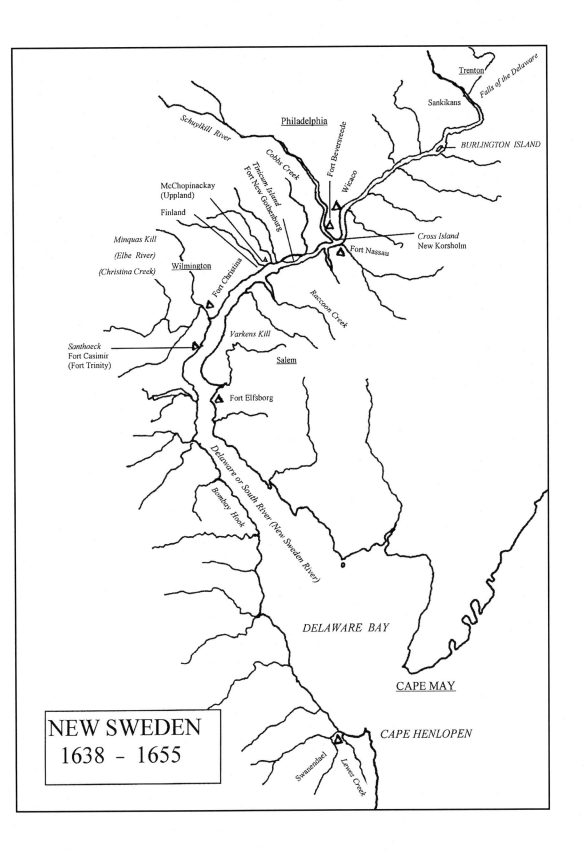

Trenton
Falls of the Delaware
Sankikans
BURLINGTON ISLAND
Schuylkill River
Philadelphia
Cobbs Creek
Fort Beversreede
Wicaco
Tinicum Island
Fort New Gothenburg
McChopinackay
(Uppland)
Finland
Cross Island
New Korsholm
Fort Nassau
Minquas Kill
(Elbe River)
(Christina Creek)
Wilmington
Fort Christina
Raccoon Creek
Varkens Kill
Santhoeck
Fort Casimir
(Fort Trinity)
Salem
Fort Elfsborg
Delaware or South River (New Sweden River)
Bombay Hook
DELAWARE BAY
CAPE MAY
CAPE HENLOPEN
NEW SWEDEN
1638 – 1655
Swanendael
Lewes Creek

equivalent to the English lord of the manor). His colonists were exempt from government taxes for ten years and were tied to the land, not able to move without written permission from the *patroon*. A patroon had the right to fish and trade anywhere in the colony. However, all imports and exports had to pass through New Amsterdam and the fur trade remained a company monopoly.

Stockholders and groups of stockholders organized colonial ventures not only in America, but in the Caribbean and South America (a large colony developed on the coast of Brazil). One group of stockholders headed by a Walloon, Samuel Godyn, and included Samuel Blommaert, organized a colony to be established in the bay of South River. An agent purchased a tract of land on Lewes Creek just past Cape Henlopen. Twenty-eight men landed at the mouth of the creek, constructed a brick house and encircled it with a palisade. They then cleared ground and planted crops to be harvested before winter. The colonists of Swanendael survived the first winter, but in 1632 they clashed with the Indians.

A second expedition arriving at Swanendael on December 3, 1632, found thirty-two corpses and the remains of horses, cows and dogs. All had been killed and the buildings burned. The two ships of the second expedition did some whaling during the winter months and explored the bay. On a trip up the Delaware they found Indians wearing English clothes taken from members of a party of Virginians that had come upriver on a sloop only to be waylaid and killed.

The expedition obtained some whale oil by hunting in the bay and traded with the Indians for furs, but not enough to pay for the venture. The investors called it quits and sold all rights to the Dutch West Indies Company. Thus, the Dutch presence on the lower Delaware below Nassau had evaporated by the time of the Swedes' arrival.

Swanendael did accomplish one thing. It prevented the incorporation of the area into the colony of Maryland. In 1632 King Charles I of England granted Cecilus Calvert, the second Lord Baltimore and a Catholic, a tract of land to settle running north from the Potomac River. This may have included land along the Delaware, but a clause in the charter said only "hitherto uncultivated land"[3] (meaning by Europeans) could be claimed. Thus, the crops planted at Swanendael removed this area from Baltimore's claim.

In early March 1638 the *Fågel Grip* and *Kalmar Nyckel* nosed into Delaware Bay. After a 600 year absence, a Scandinavian presence had returned to North America in a second attempt to establish a colony. After two months at sea the sight must have been wonderful to those on board. The west shore was sandy with stands of tall pine trees. Farther into the bay the sandy beaches turned to marshes and numerous islands covered with reeds among cypress and cedar produced a pungent fragrance that could be smelled far out to sea. The interior was heavily forested with oak, beech, chestnut, walnut, hickory, maple and ash. Among the trees were raccoons, opossums, rabbits, squirrels, deer and elk hunted by the predators: fox, bear, wolves, panthers and bobcats. Rattlesnakes, something new to the Europeans, were prevalent, but so were beaver, otter, mink, weasels and muskrat. The marshes and streams held a treasure in furs.

In the forests were occasional open areas where the Indians cultivated corn, beans and squash. The Delaware Indians of this area lived in wigwams (bark huts) arranged in small semi-permanent villages. The leader of each community was a *sachem* who held varying degrees of power depending on his political abilities. These Native Americans survived by fishing, farming and hunting, and were generally peaceful, though unpredictable. They spoke a dialect of the Algonquian language as did most of the Indians up and down the coast. To the north and northwest, however, lay the land of the Iroquois. A tribe of this linguistic group, the

Minqua, lived in the Susquehanna Valley, but had for some time raided the Delaware for food, women and slaves. By the time the Swedes arrived the Minqua had established a loose control over the lower Delaware. Similarly, the upper Delaware had become subject to the powerful Iroquois tribes of the Five Nations. Rattlesnakes and Indians were things the newcomers would have to learn about, but for the moment the scene was of trees and an occasional sighting of wildlife.

To the Dutch this might have seemed a strange land, but to the Swedes, never far from their country's ubiquitous forests, it would have looked familiar. The smaller *Fågel Grip* led, picking its way past submerged shoals that could rip a hole in a ship's bottom. Soundings were constantly taken as the vessels crossed the bay and proceeded up the river to the mouth of a creek known to the Dutch as the Minquas Kill for it was a favorite path of raiding parties headed for the Delaware villages. Here Minuit anchored his ships. This location, of present day Wilmington, had a rock ledge on the west bank next to deep water forming a natural wharf where cargo and passengers could debark directly from ship to shore.

The sloop was unloaded and assembled. A scouting party was sent up the Minquas Kill which was renamed the Elbe River, memorializing the river by the same name in Germany. Several trips were made up the Elbe to be sure there were no "Christian people" in the area. The closest Europeans would be the traders and soldiers of the Dutch West India Company at Fort Nassau a few miles upstream.

Minuit had a cannon of the *Kalmar Nyckel* fired, which brought a score of curious Indians to the site. Eventually, five sachems were located and brought aboard the *Kalmar Nyckel*. In exchange for iron pots, metal axes, glass beads, cloth and distilled spirits, the Indians deeded to the Swedes the land from the Schuylkill River to the north downriver to Bombay Hook, some fifty miles of waterfront. The Delaware Indians, who called themselves Lenape or "the Common People," understood this to mean they were granting the privilege of sharing the land with the colonists, not turning it over to them. Such misunderstandings were to lead to problems later, but for the present relations with the Lenape were good and Minuit began to construct a fort on the spot.

Four bastions were built of logs with a wall between each made of poles stuck vertically in the ground and pointed at the top. Three sides were protected by marsh and creek. The main gate opened toward the rock wharf. Inside the fort two log houses were built with fireplaces and ovens made from bricks brought from Europe. One cabin was the barracks for the men and the other a storehouse for food, supplies and Indian trade goods.

These two log buildings were the first seen in America of the Lincoln Log style construction, that is, with the logs parallel to the ground, the ends notched to fit and hold the walls in place. Until the Swedes arrived in Delaware this construction was unknown in the New World.

Immigrants from France, the Netherlands, England and Spain built houses of clapboard, boards and plaster. Later, brick and stone were used when there was true affluence.

The Swedes and Finns were woodsmen in addition to any other vocation they followed. The log structure was a staple of their construction and would become so in North America. The Swedish log cabin spread from the Delaware valley across the Appalachians to Tennessee and Kentucky, then the Ohio and Mississippi valleys. On the Great Plains it was replaced by the sod home, but reappeared as Americans approached the Rocky Mountains where trees were again abundant. The log cabin, along with the covered wagon, has become, perhaps, the most recognized symbol of the American pioneer.

Minuit named this first outpost Fort Christina in honor of the twelve-year-old queen and daughter of the great Gustav Adolf. Eventually the creek picked up the name also, but to the Swedes and Dutch it remained Minquas Kill.

It didn't take long for the commander of the Nassau garrison to discover the presence of the Swedes. Since he had fewer men than Minuit, he could only pass word of the encroachment on to the director-general at New Amsterdam, William Kief.

Kief sent a protest to Minuit, then passed the information of the new arrivals up the chain to Dutch West Indies headquarters in the Netherlands. None of this fazed Minuit who was concerned only with acquiring enough cargo to show a return on the company's investment.

He sent the *Fågel Grip* to Jamestown to buy tobacco, but the Virginians refused to sell. Upon its return, the ship was refitted and sent, on May 20, to the Caribbean to capture a Spanish ship carrying gold or silver. Minuit sent the sloop up the Delaware repeatedly to trade with the Lenape, outbidding the Dutch for pelts.

By the end of June Fort Christina was finished. Minuit felt he should get back to Gothenburg and report. The *Fågel Grip* had not yet returned and he had only a partial hold of furs, but he still had a supply of liquors and wine that might be traded in the West Indies.

Leaving Måns Kling in command of the twenty-four men at Fort Christina, now busy clearing fields and planting grain, Minuit sailed on the *Kalmar Nyckel* to St. Christopher in the Leeward Islands. There he was able to trade the wine and liquor for a cargo of tobacco.

While in port, Minuit and Captain van de Water were invited to dine aboard another anchored ship, the *Flying Deer* out of Rotterdam. During the visit a hurricane struck the island and the *Flying Deer* was swept out to sea and lost. The *Kalmar Nyckel* survived the storm and sailed to Gothenburg under its first mate Michel Symonssen.

The *Fågel Grip*, meanwhile, returned from its cruise in the West Indies without a Spanish prize, gold or otherwise. The crew acquired some tobacco and a black man originally from Angola named Anthony. He was the first African American to come to New Sweden. Loading additional furs, the *Fågel Grip* sailed for Gothenburg in April 1639.

Gross proceeds from the two cargos came to 34,000 florins, but the expedition had cost 46,000. The Swedish investors were much encouraged and believed the enterprise off to a good start. The Dutch financers, however, had higher expectations. Surprisingly, the tobacco brought more than the furs. Sweden was just beginning to acquire a taste for the leaf, first for medicinal properties, poultices, inhalants and as an analgesic, then for recreation. It was smoked, chewed and sniffed. Peter Minuit realized its potential in the Swedish market and intended to use it to finance the building of a Swedish nation in the new world. His death was a severe blow to the dream of a fast growing, vibrant New Sweden.

Minuit's untimely death was also a blow to the New Sweden Company. Its director, Admiral Fleming, pushed for a larger second expedition and received the backing of Blommaert, Spiring and Oxenstierna, but the other Dutch investors refused to sink that much money into a second voyage. After her return, the *Fågel Grip* was wrecked by a gale while at anchor. The second expedition was reduced to just the *Kalmar Nyckel*. A Lieutenant Peter Holnder Ridder, also Dutch or German, but serving in the Swedish navy, would replace Minuit as commander at Fort Christina, superseding Måns Kling. The directors hired another Dutchman, Joost van Langdonk, to manage the commissary, replacing Hendrick Huygen. He would be assisted by Gregory van Dyck, a Swedish subject though born in The Hague. Van Dyck would stay with the colony, becoming prominent a few years later. Again, most of the crew was from the Netherlands while the colonists were Swedes. Life was good in Sweden at that time and the country had its own frontier to develop. Craftsmen and artisans were in demand and had no need to search for greener pastures an ocean away in New Sweden. To complete the enlistment of colonists, the crown agreed to draft army deserters and soldiers convicted of minor offenses. Families were allowed to join this expedition. The company included blacksmiths, soldiers, shoemakers, carpenters, coopers, bricklayers and a Lutheran minister, the Reverend Reorus Torkillus. Six horses were part of this cargo for the young colony.

The *Kalmar Nyckel* sailed from Gothenburg in early September 1639 on what proved to be a difficult and contentious voyage. At sea the captain did not maintain tight discipline and crew members harassed Reverend Torkillus. The Swedish colonists, all Lutherans, sided with their pastor while the Dutch sailors and captain, Dutch Reformed Church members (Calvinists), banded together. The ship encountered several storms on the crossing, finally limping into Delaware Bay and landing at The Rock on April 17, 1640. All parties, Swedes and Dutch, aboard and on shore were much relieved at the ship's arrival at Fort Christina.

Kling had done an excellent job as chief of the little community. He had been able to control the animosity between the Dutchmen and Swedes. He had stayed on good terms with both the Lenape and Minquas, through they were enemies to one other, and he had accumulated a pile of pelts from trade with both. Thanks to Minuit's stocks of trade goods he could outbid the traders at Fort Nassau, which caused threats to be issued from both the fort and New Amsterdam. Kling ignored the warnings, knowing the West India Company would be reluctant to start a conflict that might spread back to Europe and involve the Netherlands in a war with the most powerful military on the continent.

The *Kalmar Nyckel* sailed for Sweden on May 14, 1640, bearing a cargo of furs and some tobacco acquired from independent Dutch and English growers who brought the bales of leaves to Fort Christina for trade. Hendrick Huygen and Måns Kling were also aboard. About forty to fifty people remained at New Sweden to hack out an existence on the edge of this untamed wilderness.

Arriving at Gothenburg with a full hold pleased the Swedish investors, but made the Dutch uncomfortable. Though technically both New Netherlands and New Sweden were commercial enterprises only, nationalism was beginning to touch the Dutchmen's consciences, and the Dutch West India Company was bringing pressure to bear on their countrymen and rivals.

Ridder, meanwhile, was busy extending the perimeter of Fort Christina, moving the walls out and adding more log buildings. He was also developing a community of log cabins outside the fort. He "purchased" from the Lenape additional land to the north and south of Minuit's original colony. Deeds now showed New Sweden extending from the Sankikans (site of present day Trenton, N.J.) to Cape Henlopen. The area included present day Philadelphia. The "deeded" area also included land on which several large Lenape villages were located. The Lenape certainly would not have sold this area had they understood the European concept of land ownership. This land grab and the dent the Swedes were making in the Dutch fur trade was about to bring the two rivals to a confrontation when a third and more dangerous competitor appeared.

In the spring of 1641 a sloop with twelve Englishmen on board slipped into Delaware Bay. The newcomers were from the New Haven Colony on the Connecticut River, an extension of the Massachusetts Bay Colony. The settlement had been established as a fur trading post, but found it slim pickings due to other New England competition and inroads made by New Amsterdam. Investors from the colony formed the Delaware Company to develop a fur trade on that river, which was much less exploited. The newcomers explored the river, did some trading with the Lenapes, bought land on the east bank of the river around the Varkens Kill and left a few men there when they sailed away. In 1642 George Lamberton and Nathaniel Turner, two leaders of the New Haven, Delaware, Company, returned with more colonists, including families. The colony, near present day Salem, was expanded and the English "purchased" land along the Schuylkill River on the west bank, land already deeded to New Sweden. Here they built a blockhouse and a few dwellings.

The Schuylkill site was particularly advantageous for trade with the Lenape and it lay at a crossroads of the Minquas coming to trade at both Fort Nassau and Fort Christina. The English could intercept trading parties and they were offering more goods per pelt than either the Dutch or the Swedes. The English also discovered the Varkens Kill area was suitable for growing tobacco. It looked like the English were there to stay.

At the same time the English first appeared, Ridder was negotiating with the Lenape on deeds to land on the east bank from Raccoon Creek, just below Fort Nassau, to Cape May. With deeds in hand he visited the Varkens Kill settlement and demanded Lamberton and Turner remove their people from Swedish territory. The English, of course, had purchased some of the same land and refused.

The Dutch were in a stronger position than the Swedes in dealing with this new threat to the fur trade. Kief sent two armed sloops to Fort Nassau with orders for the commandant to remove the English from the Schuylkill site, by force if necessary. The settlers at Schuylkill were herded on board the sloops at gunpoint and taken back to New Haven. The blockhouse and other buildings were burned to the ground. The dozen families at Varkens Kill were left alone as they presented no threat to the fur trade. The English encroachment into the Delaware had been turned back.

While Ridder was expanding Swedish territory along the Delaware and the Dutch were expelling the English, the New Sweden Company was organizing a substantial expedition. The *Kalmar Nyckel* was readied at Gothenburg. It would be the warship and passenger carrier of the expedition. A second ship, the *Charitas*, was fitted out at Stockholm and would be strictly a cargo ship, lightly armed. On board were horses, goats, cattle, farm implements, seed, and trade goods.

Måns Kling, promoted to lieutenant, was returning with his wife, a servant girl and a child, as was Henrick Huygen, who agreed to replace van Langdonk, who had proved to be incompetent, as a commissary officer. Perhaps as many as 50 to 60 people were recruited for the voyage including laborers, soldiers (some sent as punishment), a tailor with his wife and two teenage daughters, a millwright with his wife and two small children, a bookkeeper, an army deserter, a Lutheran preacher, a young nobleman, an adventurer, a constable for the settlement and his wife, and a prospective tobacco farmer.

As enough volunteers were not available, additional colonists were found among Finnish immigrants to Sweden's north country. These were Finns who had crossed the Bothnia to the dense forests of northern and central Sweden where they practiced a slash and burn agriculture or just roamed as hunters. The overt destruction of forest was appalling to the Swedish government and some of those Finns were rounded up and sent on the expedition.

On November 7, 1641, the two ships arrived at Fort Christina after a three month voyage. By the summer of 1642, grain and vegetable fields were producing, the livestock flourished and New Sweden had its first windmill, used to grind their grain into flour.

The colony was progressing toward self-sufficiency, but the investors wanted a return. The temporary intervention of the English had destroyed the fur trade for a couple of years. Gregory van Dyck sailed with the two ships returning to Sweden with almost empty holds.

For the profit conscious Dutch this dismal showing was the last straw. In February 1641 the Swedish government returned the original Dutch capital investment with interest. The action made the enterprise totally Swedish and brought the government into direct involvement. The chief officers of the company, Oxenstierna, Fleming and Spiring were paid by the government, receiving no salary from the company. In addition to profit there was now much interest in establishing a Swedish presence in the Americas, with Swedish customs, traditions and the Lutheran religion.

With this shift in motive and an administration firmly established, a new expedition was planned. Two ships were made ready, the *Fama*, about the size of the *Kalmar Nyckel*, and a larger ship, the *Swan*. Their cargo was tools, wine malt, grain, fish net, muskets, fabrics, horses, sheep and chickens. New colonists included Gregory van Dyck (returning) and two Lutheran pastors. Again, recruits were hard to acquire. In addition to volunteers, poachers, deserters, insolvent debtors, and more of the forest-burning Finns were pressed into service. The total complement was less than one hundred.

A new governor was selected by the company, one Johan Printz from Bottnard, Småland, the former officer in the Thirty Years' War. He was given orders that reflected the new emphasis — to organize government and administration in the name of her royal majesty, seventeen-year-old Queen Christina.

Printz was a career military officer reaching the rank of lieutenant colonel and had been knighted. He was deeply religious, the son of a minister. Described as headstrong, overbearing, arrogant and unjust, he was also intelligent, resourceful, brave, shrewd and an able administrator. He was noted for being a big man, supposedly topping 400 pounds. At age fifty he was embarking with his second wife and six children from his first marriage. He brought with him Gustav, his son, and five daughters, Armegot, Catharina, Christina, Elsa and Gunilla.

After an arduous three month voyage the *Fama* and the *Swan* arrived at Fort Christina on February 15, 1643. Two months later the two ships weighed anchor for Gothenburg with a load of beaver and other pelts. They picked up a consignment of salt in Portugal and sailed on to Sweden carrying the returning Peter Ridder who had performed his service as governor admirably.

Upon its arrival at Gothenburg, the *Fama* was refitted and returned with a few colonists, but a cargo of mostly trade goods, copper kettles, axe heads and other metal tools the Indians now demanded. Cloth, linen, shoes, bricks, flour and wine for the colonists were included per Printz's orders. The ship arrived on March 11, 1644, and was reloaded with beaver pelts and tobacco for the return voyage. The tobacco came from trade with the Virginia colony, Connecticut people at Varkens Kill, and a small quantity from the Swedes at Fort Christina.

Printz wasted no time in establishing his authority and rearranging the colony according to his plan and the director's instructions. He built a second fort across the river to the southeast just below the Connecticut settlement at Varkens Kill, which had grown to some sixty individuals. Fort Elfsborg was meant to command the river and be capable of stopping any ship coming upriver. He armed it with his heaviest guns, eight 12 pounders and a mortar. Thirteen soldiers were stationed there permanently with Lieutenant Sven Skute, Printz's deputy, in command and Gregorius van Dyck as chief of the guard.

Next, Printz moved the seat of government north to Tinicum Island near the Schuylkill River where he constructed another fort, Fort New Gothenburg, arming it with four small coppers pointed toward the river. He stationed two gunners and eight soldiers there. On the island he also built a storehouse, a *badstu* (for sweat baths), and his private mansion, Printzhoff (Printz Hall). This was a two story log structure complete with glass windows, an item previously unknown in New Sweden. The governor's mansion was surrounded by a garden and orchard.

Printz also renovated Fort Christina, strengthening the walls and bastions. He placed Lieutenant Johan Papegoja in command with only a few soldiers, Hendrick Huygen as commissary officer and his cousin Gottfried Harmer as interpreter.

A blockhouse was built at McChopinackay, two miles south of Tinicum Island, an area that came to be known as Uppland for the number of families from that province settling there. To the south of Uppland was an area called Finland because of its Finnish settlement. Additional blockhouses were constructed at Hya Vasa on the Kingsessing and at New Korsholm on Cross Island at the mouth of the Schuylkill where Lieutenant Måns Kling was stationed. Settlements sprang up around all these defensive posts.

Settlers also moved to Tinicum Island and built cabins. Printz applied for and received title to the island, becoming the first private landowner in New Sweden. Generally, the land of New Sweden was owned by the company although colonists farmed and ran livestock on it without paying rent or taxes.

Printz had a water powered gristmill built at Cobbs Creek, today's Woodland Avenue Bridge over Cobbs Creek in Philadelphia. Finally, he constructed a Lutheran church on the south end of Tinicum Island, the first in the colony. Worshipers traveled to the church from all over the colony to receive communion. Printz's oldest daughter, Armegot, was married in this church to Lieutenant Papegoja. The newlyweds took up residence at one of the new cabins on the island. They would have five children. Though Papegoja would spend much of his time on family estates in Sweden, becoming a captain in the Swedish navy, Armegot preferred America, eventually moving back into Printzhoff and reigning as the grand dame of the colony.

One of the interesting colonists was the Reverend Johan Campanius, preacher for five years at the log church on Tinicum Island. Not only did he serve Printz and the Lutheran community of New Sweden, but he worked hard to convert the native population to Christianity. Within two years of his arrival he had mastered both the Lenape and Minqua languages. He worked out a method of writing the tongues using the phonetic sounds of the Swedish alphabet. Finally, he began translating the Martin Luther Catechism into Lenape. By 1646 he had completed the work. He used his book to proselytize among the Indians for the reminder of his time in the Americas. He had some converts, but never achieved the wholesale acceptance he had envisioned. After five years Campanius returned to Sweden where he could more easily feed his several children. Though his manuscript was published in 1696, he never received the recognition due him for his pioneering work in reducing the Indian languages to a written form or his missionary work among the American natives.

Governor Printz had accomplished much during his administration in New Sweden, extending the occupied territory of the colony and constructing defensive works to protect the widely dispersed settlements, but such progress came at a cost. Some colonists moved from the colony to Maryland to escape Printz's authoritarian rule. These desertions would not have been a serious problem, but at the same time support from the mother country waned. Between 1644 and 1648 only two ships arrived from Gothenburg, the *Gyllene Haj* (*Golden Shark*) in October 1646 and the *Swan* in early January 1648. Both ships brought supplies and trade goods, but few new colonists. They returned with cargoes of tobacco and the *Swan* had a large inventory of pelts as well, but even this did not stir new enthusiasm.

Neglect of the colony was due to the changing circumstances in Europe. Already stretched thin because of the Thirty Years' War in Germany, Sweden was pushed still harder by a new war with Denmark. Worse, Admiral Fleming, the colony's chief supporter, was killed in action leaving Oxenstierna as the main advocate for New Sweden. In 1644 Christina became queen in fact, cutting into the chancellor's political power. Though both the Danish and German wars were ended under the new queen, freeing resources that might have been used to build the colony, Christina showed little interest in her American possessions. Her main concern was in developing Stockholm into the "Athens of the North." She spent lavishly in perusing this goal and little was left for New Sweden.

On July 31, 1649, a single ship, the *Kattan* (*Cat*) sailed from Gothenburg with seventy passengers and supplies. At Puerto Rico it ran aground. The Spanish, who had been fighting Sweden in the Thirty Years' War, confiscated the cargo, burned the ship and carried off the passengers and crew. Nearly all died. Only nineteen eventually made it back to Sweden. The disastrous voyage was a catastrophe for the colony. After the *Swan's* arrival in early 1648, no ships were seen for six years, not even a communication. The little colony was all but forgotten, left to survive on its own.

Printz did his best to keep his charges alive. He cut trade with the Indians and the raising of tobacco, concentrating on grains and livestock feed. What pelts he did accumulate were traded to the Virginians for food and supplies. Even so, there was starvation in years when crops were poor. His rule became more harsh and more autocratic. He even executed Anders Jönsson, a leader of an opposition group, for treason. More colonists left New Sweden to settle in Maryland. The colony dwindled to a population of less than one hundred men, women and children.

Meanwhile, Printz's aggressive expansion of settlements into new areas alarmed Dutch officials in Amsterdam, the faction of the Dutch West India Company overseeing New Netherlands. As the Dutch Delaware fur trade was cut into more and more by the Swedes, the directors began pressing Kief for action. But the governor-general was completely occupied holding the New England colonies at bay and keeping the Indian situation under control. As long as Printz did not threaten Fort Nassau, he did what he could to maintain good relations with the Swedes. In retaliation for Indian raids in the Hudson Valley, Kief ordered reprisals against Indian villages in the area. Women and children were massacred in a wanton orgy of burning and pillaging. This was unacceptable to the Amsterdam directors. Kief was recalled. On his return voyage his ship wrecked and he drowned.

The new governor-general was the famous Peter Stuyvesant. He arrived at New Amsterdam with his wife on May 11, 1647. Only 36, he had already served the West India Company with distinction in Brazil and the Caribbean, losing his right foot from a Spanish cannonball during a siege on the island of Saint Martin. A silver decorated peg leg slowed him down not at all. He was fiery, energetic, intelligent, and like Printz, deeply religious. As supervisor of New Netherlands, he also retained governorship of the Dutch Caribbean possessions, Curacao, Buenaire and Aruba. Among his instructions from the Amsterdam directors were orders to curtail Swedish interference with the Dutch Delaware fur trade.

Before he left, Kief had sent a new commandant to Fort Nassau, Andries Hudde. The two had started a project to persuade Dutch colonists from New Amsterdam to move and settle in the Schuylkill area in what is now a suburb of Philadelphia. Hudde recognized, as the English had earlier, that this was the key to dominating the Minqua fur trade. To entice settlers, Kief afforded land ownership and the right to trade privately for furs. A few entrepreneurs moved to the Schuylkill, laid out farms and began an aggressive trade with the Indians. They outhustled the Dutch at Fort Nassau and the Swedes, both of whom maintained the company monopoly on fur trading. When Stuyvesant arrived he continued the effort to settle the Schuylkill, even constructing a blockhouse on its east bank naming it Fort Beversreede (Beaver Road).

Printz was furious at this intrusion into Swedish territory, but he didn't have a force large enough to oust the interlopers. All he could do was launch surprise raids against the newcomers to harass them. The Swedes knew the area intimately and could range throughout the forests without being detected. They tore down fences, and even the stockade around Fort Beversreede. Hudde could do little to prevent the harassment and gradually the Dutch settlers became disenchanted with their prospects at the new site.

The settlement tactic wasn't working. Stuyvesant studied the situation and devised a new solution. He organized a force of 120 men, an army in this part of the world, perhaps 10 percent of the total population of New Netherlands. He marched this force overland to Fort Nassau while sending a fleet of eleven ships from New Amsterdam to Fort Nassau. Fort Elfsborg, established to block unwanted traffic passing up the Delaware, did not fire a shot in response to this awesome display of military power. The five or six soldiers at the fort merely watched as the ships passed by, firing cannon for show.

Stuyvesant had demonstrated his military superiority and could now do what he liked on the Delaware. He did not attack or molest the Swedes directly, but merely moved the location of the Dutch fort on the river. Printz had effectively emasculated Fort Nassau by locating forts and blockhouses in strategic locations along the river, but Stuyvesant was an experienced military officer and had spotted a weakness in the Swedish defenses.

Six miles below Fort Christina was an earthen promontory that jutted out into the river. It was called Santhoeck meaning "Sand Point," and was located where New Castle is today. Like The Rock, it rose vertically out of the deep water in the river so that ships could dock and unload without the need for small ferry boats. Stuyvesant bought Santhoeck and the surrounding area from the Lenapes, land already sold to the Swedes. He put his army and navy to work constructing a new citadel which he named Fort Casimir. The move was a stroke of genius. A high area located out in the river with a natural wharf, it was the strategic point on the lower Delaware. Artillery here would command the river. Fort Elfsborg was rendered impotent. Fort Christina and Fort New Gothenburg could be cut off at Dutch discretion.

Fort Nassau was dismantled. Cannon, supplies, company traders and soldiers were moved to the new stronghold. Even Fort Beversreede was torn down and the Dutch settlers along the Schuylkill moved to Santhoeck where Stuyvesant envisioned a Dutch enclave developing on the order of New Amsterdam. Work on the fort began in mid–July 1651 and structures were near completion by month's end. Stuyvesant left sufficient soldiers in the garrison to discourage any mischief from the Swedes. To make sure he stationed two of the armed vassals at the wharf. Printz had been outmaneuvered.

Outflanked defensively, supplies long since exhausted, colonist numbers declining due to disease and desertions, Printz was at the point of desperation. Finally, in October 1655 he left New Sweden with his wife, four of his daughters and 25 soldiers and settlers including Hendrick Huygen. The party traveled to New Amsterdam where Printz arranged passage to Amsterdam on a Dutch vessel. Lieutenant Papegoja was left in charge of the colony. His wife, Armegot, Printz's eldest daughter, also stayed. The governor's plan was to raise a new expedition to America bringing trade goods, supplies, and settlers.

Fortunately, for the colony, Stuyvesant did not follow up his advantage on the Delaware. He was being pressed more and more by an ever expanding New England colony made doubly dangerous by a new war between England and the Netherlands. He had to strengthen his defenses at New Amsterdam and along the Hudson, even recalling some of the troops he'd left at Fort Casimir. All warships were pressed into service to guard the waters around the North River. The settlement at Santhoeck never developed the way Stuyvesant planned. So the question of control of the South River remained unsettled and both factions languished in neglect from their sponsors.

Renewed interest in the settlements along the Delaware came first in Sweden. Management of the New Sweden Company was entrusted to the Commercial College, a branch of the government similar to the U.S. Department of Commerce. It was headed by Eric Oxenstierna, son of the chancellor. He took an interest in the American colony and appointed Johan Rising, secretary of the college, as commander of an expedition to the Delaware. The *Örn* (*Eagle*), a 40 gun warship captured from Denmark, was fitted out and loaded with supplies and 350 passengers. This time law-breakers were forbidden from taking part. The formerly booming economy in Sweden had subsided and there were far more would-be colonists than there were accommodations. An epidemic in eastern Sweden prompted additional families to leave.

An overcrowded ship sailed from Gothenburg on February 2, 1654, with Rising in charge. He was an economist and recognized authority on commerce, trade and agriculture having studied in several European countries. He was to be assistant to Printz whose departure was unknown in Sweden. Before leaving he was knighted by the queen and given the right to a tract of land in the colony, only the second time private property had been allotted by the company.

While Printz was sailing to Amsterdam, the *Örn* battled its way across the Atlantic through storms and a plague that broke out aboard ship. More than one hundred people died and were buried at sea. On May 20 the exhausted crew and passengers pulled into Delaware Bay. They anchored opposite Fort Elfsborg, which they found to be deserted and in ruins. Neglect and mosquitoes had driven the last of the soldiers from their posts and the structure had crumbled. Nearby Fort Casimir had fared little better.

The commandant, Sergeant Gerrit Bieker, had only nine Dutch soldiers to man the thirteen cannon intended to control river passage. With a fort fallen into disrepair and without powder for cannon or musket his position was extremely weak. He sent a boat with five Dutchmen out to the warship flying the Swedish colors.

On board Rising received the delegation warmly and learned that Fort Christina and Fort Gothenburg on Tinicum Island were still in Swedish hands. The next day was Trinity Sunday. After church services aboard ship Rising moved the *Örn* to the Santhoeck wharf and fired his cannon. There was no answer from the fort. He sent Captain Sven Skute, his military commander, and Lieutenant Ekias Gyllengren ashore with twenty musketeers to call on Sergeant Bieker. An exchange of messages began between Bieker and Rising that culminated in the surrender of the fort by day's end. The flag of the Netherlands was lowered and replaced by the Swedish colors in a bloodless coup.

The twenty or so Dutch families that lived in and around the fort were unmolested, but were required to pledge their loyalty to the Swedish crown as were Bieker, Hudde and the soldiers at the fort. Six of the soldiers chose to leave for New Amsterdam.

The fort was renamed Fort Tefldighet (Fort Trinity) in honor of the day. Rising left Lieutenant Gyllengren in command with the twenty musketeers while he sailed upriver to Fort Christina where the passengers disembarked. They were taken into the homes of the remaining colonists, who were overjoyed at having the new arrivals with supplies and news from home. The colony's population jumped from less than one hundred to over three hundred. However, the plague that had dogged the passengers and crew quickly spread to the colony, then to the Lenapes where entire families were wiped out, increasing the animosity between the two cultures.

Rising established a provisional government with himself as director, Captain Skute as military commander and Johan Papegoja as vice director. Andreis Huddle was hired to assist Rising in making maps and arranging affairs with the Indians. Captain Skute, assisted by 21-year-old Peter Lindeström, who had studied mathematics and the science of fortifications at Uppsala University, began repairing and remodeling Fort Trinity. The Dutch around the fort were pressed into contributing fourteen days of labor to this work, which caused discontent. The Reverend Peter Hiört, a passenger on the *Örn*, was assigned as the Lutheran pastor at Fort Trinity where there was no Dutch Reformed minister. This, combined with the imposition of the Swedish legal system, made the Dutch settlers uncomfortable and one by one the families left for New Amsterdam. Their homes were quickly occupied by the new Swedish arrivals until by June 1655 all the Dutch had left Santhoeck.

Rising was an economist by training and recognized the need to unleash the power of free enterprise. He granted the colonists the right to trade with the Indians and other Europeans for furs. They were also allowed to purchase their own land from the New Sweden Company or from the Indians. The land use had never been a problem for the colonists, but this new right was greeted with enthusiasm. The freedom to trade in furs led to a boom in this industry, cutting further into the Dutch fur business as the Swedes extended their activity beyond the Lenapes and Minquas into Mohawk territory, formerly the preserve of the Dutch at Fort Orange (Albany).

Rising moved the capital of the colony from Tinicum Island back to Fort Christina. He laid out his own tract of land north of Brandywine and Skillpaddskylen creeks and here he built his own two story mansion. Armegot Printz Papegoja moved back to Printzhoff with her children when her husband returned to Sweden. She would reign as the unofficial queen of the colony until her death. Though food was short because of the new arrivals and Rising had to buy supplies from the Lenapes, Virginians and New Englanders of Connecticut, he was optimistic. The supply ship *Gyllene Haj* (*Golden Shark*), which was to have sailed with the *Örn* but had been delayed, was expected any day. Where the *Örn* had brought the bulk of the colonists, the *Gyllene Haj* was loaded with food, tools, clothing and trade goods which would supply New Sweden through the coming winter.

In June 1655 Jacob Swensson returned from the Susquehanna country with four Minquas chiefs who offered land along the river as a gift. In return they wanted trading posts, blacksmiths and gunsmiths settled in this more westerly extension of New Sweden. This would also provide the Swedes with direct access to Minquas furs, further undercutting the Dutch and English. The colony's future seemed assured. Then the first of a series of devastating events occurred.

In September Rising learned from merchants in Hartford that the much anticipated *Gyllene Haj* had put in at New Amsterdam on its way to the Delaware. Stuyvesant, furious at Rising's capture of Fort Casimir, had taken the ship. The cargo was sold off and the passengers put ashore on Manhattan Island. The ship was put into service with the Dutch company. Only five people managed to find their way overland to New Sweden: Nerick Van Elswidk, the ship's captain, Lieutenant Sven Höök and another soldier, a servant and a clerk. The colony would begin the winter on the verge of starvation.

Next, Rising learned that in July 1654 England and the Netherlands had ended their war, meaning that Stuyvesant could turn his attention from defending New Netherlands from New Englanders to his Swedish problem on the Delaware. Even worse, he was told that Queen

Christina had abdicated in favor of her cousin Karl X and that Sweden was deeply involved in a war with Poland, diverting resources and focus from the struggling colony. Finally, he discovered that Stuyvesant was mounting an expedition to invade the Delaware. He assumed, wrongly, that the object of the Dutch action was the retaking of Fort Trinity (Fort Casimir). But with Sweden now preoccupied by a European war and the Netherlands free of such encumbrances, the director-general had bigger plans.

Stuyvesant had been in communication with the Amsterdam group in control of New Netherlands for the Dutch West India Company. His instructions were to remove the Swedish colony as a threat to the company's territory and impediment to the fur trade. Such a wide ranging threat had not occurred to Rising.

The New Sweden director was concerned with defending Fort Trinity and to that end he transferred most of his soldiers from Fort Christina to Fort Trinity along with 150 pounds of gunpowder, muskets, swords and pikes. Captain Sven Skute was placed in command with Lieutenant Gyllengren, Ensign Peter Wendell and Peter Lindeström as officers. Supplies of rye, brandy and beer were laid in. Fort Christina was left with a small garrison under Van Elswick with Lieutenant Höök second in command. After a winter of starvation, the little colony had recovered sufficiently to mount a significant defense. What Rising was not prepared for was the scope and size of the impending invasion.

Stuyvesant assembled a fleet of seven ships, a front line battleship (the *Wagh*) and six lesser armed ships. The *Wagh* carried 32 guns and was the largest ship owned by the city of Amsterdam. The other craft carried at least four cannon each. On board were 317 soldiers, a total attack force of about 400 men, more troops than the total population of New Sweden.

At the end of August 1655 the armada entered Delaware Bay and approached Fort Trinity. Skute's orders were to dispatch a boat to meet the ships and inquire as to Stuyvesant's intentions. If the Dutch were determined to be hostile, he was to prevent their passage even to the point of firing on them. But for some unknown reason Skute did neither, letting the Dutch ships pass by the fort unchallenged. This lack of action sealed the fate of the Swedish colony.

Lieutenant Lindström later accused Skute of treason for not resisting the Dutch advance up the river. Lieutenant Gyllengren likewise held the commandant responsible for not mounting some kind of a defense.

Stuyvesant passed the fort, then put into shore and had his men begin to construct a fortified beachhead. Troops were landed, effectively cutting off communication between Fort Trinity and Rising at Fort Christina. Skute first sent an emissary to Stuyvesant, then met with the West Indies director-general in person. In the end the Swedish commander surrendered the fort without firing a shot.

Stuyvesant took control of the fort, restoring the name Fort Casimir, and ran up the Dutch colors. He put the officers under house arrest and forced the thirty Swedish soldiers aboard one of his vessels as prisoners of war. They were transported to New Amsterdam. In a single stroke he had wiped out the corps of the Swedish military power in America.

Rising was furious when he learned of the bloodless fall of Fort Trinity. Yet he was still of the mistaken notion that recovery of the fort was the extent of Stuyvesant's objective. The Swedish director sent van Elswick to Fort Casimir to open negotiations with the Dutch as to terms and boundaries to be observed. But the Swedish delegate was informed that Stuyvesant's mission was nothing less than the complete conquest of New Sweden.

Upon the return of van Elswick, Rising put his men to work night and day in strengthening Fort Christina for the expected assault. Stuyvesant did not disappoint. Having secured

Fort Casimir he sailed his flotilla upriver to Rising's headquarters. The *Wagh* and a smaller vessel blocked the mouth of the Minquas Kill. The Dutch now controlled the Delaware River. Stuyvesant landed his troops and began constructing siege works encircling the fort. Powder and guns were brought ashore to reinforce the breastworks and bombard the fort when hostilities opened.

Finally, the Dutch began looting and destroying Swedish property. Cattle and horses were shot. Houses were robbed and a few settlements were burned to the ground. Stores of grain and goods were carried off or destroyed. Even Printzhoff, where Armegot Papegoja had gathered women colonists and families in an attempt to protect them, was invaded and plundered. These unfortunate excesses would leave a lasting animosity for the Dutch among the Swedes.

As the grip of the siege tightened on Rising and the tiny Fort Christina garrison, conditions inside the fort became desperate. On September 13 Rising offered to confer with the Dutch governor-general and the two met for the first time in Stuyvesant's tent. Rising learned his worst fears were well founded. The Dutch were determined to end the Swedish presence on the Delaware once and for all.

On September 14 a second meeting was held, but this time Rising, having concluded further resistance would only end in a waste of lives, brought his own terms of surrender to be used as a basis for negotiations. To the Swede's surprise Stuyvesant accepted the terms as presented. The following day the treaty was signed ending Swedish control of her American colony. By the terms of the treaty Rising and his soldiers left the fort under arms with flags flying, relocating to Tinicum Island. Under the terms, all colonists who wished to return to Gothenburg were free to do so. Those remaining would retain their homes and land, and would be free to practice the Lutheran religion, but they would have to take an oath of allegiance to the Netherlands and be subject to the government in New Amsterdam and Dutch law. Thirty-seven men, mostly soldiers, took the offer to return to Sweden or Finland leaving some 300 people behind.

It was only after the surrender was signed that Rising learned the reason for Stuyvesant's quick acceptance of terms. When the Dutch force left New Amsterdam for the Delaware, the Indians in the area recognized an opportunity to avenge the rape and rapine that had been perpetrated upon them by the Dutch under the Kief administration. A fleet of 64 canoes carrying some 500 warriors made a surprise attack on New Amsterdam. The few guards were quickly overcome. By evening another 200 warriors had joined the assault. The town lay open to them and they robbed, murdered and pillaged at will until the burgher militia was able to form up and drive the invaders from the island. The Indians crossed over to Staten Island and the Pavonia settlement where they continued their rampage for three days. In the end some fifty colonists were killed with twice that many, mostly women and children, carried off as captives. Another 200 were left homeless and many more lost possessions and, most importantly, their food supplies. Stuyvesant and his army had to return to the capital without delay. Having settled the treaty conditions, Stuyvesant left only a few soldiers at each of the two forts and sailed for New Amsterdam.

Before Sweden learned of the fall of New Sweden, another expedition was organized and sent to the colony from Gothenburg. On March 14, 1656, the *Mercurius* put in at Fort Casimir with 110 passengers mostly from northern Sweden. Again there were many more applicants than space aboard ship. There were more Finns than Swedes on the passenger list, which included Johan Papegoja and Hendrick Huygen as co-commanders. They must have been shocked to find both Fort Casimir and Fort Christina flying the Dutch colors.

When Stuyvesant learned of the new Swedish ship on the Delaware, he sent word that it was not to be allowed to land, but was to proceed to New Amsterdam. Papegoja and Huygen ignored the instructions and sailed to Tinicum Island where the ship was unloaded. When the vessel didn't immediately comply with his orders, Stuyvesant dispatched a squad of soldiers overland to take charge. But the supplies were hidden and the passengers who had relatives on the island melted into the population. The rest took to the forests where they were quite at home, much more so than the Dutch. By the time the troops arrived their trail was cold.

Eventually, a town developed around Fort Casimir. It would become the thriving city of New Amstel, later New Castle, before there was a Wilmington or Philadelphia. On the Delaware, Tinicum Island became the center of the "Swedish Nation." Here was located the only Lutheran church with Swedish pastors. Eventually, Stuyvesant appointed Gregory van Dyck deputy *schout* for the Swedish Nation along with Swedish magistrates to preside over their own courts. The former Swedish colony raised its own militia, officered by Sven Skute as captain and Lieutenants Anders Dalbo and Jacob Svensson. Stuyvesant did curtail Swedish autonomy somewhat, afraid too much independence might lead to a revolt.

In 1664 James Stuart (later James II), duke of York, conquered New Netherlands and the Swedish Nation became part of the English colonies. They were then required to shift allegiance to the king of England, not a problem for the Swedes and Finns as they had never been entirely comfortable under Dutch rule. All land patents were recognized, religious freedom observed, and they were given full rights as English citizens. On June 4, 1699, a new Swedish Lutheran church was dedicated at the site of what had been Fort Christina. Named Trefeldighets Kyrckia (Holy Trinity Church), it still stands today in Williamsburg, now called Old Swedes Church.

Thus Sweden's colonial effort in America ended, but not the Swedish adventure in this New World. New Sweden would be instrumental in the formation of a new nation. On July 1, 1776, the Continental Congress took a vote on the Declaration of Independence. Only nine of the thirteen colonies voted in the affirmative. Pennsylvania and South Carolina voted against acceptance, Delaware was deadlocked and New York, the old New Netherlands, abstained. Benjamin Franklin's admonition of, "We must all hang together or we shall all hang separately,"[4] described the situation.

The final vote was postponed until the following day. On July 2 South Carolina voted to join the rebellion. Then John Morton, a Pennsylvanian of Swedish descent, switched his vote swinging his state to the affirmative. Late in the day Caesar Rodney, Delaware's third delegate, galloped up to the statehouse after an eighty-mile ride through the night and a thunderstorm to break his state's deadlock and bring it into the Declaration of Independence camp. It was enough. The Continental Congress spent the next two days finalizing the document that would create the first independent nation of Europeans in the Americas.

Swedish immigrants would continue to come to these shores for another two hundred and fifty years. They pushed inland, generally preferring their own farms away from the large settlements, a characteristic of Swedish immigrants to the United States. Swedes arriving in the 1800s and early 1900s did not congregate in the eastern cities as other Europeans often did. They pushed on to the farmlands of Michigan, Minnesota, Iowa, Illinois, Kansas, Nebraska, Texas, the Dakotas and Montana. They arrived at the rate of 37,000 per year in the 1880s, inhabiting the frontiers as fast as new lands were opened to them until the northern forests, plains and Rocky Mountains were settled. Today there are some eight million Americans of Swedish decent, a strong and energetic people who have contributed much to their adopted country's development and prosperity.

There is one last footnote to Sweden's attempts at colonization. In 1784 King Gustav III of Sweden acquired the Caribbean Island of St. Barthelemy from France in exchange for trade privileges. The Swedish West Indies Company was formed in the hope of using the island as a base for exporting iron to the Americas. The chief city and harbor on the island was named Gustavia and declared a free and neutral port. During the Napoleonic wars the city thrived and grew rich from trade. As the European wars subsided, commerce dwindled and the island was sold back to France in 1878. However, the name of the capital and tourist center of the island remains Gustavia to this day, a last reminder of Sweden's colonial ventures in Africa, North America and the Caribbean.

22. Karl XI and the Scanian War

Karl X died February 13, 1660, having ruled the Swedish Empire at its height. By the Treaty of Roskilde Denmark turned over Trondheim (in Norway), Blekinge, Skåne, Halland (permanently), Bohuslän and Bornholm to Sweden. Karl had conquered and then lost Poland. He had lost Sweden's colony in America and her trading posts in Africa except for Karlsborg, which would succumb within three years. He did manage to keep Sweden's Baltic possessions and those in northern Germany, but these were threatened by wars in Livonia and Swedish Pomerania.

Peace negotiations had been ongoing for a year with France as primary mediator. The biggest impediment to progress was Karl himself insisting on terms even more generous than those of Roskilde. Once this obstacle was removed, negotiations proceeded rapidly.

The Peace of Oliva was signed on May 3, 1660, between Sweden and Poland-Lithuania, Austria and Brandenburg. Sweden retained Bremen, Verden, Wismar and Swedish Pomerania. In addition, her possession of Livonia was finally recognized by the Commonwealth. For the first time a Polish king, John Casimir, officially withdrew his claim to the Swedish throne, though he would use the title of king of Sweden for the rest of his life. The Vasa feud was finally ended.

On June 9 the treaty of Copenhagen established peace between Denmark and Sweden. By its terms Denmark regained Bornholm and Norwegian Trondheim, but Sweden kept Blekinge, Skåne, Halland and Bohuslän, as well as previously won Jämtland and Härjedalen. Though he lost Poland and Prussia, Karl X had pushed the contiguous territory of Sweden to its present borders at the expense of Denmark.

The war with Russia was concluded at the settlement of Kardis in 1661 with Muscovy returning the parts of Livonia, taken including Dorpat. Thus Swedish Baltic possessions were also preserved, including Livonia, Estonia, Ingria and Kexholm.

All in all Sweden emerged from the war and the peace negotiations in an excellent position. This was due in part to her ally France being the mediator, but also because her military reputation was at its height. The near conquest of Poland had certainly caught the attention of the European states and the speed with which Karl had crushed Denmark was astonishing. Only the united forces of several nations had saved Denmark from annihilation.

It had taken the combined navies of Denmark and the Netherlands to blunt Swedish domination of the Baltic and the Sound. Sweden's military prowess was respected and feared. It was her lack of population and substantial economy that were her weaknesses. This was to become apparent during the coming peace.

Meanwhile, Poland and Russia, freed from Swedish wars, hammered away at one another for another five years. Finally, the two exhausted protagonists concluded a thirteen and a half year truce on January 30, 1667. A period of peace settled over northern Europe for the first time in centuries, marred only by the Dutch war with France (1667). Sweden and her neighbors were given a breathing space to recuperate from the devastation and deprivations of war.

The death of Karl X left Sweden, once again, with a child monarch. Karl XI was just four years old. His mother, Hedvig Eleonora of Holstein-Gottorp, was staunchly anti–Danish. He had the best of tutors, but struggled in his studies, probably due to some form of dyslexia. He would become proficient in only Swedish and German. As an adult he was naturally shy and entertained at court only when required for state occasions. This reticence would cause problems in his marriage to the Danish princess. She was fond of lavish social events and entertainment, functions Karl did not enjoy and considered frivolous. His aversion to studies meant that he spent much of his youth in outdoor activities. Hunting and playing war games with his companions occupied his time. He took little interest in government, leaving the country in the hands of the Regency.

Chief of this governing group was Magnus Gabriel de la Gardie, son of Jakob de la Gardie and Ebba Brahe. As part of his education Magnus spent time in France where he became a great admirer of French culture and acquired a social polish not common in Sweden. He returned to his native country in 1644 at the outbreak of war with Denmark intending to launch a career in the military, but his French manners, sophistication and handsome presence made an impression on Christina. The queen kept him at court, showering him with favors. He was made a colonel in the Lifeguard and betrothed to Enfrosyne, the queen's cousin and sister of the future Karl X. Christina played him off against Axel Oxenstierna as she made him a member of the Council of State at twenty-five. In 1648 he became second-in-command to Field Marshal Karl Gustav Wrangel in Germany and participated in the siege of Prague. A year later he was made a field marshal and governor-general of Livonia. At thirty he was state treasurer. Along with his political rise he was given lands, several hundred farms in Sweden, the islands of Wollin and Ösel, and the county of Pernau in the Baltics.

In 1652 de la Gardie became ill and was bed-ridden for some six months. When he recovered he found he was no longer one of the queen's favorites. He was shunted aside, even losing his office of treasurer. At Christina's abdication Magnus hoped to regain his former status at court. He was returned as treasurer, but was employed in diplomatic missions by Karl X which kept him abroad.

In June 1655 de la Gardie was again made governor-general of Livonia and put in command of all forces between the Düna and Lake Ladoga. He proved to be a poor military commander and suffered several reverses during the war. As the war in the Baltics wound down he was given the diplomatic commission of conducting the peace negotiations at Oliva and here he showed considerable aptitude.

De la Gardie returned to Stockholm in June 1660 to find the government in the midst of a quarrel over who would run the country until Karl XI's maturity. The dead king (Karl X) had left a will naming a Regency consisting of the queen mother, Karl X's brother, Duke Adolf Johan (who was to be high marshal), Per Brahe (high steward), Magnus de la Gardie (chancellor), Herman Fleming (treasurer) and Karl Gustav Wrangel (high admiral). The House of Nobility objected to the choices. They didn't like Adolph Johan because he was a difficult man and detested Herman Fleming for his zealous advocacy of the reduktion. In the end the Noble Estate won out. Johan was replaced by Lars Kagg and Fleming by Gustav Bonde as treasurer.

De la Gardie, as chancellor and head of government, was saddled with a cabinet he had no voice in selecting and didn't like. In addition to the members of his own Regency, Magnus's leading opponent was Johan Gyllenstierna, who did not have de la Gardie's admiration for France and favored an alliance with Denmark and the Netherlands.

Given the strong divisions in the Swedish government it would have taken an Axel Oxenstierna to gain control and impose his will. Magnus was no Oxenstierna. Though at times he showed great energy and resolution, was skilled in debate and knew how to use the authority of his office to effect, he lost heart easily when things went badly. He often wearied of the demands of his office and sought refuge outside Stockholm at his estates where he indulged in building projects, collecting art and landscaping design. During these absences, the other members of the Regency would take over and move the government on a different path. This situation meant Sweden had a government that shifted direction, not staying on one even course in either foreign policy or domestic affairs. Both these areas were affected by Sweden's financial crisis.

Christina's extravagance and Karl X's wars had left the country deeply in debt. The new treasurer, Gustav Bonde, came up with an austere budget so that the debt could be paid by the time Karl XI reached maturity. One of the areas cut was the military, a military Sweden needed to maintain peace with her neighbors. But during the Regency's rule Sweden's army and navy suffered a decline in readiness.

De la Gardie argued for an alliance with Sweden's traditional ally France as the best way to stay out of war, but Johan Gyllenstierna led an opposition that urged an alliance with the maritime countries of the Netherlands and Denmark. Direction in Sweden's government was not consistent.

In 1666 Bonde died and de la Gardie was able to influence the country's financial policies to a greater extent. But his adversaries won a political triumph when Sweden joined an anti–French Triple Alliance with England and the Netherlands in 1668. However, de la Gardie engineered an alliance with France, signed in April 1672, that guaranteed a subsidy of 400,000 riksdalers per year to maintain a 16,000 man army in Pomerania. This was to be raised to 600,000 if Sweden was at war, presumably with enemies of France.

Denmark, that same year, joined a coalition of Leopold I (holy Roman emperor), Brandenburg, Brunswick-Celle, Brunswick-Wolfenbüttel and Hesse-Kassel. In May 1673, Denmark signed a treaty with the Dutch, who agreed to subsidize a war fleet of 20 vessels and a 12,000 man army.

The tension between Sweden and Denmark was exacerbated by Sweden's promotion of ties with Holstein-Gottorp, one of a patchwork of duchies at the base of the Jutland Peninsula. Swedish interests in the area dated back to Viking Hedeby and, more recently, to Karl X's marriage to Hedvig Eleanora of Holstein-Gottorp. This was a region Denmark intended to dominate.

1672 also saw Karl XI reach the age of eighteen and become the head of state. That same year war broke out between France and a coalition of England, the Netherlands and Brandenburg. Both Denmark and Sweden tried to remain neutral, even attempting to act as mediators between France and Brandenburg. Both were threatened with non payment of subsidies if they didn't join the conflict.

In 1674 England withdrew from the war, but the Empire and Denmark joined the anti–French coalition. More pressure was applied by France for Sweden to engage her enemies. By September 1674 Sweden had 22,000 men under arms in her German territories thanks to French money. The war threatened Bremen and Verden. Sweden could not maintain a large army in Pomerania much longer. She had to act.

In December 1674 Karl Gustav Wrangel pushed into Brandenburg with 13,000 troops. Another 25,000 men were scattered in garrisons in Swedish German territories. The thrust into Brandenburg was rather tentative by Swedish standards, as if the country's heart was not really in this conflict. Wrangel fell ill and his deputy, Helmfelt, also was incapacitated. Command fell to Mardefelt, a fortifications engineer, not a field general.

Frederick William retreated in the face of the vaunted Swedish military machine, burning crops and supplies before the advancing army. On June 18, 1675, the main Swedish force had taken up a position at Alt-Brandenburg above the Havel River near Berlin. Volmar, Wrangel's half-brother, bivouacked on the other side of the river.

Frederick William saw his chance and drove a column between the divided Swedish army, capturing the bridge at Rathenow. In an attempt to rejoin the main army, Volmar moved his troops to Fehrbellin, but found the bridge destroyed. While repairing the structure, the Swedes were caught in the valley where Frederick shelled them with his artillery, then attacked with cavalry and infantry. The Swedish rear guard held off the Brandenburgers until Volmar could get his troops across the repaired bridge. Though not a major battle the Swedes did lose 600 men and retired from the field, technically a defeat.

Frederick William trumpeted his victory at Fehrbellin across Europe convincing many the Swedish Army was impotent. Sweden's old enemies quickly joined the fray. Emperor Leopold I, the Netherlands, even Christoph Bernhard von Galen (bishop of Münster) declared war on the great northern power. Christian V of Denmark formally entered the war against Sweden, imprisoned his brother-in-law, Christian Albert of Holstein-Gottorp, then rushed south with 9,600 infantry, 5,500 cavalry, 1,200 dragoons and 312 guns to help Frederick William drive the Swedes from Germany, closing Denmark's back door in preparation for an attack to recover the lost provinces on the Scandinavian Peninsula.

At sea the center of power was also shifting. During a decade of Regency rule in Sweden (1661 to 1672) the country had built fifteen warships of 17,000 tons. Denmark, which had been ruled by Christian V as absolute monarch, had constructed twenty-four battleships of 18,000 tons during the same period. This considerably strengthened navy was supplemented by Dutch warships, forcing the Swedes to turn to converting merchantmen into ships of war, a practice completely outdated by the advances in naval technology.

In October 1675 a Swedish fleet under Gustav Otto Stenback was defeated by the coalition. Danish Admiral Niels Juel defeated a Swedish fleet between Bornholm and Rügen in May 1676, opening access to the northern Baltic and a potential Swedish blockade. A mainly Dutch fleet under Admiral Cornelis Tromp defeated the Swedes off Öland in June 1676 and again at Köge Bay effectively ending Sweden's domination of the Baltic. Sweden lost 20 warships and 4,000 casualties. No longer would the Swedes be able to swoop down from the sea and attack Baltic coasts at will. The movement of troops and supplies from one port to another became problematic. Sweden was constrained from reinforcing and resupplying her German possessions.

Christian V attacked Wismar and Bremen while Frederick William invaded Swedish Pomerania. France could offer only money. England and Hamburg sided with Sweden, but provided no troops. Wismar fell in late 1675, Bremen followed and Brandenburg took Stralsund and Stettin. With the fall of Greifswald in November 1678 Sweden lost her last stronghold in Germany.

Christian had the upper hand both at sea and in Germany. It was time to pursue his real interests, the lost Danish provinces in Scandinavia. In June 1676 he launched a two pronged attack. A Danish-Norwegian force entered Bohuslän from Norway and on June 29 Christian landed at Helsingborg with a large, well equipped army of Danish conscripts, German mercenaries and Dutch auxiliaries. The population of Skåne, particularly the peasants of the northern woodlands, rose up against the Swedish occupiers. On July 24 a Swedish train of some 250 wagons bound for the army was ambushed at Loshult on the Småland-Skåne border by these partisans. A war chest of 50,000 silver coins was taken. These kinds of attacks were to continue for the remainder of the war.

As the Danish-Norwegian army continued to advance through Bohuslän into western Sweden, Christian swiftly took Helsingborg, Kristianstad, Lanskrona, Lund and Ystad, securing Skåne except for Malmö, which resisted a Danish siege.

King Karl XI, now twenty-one years of age, had not taken a strong hand in the government, allowing the Regency to continue its rule. With the homeland in imminent peril, however, Karl finally stepped in to take an active part. He raised a new army of mostly conscripts and headed south to intercept Christian. The Danish king had sent a force west, possibly to connect with the Norwegian-Danish army in Western Sweden. Karl moved to intercept. The two armies met at the Battle of Fyllebro four miles from Halmstad in Halland. The Swedish conscripts should have been routed by the well equipped Danish professionals, but Karl's advantage in cavalry proved decisive. The Danish army was crushed and sent in flight back into Skåne.

Karl XI pursued, but the going was tough. As Christian retreated in the face of the Swedish advance, he laid waste to the countryside depriving the Swedes of food and forage. Partisans harassed and ambushed Karl's troops. That autumn was unusually cold and wet. Torrential rains flooded fields and turned roads into bogs. Christian could supply his troops by water, but Karl was forced to rely on the scanty road network back to the Swedish heartland. His momentum stalled. On November 20 Christian decided it was safe to let his troops go into winter quarters. He selected an ideal location north-east of Lund. Karl hunkered down with his starving, ill supplied army about seven miles away, north-west of the town.

On November 30 a cold snap froze the swollen streams and rivers. Karl decided to try one last battle before year's end. On paper Christian had all the advantages. His well fed and equipped troops numbered 5,000 horse, 1,300 dragoons, 6,000 foot and 56 heavy guns. Against this Karl could hurl only 6,000 cavalry, 2,000 infantry and 8 guns. He needed the element of surprise to have a chance.

At 4:00 A.M. on December 4, 1676, Karl moved his army across the Kävlinge River and launched a daring pre-dawn assault. The Danes were caught by surprise, but quickly rallied and brought the Swedish advance to a halt. The fighting was furious with Karl in the thick of it. His battle horse, Thotten, was shot out from under him. After eight hours of slugging it out in a battle of attrition, a battle the numerically inferior Swedish force was going to lose, Karl mounted a cavalry charge against the Danish left wing. The Danish left, made up mostly of horse, collapsed. The usually disciplined Swedish cavalry pursued the fleeing enemy back to their camp which the Swedes proceeded to loot. It took an hour and a half for Karl to round up nine squadrons of cavalry and return to the field of battle.

Meanwhile, the Swedish infantry and artillery were being steadily pushed back until they were pinned against the walls of Lund. They were on the verge of being overrun when Karl appeared at the Danish rear with his cavalry. Caught in the vise of the two Swedish wings the Danes were slaughtered until Karl called for a ceasefire and gave quarter.

It was the bloodiest battle of the Swedish-Danish wars. On the field lay 6,000 Danes, German mercenaries and Dutch Marine Infantry, half of Christian's army. Another 2,000 were prisoners of war. The Battle of Lund broke the back of the Danish invasion and made Karl a national hero.

After Lund, Karl moved on to take Helsingborg, but was unable to do more. His activity did, however, take the pressure off Malmö and it remained in Swedish hands for the rest of the war. At the end of the campaign season Christian held only Landskröna and Kristianstad, little enough considering he controlled the seas and had come with a large, well supplied army.

The year 1677 saw no significant action. Christian failed in two attempts to retake Helsingborg and was driven back at Malmö. Danish forces were defeated outside Landskröna in July and thereafter avoided open pitched battles with the Swedes. To the west Magnus de la Gardie took over command of Swedish forces in Västergötland fighting the Norwegian-Danish army. He suffered a severe defeat at Uddevalla damaging his reputation. This would have far reaching political consequences for both himself and Swedish foreign policy.

By 1678 the Scanian War had ground to a stalemate. With his bigger and better provisioned army Christian was able to retake Helsingborg, but lost Kristianstad in spite of a 12,000 man relief force sent to rescue it. The non–Scandinavian belligerents were pushing hard for a settlement with France as the mediator.

With Karl constantly at the front, a power struggle was emerging in Stockholm between de la Gardie and Johan Gyllenstierna. Magnus was losing ground and his descent got a kick with his defeat at Uddervalla. This combined with his pro–French foreign policy that had gotten Sweden into a devastating war led to his down fall. Karl took Gyllenstierna as his chief advisor. Johan favored a foreign policy aimed at developing an alliance with the northern maritime powers of the Netherlands, England and Denmark, cutting out Sweden's dependence on France. It was a policy that seemed logical, but ignored the long standing animosity between the two Scandinavian countries.

In early 1679 peace with the emperor was arranged. Brandenburg settled in July and in August King Louis XIV arranged a peace between Denmark and Sweden. The treaty was signed at Lund in September 1679. Sweden emerged from the negotiations almost unscathed due to French maneuvering on her behalf and Denmark's weak bargaining position. Sweden's German possessions were returned except some minor counties. She retained all her Scandinavian territory and exemption from the Sound toll. Denmark gained nothing, even losing what control she had over Holstein-Gottorp. It was nearly a total victory for Sweden and a crushing defeat for Denmark.

As part of the negotiations, the Swedish and Danish delegates, guided by Gyllenstierna, arranged a political alliance between the two countries to be sealed by the marriage of Karl XI to Ulrica Eleonora, youngest sister of Christian V. The shift in Swedish foreign policy was complete. De la Gardie and the French were out; Gyllenstierna and the northern alliance were in.

The Scanian conflict had demonstrated clearly Sweden's unpreparedness for the war. Christian's absolute monarchy had allowed him to raise a large army and build a strong navy. He had been able to direct the military and the country's resources for greatest effect. Sweden's ruling Regency, on the other hand, had allowed the country's military to degenerate to that of a second class power. De la Gardie's dependence on French subsidies to maintain defenses had proven woefully inadequate and had turned Sweden into a French client state, dragging her into an unwanted war.

Newly acquired Danish provinces, particularly Skåne, had evidenced loyalty to their former country. But most of all, the state of Sweden's army and navy were revealed to be appalling. Only Karl XI's ability to raise troops through Sweden's *förläning* (assignment of farmland to a soldier), *utskriving* (Swedish conscription system) and *indeling* (system where soldiers were assigned to individual farms and officers were given farms to operate in peace time) had saved the country. All these deficiencies had to be dealt with and Karl XI set about making corrections with determination.

His leadership in the successful defense of the homeland had made him popular among the people. He capitalized on his status to push for more political power. In December 1680 the Riksdag granted the king full powers, effectively canceling the aristocracy's hard won 1634 Form of Government. Further, Karl was released from consulting the Råd and was declared responsible to God alone. Karl had his authority, now he moved to secure his domain.

Of the provinces acquired from Denmark, Härjedalen, Jämtland and Gotland had been assimilated without serious problems. Of particular importance was the replacement of Danish clergy with Swedish, accomplished through attrition and appointment from Stockholm. These were areas with mostly peasant populations and never tied closely to Denmark. The provinces at the southern end of the Scandinavian Peninsula were another matter. While Bohuslän was more Norwegian and Blekinge had ties to Sweden through centuries of trade and cross-border marriages, Halland and particularly Skåne were long time Danish subjects. Unlike the other provinces Skåne was mostly fertile plain ruled by an oligarchy of some forty noble families. Danish rule favored these nobles more than did Swedish rule. Resistance was strongest here. Karl appointed Gyllenstierna governor-general of the province and he began a program to remedy the situation.

Skåne's partisan activity had been met with summary executions and the burning of farms and villages. But with the peace, Karl showed great leniency requiring only an oath of loyalty for return of individuals and families to his good graces, a goodwill gesture that was not reciprocated.

Gyllenstierna's plan was one of forced assimilation. About a third of the farms in Skåne were empty due to the devastation of the war. The governor-general invited Swedes from the north to come and settle this land. By the terms of the peace treaty any inhabitants that wanted to leave the province and emigrate to Danish territory were allowed to leave. Gyllensteirna encouraged such moves freeing still more land for Swedish occupation. In short Gyllenstierna's program was one of ethnic cleansing. His early death in 1680 ended the project before it could be carried out.

Karl next appointed Rutger von Ascheberg governor-general. His approach was entirely different. Instead of bringing in Swedes, he elevated local individuals who showed loyalty to the Swedish king. He encouraged cross-border marriages with Swedes. Gradually he reorganized the church along Swedish lines encouraging the use of Swedish hymnals and catechisms. He pressured families to petition the king for status as full Swedish citizens. Karl responded by canceling the investigations into war crimes. Within a few years the territories conquered from Denmark were fully assimilated as Swedish provinces.

At the same time Karl was pressuring the Riksdag to resume the reduktion. Here he could play the lower Estates off against the high nobility. The lesser nobles were lobbying for a Table of Ranks based on government service rather than land ownership. The aristocracy was divided. The clergy and burghers hoped the reduktion would reduce their tax burden. Finally, the peasants would rather work for the crown than the oppressive nobility. Karl pushed the Table of Ranks and the reduktion through the Riksdag in 1680. A second and even more severe reduktion was passed in 1682. Fully one-third of the aristocracy's lands were returned to the crown. Hardest hit were the great magnates including the de la Gardie family. The power of the great land magnates of Sweden was forever broken. The peasantry, on the verge of domination by the nobility, perhaps being forced into serfdom common in other European countries, was set free. Never again would the peasants' traditional freedoms be seriously threatened.

The newly acquired crown lands brought in 4 million riksdalers annually. Karl used this money to reduce the national debt from 40 million riksdalers in 1681 to 10 million in 1697. Most importantly, Karl now had money to pay an adequate civil service and build his military.

In terms of recruitment, Karl worked on refining the förläning, utskriving, indeling system already in place. Under his plan each province was responsible for maintaining a certain number of regiments of a fixed size (1,200 men in the case of infantry). For infantry, farms were grouped in pairs called *rota* (files). Each rota was required to provide and equip one soldier. As to cavalry, one or more prosperous farms made up a *rusthåll* which supplied one or more cavalrymen. Karl extended the system from just crown peasants to tax paying peasants as well distributing the load more evenly. There were incentives for farmers to enter into the arrangement. Special tax privileges were extended to participants and the soldiers were obliged to work as farm hands when not at war or in training. The whole system was known as the *indelningsverk*. One of the advantages over the old system was that uncertainties were removed. The requirement was constant in war or in peace.

By 1697 this system provided 11 cavalry regiments and 23 infantry, that is 11,000 horse and 30,000 foot of native, well trained and equipped troops. Money freed by the system allowed the government to hire an additional 25,000 mercenaries for overseas garrison duty.

The indelningsverk and reduktion also made funds available to reconstitute the navy. By 1700 Sweden had a fleet of 53,000 tons compared to Denmark's 46,000. A new naval base was constructed at Karlskrona providing an ice-free port earlier in the year than at Stockholm. This build up of the military was designed to keep Sweden out of wars. This was Karl XI's intention and the centerpiece of his foreign policy, armed neutrality.

At the death of Gyllenstierna in 1680, Bengt Oxenstierna, as chancellor, assumed direction of foreign policy. The next year he and the king formed alliances with the emperor and the Netherlands to contain Louis XIV. To the east, Russia and Poland were occupied trying to hold the line against the Ottoman Turks and various Tartar inclusions.

In 1683 Denmark threatened an attack on Sweden backed by the French fleet and several German states openly discussed joining the attack on what they believed was as yet a weakened Sweden. That same year the Turks drove all the way to Vienna and laid siege to the city. The attack on Vienna failed and marked the high tide of Turkish advance into Europe.

Denmark finally threw down the gauntlet to Sweden by seizing portions of the Duchy of Holstein-Gottorp. Karl did not take the bait, but looked for other avenues to resolve the issue. In 1686 the League of Augsburg was formed against Louis XIV at the instigation of the emperor, Leopold I. The emperor was joined by the Palatinate, Bavaria and Brandenburg. The German states gained the alliance of Portugal, Spain and the Netherlands. Sweden joined the league and in return the emperor arranged the Conference of Altona to settle the Holstein-Gottorp question. However, Denmark hung tough and the conference accomplished little.

Louis XIV's aggression, in 1688, in the Palatinate-Rhineland area of Germany resulted in the Nine Years War involving all the major powers of Europe except Sweden. In launching the war the French king had expected England's James II, a Catholic and French sympathizer, to tacitly support him. But that same year the English people rebelled against their king in favor of his sister, the protestant Mary. Mary's husband, William of Orange, a *stadtholder* (governor) in the United Provinces, invaded England with an army of 14,000 men. London fell to the Dutch force which was supported by most of the population. James II fled to France and Mary took over the English throne jointly with her husband as Mary II and William III. William and Mary joined the Grand Alliance and declared war on France in May

1689. The war, called the War of the Grand Alliance, the War of the League of Augsburg or the Nine Years War, is known as King William's War in America and was the first of the French and Indian wars in the colonies.

By 1689 Karl had lost patience with Danish foot-dragging and convinced the Riksdag to authorize funding for war. He mobilized Swedish forces against Denmark. Just as war seemed imminent, Christian backed down, restoring the lost territory to the Duchy of Holstein-Gottorp.

In 1692 Louis XIV reached the peak of his war successes and there was a movement in Sweden to join his cause. Karl, however, squelched the pro–French drive and stuck with Oxenstierna's policy of pro-Empire, pro–Dutch alliances that had kept Sweden out of war for several years.

Queen Ulrika Eleonora died in 1693. That same year the king announced the budget to be in surplus and declared extraordinary taxes would no longer be needed in peacetime. The Riksdag passed a resolution called the Declaration of Sovereignty confirming the Swedish monarchy to be absolute. Swedish law was rewritten to accommodate the rule of absolute sovereignty.

Karl XI had accomplished much of his agenda and he added a final triumph, his positioning Sweden as mediator to end the Nine Years War. France's initial successes had been nullified as the war dragged on. In 1693 all belligerents accepted Karl as mediator for a general peace. Negotiations began in 1695 at Rijswick. Two years later in September 1697 a treaty of peace was concluded.

Karl XI did not live to see the culmination of his peace efforts, however. He died April 5, 1697, of stomach cancer. He was forty-two years old. He had accomplished much to strengthen his country's position in the world. He had reestablished the monarchy as absolute. Sweden now had a powerful army and navy with a support system to maintain them. If not quite the dominant military power of a half century earlier, Sweden's prestige was at a high point as mediator of the Nine Years War. Karl XI bequeathed to his son and heir a country sound financially and militarily. Sweden, at peace now for eighteen years, watched a rapidly evolving Europe and waited to see what path the new king would take.

Sweden maintained a commercial and territorial empire around the Baltic Sea. But the nation was surrounded by neighbors with far greater resources who gazed upon Sweden's possessions with envy. Peace had been possible only because those countries respected Sweden's king and his military might. A change in circumstance, particularly a replacement in leadership, was sure to invite probing to determine any shifts in Sweden's position. A test of the new king's resolve and abilities could not be far away.

23. Karl XII and the Great Northern War

Karl XI's premature death left Sweden, once again, with a young monarch. At least this time he was not a child. Karl XII was fifteen and the only surviving male heir. He inherited an absolute sovereignty. The only question was one of maturity.

Karl XI had left a will in which he delayed his son's majority until the age of eighteen. He designated his own mother, Hedvig Eleanora of Holstein-Gottorp (Karl X's widow), regent along with a five-man council. The ambitious queen grandmother, in hopes of a long *de facto* reign, kept her grandson away from state business as much as possible, allowing him his youthful pursuits of hunting and reviewing the troops.

Voltaire, the French author and philosopher, writing only forty years after the incident, tells of Karl XII's usurpation of his grandmother's power. In November 1697, only a few months after his father's death, Karl is reviewing several regiments with Privy Councilor Piper at his side. He is deep in thought and Piper asks, "'May I take the liberty of asking what Your Majesty is contemplating?'

"'I was thinking,' replies the king, 'that I feel myself worthy to command these brave fellows, and I am unwilling that either they or I should take orders from a woman.'"[1]

Piper seized the opportunity to elevate his position and contacted Count Axel Sparres to set in motion a plan advancing the king to his rightful seat of power. They convinced the five-man regency that it was in their best interests to cooperate. This group took the proposal to the queen who was caught by surprise. Before she could mount a defense, the Estates General was convened and a motion to empower Karl XII was passed so quickly no one had a chance to oppose it. Three days after his remark to Piper, Karl XII was king in fact as well as in name. Hedwig Eleanora's power base collapsed and she was forced back into private life.

Voltaire records that "He [Karl XII] was crowned on December 24, 1697. He entered Stockholm on a chestnut horse with silver horseshoes carrying his scepter and wearing his crown to the acclamation of an entire people, worshipers of anything novel and invariably filled with great expectations of a young prince."[2]

Karl XII was one of a whole new generation of monarchs mounting thrones across Europe. In 1701 the childless Charles II of Spain would die, initiating a scramble for his throne, and the War of the Spanish Succession began pitting France against England, the Netherlands, Prussia, Austria, the emperor and several German states. A year later, William III (last of the William and Mary dual monarchy) would die, passing the English crown to his sister-in-law Anne. Louis XIV would hang on for another fourteen years, but spent most of that time embroiled in the Spanish Succession War. Christian V died in August 1699 and was succeeded by his son Frederick IV of Denmark who carried on the Danish thirst for recovery of territories lost to Sweden. Frederick William of Brandenburg died in 1688 leaving the electorate to his son, Frederick III. But the new ruler obtained permission from Emperor Leopold I to be crowned Frederick I of Prussia-Brandenburg.

In Poland Karl X's old antagonist, John Casimir, had abdicated in 1648 and been succeeded by Michael Korybut who was replaced in turn by John III Sobieski. It was Sobieski who was one of the key players in stemming a new tide of Turkish invasion of Europe. His passing in June 1696 opened the way for the election of Augustus II, elector of Saxony, to the Polish throne creating a formidable alliance and a potential problem for Sweden.

The biggest changes, however, were occurring in Russia. Alexis, whose Baltic ambitions had been thwarted by treaties and a preoccupation with the Ottomans and Tartars, had left his empire to two young sons and an ambitious daughter. Ivan V died in February 1696 leaving his half-brother, Peter, as sole Tsar — sister Sophia was hustled off to a nunnery. That same year Peter took the Turkish fortress of Azov at the mouth of the Don River. The twenty-four-year-old was already demonstrating his military abilities.

Peter made his famous tour of Western Europe in 1697–98 to learn of the West, make contacts and promote an alliance against the Turks. But when Austria, the Commonwealth and Venice settled with the Ottomans at Carlowitz in January 1699, Peter was not long in following suit. Now both Poland-Lithuania and Russia were free to turn their attention to the north and retake lost territory from an adolescent king.

Though Karl XI had certainly improved the country's position financially and militarily, Sweden's hold on her overseas provinces was still precarious. The reduktion which had been so successful in Sweden proved to be something else across the sea. The reduktion in the German provinces produced much less crown revenue than expected, but did stimulate opposition to Swedish rule.

In the Baltics it was even worse. The tangled history of land ownership made it impossible to judge fairly what lands should be returned to the crown. In Livonia 72.3 percent of the land wound up in crown hands compared to just 1.25 percent prior to the reduktion. In Estonia 53 percent of the estates were impacted. Local tolerance for Swedish rule received a setback. On top of all these negatives there were a number of European states still unhappy with Sweden for her neutrality during the Nine Years War. The war clouds were gathering and Sweden was in the eye of the storm.

The envying and resentful gazes turned toward Sweden saw in its youthful king an opportunity to settle old scores. Karl XII, though only a boy, had received all the advantages an heir apparent would ordinarily get in Europe. His instruction in languages was well grounded. He spoke and wrote German, French and Latin fluently and could converse in Finnish, Italian and Polish. Later he picked up Turkish as well. His Greek, however, was never more than rudimentary. His Lutheran instruction was not neglected and he remained devoutly religious all his life. He had a thorough knowledge of history both ancient and modern. He excelled in mathematics and its application to the martial arts. Artillery and fortification design became great interests of his. He had a complete knowledge of recent Swedish campaigns and battles. Karl could place every regiment and describe their movements at the Battle of Lützen from memory. His education was cut short by his father's death. Philosophy and political science were to be addressed between his fifteenth and eighteenth years and therefore were never covered.

Karl loved hunting and other outdoor activities. He was never comfortable in the presence of women except those of his family. He was particularly attached to his older sister,

Hedwig Sophia. He handled himself well when dealing with nobles and diplomats, but was most at ease with fellow officers. Small talk with the sergeant of the guard or the soldier in the field were more his style. Life in the open shared with his hardy comrades in arms was entirely to his liking. He was a born campaigner.

The death of Karl XII's mother in 1693, when he was only eleven, was devastating. Ulrika Eleanora, the Danish princess, passed away after a couple of years of declining health involving fevers and progressive weakness. She refused to go abroad for treatment because she could not bear leaving her family and slipped away at thirty-six years of age. Karl XI fainted upon the news and Prince Karl took to bed with a fever. Sorrow hung over the whole country. Karl XII would lose both parents before he turned fifteen.

As a child Karl XII was precocious. As a boy-king he could be truculent and haughty, traits that disappeared with maturity. Not a natural student, Karl did continue to study languages and the military arts after becoming king. There was much to keep abreast of—technology was changing the face of war.

The two major developments in arms were the improved flintlock and the bayonet. The flintlock, now lighter and faster firing, had completely replaced the matchlock and wheel lock in the field. The combination of flintlock and bayonet made the infantry the queen of battle. The pikemen were no longer needed. A well drilled line of infantry could stop a cavalry charge in its tracks with the faster firing flintlock musket and bayonet. Training in reloading and maintaining orderly lines while maneuvering in combat became all important. The western European style of fighting was one of arranging both sides into uniform lines of infantry facing each other and banging away with musket fire until one side broke and fell back. Advances were made in an orderly fashion to the beat of drums and perhaps a fife or bugle. Artillery was added to the lines and battles became defensive in nature. If one side was dug in or in a fortified position, an open field attack by the other side was expensive in terms of losses of men.

Karl XII, however, had been raised with the Swedish style of aggressive warfare. Swedish infantry was equipped with the very best in flintlock muskets and their bayonets, having a better mount system, were superior to most western versions, but Karl retained the pikeman. A third of each battalion was made up of troops with this weapon. In addition, each infantryman carried a sword which Karl personally designed. The musket was to be fired at close range and the attack then carried home with cold steel. If the cavalry charge could be dismantled by musket fire and the bayonet, an assault by close packed infantry might not.

This style of warfare required a disciplined and well trained soldier. In this Karl had, perhaps, the finest in Europe. Voltaire says, "The Swedes are handsome, robust, agile and capable of enduring the hardest labor, hunger, and poverty. They are born soldiers, extremely proud, [and] courageous."[3]

Eyewitness accounts tell of Swedish infantry attacking at a dead run. In many battles the Swedish foot did not even bother to fire, but crossed the last hundred yards first on the double, then at a run. The enemy might get off two or three artillery salvos and one or two musket volleys, but the Swedes would be among them with sword, pike and bayonet. Karl XII had taken his father's tactic of an all-out cavalry assault with cold steel and applied it to his infantry.

Having secured control of the Swedish Empire, Karl XII settled back into his old ways, hunting, attending to military matters and indulging in balls, banquets and parties. It was rumored he also had a torrid affair with a lady of the court. He relied on Piper to run things, making him a count and elevating him to the position of prime minister in all but name. Karl did attend council meetings now and then, but exhibited an air of indifference and was inattentive. This led to indecisiveness in the government, but events on Sweden's borders would soon force an end to this situation.

The opening salvo of the Great Northern War was fired by Frederick a month after Karl XI's death. Denmark invaded Holstein-Gottorp and razed the fortress at Schleswig built by the duchy to defend itself against Danish aggression. The Swedish Regency did nothing but wring its hands, encouraging the view that Sweden was now impotent.

Unbeknownst to Sweden, diplomacy by her enemies had for some time been building coalitions against her. In March 1698 the Danes and Saxons had signed a defensive pact. Frederick IV's ascension in 1699 gave new vigor to the Danish reconquest appetites, but the country was not foolish enough to commit to a war without allies. The western European powers were embroiled in the international politics of the Spanish Succession so Frederick turned to the east. In April 1699 Russia and Denmark had signed a defensive agreement to be effective upon Russia's peace with Turkey. Frederick gained the crown in August and in September he signed a new defensive treaty with Saxony in Dresden. Meanwhile Augustus II also signed a treaty with Peter that same month which committed Russia to an invasion of Ingria in 1700. Frederick had his coalition. Sweden's old enemies Saxony-Poland-Lithuania, Denmark and Russia were poised for the kill. Sweden and her new king were quite alone.

The Råd dithered knowing trouble was brewing, but not understanding the extent of the coming disaster. Karl seemed quite unconcerned until one day while attending the council, he suddenly stood up and, according to Voltaire, made a short speech.

"'Gentlemen,' he said with an air of gravity, self-confidence and determination, 'I have resolved never to fight an unjust war, nor finish a lawful one except with the destruction of my enemies. My mind is made up; I shall attack the first to reveal his intentions, and when I have beaten him, I hope I shall give a little fright to the rest.'"[4]

Voltaire says Karl XII, from that point on, completely changed his ways. His ostentatious dress was exchanged for a private's uniform. He renounced women — Karl would never marry — and strong drink. In camp he did not wear a wig and was easily recognized, standing out among his generals with their silk, lace and pronounced wigs, the fashion of the day. Karl ate what his men ate and slept on the same style cots. He would live simply and share the soldier's life with his troops. His conversion was none too soon.

In February 1700 Saxon troops under Generals Flemming and Carlowitz crossed the border into Livonia and stormed Fort Kobron without a declaration of war. The Saxons then attacked Riga. Seventy-eight-year-old Count Erik Dahlberg, the Swedish commander at Riga, sent a courier around the Gulf of Bothnia, the sea being ice packed, to inform the king. Word reached Karl in March. It was no surprise when the young monarch next learned that Denmark had invaded Holstein-Gottorp for a second time. The Great Northern War was now a shooting war.

Karl gave the word to mobilize. The call-up system so carefully designed and organized by his father went into action. Coats of the Swedish soldier were donned by men from one end of the country to the other including new units such as the Regiment of Scanian Dragoons made up of troops from the country estates and manors of Skåne, Halland and Blekinge. Companies were organized, then marched to assembly points to become battalions and finally regiments, the Dalarnian, Västermanland and Uppland infantry regiments. Well-equipped cavalry units formed up, the West Gotlander, Smålander, East Gotlander and Household Regiment of Horse. Also called up were the North and South Scanian Cavalry Regiments. There were the king's special troops, His Majesty's Drabants of Köping and Arboga that Karl

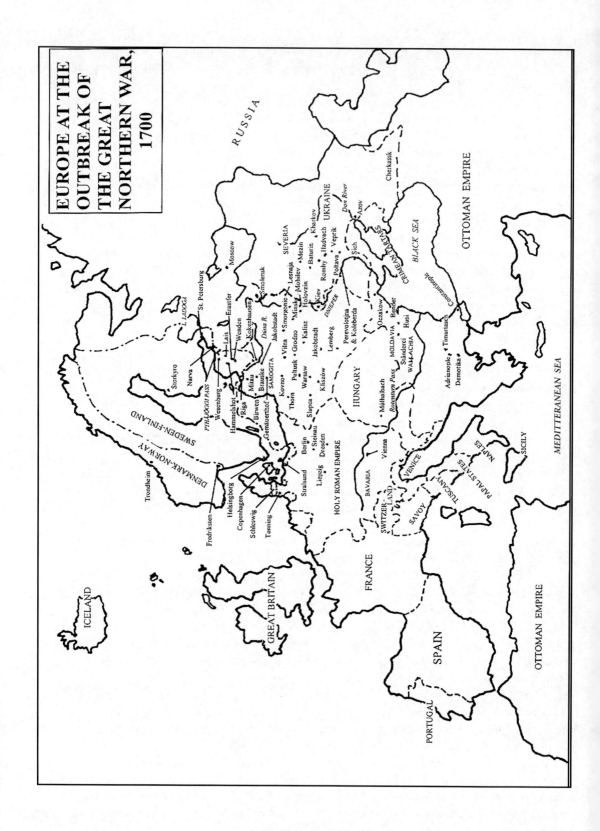

EUROPE AT THE
OUTBREAK OF
THE GREAT
NORTHERN WAR,
1700

had selected and trained himself. These 200 men acted as his staff. All officers, they could be sent to take command of units with fallen or incapacitated leaders. There were the Guards from Stockholm, regiments of double strength that always accompanied the king. Last to arrive were the tough troops from Västerbotten, coming 350 miles by sleigh to reach final assembly points. Karl had his army, an army constructed by his father. It was, perhaps, the finest army in the world. But did the teenage king have the ability to make use of it?

In the overseas provinces the same mobilization was taking place. As Finnish and Estonian troops formed up they were sent south to aid Riga. Karl dispatched a contingent to General Nils Gyllenstierna, Swedish governor of Bremen, to join operations against the Danes in Holstein-Gottorp. Eight thousand troops were sent to Pomerania adjacent to the threatened duchy.

Danish troops had already taken Gottorp Castle and were besieging the city of Tönning. Frederick himself left for the front to witness the final conquest. Troops from Saxony, Brandenburg-Prussia, Wolfen-Büttel and Hesse-Kassel were marching to reinforce the Danes and get in on the kill.

However, England and the Netherlands were also guarantors of the Treaty of Altona along with Sweden and now they began to act. The United Provinces sent three regiments to Holstein-Gottorp and Hamburg joined with a small force. England and the Dutch each dispatched a fleet to the Baltic. Karl had some allies and he made use of them.

The garrison at Tönning, holding on stubbornly, was commanded by the Swedish general Johan Gabriel Baner. Gyllenstierna brought a small Swedish force up from the south to assist. The Dutch and Hamburg army was commanded by George of Hanover (later to be King George I of England), also moved north. The allied army forced the Danes to raise the siege of Tönning.

The combined English-Dutch fleet finally arrived at Gothenburg. Karl put to sea with his magnificent Swedish fleet from Karlskrona. The Danes, however, had placed their fleet in the main channel of the Sound with orders to prevent the two fleets from combining at all costs. There was an alternative route, but it lay through a hazardous strait used only by shallow draft boats. Karl ordered his admiral, Hans Wachtmeister, architect of the great fleet, to pass through the strait. Wachtmeister hesitated, afraid of losing some of his fine ships. Karl railed and the admiral finally complied on July 5. Thirteen of the largest ships were left behind and five ships ran aground, but the main body passed the Sound and joined the allied fleet. The Danish navy, now badly outnumbered, scurried into Copenhagen Harbor where it could hold off an attack.

Next, Karl made a wholly unexpected move. He ordered the combined allied fleet to blockade Copenhagen while he led a landing force of 4,000 men onto the beaches of Zealand at Humleback, seven miles from Copenhagen. He encountered strong earthworks, but they were manned by militia which were easily scattered. The Danish army was in Holstein-Gottorp and Karl had an open path to a poorly defended Copenhagen. An additional 9,000 troops were ferried across from Skåne. Karl marched on the Danish capital at the head of 11,000 men.

Frederick knew when he was beaten. He quickly settled with Holstein-Gottorp in the Treaty of Travendal, giving back all he had taken. Karl had his first victory, a war begun and ended in less than six weeks. The Swedish king controlled Zealand and stood at the gates of a nearly defenseless Copenhagen. Here was an opportunity to crush Frederick and remove the Danish menace once and for all. But the Dutch and English had no desire to see Sweden swallow up Denmark and informed Karl the war was over. The English and Dutch fleets sailed home. Karl's fleet was still divided and either part would be easy prey for the united

Danish fleet. So Karl withdrew his troops and turned his attention to the other end of the Baltic. It is worth noting that the Danish population was favorably impressed with the Swedish troops. Discipline was maintained so well that there was no looting or other offenses usually associated with an occupation force. All food and supplies were paid for by the army and personal items were bought by the soldiers. In fact local merchants catered to the foreigners because they were willing to pay more than Danes.

Augustus II had hoped to take Riga by surprise, sending a Saxon army of three infantry and four dragoon regiments (5,000 men) across the Düna in February to attack the city. Unfortunately for him, his Saxons ran into Count Erik Dahlberg, the tough old (75) Swedish governor-general of the province who had earned the title "The Vauban of Sweden" for his skill in fortifications. It was he who had discovered and marked the path across the Danish islands for Karl X in his first invasion of Zealand. Dahlberg organized a stout defense of the well fortified city and threw the Saxons back though they did manage to take the small fortress of Dünamünde at the mouth of the Düna. Dahlberg then proceeded to defeat the invaders in two battles, at Wenden and at Neumühle. The Saxons had had enough and retreated back across the Düna.

In May Augustus sent his Saxons into Livonia again, but now Finnish and Estonian troops had arrived. Again the Saxons were defeated and driven out. In July Augustus sent his Saxon army into Livonia a third time. By then much of the Swedish army had returned north. Livonia had been suffering from famine and drought for two years. There was no food, forage or money to sustain a large army. The Saxons were able to cross the Düna without serious opposition and move on Riga, laying siege to the city.

By August Peter had settled with the Ottomans and set his army in motion to win his dream of a corridor to the Baltic. Karl spent two months readying his army for the trip to the east while Peter's army of some 40,000 troops marched on Narva. The Saxon investment of Riga, meanwhile, had not gone well. The heavy siege artillery was supplied with the wrong caliber of ammunition. There was no way for the Saxons to stop the city from being supplied by sea. By the end of September the Saxons had raised the siege and recrossed the Düna to winter quarters. Augustus even sent emissaries to Karl with offers of peace, but the young king was incensed over the Polish king's treacherous invasion and would not consider the proposals. Peter arrived at Narva, built extensive siege works and began the bombardment at the end of October.

Karl reached Pernau on October 6 while his main army debarked at Reval. He made his headquarters at Wesenburg and spent five weeks collecting and organizing his forces. Karl's generals and the French ambassador tried to dissuade him from the Narva relief effort. It was a seven day march to the besieged city over roads now turned into muddy bogs. Peter had sent General Sheremetev with 5,000 men to Wesenberg to destroy Swedish stores there. Sheremetev had been turned back short of his goal, but he had laid waste to everything from there back to Narva. Karl had scarcely 11,000 men to throw against a well entrenched army of at least 35,000 troops. Karl's comment was that he had to stop Peter or the whole Baltic coast would be flooded with Russian troops. He had come too far and Swedes were always fighting much larger Russian armies. On November 13 he began his march to Narva.

The Swedish relief army waded through mud that reached to their knees sapping the strength of man and horse. Food and fodder were scarce and both the troops and the horses were hungry, cold and wet. Karl had to navigate three passes, any one of which could have been easily defended. The first two were unguarded, but at the third, Pyhäjöggi Pass, the Swedes discovered Sheremetev with his 5,000 men in a strong position. Karl personally led a cavalry charge to dislodge the Russians and found only a rear guard covering the departing brigade.

The skirmish at Pyhäjöggi Pass was a real morale booster for the Swedish army. Their king and general had selected the point of attack well, so that the enemy guns had fired harmlessly over their heads. He had led the attack and driven off the Russians. Word spread among the Swedish troops that this was a leader of promise. Guns and supplies left behind were welcome additions to the army. The road to Narva now lay open.

By November 19, 1700, Karl was within a mile and a half of Narva. He fired a series of cannon shots in a prearranged pattern as a signal to Henning Rudolf Horn, the commander of the city. Peter had left the Russian siege army the day before expecting there to be a lengthy buildup of digging earthworks before an attack was attempted. The Swedes claimed he fled in panic as their army approached, even striking a coin later showing the tsar cowering in fear.

In any case Tsar Peter was not there when Karl and his small army marched into a wooded area near the Russian camp. This fortified camp was on the south side of the town and well protected. Peter had constructed earthen walls nine feet high behind six foot wide ditches. One hundred and forty cannon were mounted along the walls manned by 26,000 troops (25 regiments). Another two infantry regiments, two dragoon regiments and some 5,000 cavalry, including Cossacks, were manning the siege trenches and flanking the camp.

Though the Russians expected a slow buildup Karl could not tarry. He did not have the supplies for a drawn out conflict and it wasn't his style, nor was it the Swedish army's way of fighting. Though tired and hungry, they were ready for action. The long march had created pent up expectations.

Karl allowed Karl Gustaf Rehnskiöld to lay out the plan of battle. The field marshal set the Swedish guns on a slight incline to cover his troops as they moved out of the woods and formed up on November 20. The Swedes offered the Russians the opportunity to attack them in the open, but the Magyar prince Charles Eugene du Croy, left in command by Peter, held his troops within his earthworks. Karl would have to storm the camp.

By 2:00 p.m. Rehnskiöld had the army ready for the attack. He commanded the left wing himself while Karl took up his station with his Drabants commanded by Count Arvid Horn. The right wing was commanded by Count Otto Vellingk. Just as the Swedes began advancing a snowstorm struck blowing into the faces of the defenders. The Swedish cavalry quickly drove off the Russian horse and in fifteen minutes the Swedish foot was inside the entrenchments. The Russian right broke first and the fleeing soldiers crowded onto a bridge until it collapsed, drowning hundreds. The Swedish well disciplined left wing wheeled and rolled up the line. The rest of the Russian army retreated to an area of the camp where hundreds of wagons were parked. Using these for cover they fought on until dawn. The sunlight revealed the Russians' complete encirclement and the commander surrendered.

Karl found himself with more prisoners than he had troops. He could do nothing but disarm them and send them home. All the next day a steady stream of men headed eastward from Narva. Karl had lost 2,000 men. Russian losses are estimated to have been between eight and ten thousand. The Swedes took 140 guns and other much needed supplies. Karl, who had been in the thick of the fighting, had won his second quick victory, this time in a major battle.

Historians have often blamed the defeat of a superior, entrenched army by a half starved and freezing Swedish force on the Russians being inexperienced, untrained rabble (a picture Peter even encouraged), but this was not the case. Many of these same Russians had been in the battles against the Turks where Sweden had not fought a war for almost twenty years. True, many of the high ranking Swedish officers had served in various armies during the Nine Years War, and a few units had been hired out to one belligerent country or another, but in general the Swedish soldiers had not been in battle before.

Furthermore, the Russian army had been reorganized and in training for the last fifty years. In 1696 there were 47 foreign cavalry colonels in the army, 77 in the infantry. Altogether, 560 foreign officers were serving in the Russian army at the time, training and drilling Peter's soldiers. Nor was their equipment inferior. Russia had its own factories supplying flintlocks and cannon, as good as any in Western Europe. Russian artillery manufactures had switched from clay molds to iron about 1690, even before the French had made this modernization step.

The Russian defeat at Narva was not so much the fault of an inadequate Russian military as it was the superior Swedish army it encountered. The aggressive tactics and iron discipline of Karl's troops made the difference. Mid-level and junior Swedish officers were adequate and professional, but the senior officers were as good as or better than any in Europe at the time. As much as anything the battle was an affirmation of Karl XI's plan and organization of a reserve army trained and ready for war. This Swedish army was his father's creation, and Karl XII had demonstrated he could employ it effectively.

24. Karl XII and War in Poland

Karl XII had been able to focus his attention on Peter partly because of Erik Dahlberg's stout defense of Riga and partly because of French efforts to mediate a peace between Sweden and Augustus. As all sides lined up for the coming struggle over the Spanish throne, Louis XIV felt he could get Sweden's help and maybe Augustus's in obtaining some part of a partitioned Spanish Empire.

On November 1, 1700, Charles II of Spain died leaving no heir. In his will he nominated the duke of Anjou, Louis XIV's grandson, to take the throne. If the French duke would not take the entire domain, it was to pass to the Austrian Hapsburgs. Suddenly, Louis XIV had a shot at obtaining control of the entire Spanish Empire instead of just a piece of it. A united France and Spain, with all their American possessions, would make Louis XIV the most powerful monarch on earth, dwarfing the other western European nations.

The potential for such a superpower immediately turned the Maritime Nations against France and led to the outbreak of the War of Spanish Succession. Louis was now afraid that Sweden would join the maritime powers against him and that even Poland-Lithuania might take their side. He was better off letting them fight among themselves.

As pro-French and anti-French sides began to take shape, Sweden's position became complicated. She had historic and diplomatic ties to France. Yet, Karl needed the Maritime Nations' guarantee of the Travendal Treaty to keep Denmark from becoming an aggressor at Sweden's back door. At the same time the nineteen-year-old king was trying to decipher the complicated world of international politics, he had an army to manage.

Following the Battle of Narva, the Swedish army had moved into the comfortable tent city left to them by the evacuating Russians. But pestilence, which had begun to be a problem for Peter's troops, now broke out with a vengeance among the Swedes. As Karl watched his troops being ravaged by disease, he resolved to never again allow his army to be quartered in a closed camp. He moved the army to Estonia and Livonia for winter quarters where they could exercise and train. His headquarters was in Lais, north of Dorpat. He sent detachments to the east and northeast to test Peter's strength along the borders. It would be spring before he could get reinforcements to begin another campaign.

With Western European nations lining up for the Succession War, Augustus and Peter arranged a conference at Birsen in February 1701. The subject was a coordinated war on Sweden and a division of the spoils afterward. By the Treaty of Birsen Augustus would get Estonia and Livonia when Sweden was defeated and Russia would take Ingria. In addition the tsar would furnish 14 thousand to 20 thousand men to help Augustus in this conquest. Augustus had been waging his war against Sweden using troops available to him as duke of Saxony, some 26,000 experienced, well trained soldiers. He had been unable to get the Sejm to sanction the war and provide Commonwealth troops. In fact a substantial party in Poland-Lithuania wanted to cooperate with Sweden against Russia in order to recover lands lost to Russia, particularly in the Ukraine including the city of Kiev. Leading this group was the commander of the Commonwealth army, Jablonowski, and his son-in-law Rafal Leszczyński. The country was divided between the pro-Swedish party and the pro-Russian party. A third group, headed by Prince Radziejowski and larger than either of the first two, was intent on maintaining aristocacy power. This aristocracy party wanted to limit crown authority and eschewed both war and foreign alliances.

Even within Lithuania there was civil unrest. The Sapieha family, which wanted to gain the commonwealth throne, was in a political struggle against the Lithuanian Crown Army supported by an opposition party known as the United Families. In December 1700 this conflict flared into open warfare. The whole commonwealth was teetering on the brink of civil war.

During the winter of 1700-01, Karl had to decide which enemy to attack first. He did not have sufficient forces to engage both Peter and Augustus at the same time; he had to deal with one quickly, freeing himself to attack the other.

Narva had crippled Peter temporarily. Though an efficient system of recruitment was a problem, Peter had no shortage of manpower to draw from. The Russian Empire at that time contained 10 million to 12 million people as compared to 3 million to 4 million in all Sweden and its possessions. Guns, munitions and cannon were Peter's real problem. He scrambled to replace those lost at Narva to the point of melting down church bells for iron to feed his artillery factories.

Historians and military strategists have often argued that if Karl XII had gone after Peter in 1701 he would have been able to defeat him and force a peace treaty. It must be remembered, however, that Karl had two active enemies to deal with and a third, Denmark, waiting for an excuse to reenter the war. He had dealt Russia a blow and his frontier garrisons along the east side of Ingria, and Livonia were containing Peter's incursions whereas Augustus's Saxons continued to raid into Livonia from Kurland during the winter. Also, the political divisions in Poland-Lithuania appeared to provide more opportunity for a quick victory than the huge expanse and comparatively politically monolithic domain of Peter's Russia. By the end of 1700 Karl had decided to move against Augustus first, hoping for an early decisive victory that would allow him to turn against Peter in the same campaign season.

Karl's first problem was crossing the Düna. South of the river Field Marshal Steinau, the Saxon commander, had 9,000 crack Saxon troops and another 10,000 less reliable Russians under Prince Anikita Ivanovich Repnin. These had to be spread along the river until he could be certain of the crossing point. Then he could concentrate forces to crush the landing party. Ramparts and artillery were placed along the river at strategic points.

In April 1701 Karl ordered the 76-year-old Count Dahlberg, still governor-general at Riga, to gather boats and build a pontoon bridge that could be floated into place for the crossing. Karl would attack at a point near the city.

In May 10,000 soldiers arrived at Reval. On the king's nineteenth birthday, June 17, the army was ordered out of quarters for the march south. Karl's army of 18,000 men marched through Walk and Wolmar, but at Wenden it turned toward Kokenhausen and a cavalry regiment was sent ahead to threaten the fortress. Steinau reacted by moving a substantial force to that point ready to reinforce the garrison.

However, on July 3, just three miles from Kokenhausen, the marching columns turned right and in a series of forced marches arrived at Riga in four days where Dahlberg had all in readiness for the crossing. The night before the attack Karl sent a detachment down river to threaten Dünamünde, drawing off additional Saxon troops.

At dawn on July 9 Karl led the attack across the river in the lead boat. Dahlberg, the wily old general and engineer, had done his preparation work well. The larger landing craft had ramps at the bow that would be lowered onto the beach for the soldiers to cross over. During the crossing the ramps were in a vertical position, protecting troops on board from shore fire. Transports were fitted with leather curtains or "sails" to stop shot and shell. The smaller lead boats had bales of straw and grass stacked at the bows providing protection. A smoke screen from fires fed with green foliage drifted across the river and from specially designated boats which obscured the crossing flotilla, enabling them to get close to shore before receiving any effective enemy fire. Guns from the Riga fortress and armed merchantmen in the river pounded the shore with a heavy barrage.

Karl leaped out of his boat as soon as it was near shore, not waiting for it to beach. With him was the Grenadier Battalion of the Life Guards. They dashed through the water on foot to attack the palisades along the shore. They were hit by fire from the few artillery pieces at that point and shots from the defending musketeers. The shoreline defenses were quickly taken out as battalions from the Västermanland, Uppland and Dalarnian Regiments, about 6,000 men, joined them.

Defense of the area was commanded by Lieutenant General Paijkull, a Livonian by birth. He formed up his Saxons for a counterattack with the splendid Saxon cavalry on the flanks. They advanced, discharging their volley at 100 yards. The Swedes fired at 50 with devastating effect. Paijkull was driven back. A second charge was repulsed by bayonet and pike. Steinau arrived with reinforcements and led a third attack. This time the Swedish right wing was enveloped by the Saxon cavalry. A detachment of grenadiers was thrown into the melee, then all the horse the Swedes had on shore, 150 Drabants and 50 troopers from the Household Horse Regiment. They charged the Saxon cuirassiers without firing a shot, bringing home the cold steel. The wing wavered, but held. A Västerbotten battalion charged in, having just arrived from their boats. The Saxons were thrown back. The Russians under Prince Repnin turned tail. Steinau organized his troops for a fourth assault, but decided the situation was now hopeless and pulled back. The Swedish beachhead was secure.

Phase II was to bring about the destruction of the Saxon army. The pontoon bridge was floated into position to provide a bridge for the main army to cross the 600 yards of water. But a violent storm blew in dispersing the parts of the floating bridge before it could be secured. The main part of the army had to be ferried across piecemeal allowing Steinau time to evacuate his army. The Saxons and Russians escaped. The destruction of the Saxon army was incomplete. Karl had lost his opportunity to bring the conflict to a quick conclusion.

The Swedes had lost 500 men dead and wounded in the battle. The Saxons had 800 casualties with another 700 taken prisoner. This was a substantial victory by European standards. It impressed the crown heads and military experts more than Karl's victory at Narva because this was against the vaunted Saxon army. But the Swedish high command was sorely disappointed and set out immediately to find the Saxons. Steinau, however, had moved south into Poland proper assuming the Swedes would not dare to follow.

Karl was undaunted by the commonwealth's boundary, but he did need to secure Livonia and Kurland before he proceeded. The garrisons at Kokenhausen and Kobron abandoned their positions upon hearing of the Swedish crossing of the Düna and the Swedes took them over. Dünamünde was besieged, but held out until December. Mitau, the Kurland capital, was occupied and the main army moved on to take Bauske and Birwen. Kurland was secured and was treated as any other province of the empire.

Lands were surveyed on the Swedish pattern, taxes levied using the Riga base, and all officials were required to take an oath of loyalty to Karl. The Maritime Powers and Prussia were dismayed and alarmed at Karl's lightning conquest of the territories south of the Düna. The prospect of Swedish control of the entire eastern Baltic was unsettling and this strained relations between Sweden and these countries.

Karl was in a quandary. He still planned a winter campaign against Peter (1701-02), but could not proceed until he had secured his flank (Poland-Lithuania) and neutralized the Saxon army. He did not want to be pulled into the commonwealth's political morass, but he needed to get to the Saxon army now in Poland. Augustus, as duke of Saxony and king of Poland-Lithuania, was the key, but how to deal with him and the politically fractured commonwealth was the question.

Karl's presence on the commonwealth's border also increased the political chaos within the country. The aristocracy played the Swedish card to obtain concessions from Augustus including the removal of Saxon troops from Polish soil. Jablanowski, Leszczyńsli and their supporters were in touch with the Swedes. A party supporting James Sobieski, who had been defeated by Augustus in the 1697 bid for the Polish crown, tried to entice Karl to interfere in his behalf. A neutralist party headed by Cardinal Radziejowski, who was also chancellor, was trying to hold things together and keep Sweden out of the commonwealth. The cardinal, with Augustus's support, wrote a letter to Karl on July 25, 1701, asking for a promise not to invade the country.

Karl, not knowing about the king's involvement in the communication, saw this as an opportunity to deal with Augustus. He replied on July 30 demanding that the commonwealth dethrone Augustus, promising not to pursue the Saxon army into Poland until he heard from Radziejowski. To Karl's consternation, the cardinal made the letter public then brought the demand before the Sejm in December 1701.

As the Spanish Succession War advanced toward open hostilities, Sweden's participation was solicited by both sides. Louis XIV appealed to Karl based on past French-Swedish alliances and treaties. The maritime powers cited mutual interests and present treaties (Travendal). William III even put Karl forward for the office of supreme alliance commander. But the Swedish king determined to stay clear of that war. He had quite enough to handle in Eastern Europe.

In September a Russian army moved west to link up with Augustus's forces. A Swedish contingent under General Schlippenbach intercepted the Russians and defeated them. A month later Schlippenbach was beaten at the Battle of Erastfehr by a Russian army of overwhelming numerical superiority. Peter was growing stronger. The sooner Karl could dispatch Augustus and turn to deal with Peter the better would be his chances.

By year's end Karl received the reply to his letter of July 30. It came in the form of a letter from the Sejm and its central theme was, stay out of Poland and Lithuanian territory and out of our business. Radziejowski had used Karl's letter to unite some of the factions against the potential invader, temporarily at least.

In Lithuania the United Families had defeated the Sapieha family, forcing the heads of that clan to flee to Prussia. Fearing the United Family Party would then devastate or even confiscate their family holdings in Samogitia, the Sapiehas petitioned Karl to intercede on their behalf. James Sobieski was in constant communication with the Swedes, presenting strategies for neutralizing the elector-king.

Karl made no commitment to these parties, but in December 1701 he led 400 horsemen in a reconnaissance-in-force deep into Samogitia, the northern province of Lithuania just across the border from Kurland. His next move was to bring his main force, 15,000 men into the province in January 1702. This meant that Karl was postponing a showdown with Peter. Schlippenbach's army was reinforced and militias organized throughout the Baltic provinces in the hope of holding the Russians at bay until Karl had time to deal with them. 4,000 troops were left under Stuart's command to protect Kurland and Riga.

Augustus reacted to the Swedish incursion into commonwealth territory by sending two envoys to the Swedish king. The first was Maria Aurora von Königsmark, a famous beauty, witty and charming. She was born of Swedish nobility, but had spent her adult years at various European courts, bearing Augustus a son in her younger years. Though now thirty-nine, she was still noted for being an intelligent, accomplished and handsome woman, one of the celebrated emancipated women of European society. Karl referred to her once as "that royal whore."[1]

Her family did have land in Livonia and she had several relatives among the officer corps of Karl's army. So she had reason for a visit, but gossip in the European courts passed the word that Augustus sent her to Karl to seduce him and divert his attention from his Polish campaign. If this was the case, the elector-king badly miscalculated. The twenty-year-old king was deeply religious and his father had passed on to him his belief that adultery was a mortal sin. Karl considered even permitting an audience with the lady an act of condoning her lifestyle. Though she tried repeatedly, he would not see her. Finally, she arranged to position herself along a trail the young king used habitually for early morning rides. When he approached, she presented him with a deep curtsy meant to reveal certain of her charms. The king merely doffed his hat politely and moved on. Aurora left for Poland the next day.

Augustus's second emissary was even less successful. The Saxon official was arrested for not having proper credentials and ejected from the headquarters. Did the commonwealth king have serious intentions of negotiating some kind of peace at this point? Probably not. He had a treaty with Peter and was in the final stages of building a new 20,000 man army in Saxony. Another eight thousand troops promised by the emperor were stationed in Bohemia and could be called upon as reserves. He was just playing for time.

Crossing into Lithuania had certainly grabbed the attention of the Oriński and Wiśniowieski clans. These members of the United Families began conducting guerilla warfare on the Swedes, the most serious attack being the massacre of a detachment of 400 troops by 6,000 Wiśniowieski militia. Due to this harassment Karl opened talks with the Sapieha family in March 1702. Karl offered military protection in exchange for commitment to the Swedish dethronement policy. With an ally inside the commonwealth, Karl could move on expeditiously.

The Swedish king left a few regiments in Samogitia to protect the Sapiehas as agreed. He stationed Mörner with 4,000 men at Vilna, a Wiśniewiecki stronghold, and ordered Nils Gyllenstierna to collect all available troops in Swedish Germany and march to his aid. New recruits were coming from Sweden to Riga and these were placed under Maidel's command. Karl, with the main body of his army, advanced on Warsaw hoping to get there before Augustus's Saxons.

The maneuver was carried out without mishap. The Polish army made no attempt to interfere. Karl's well disciplined men passed through the countryside without the stealing and looting common to invading armies. He arrived at the commonwealth's capital on May 14, 1702.

While occupying Warsaw Karl called upon Radziejowski to induce the Sejm to dethrone
Augustus and elect a new king. Augustus, meanwhile, had slipped out of the city ahead of
the Swedish arrival and moved to Krakow. The good cardinal played for time while the neutralist party tried to negotiate with the Swedish king.

Augustus convened a Sejm in Krakow and persuaded the commonwealth's Senate to give
him permission to bring Saxon troops into Poland to confront the Swedes and he was given
command of the Polish Crown Army to use against Karl. The elector-king ordered his Saxons to meet him in Krakow and he set the Polish Army under Luomiski in motion.

Karl ordered Gyllenstierna in Swedish Pomerania, who had almost 10,000 troops, to
head for Krakow. The same order was passed to Mörner with his 4,000 men. Karl left Warsaw leading 8,000 soldiers en route to Krakow. He wanted to intercept the Saxon army before
the Poles arrived. Spilling Polish blood would only complicate his situation. Augustus, on the
other hand, wanted to meet Karl before Gyllenstierna could join him.

By mid–June Augustus was encamped at Pinczów with 14,000 Saxon troops. Karl was
near Kliszów waiting for Mörner to arrive. Augustus moved closer to the Swedish camp. He
had time. Gyllenstierna was still in Brandenburg and would not arrive until sometime in
August. The elector-king was confident of victory. He was only waiting for Lubomirski, who
had asked Augustus to hold off until he got there so as to cover his army in the glory of the
victory. Having superior numbers and the renowned Saxon army, Augustus and his staff
expected to take the offense and initiate the battle on their terms. They were quite surprised
when, on July 9 at mid-day, what they thought were reconnaissance patrols turned out to be
King Karl XII and the main Swedish army on their front. The Saxon officers, about to take
noon meal, ordered their servants to hold lunch while they took care of a few Swedes.

Mörner had arrived at the Swedish camp the night of July 8 after two days of forced
March. Karl passed the word they would attack the next morning. Piper and some of Karl's
staff counseled waiting until the fresh arrivals had time to rest, to which the king retorted,
"hungry dogs bite best."[2]

After a hot evening meal, the first in days for Mörner's 4,000 men, and a good night's
sleep the troops were rolled out at 6:00 a.m. for morning prayers. The troops fell into line as
reports came of a Saxon advance. When this proved false Karl ordered a march on the Saxon
camp. Four columns navigated the five miles of woods without drum or fife in order to surprise the enemy.

Exiting the woods in front of the Saxon camp the Swedes deployed in the usual manner, infantry in the center flanked by cavalry. The surprised Saxons quickly formed up with
infantry and artillery in the center, horse on the right and left. But the Swedes also got a surprise, for on the Saxon far right Hieronymus Lubomiski pulled into position with his
magnificent Polish Crown Army. There were four lines of the famous Polish cavalry resplen-
dent in scarlet tunics and shining armor, on their big powerful war horses. There were the
aristocratic Hussars with lance, sword and engraved musket, and the chain-mailed Panzers
with spear and mace.

In all, Augustus had 9,000 Saxon cavalry, 7,500 infantry, 8,000 Polish cavalry and 46
guns. Karl could muster only 8,000 foot and 4,000 horse. His artillery was still struggling
through the woods. He had a total of 4 three-pounders that had caught up with him. His
right wing was commanded by Rehnskiöld and his left by his brother-in-law Frederick, duke
of Holstien-Gottorp. Karl, with almost no field guns, was outnumbered two to one.

The young king surveyed the situation. The Saxon left wing was anchored against the
river and had a marsh running in front of it as did the center. Only in front of the right wing

was there a clear field though even here the enemy had an advantage of being on higher ground than the Swedes. Karl shifted his infantry, especially pikemen, from the center to the left and advanced his left wing to take the high ground.

The Saxon guns opened up on the Swedes and Frederick was cut in two by a cannon-ball. Karl took personal command of the left wing as the Polish cavalry charged home. They were met by Småland and Scanian cavalry under Vellingk interspersed with units of infantry led by Stenbock. Pikemen in the front brought the Polish charge to a halt and repeated musket volleys from the rear decimated their ranks. The Polish cavalry wavered then fled, exposing the Saxon right wing to a flank attack. The whole right wing collapsed and was scattered.

Meanwhile the Saxon left wing had worked its way through the marsh and was assaulting the Swedish right. With over 4,000 horse against the Swedish 2,000 they had outflanked the Swedes and were pressing in on three sides. Rehnskiöld ordered his rear ranks to turn about so that he had parallel lines back to back. At the end of the lines, the Drabants made a link between the two lines forming a U-shaped defense. The situation appeared bleak for the Swedes, but the Saxon horse had been schooled in the *caracol* cavalry tactic of trotting to the front, discharging pistol and carbine, then falling back to allow the next rank to perform the same maneuver.

Rehnskiöld unleashed his mounted troops in their accustomed full-gallop close-order charge. Firearms were discharged only at point blank range and only if they did not slow the attack. The Saxon squadrons fell back and then fled in disorder. They ran for the marsh and the river. Horses sank in the bog, spilling riders and leaving them afoot. In the river many a horse and trooper were drowned.

Even the weak Swedish center charged the Saxon infantry at a run. Six battalions led by Major General Posse struggled across the marsh under heavy fire, then dashed into the midst of the Germans. Heavy hand-to-hand combat marked this portion of the front and it was here that most of the Swedish casualties were sustained. But once Karl had secured the left he began sending squadrons of cavalry into the center. The Saxons were driven back from their guns which were taken and employed by the Swedes. The Saxon infantry broke. Some fled into the marsh at their backs. The rest were surrounded.

In all, 2,000 Saxons and Poles lay dead on the field. Another 1,000 were prisoners. Karl lost 300 dead, including his brother-in-law Frederick, and 600 wounded. Credit for the victory goes to the aggressive tactics of the Swedish army, the training and discipline of the troops, the professionalism of the officers and generals, but above all it was Karl's triumph. His cool headed shift to the left of the army, his handling of the unexpected arrival of the Polish Crown Army and his performance as general-in-the-field were nearly flawless and made the difference.

Karl made his headquarters in Krakow. Augustus, who had escaped across the marshes, slunk back to Lamberg in south-central Poland to collect his scattered army. The emperor tried to negotiate a Swedish-Saxon peace, but the elector-king showed no sign of willingness to compromise. The tsar sent troops into Lithuania proclaiming himself protector of the grand duchy. More Russians moved up the Dnieper into Poland and Peter sent troops to Augustus's army.

In late 1702 the elector-king moved his army north across the Vistula for safety. Peter, meanwhile, had been busy in the Baltics. He built a navy on Lake Ladoga and sent it against the Swedish flotilla. The Swedes were routed giving the tsar control of the lake. Russian forces had defeated Schlippenbach at Hummelshot in July confining Swedish control to the cities and fortresses. Peter brought in Asiatic tribesmen, including some of the Crimean Tartars, to loot, sack, burn and carry away captives for sale as slaves. One of these Livonian peasant girls wound up among the Russian soldiers and eventually became Peter's wife and later empress as Katherine I.

The devastation was so complete that the Baltic provinces ceased to be a source of supply for the Swedish army. Peter next invaded Ingria, storming the fortress of Nöteborg in October 1702. In May 1703 Peter would move down the Neva to its mouth where he captured the small fort of Nyeuschantz and renamed it St. Petersburg. This would be his capital, Russia's window to the West. He built a fort on an island in the mouth of the Neva to protect his city and extended control along the south shore of the Gulf of Finland, taking Koporé and Jama. In 1704 he took the university city of Dorpat and finally he captured Narva.

To try to intimidate the Russians, Karl moved his army north to Praga just east of Warsaw. Augustus, afraid of being encircled, sent his infantry to Thorn, already held by a Saxon garrison. His cavalry, under Steinau, he sent east to link up with the Wisńiowiecki forces in Lithuania.

Karl led 3,000 cavalry and dragoons in a drive east to catch the Saxons. At Pultusk the two sides fought it out on a bridge leading to the city and in the city streets. Steinau fled leaving 200 dead and 800 taken prisoner. Karl lost less than 20 men. It was Karl's first battle in complete command without any of his senior generals in support. He returned to the main army and proceeded to Thorn where he laid siege to the town and the 6,000 Saxons inside.

While Karl besieged Thorn, Rehnskiöld with 8,000 Swedes combined with Stanislaus Leszczyński leading an army representing the nobility of Great Poland (northwestern Poland). They cleared Great Poland, fighting Augustus backed by the Saxon cavalry, the Lithuanian and Polish Crown Armies. During this period Karl also received word of a convention signed by the United Provinces and the New Queen Ann of England guaranteeing the Travendal Treaty. Denmark would be held in check a while longer.

By September 14 the heavy guns had arrived from Kurland via Danzig where they were held up-the free city demonstrating its independence. The assault planned for the end of the month was not needed. On October 4, 1703, the city and fort surrendered. Five thousand Saxon soldiers were sent to Sweden. The city paid 100,000 *thaler* in indemnities and turned over all artillery and other war materials. Augustus's Saxon army was now down to 4,000.

The elector-king needed help and again he turned to his Russian ally. On October 10, 1703, a new treaty was signed promising Russian subsidies to Augustus for building a new Saxon army. These troops plus the commonwealth's forces were to join a Russian army in a war against Karl to be fought on Polish soil.

This was too much for the neutralist party and Cardinal Radziejowski. In January 1704 the cardinal called the Sejm in to session at Warsaw. Augustus was declared to have forfeited the commonwealth crown. Now Karl pushed for an election session to be called so that James Sobieski could be duly elected and a government favorable to Sweden would be in place. But Augustus still had a trick or two up his sleeve.

In February James was captured by Saxon soldiers as he left his castle in Silesia to return to Poland. He and his brother were whisked away to Saxony as prisoners. The clear successor to the commonwealth throne had been kidnapped by Augustus himself and now the various Polish parties were completely divided as to a selection. So Karl presented his own choice, Stanislaus Leszczyński. The Swedish king sold his candidate on the offer only after making many concessions and guarantees, one of those being that upon James's return Stanislaus could step down in James's favor.

Next, Karl had to persuade Radziejowksi to hold a coronation session of the Sejm, but the good cardinal balked. The pope (Clement XI) objected to so close a friend of a Lutheran king being crowned and there was still Augustus and his Saxons and the Russians to be removed from the country.

Leaving Stanislaus and his Polish army to guard Great Poland and Avid Horn with a small garrison at Warsaw, Karl and Rehnskiöld with the main army moved southeast to secure that part of Poland and drive out the Russians. They took Lemberg while Lewenhaupt and the Sapiehas defeated Wiśniowecki and his Russian allies in July at Jakobstadt in Lithuania. As a consequence of his success Count Adam Ludwig Lewenhaupt was given command of all Swedish forces in the northeast (Lithuania, Kurland and Livonia) and ordered to keep Russian troops at bay.

At Lemberg Karl received bad news. It was here he learned of Peter's conquest of Dorpat and Narva. Furthermore, Augustus, with 3,000 Saxons and 9,000 Russian troops had taken Warsaw. Stanislaus's Polish army had pulled back and not come to Horn's aid.

Karl and Rehnskiöld moved back to the northwest and chased the enemy out of Great Poland. Augustus and his Saxons left Warsaw crossing the Vistula. Another 4,000 Saxons under Lieutenant General Johann Matthias von der Schulenburg slipped across the border into Silesia. Most of the Russians and Cossacks headed east out of harm's way. Those that Karl did catch he cut down.

The 1705 campaign season saw two attempts to disrupt the coronation process. A large Russian army 50,000 strong under Sheremetev entered Kurland headed for Poland. Lewenhaupt met them at Gemäuerthof and defeated Sheremetev in a brilliant victory; 9,000 Swedes fought 45,000 Russians in a battle lasting a day and a half. The Swedes lost 1,000 men while Peter suffered 17,000 casualties and the loss of all their guns and train. Peter halted his troops in Kurland while Lewenhaupt withdrew into Livonia. Though the Swedish general had won the battle and held the field, he did not have sufficient strength to occupy Kurland and resist the Russians that were pouring in.

Augustus sent General Paijkull to attack Warsaw with all the Saxons and Poles he could gather. Swedish major general Nieroth defeated them with a much smaller army taking Paijkull prisoner. On September 14, 1705, Stanislaus was crowned king of Poland-Lithuania in Warsaw. This was followed by a treaty of mutual cooperation against Tsar Peter and against any attempt by Augustus to retake Poland.

Karl now split his army. Leaving 10,000 men with Rehnskiöld in Western Poland, he took 20,000 and marched east to either meet Peter in a major battle or link up with Lewenhaupt at Riga. To the west on the Polish border Schulenburg had 20,000 troops, Saxons, Russians, and mercenaries, Swiss, German and French ready to invade if the opportunity presented itself.

Karl, accompanied by Stanislaus's Polish-Lithuanian army, moved fast. He left the Warsaw area at the end of December 1705 and by the middle of January 1706 was near Grodno where he surprised a Russian, Saxon and Polish army under Augustus and the Russian general Ogilvie. The enemy refused to give battle and divided. Ogilvie took his 20,000 Russians into Grodno, a defensible position. Augustus headed west to catch Rehnskiöld from the rear. Karl scouted north toward Kovno and ordered Lewenhaupt to march toward him, hoping to force the Russians in Kurland to battle.

Rehnskiöld, meanwhile, was in trouble. He had Schulenburger with an army of 18,000 crossing the border and marching toward him from the west, while Augustus with 8,000 approached from the east. Indeed, as the deposed Polish king marched toward Warsaw he picked up additional loyal troops. They would crush Rehnskiöld between them, then turn on Karl at Grodno. Russian forces in Kurland would move south, Ogilvie would come out of Grodno and Augustus would wipe out the Swedish menace.

Rehnskiöld, however, was not about to be trapped. He took the offense, driving toward the Silesian border until he contacted Schulenburg. Both sides maneuvered for position, then Rehnskiöld feigned panic and retreated, looking for more favorable terrain. He found ground near Franstadt to his liking, better for cavalry where he had the advantage. He had 5,700 horse and 4,500 foot against Schulenburg's 2,000 cavalry and 16,000 infantry.

Having engaged with the Swedes, Schulenburg deployed his troops with infantry and guns in the middle, cavalry on both wings anchored by a town at each end. He had a ditch dug in front of his line and mounted the stakes used to repel cavalry attack. These were improved, linked by chain and with knives at the end instead of just a sharp point.

Rehnskiöld formed up with a thin line of infantry in the middle; he had no heavy guns. His best weapon was his cavalry placed on both flanks. His only reserves were a few squadrons of Bremen and Verden dragoons forming a scanty second line.

At noon on February 3, 1706, the Battle of Fraustadt began. Though outnumbered almost two to one, Rehnskiöld took the initiative charging forward all along the front. The Swedish cavalry quickly drove off the Saxon wings of horse, then turned on the center already engaged by the Swedish infantry. It was over in two hours. Eight thousand Saxons, Russians and mercenaries were cut down. Four-fifths of the enemy were killed or captured. Schulenburg's army ceased to exist.

Instead of trapping Karl's forces, Augustus was left wandering in central Poland between two Swedish armies. Peter was now in a panic. He had uprisings at home and his two main armies were in danger of being cut off by Swedish forces. He ordered Ogilvie to retreat from Poland any way he could and he ordered his troops in Kurland and Livonia to evacuate.

Ogilvie slipped out of Grodno when in spring the ice broke up, taking out Karl's boat bridge on the Niemen. His 20,000 men had been reduced by half through disease and starvation. Russian cannon and ammunition were dumped into the river as the troops fled toward the Ukraine. Flooded streams and rivers impeded Karl's pursuit and Ogilvie didn't stop until he reached Kiev.

Though he didn't bring any major Russian force to battle, Karl did free Livonia and Kurland. He linked up with Lewenhaupt and induced the Lithuanian nobility to support Stanislaus, at least temporarily.

Rehnskiöld was rewarded with the rank of field marshal and given the title of count. He was also informed of Karl's next move, the invasion of Saxony.

Karl had to bring Augustus to heel and the invasion of his seat of power was the obvious way to do it. Earlier he had been reluctant to attack the German state as it would be seen as aiding Louis XIV's fight against the emperor which had gone well for the French in 1702 and 1703. The French had thrust deep into German territory and were assisted by attacks against the empire from another Louis, the elector of Bavaria, and Rákóczi, leader of the Hungarian independence movement.

By 1706, however, the tide had turned. Louis XIV was being pushed back by the emperor's forces. Bavaria had been crushed and Flanders was in jeopardy. A new champion had arisen to lead the allies. This was the brilliant, John Churchill, duke of Marlborough. His victories at Blenheim and Ramillie put Louis clearly on the defensive. Now Karl felt he could attack Saxony without upsetting the Maritime Nations.

On August 28, 1706 the main body of the Swedish army crossed into Saxony. There were few soldiers in the country and no organized resistance. Karl put Swedish garrisons in Dresden and Leipzig, then made his own headquarters in Altranstädt Castle outside Leipzig. He had left Swedish general Mardefelt with 4,000 men (many were French battalions that had taken service with Karl after Fraustadt) to support the Polish-Lithuanian army under Potocki that served Stanislaus.

The *Geheimrat* (Saxon Council) signed the Treaty of Altranstädt with Karl recognizing the dethroning of Augustus, the kingship of Stanislaus and end of the Saxon alliance with Russia. The treaty was carried to Augustus who was invading Poland from Lithuania at the head of a Saxon-Polish-Russian army while Peter was busy besieging Viborg in Finland. On October 10 he signed the treaty, but nine days later his army attacked Mardefelt and Potocki at Kalisz. Potocki's Poles and Lithuanians fled leaving the Swedish army to be cut to pieces. Over half the troops were killed or captured. Russia was now free to occupy the commonwealth from the east.

Karl retaliated by making the treaty with Augustus's signature public. Stanislaus, having lost Poland, fled to Saxony and Karl's protection. Augustus, now exposed as having made peace with Karl, also left Poland for Saxony. Karl finally had his peace with Saxony and the commonwealth, only Russia now controlled Poland and Lithuania.

Meanwhile, the Swedish army was doing well enough in Saxony. Strict discipline was maintained so there was no looting or pillaging. After the initial shock, soldiers and civilians got along well. German customs and language were more familiar than those in Poland. While Karl did extract a large contribution from the Saxons to sustain his army most of it was cycled back into the local economy through wages spent and supplies purchased. Large numbers of non-Swedes enlisted in the army of the successful king-general, swelling the rolls.

During his stay at Altranstädt Karl, though a shy person by nature, received many visitors of rank from all over Europe who came to see the young phenomenon. Most probably came out of curiosity, some to promote schemes or alliances. Among his visitors was the duke of Marlborough. At the same dining table sat the two greatest generals of their time, one a twenty-four-year-old king, the other a fifty-seven-year-old general and statesman. Marlborough was looking for guarantees, on behalf of Queen Ann, that Karl would soon be leaving Germany. Karl wanted further assurances of English support for the Treaty of Travendal, keeping Frederick IV of Denmark restrained, and he wanted recognition of Stanislaus as commonwealth king. That the two men respected each other there can be no doubt. That they had much in common and much to discuss is certainly true. Did they share stories and information or did they keep a formal stiffness, engaging only in diplomatic exchanges? If ideas, theories and experiences were not shared, it was, indeed, an opportunity lost.

25. Karl XII's Russian Campaign

News from Russia indicated it was time for Karl to begin his long delayed campaign against the tsar. Muscovites were restive, unhappy with many of Peter's reforms. The Astrakhan Cossack revolt, which commenced in 1705, was gathering steam. In 1707 the Don Cossacks under Bulavin challenged Russian authority and there was the uprising of the Zaporozhian Cossacks. With all this unrest, Ivan Mazepan of the Ukrainian Cossacks was looking for an opportunity to secure Ukrainian independence from Russia and Poland. It was time for Karl to move.

The size of the army which Karl had assembled was unimpressive, 33,000 troops. With non-combatants, medical people, civil servants, clergymen, et cetera, the total may have been close to 44,000. He had volunteers from various German Protestant states who were organized into regiments of dragoons. Sweden sent 9,000 new recruits which landed in Pomerania and caught up with him at Slupca, Poland. In all he had 7,100 cavalry, 9,600 dragoons, 14,200 infantry, 1,500 *Vallochi* (light cavalry, mostly Polish, used for scouting and patrols), 150 Drabants and 150 artillerymen. Besides the main army, there were 11,400 troops in the Baltics under Lewenhaupt, and 14,000 in Finland under Lybecker. Another 11,000 troops were stationed in the Baltics on garrison duty, 11,000 in the German provinces and 17,000 left to guard Sweden.

The soldiers were armed with new swords designed by Karl to be lighter, more akin to the rapier. All were now armed with the flintlock musket and bayonet. The cavalry carried flintlock pistols. Uniforms were the familiar blue and yellow with a dark blue cloak. In some regiments the cloak was replaced with a greatcoat. The army marching into Saxony had been in tatters, but now the uniforms and shoes were new and the army shined.

The king sent two of his most trusted officers, Stenbock and Arvid Horn, to Stockholm as councilmen. He wanted to strengthen his hold on the government. Rehnskiöld was kept in the field as Karl's chief military advisor and Piper as counselor on political matters. On September 7, 1707, the Swedish army crossed the Oder at Steinau entering Polish territory. They found before them a land of desolation.

Peter planned to fight this war outside Russia if possible and had instructed Menshikov to lay waste to the country west of the Vistula and take up positions behind the river. The Swedes were shocked at the corpses of would-be home defenders left behind. Towns were razed and wells poisoned. The Swedes paused at Slupca to reorganize, but then kept moving through the ravaged countryside.

Menshikov garrisoned the towns around the bridges over the Vistula, particularly Warsaw and vicinity. But Karl swung north, crossing unopposed between Thorn and Plock in the bitter cold of late December. He took the entire army though an area known as the

Masurian Woods, a stretch of swamps and marshes north of Pultusk, considered impenetrable by a military van. On January 28, 1708, Karl and 600 men road into Grodno which Peter had just evacuated a few hours earlier. A counterattack that night by Mühlenfels and 3,000 troops was beaten back. Karl had completely outflanked the Russian line in central Poland and forced a pullback into Lithuania. He had strengthened Stanislaus's hand immeasurably and gained a position from which he could move either north into the Baltic region or east into Russia.

Peter figured Karl's next move would be to free the Baltic provinces so he deported the population of Dorpat to Russia and razed the city except for the fortifications. Ingria was likewise ordered to devastate the countryside. In case the Swedes turned east Tsar Peter had a 150 mile wide strip from Pskov to Smoleńsk to Cherkassk turned into a no-man's land. Peter had no problem with laying waste to his own territories to deny the enemy support.

The Swedish king moved to Smorgonie, between Vilna and Minsk, forcing the Russians still further back. Karl assigned 8,000 German mercenaries posted in Pomerania, Elbing, Posen and the Danzig area under the command of General Krassaw to support Stanislaus. Soon the Lithuanians came over to Karl as did the Polish Crown Army. The commonwealth, Karl's flank, was becoming more and more secure. Good news arrived in May 1708; the Bulavin rebellion was now an open war with 60,000 Cossacks fighting for Ukrainian independence.

Peter put into effect an even more severe scorched-earth policy. Whichever route the Swedes took, every building, field, pasture, granary and haystack was to be burned. The Swedes were to be presented with a desert to march through. To counter this tactic that had cost Karl's army dearly in misery and lives, the Swedish king ordered Lewenhaupt to build a supply train and bring it to his army along with the 12,000 troops he commanded in the Baltics.

Meanwhile, Karl pressed on, to Minsk, then to Berezina and to Bialenicze where he heard that a large Russian force was gathered at Holovzin on the Vabich River. Here, 38,000 troops were stationed in two camps separated by woods and a marsh. Karl collected nearly 18,000 of his men intent on an attack through the woods to keep the Russian camps from supporting each other. He would cross the river into the wooded area then turned on the southern camp commanded by Repnin. It would be difficult to maintain order in the woods, but this would avoid the well prepared earthworks facing the river. The biggest danger was a large body of cavalry south of Repnin commanded by Goltz.

Through the night, in a downpour, the Swedes moved into position. Artillery was pushed up to the river opposite Repnin's camp to pound his works. Karl led the assault group composed of the grenadier battalion of the Guards first followed by the other three battalions and one battalion of Dalesmen. The second group, commanded by Axel Sparre, consisted of the remainder of the Dalarnian Regiment, the Västermanland, Uppland and East Gothland Regiments. Spaced well back was the cavalry under Rehnskiöld. Wading through the deep mud Karl's lead group didn't reach the river until dawn so their crossing aroused the defenders.

The Swedish artillery opened up, dropping shell and bomb into Repnin's works. The Russian general sent urgent cries for help to Scheremetyev commanding the other camp to the north and to Goltz. Karl's infantry was still struggling through the swamp and woods. Repnin pushed some cannon in line and began to shell the first waves. He still had numerical superiority though in the dark and storm he probably had little knowledge of the Swede's numbers. Without any help coming from Scheremetyev or Goltz, Repnin began to withdraw. Most of his Russian regiments retired in good order. As the Swedes began to attack, they would loose a volley, then retire to reload, covered by the next rank. As they backed into the wooded area to their rear their ranks finally broke and they fled.

The second Swedish group, meanwhile, had reached Repnin's works and quickly drove out the last Russian troops. Goltz, finally aroused enough to take action, sent two dragoon regiments to support Repnin. They arrived in time to attack the Swedes who were busy cleaning out the camp. Before they moved in, Rehnskiöld arrived with the first of his cavalry, two squadrons of Household Dragoons followed by the Drabants. They fought resolutely against the two Russian regiments until the rest of the Household Regiment and some of the Småland Regiment of Horse arrived. The Russian dragoons broke and fled. Goltz fed the rest of his three brigades into the fight. One by one they were routed. 2,500 Swedish cavalry had bested Goltz's 10,000 horse and driven them from the field.

With the fury of the battle raging to the south, Scheremetyev in his northern camp decided to raid the Swedish baggage train. He advanced on the bridge the Swedes had constructed for their last foot and horse to across the river. Arriving at the bridge, Scheremetyev found the Västebotten Regiment on station after a forced march. Scheremetyev retreated and prepared to evacuate his camp. He might have been routed by Karl, who was forming up his army to attack the north camp, but a false message indicating Rehnskiöld's cavalry was in trouble diverted the king and Scheremetryev escaped.

The Battle of Holovzin was not the decisive conflict Karl needed. Once more the Russian Army had slipped away. Karl lost 267 dead and 1,000 wounded. Official Russian records show 977 killed or missing and 675 wounded, but their losses were certainly much higher. The fight did, however, clear the way to the Dnieper.

The Swedes had prevailed, but there had been a noticeable improvement in the Russian soldier. For almost 60 years the Russians had been employing foreign officers, as low as captain, to modernize and train their armies. Gradually, these were replaced by trained, experienced Russian officers until Peter's army was now a Russian Army. The private soldier had also developed, along with training methods and a corps of NCOs. Repnin's soldiers had mostly retired in order, exhibiting courage and discipline. The outcome might have been different had he not decided to bolt at the beginning of the battle.

The king encamped at Mohilev on the Dnieper on July 9. The rains continued and illness spread in the army. Ostensibly Karl stopped to rest his troops, but perhaps more importantly he was waiting for Lewenhaupt with his supply train and 12,500 troops. The Livonian commander had left Riga the end of June, but the rain and mud had slowed the progress of his heavy wagons to a crawl. Karl needed the supplies. In the distance stretched fire and smoke as far as the eye could see. How maddingly close, 35 miles to Smoleńsk, 150 to Moscow, but he would require Lewenhaupt's supplies to get there.

The lack of food for the troops and fodder for the horses was becoming critical. Karl made the decision to turn south into Severia, an area neither decimated by war nor burned by Peter. And so a race began for the strategic points in the province or so Karl thought. Actually, Peter had left contingents there from an earlier campaign against the Ukrainian Cossacks and the important fortresses were taken over by these troops. Peter needed only to rush reinforcements to them to hold the province. Still the Swedes did find provisions in the province. But the move south also widened the distance between Karl and Lewenhaupt. Peter watched the movement of the two Swedish elements and recognized the opportunity presented to the Russians.

He detached a force of 6,795 dragoons and 4,830 infantry, which he mounted, to intercept the reinforcements and supplies. Peter tried to catch Lewenhaupt before he crossed the Dnieper, but he was too late. Peter's column met the train at Lesnaja and attacked. The battle raged all day. The Swedes did their best to protect the wagons, but many were destroyed.

At nightfall both sides broke off the engagement. Lewenhaupt made a night march to Propoisk which proved to be a disaster. Between the battle and the march he found his forces halved. Of his original 12,000 men only 6,000 remained. Some had been killed in the battle, some were captured and some deserted. About 1,000 eventually found their way back to Riga. The Swedes had fought well, but so had the Russians. Peter considered this his first real victory over a regular Swedish force.

Lewenhaupt burned what was left of the supply train, convinced he could not protect it with so few men. Then he left to rendezvous with Karl. Unencumbered with the wagons, Lewenhaupt traveled fast, catching up with Karl in Severia. The king showed no sign of displeasure. He maintained the general had acquitted himself well, both in the movement of the train and in the battle. Karl praised him for his stand.

The loss of supplies at Lesnaja decided Karl's next move. On October 11, 1708, he sent his vanguard into the Ukraine. The king followed, joined by Mazepa (who conversed with Karl in Latin) and 2,000 Cossacks at the border. On November 2 Karl forced a crossing of the Desna River into the Ukraine at Mezin against considerable Russian resistance. However, that same night Menshikov besieged Baturin, Mazepa's capital. The next day Baturin fell to the Russians, who burned the town and destroyed the arms and ammunition the Swedes needed. Food and forage, on the other hand, were not a problem. There was grain, fruit, tobacco and livestock in abundance. It is for good reason the Ukraine is called the breadbasket of Eastern Europe. Karl beat the tsar to the fortified towns of Romhy on the Sula River and Hadyach on the Psiol thanks to Mazepa's knowledge of the country and the people.

It was easy living for the Swedes that summer, but the winter of 1708–09 was one of the most severe in Europe in a century. The Sound froze so deep that heavy wagons could cross on the ice, fruit trees were killed in Germany, and the canals of Venice were covered with ice. In the Ukraine snow covered the ground from the 1st of October to the 5th of April. Disease and malnutrition stalked the army and many died. There were also skirmishes with Russian troops that further reduced Swedish numbers. Peter sent garrisons to towns between the Swedes and roads leading to Moscow. One of these was Poltava, and another Veprik. Karl's plan was to move north toward Moscow when the 1709 campaign season opened. To prepare he began attacking these outposts that stood between his army and the Russian capital. He took Veprik at the cost of 400 men, mostly from the fire of Cossack riflemen who could far outrange the Swedish smoothbore muskets.

In March the hetman of the Zaporozhian Cossacks, Konstantin Hordienko, joined Karl bringing 1,500 men. More importantly he had munitions at the strongholds of Koleberda and Perevolotjna, and a fleet capable of carrying 3,000 men that would be invaluable when the campaign season began. But again Russian troops and allied Cossacks raided the two strongholds upon learning of Hordienko's move to the Swedish camp and they burned the fleet.

In April Karl moved against Poltava. By early May he had begun building the siege trench works. By the end of May he had his main army around Poltava. The Swedish army had been reduced from the original 33,000 men to about 25,000. Peter had suffered even worse, but he was in a position to refill his ranks. Karl cast about for reinforcements.

He asked King Stanislaus and General Krassaw for help. However, the commonwealth's king had all he could handle with Sieneawski gaining the upper hand thanks to the support of Russian forces under Goltz. Krassaw had moved toward Pomerania to protect new recruits expected from Sweden. Karl turned to Devlet-Grei, khan of the Crimean Tartars, through negotiations sponsored by Mazepa and Hordienko. All seemed to go well. The khan even had troops at the Ukrainian border, but they would get no further. On May 14 Peter's troops struck the Zaporozhian capital of Sich and destroyed it. This was a not very subtle suggestion of how the tsar dealt with anyone supporting the Swedes. He next made a display of increased activity at his naval base at Azov, an open threat against the Ottoman porte. The Turkish ruler passed the order down to the khan to stay clear of the Swedes. Karl was not going to get help from the south.

By the end of May 1709 Poltava on the west bank of the Vorskla River was fully invested. Peter moved the main Russian army to the opposite side of the river in an attempt to lift the siege. In mid–June the Russians tried to cross the river at Poltava and relieve the siege, but were thrown back. If Peter was to save the town and its garrison he would have to cross far enough away to evade the Swedes. Then he could build a fortified camp and force Karl to attack him in this strong position or, if the Swedish king did not, Peter could raid and harry the already weakened Swedish army until it lifted the siege. Either way the road to Kharkov, and Moscow, would be blocked.

Peter would have to hurry for he received word from the Poltava garrison commander that he could not hold out much longer. The crossing was scheduled for the night of June 16–17 and would be made at Petrovka north of Poltava. Diversionary assaults at Poltava and further downstream would hold the Swedes in place long enough for the advanced corps to dig in.

The Swedes were well aware of the Russian plans from deserters, spies and reconnaissance by the Vallochi. Karl had his own plan. The Swedes would let a large part of the army cross then attack and annihilate the first section, sealing off the landing site. In this way they could wipe out a sizable part of Peter's army and discourage further attempts to relieve Poltava.

Rehnskiöld moved to Petrovka with ten cavalry and eight infantry regiments. Karl remained at Poltava to drive back the other assaults. The night of June 16–17 crossings were made at three points. Rönne crossed north of Poltava at Petrovka, an assault was launched from directly opposite Poltava and a third to the south where General Hallart was crossing. Troops at Poltava threw back the attack. The king, on the morning of his twenty-seventh birthday, took a battalion of Dalesmen south and drove back the vanguard of Hallart's troops. Having cleared the river bank, the Dalesmen came under rifle fire from Hallart's Cossacks occupying an island in the river. Karl called in some of his own Zaporozhian Cossack riflemen and watched from the shore as the two sides popped away at each other. It was a brisk exchange with casualties on both sides. A Drabant aid beside Karl was shot dead during this exchange. As Karl turned and rode up the bank a rifle bullet hit the king in the foot. The projectile entered Karl's heel and passed diagonally through the foot, breaking a number of bones and exiting near the big toe. It was the shot that, quite literally, brought down an empire.

The wound occurred at 8:00 in the morning as the king was leaving the river to review the defenses around Poltava. He did not let the injury deter him. At 11:00 he finally reigned in at his headquarters. By then his foot was soaked with blood. Blood oozed from his boot leaving a crimson trail along his route and a pool of blood wherever he stopped. As he dismounted, he fainted from pain or loss of blood and was carried to his cot. His surgeon picked out the pieces of bone fragments and dressed the wound. By the next day infection had set in. From the 19th to the 20th, the king was feverish and his life hung in the balance. At one point his doctors gave him but two hours to live.

Meanwhile, command passed to Rehnskiöld who counseled with the other senior officers on whether to carry out the plan to attack the Russians at Petrovka. The decision was made not to risk battle partly because the enemy was found to be strongly entrenched, but the primary reason was the uncertainty of the king's condition. The Swedish command structure was paralyzed at a moment in history when only decisive action could save the nation.

Peter did not delay in taking advantage of the situation, of which he was fully informed. Between June 19 and 21, while Karl's fever was at its height, he moved nearly all of his army across the Vorskla and built a strong fortified camp. On the 26th the Russians moved closer to Poltava, within cannon range, and built an even more extensive works. It was clear Peter was not going to meet the Swedes in open battle, but would force them to attack him in his fortified stronghold. This was the exactly the situation Karl had been waiting for: the Russian army was cornered, in a position where he could not only force a battle, but one from which there was no escape route. Except Karl would not be there to lead the army.

Operational command passed to Field Marshal Rehnskiöld, who did not get along with Lewenhaupt. This disrupted the communications flow within the command structure, problems that did not exist when Karl was in charge.

The Russian position was strong. The camp was well fortified with earthworks mounting seventy cannon. Inside were 30,000 infantry. Having learned the lesson of Narva, the walls were built with gaps so troops could be moved to the outside rapidly. Surrounding the camp was a series of impenetrable woods and marshes except to the southwest where a gap existed. Across this space Peter had constructed six redoubts to break up any coordinated attack. Being built at a right angle to these structures was another series of four redoubts forming a T. Passing enemy troops could be raked with musket fire if they tried to pass without taking this first line of defense. Between the redoubts and the camp were 10,000 Russian cavalry. It was a solid defense, but deemed not impregnable by the Swedes.

By June 26 Karl had recovered sufficiently to participate in the planning of the attack. The army would form up in the night and slip past the redoubts before sunrise. The cavalry would be brought in to drive off the Russian horse, then the infantry would charge the works where the Russians were crowded into a small space, forfeiting much of their numerical advantage. The plan was daring, but no more so than other attacks Karl had led successfully. Lewenhaupt was in charge of the 9,000 infantrymen. Creutz took Rehnskiöld's position as commander of the 13,000 cavalrymen. Karl would accompany the infantry borne in a litter carried by two horses. The fever had lifted, but he was still too weak to raise himself.

In the early morning hours of June 28, 1709, the infantry rolled out and began to form up. But Creutz's cavalry did not arrive until after 3:00 a.m., delaying the assault. In the meantime the extent of the redoubts projecting forward was discovered and the original infantry line formation changed to columns to get past the redoubts. Lewenhaupt, who should have been coordinating all this with Rehnskiöld, was on the far right, totally left out of the chain of command. The infantry reformed into five columns with Major General Stackelberg, commanding the middle column, given orders to attack the first two partially constructed redoubts.

By the time all was made ready, it was dawn and the element of surprise was lost. The infantry started forward with the cavalry to the rear. Stackelberg easily took the first two redoubts, but then Major General Roo with six battalions attacked the third and fourth redoubts and got so caught up in the assault the rest of the army passed him by without his noticing.

As the infantry passed the last redoubt, they were attacked by the Russian cavalry. The Swedish horse charged in and a vicious cavalry fight ensued. Finally, the Russian cavalry was swept from the field and the infantry began to form up in front of the camp for the assault. This organization took place in a low area where the troops were not vulnerable to the camp's heavy guns. Lewenhaupt, who had wandered off to the right with his column after passing the redoubts, had finally rejoined the main force, but Rehnskiöld discovered they were still short a third of the infantry. Rehnskiöld waited for two hours for Roo's regiments, all in vain.

Roo had finally given up on his attack on the redoubts, but by then he had completely lost contract with the rest of the army. Because of the poor communication, he wasn't even sure where he should be or where the other regiments had gone. His force of 2,600 men was down to 1,500 and he pulled back, retreating to the south instead of following the rest of the infantry through the redoubts to the interior of the fort. He tried to make the lines around Poltava, but the Russians got word of his predicament and dispatched Menshikov with an infantry and cavalry detachment that surrounded him, cutting his units to pieces and eventually forcing him to surrender.

The loss of Roo's infantry was decisive. The news boosted the morale of the Russians and they now began to leave their fortifications and form up in the open. They were arranged in two lines, 22,000 Russians backed by 70 cannon, opposite Rehnskiöld's 4,000 Swedes. Even so the Swedes charged. Lewenhaupt's right wing drove the Russians back enough so his men captured a few field guns which they turned on the enemy. But a gap opened between the right and left flanks, and the Russians poured through it.

Within half an hour the battle was lost and the Swedes began to fall back. The king's litter was shot to pieces. He was put on a horse and it was killed. A second mount finally carried him from the field along with his fleeing soldiers. The Swedish baggage train at Pushkarivka was guarded by a cavalry regiment. The remnants of the Swedish army collected there. Mazepan and Hordienko set up defensive positions at that point and the Swedish artillery was brought up. The two regiments left at Poltava cut their way to Pushkarivka. Russian pursuit was halted in its tracks.

Rehnskiöld, Piper and Prince Maximilian (a colonel of dragoons) were prisoners. The Swedes lost 6,901 dead and 2,760 taken prisoner. Russian losses were 1,345 killed and 3,290 wounded. Karl gathered his remaining 16,000 men for an orderly retreat.

By the afternoon of the 28th the baggage train was on its way toward the Dnieper, followed by the infantry and cavalry. They marched well into the night, quite a feat for an army that had just fought an exhausting battle. While the troops rested Creutz brought horses to the remaining infantry so that all were mounted for greater speed.

The army reached the Dnieper by June 30 at Perevolotjna, but news arrived that the Russians were in pursuit. Not everyone would be able to across the river as there were only small fishing boats available to carry the troops. It was agreed that as many of the Cossacks as possible should be transferred as the Russians would treat them badly if captured.

Mazepan, Hordicuko and many of their Cossacks swam across the river led by the Zaporozhians, who knew the river's currents. Karl was ferried across on the night of June 30 along with the other wounded. Also crossing were the Drabants (the 80 left), 700 other cavalry and 200 of the Södermanland Foot. The rest of the army and 5,000 Cossacks were to march to the Crimea for a rendezvous with Karl in a month. But at 8:00 on the morning of July 1 Menshikov with 6,000 Russians and 2,000 Cossacks appeared on the heights above the river trapping the army below. Many of the Cossacks bolted and escaped. Lewenhaupt and Creutz made no attempt to fight. They surrendered the last of the Swedish army, 1,161 officers and 13,138 men. It was indeed an ignoble end to an army that had fought for nine years, seen great victories and marched over so much territory.

After being paraded through Moscow in Peter's victory procession, reminiscent of a Roman triumph, the Swedish officers were distributed to remote corners of the empire. The men were pressed into the Russian Army, or into labor battalions to build fortifications, or work in the mines. Many died, some escaped and some made it back to Sweden thirteen years later when the Peace of 1721 was signed between Sweden and Russia. But by then the troops of Karl's great military machine were old men. Sweden's magnificent field army and its exceptional officer corps had been destroyed.

26. The End of Empire

Karl and his band left Perevolotjna pushing out into the hostile Eurasian Steppes. It was hot, dry and inhospitable. There was grass, but water was scarce. The soldiers lived on berries, roots and horse flesh. Finally, they arrived at the Buh River, near the Black Sea, and the Turkish town of Oczakow. Getting across, however, proved problematic as the local chief haggled over the price of the boats to ferry the little army across the river. Karl finally lost his temper and confiscated the craft, but the delay allowed his Russian pursuers to catch up and 800 more men were cut off and captured. Only 500 survivors made it to the sultan's major fortress of Bender on the Dneister in Moldavia. The country was lush with beautiful green fields, fruit orchards, and an abundance of food. The little troop could finally rest in safety. The sultan, Achmed III, had granted the Swedes and Cossacks asylum in accordance with Muslim law.

It was here that Karl learned of his favorite sister's death, Hedwig Sophia, duchess of Holstein. Karl, who was stoic about everything, victory, defeat, hunger and want, even joking about his excruciating foot wound as a little fever in the foot, was now devastated. He was inconsolable for days and would see no one so he could hide his outbursts of tears. He said later this was the one great sorrow of his life.

At Bender Karl built a stone mansion, thick and sturdy, to serve as a fort if needed. He was given an honor guard of Janissaries and maintained a chancellery with secretaries. It was a small government in exile. He had brought money with him, but was also given an allowance by the porte (sultan). A colony of Swedes, Poles and Germans collected around Bender as the sultan freed, in Karl's honor, a substantial number of the slaves that had been captured during Peter's devastation of the Baltics and sold at Constantinople. Local Muslims, officials of rank and others flocked to Bender to meet and observe the king from the north. They were favorably impressed with his habits of sobriety, celibacy and devotion to prayers.

For advisors Karl had only Axel Sparre (the last of his generals), Stanislaus Poniatowski, the Polish diplomat who Karl used as an effective ambassador at the sultan's court, and Mazepan who died in 1710. That same summer the Holstein minister, Baron Ernest Fredrick de Fabrice, joined him and served as contact with the courts of Europe.

Karl probably intended to stay in Ottoman territory only until his wound healed, but gradually he became more and more involved in government affairs of the Turkish Empire and began to promote a plan to attack Tsar Peter in a great two front war, the Ottomans attacking from the south and the Swedes and Poles from the north. This had been Peter's great fear when he was being invaded by Karl earlier, but with the Swedish threat substantially reduced, he became careless about avoiding war with his southern neighbor.

Poniatowski was instrumental in removing the Ottoman grand vizier and getting

Mehemet Baltaji appointed with the backing of the Crimean Tartar khan. The sultan, influenced by Baltaji, issued an ultimatum to the tsar demanding the surrender of Azov, the evacuation of Poland and the restitution of all provinces taken from Sweden. Peter replied in the negative and then some, where upon the porte declared war, November 10, 1710.

In 1711 Tartar hordes savaged the Ukraine and Southern Russia, burning, looting and taking captives as far north as Kharkov. Meanwhile, the grand vizier set out with an army of 100,000 men declaring he would cut a swath through Peter's empire so that the Swedish king could go home whichever way he wanted.

Peter, no less confident, headed south with his own army, pulling troops away from the north and the campaigns against the Poles and Swedes. He was promised help from Constantine Brancovanu, *hospondar* (governor) of Wallachia, and Demetrius Cantemir, hospondar of Moldavia, two Romanian princes chafing under the thumb of the sultan. Brancovanu offered provisions and 30,000 troops while Cantemir signed an alliance with the tsar.

Peter, on the Pruth with 60,000 troops under Scheremetyev, celebrated his coming victory and new alliance with Cantemir. He planned to march across the Danube and the Bulkans to the gates of Constantinople. The hospondar of Wallachia, however, was getting a little anxious and offered to mediate a settlement between the tsar and the sultan. Peter would not even listen to a proposal and sent a division of his army to take Braila, one of Brancovanu's fortresses. The hospondar of Wallachia was incensed at these high handed tactics, withdrew his support, and went over to the grand vizier with the promised men and supplies.

Peter quickly found himself in trouble. He was on the Pruth between Husi and Stânderci with his 60,000 men and no provisions. Want and then famine set in followed by pestilence. The grand vizier was maneuvering toward the Pruth with over 200,000 Turks, Tartars and Wallachians following a campaign plan drawn up by Karl XII. Baltaji closed in on the Russians until he had them completely isolated and pinned against the Pruth. It looked like Karl was about to even the score with his old nemesis. Peter's army would be crushed and the tsar imprisoned or, at the very least, he would have to buy his way out with terms very favorable to Sweden. Poniatowski, with the grand vizier, sent word to Karl who left Bender immediately for Husi to insure Swedish interests were in the forefront of any negotiations. He knew Peter would promise anything to extract himself from this trap.

But Baltaji had a healthy respect for the new Russian soldier and was leery of Austrian and Venetian hostilities reopening. Karl arrived at the grand vizier's headquarters on July 12 to find a treaty had already been signed. The Treaty of Pruth (signed July 11, 1711) allowed the entire Russian army to leave Turkey intact. In return Peter would give up Azov to the Ottomans and dismantle Tagarod (the Russian naval base nearby). Russian troops would be withdrawn from Poland and allow Karl to return to Sweden unmolested.

Karl, normally completely unflappable, was furious. As the Russian troops streamed from the camp toward the Ukraine, Karl raged at Baltaji for squandering such an opportunity. Shafirov, Peter's chief negotiator, was left as a hostage to insure compliance on the Russian's part, but Karl knew the tsar would think nothing of sacrificing a diplomat for the sake of the empire. From that moment on the Swedish king and Baltaji were enemies. Karl lost his Janissary honor guard, allowance from the Ottomans, and he received an invitation from Baltaji to leave the sultan's domain. Karl refused to move, answering that no chancellor was going to tell him when he had to leave.

Karl proved to be right about Peter's intentions on carrying out the terms of the treaty. Baltaji was replaced by a Janissary pasha and a second war was declared against Russia. But English and Dutch diplomats intervened to prevent a disruption in sea trade. The second war died stillborn. Now the sultan sent a message to Karl that it was time to leave, but again he refused.

In May 1712 Magnus Stenbock landed in Pomerania with an army scraped together by Sweden from a depleted country. Karl seized the opportunity and organized the Swedes and Poles from the refugee colony around Bender into an army. He sent them into Poland under Johann Grudzinski to join Stenbock in support of Stanislaus.

Grudzinski's small band, once in Poland, attracted adherents and his army grew to a force of 15,000. It appeared the northern campaign against Russia might finally be under way. The Janissary pasha was overthrown and a new grand vizier installed. A third war on Russia was declared as Peter had still not made good on any of his treaty agreements with the sultan.

But Grudzinski could not make contact with Stanislaus and Stenbock did not get to him quickly enough. Grudzinski's army was surrounded at Posen by Polish, Saxon, and Russian forces and destroyed. Turkey abandoned the latest war on Russia and Karl was declared *persona non grata* by the porte, who finally got serious about deporting the king.

The refugee settlement around the king's mansion and outbuildings had grown into a little town complete with shops and huts. Around this community, called New Bender, Karl had trenches and earthen walls constructed. On January 31, 1713, the porte ordered the pasha in charge of the town to evict Karl and sent a few thousand Janissaries, Tartars and Turkish soldiers to assist. As this army advanced toward New Bender, the refugees, who Karl had armed, dropped their weapons and refused to fight. Karl retreated to his mansion with about 40 loyal men. Here they found Turks and Janissaries already busy looting the place. The Swedes expelled the intruders then held the sultan's forces at bay for several hours. Finally, the king was captured when he stumbled while running from one building to another. The Turks were burning Karl's compound one building after another. The Swedes lost some 15 killed, while 40 Turks died.

This fracas was called the *Kalibalik* and caused a sensation in the courts of Europe although opinions were divided. Some credited the king with a heroic stand, while others criticized him for attacking his benevolent hosts. In any case Karl was now separated from all but a few of his small band and taken to Timurtasch near Adrianople, west of Constantinople.

After a short stay, Karl was moved to Demotika just south of Adrianople and here he stayed for almost a year. Finally, with Sweden stripped of nearly all her possessions and facing civil war, Karl determined to quit Turkey. He set out from Demotika on September 20, 1714, on a famous journey across Europe. He was going home to a drained Sweden sorely in need of a strong unifying leader.

Disguised as a Captain Peter Frisk, Karl and two companions left the Ottoman Empire, crossing into Wallachia on horseback. Twelve hundred members of his retinue followed under Sparre, but used a different route at a slower pace. The royal party rode through the Rotenturn Pass into Transylvania on October 30. At Mülhalbach, Transylvania, the horses were traded for a stagecoach which took them through Hungary to Vienna, reached on November 5. In the Hapsburg capital horses were again readily available and the trio left there mounted. Riding post-horses, they crossed Austria, Bavaria, the Holy Roman Empire and Mecklenburg, passing through Pomerania, arriving at Stralsund the night of November 11–12.

The daring ride electrified Europe. In Sweden the country went wild; the king was back, leadership and order would be restored. The hard pressed country cheered. Their legendary king had returned — well almost. Karl was in Stralsund, one of only two cities that remained in Swedish hands in Germany. Much had been lost since the king's defeat at Poltava.

The destruction of the Swedish field army at Perevolotjna on July 1, 1709, signaled to Sweden's old enemies that the carcass of the Swedish Empire was ready for plucking and the vultures were not slow in descending. In less than a month after Poltava, Augustus was back in Poland at the head of 11,000 Saxons. By October he had signed an agreement with Tsar Peter at Thorn. In November Danish troops landed in Skåne and Peter reinvaded Kurland and Liviona, laying siege to Riga. The carcass was about to be dismembered, but there was a little fight left in the old bird.

The 16,000 Danish troops that crossed the Sound quickly invested Malmö and Lund, then proceeded to the fortress of Kristianstadt by January 1710. Magnus Stenbock, governor-general of the province, had only three regiments of cavalry and could only fall back defending Karlskrona and the navy docked there. But in February, Stenback, who was a popular governor, was able to organize a 13,000 man army, though it was made up of untrained raw recruits. With these troops, derided by the Danes as "goat boys," Stenbock marched south. The Danes fell back before him until they reached Helsingborg where they finally made a stand. Stenbock's army of goat boys routed the Danes, killing 3,000 and capturing another 3,000 along with cannon and baggage. The Danish survivors took refuge inside the walls of Helsingborg, and then evacuated the province. This totally unexpected reversal stunned the rest of Europe. Sweden was not dead yet. And the old Danish province of Skåne had stood by Sweden and not rebelled as in previous wars.

But elsewhere the news was not as good. In the Baltics, being scourged by plague, resistance was minimal. Peter took Riga that summer though the long siege cost him 40,000 men. He captured Pernau in August. In September he conquered Ösel and the oldest of Swedish Baltic possessions, Reval. Kurland, Livonia and Estonia were his. He invaded Finland and took Kexholm and Viborg. With his fleet of galleys operating out of St. Petersburg he could harass and attack the Finnish coast at will. The Russian tsar was now the power in the eastern Baltic.

Sweden's only remaining field army was the one Karl had left in Poland to aid Stanislaus. It was now required to pull back into Pomerania to survive along with the Polish king. The Northern Maritime Powers looked askance at this new threat close to their territories. They had finally gained a decided advantage in the Spanish Succession War at the bloody Battle of Malplaquet (September 11, 1709) and had no desire for the Great Northern War to spill over into Germany and alter the favorable situation. England, The Netherlands and Denmark attempted to neutralize this army through a treaty guaranteeing Swedish interests in Northern Germany. The Råd concurred, but Karl vetoed the plan, beginning a drift of Swedish foreign policy away from the Maritime Nations in favor of France.

All Europe had followed the Russo-Turkish war with interest, especially when it became apparent Peter and his army were surrounded. The surprising terms of the Treaty of Pruth (July 1711) seemed to point out the failure of Karl's grand plan against Russia and Sweden's weak condition. Denmark invaded and occupied the Duchy of Bremen in 1712 while Russian, Polish and Saxon forces dismembered Krassaw's Pomeranian army. Swedish German possessions were now quite defenseless.

Karl ordered a new army be raised and the fleet refitted. He demanded a new invasion of Poland to coincide with a new campaign from the south. His people responded. The royal and noble families donated money and goods. Members of the Råd contributed and government officials took cuts in pay. Burghers and merchants sacrificed. Avid Horn, the chancellor, was able to raise an army and rebuild the navy. At the end of August 1712 Admiral General Wachtmeister left Karlskrona with the fleet and 9,000 soldiers under the command of Magnus Stenbock. They landed on Rügen Island in September, but lost a good share of their supplies, picked off by Danish raiders. Stenbock moved into Pomerania at the same time Grudzinski moved into Poland and the Ottomans had declared war on Russia for the third time.

But Grudzinski was crushed at Posen before Stenbock could help him and King Stanislaus moved into Pomerania, joining Stenbock, boosting the army to 17,000. This was not even enough of an army to attack the Russo-Polish force besieging Stralsund let alone invade Poland. Stenbock took his army into Mecklenburg where he could at least feed it. The move relieved the pressure on Stralsund and Wismar.

The king of Denmark called for a united effort to destroy this latest Swedish threat. Frederick IV took command of a large Danish army and closed in from the west while a Russian-Saxon army advanced from the east. Stenbock mounted his infantry and pushed hard to the west, catching Frederick at Gadebusch. The Danes were encamped in a strong position and outnumbered the Swedes badly. Still, with the Russian-Saxon army advancing from the east, Stenbock didn't have a lot of choice and attacked Frederick immediately.

On paper Stenbock had no chance. He had 6,000 Swedish cavalry against 7,000 Danes and 3,000 Saxons. His infantry was 7,800 compared to 9,300 Danes. He did have one advantage, however, and that was Karl Cronstedt, his artillery engineer. Cronstedt had adopted a screw device invented by Christopher Polhem (a Swedish scientist and engineer) that allowed for accurate adjustment of the height of a shot. Thus the Swedish guns were much more accurate than the Danish. A second improvement was Cronstedt's own invention. This was a strong but easily uncoupled mechanism attaching harness to the gun carriage allowing the cannon to be moved with the muzzle pointed to the front. In this way the field pieces could advance right with the infantry, be quickly unlimbered, and put into action, increasing their effectiveness dramatically.

It was a closely fought battle, but in the end the Danes were routed losing 3,000 casualties, 4,000 prisoners, 13 guns and all their baggage. It won for Stenbock the rank of field marshal. The victory also stimulated an offer of assistance.

Russian successes in the Baltic had alarmed Augustus and Frederick I of Prussia. Frederick sent a proposal to Karl at Bender meant to curb Peter's expansion. He offered to put at Karl's disposal 6,000 Prussian troops to be combined with his own and Augustus's as an army to liberate Livonia and Estonia. In return he asked for Elbing, the bishopric of Ermeland and Stanislaus's resignation as king of Poland. A Prussian-Saxon-Swedish army commanded by Karl XII seemed a way of regaining lost territories and gaining allies against the Russian-Danish-Polish coalition, but Karl would not budge even though Stanislaus journeyed to Turkey to beg for release from a throne that had only brought him misery. Perhaps Karl had seen in the victory at Gadebusch proof of Sweden's reemerging military might. If so, it was short lived.

Stenbock had a victory, but was still cornered by the Russian, Saxon, Polish and Danish coalition army. He moved to Holstein-Gottorp where Sweden's old ally let him occupy the fortress at Tønning. The coalition army invested the stronghold. Stenbock was forced to surrender with his 11,000 troops due to starvation on May 16, 1713. Sweden's last field army, built at great national sacrifice, had been destroyed. The great Swedish war machine, respected and feared by all of Europe, had finally been smashed, but it had taken a coalition of nearly every country in northern and eastern Europe.

That same year the Peace of Utrecht finally ended the War of Spanish Succession, with Philip of Anjou obtaining recognition as king of Spain, but with the proviso that Spain and

France not be united. Charles, archduke of Austria and the Grand Alliance candidate for the Spanish throne, had been elected holy Roman emperor and was, therefore, no longer an attractive alternative. As compensation, Austria was given Spanish holdings in Italy and Belgium. The end of the war freed its participants to deal with the Great Northern War. Several peace proposals were offered, but now Sweden's old enemies were moving in for the final kill.

Prussia took Stettin. The Russians took Helsingfors and Åbo with their galley fleet then defeated Karl Gustaf Armfelt at the bloody battle of Storkyro, opening the way to a complete conquest of Finland. By the end of 1714 all of the grand duchy was in Russian hands. Wismar and Stralsund were all that remained of Sweden's overseas empire. With Denmark preparing to invade from the south and Russia from the east, the defenseless country was at the point of civil war.

Although forbidden, Chancellor Horn called a Riksdag. Princess Ulrica was invited to take a seat in the Råd. The Estates met at Stockholm on December 14, 1713. There was division in the government. One party backed Ulrica to take over the government. Another remained loyal to Karl. Still others pushed for peace negotiations and another argued for constitutionalism. Using all his political skills, Horn was able to hold the government together. The political crisis did accomplish one thing; it brought the king back from Turkey.

The adulation of the king and the excitement of the people upon Karl's arrival at Stralsund on November 11, 1714, gradually turned to despair. They expected him to hurry on to Sweden and take his place as head of the government in Stockholm, but instead Karl stayed in Stralsund and ordered more soldiers be raised for its defense. The nation yearned for peace. More war is what it got. And now two more countries lined up against the beleaguered nation. First Prussia, having already taken Stettin in Pomerania, moved into Wollin and the surrounding islands. Karl collected his troops and drove the Prussians out, whereupon Frederick William I declared war on Sweden.

The second was England whose king (George I) was also the elector of Hanover and coveted the duchies of Bremen and Verden for his electorate. Thus, by mid–1715 Sweden, now exhausted, crippled and in utter despair was officially at war with six nations: Russia, Prussia, Poland, Saxony, England and Denmark. The only helping hands were from France, in the form of a yearly subsidy, and from the administrators of Holstein-Gottorp who helped out with 4,000 troops.

Karl managed to find 17,000 men with which to defend Stralsund, but it was not enough. The Prussians overran Rügen Island, the city's strength, but also its weakness if taken. The king led a stout defense for over a year, but finally, on December 12, 1715, what was left of the fortress-city fell. The king had left the day before, escaping to Sweden in a small boat. Upon gaining Swedish soil, Karl rushed to Karlskrona to mount a relief effort for Wismar, now under siege. But the fleet was in disrepair and without funds to refit the ships Wismar would be left to its fate. It fell April 8, 1716.

But Karl XII was not broken yet. In January 1716 the Sound froze over and the king seized the opportunity to invade Zealand without the need for ships. He raised 12,000 troops and rushed to the strait at Malmö opposite Copenhagen. However, before the attack could be started, a storm broke up the ice. The Danish capital was saved. Even the elements had now deserted Karl and his beleaguered nation.

At the end of February Karl led a few hundred men into southern Norway taking the town of Kristinia. In the spring his support ships were destroyed by the Danish navy and Karl was forced to evacuate.

By spring 1716 the anti–Swedish coalition had dismembered the Swedish Empire and occupied the spoils they coveted. Prussia and Denmark held Pomerania, George I had Bremen and Verden, Russia occupied Finland and the Baltic provinces, Wismar was occupied by Hanoverian, Prussian and Danish troops. What the various countries needed were treaties recognizing their new possessions, no easy matter considering Karl's stubbornness.

The coalition decided to use military pressure to bring Karl to terms. Twenty thousand Russian troops in Mecklenburg would be ferried to Zealand by Prussian transports. Then a Russo-Danish army would be taken from Zealand to Skåne. England would provide 22 ships to cover the landing. By August all was ready. An army of 53,000 Russians and Danes were at Copenhagen ready to cross to Sweden. A fleet of 19 English, 14 Russian and 23 Danish warships pushed the Swedish fleet out of the southern Baltic.

Karl had not been idle. From his headquarters at Lund, he had raised 20,000 men and strengthened all the fortresses in southern Sweden. All Europe waited expectantly for this final campaign. Would this be the end of Sweden as an independent nation?

The invasion was to begin September 21, but four days prior to the incursion the tsar declared it was too late in the season and postponed the venture until spring. Rivalries, jealousies and distrust had disrupted the coalition. By spring the alliance was in tatters and Karl had his chance to turn the tables, but his cause would have to be accomplished though diplomacy, not one of the king's strong points. Fortunately, he had just the man for such a delicate job. This was Baron George Henry von Görtz.

Görtz appears in history about 1700 as an advisor to the duke of Holstein-Gottorp. He meets Karl at Stralsund and immediately becomes the king's confidant. Karl found in Görtz the compliment to his own abilities. The king was a warrior, a general. Görtz was the consummate politician, financier and diplomat. Karl made him the de facto chief minister in charge of Sweden's government departments. He supervised all government finances. On top of this, he was the chief diplomat responsible for negotiating peace with her many enemies.

Görtz was, of course, hated by all the councilors of the Swedish government. His sudden usurpation of their power made him their enemy. This was compounded by his personal morals. He was said to be subject to all vices and totally unscrupulous, traits that did not endear him to the Swedes, but were an asset in diplomacy. However, it must be remembered that these accusations were alleged by people who detested him so it is hard to discern the truth. He was cultured, articulate, an excellent judge of people and brilliant. He was also devoted to Karl and worked tirelessly for him without pay. He gained no wealth as unofficial chief minister of the Swedish government.

Görtz played the former allies off against each other using Sweden's threat to recognize the ownership of her old territories by the new conquerors as bait. This led to a formal peace conference with Russia at Lofö, one of the Åland Islands, in May 1718. Suddenly Prussia offered to negotiate and George I sent an embassy directly to Karl at Lund.

At Lofö Görtz negotiated an incredible deal. Finland, Livonia and Estonia would be restored to Sweden in exchange for ceding Ingria with Narva, St. Petersburg, and part of Karelia to Russia. As an alternative, Sweden would recover Finland, cede the Baltics and Russia would help her recover her German possessions. Görtz was jubilant, believing he had accomplished the impossible. But Karl turned the deal down and sent Görtz back to the negotiating table.

Görtz returned with a new proposal actually signed by Peter on August 26, 1718. By this treaty Sweden would cede the Baltics, get back Finland and Russia's help in recovering territories lost to Hanover and Denmark. Again Karl rejected the proposition and sent Görtz back a third time.

Meanwhile, Görtz had propped up the Swedish economy by issuing base metal tokens and paper currency. This was meant to be a short term solution only, until peace could be restored and the country's commerce put back in order. The government tender and a spurt in the economy allow Karl to raise another army of some 70,000 men and rebuild his warships.

In the summer of 1718 Karl decided to invade Norway once again. He sent Armfelt into Trondeim with 14,000 men in August. Armfelt met little resistance and advanced all the way to the Trondeim city walls.

Karl moved into southern Norway with 22,000 men. By late November he had reached the fortress of Fredriksten. He invested the stronghold. On November 30 he was inspecting his works when he was hit in the left temple by a ball that exited the skull on the right side. He died instantly. Karl XII left his country embroiled in the Great Northern War, a war in which Sweden was on one side and most of Northern Europe was on the other, a war which had broken the Swedish Empire.

Will and Ariel Durant, the historians, summed up Karl's life eloquently: "He died as he had lived, stupefied with bravery. He was a great general, and won unbelievable victories against great odds; but he loved war to intoxication, never had victories enough, and, in search of them, planned campaigns to the verge of insanity. His generosity was spoiled by his pride; he gave much, but demanded more; and time and again he prevented peace by refusing concessions that might have saved his empire and his face. History pardons him because it was not he who had begun this 'Great Northern War' that he refused to finish except with victory."[1]

Karl XII was thirty-six years old and had reigned for twenty-one years. He had presided over the collapse of the Swedish Empire. He was the last of Sweden's warrior kings; indeed, he was more warrior than king. In spite of Karl's military abilities, he had lost nearly all Sweden's hard won possessions. He had squandered several opportunities that might have saved much of his nation's territories. He was probably the greatest general of his day, but he had failed as a king.

Perhaps Voltaire had it right when he said of Karl: "For where is the monarch who can say, I am braver and more virtuous than Karl XII; I have a more resolute spirit and a sturdier body; I have a greater understanding of warfare; I have better troops than he?"[2]

But it was not enough. Karl could destroy army after army thrown at him by five countries, but he had to be defeated only once. Sweden didn't have the resources to recover. Eventually, Sweden was going to be overwhelmed and pulled apart by so many enemies. Sweden's age of greatness had drawn to a close.

Epilogue

Karl XII was the last of Sweden's warrior kings. Never again would a Swedish monarch ride at the head of his army into battle. With his death came the end of Sweden's age of greatness and role as the dominant power of Northern Europe.

Karl is often accused of devastating his country to feed his own megalomania. Statistics are tossed around about how two-thirds of the farmland had ceased to be cultivated for lack of laborers by the end of his reign, and that most of the fisheries had been abandoned because the fishermen had been taken as sailors. Foreign trade had been ruined due to blockage of the Sound and the blockades of Swedish ports. There was a dearth of meat, butter, salt and tallow in the towns and cities. Artisans, merchants, and businessmen could work only for a few hours in winter for lack of candles. Most telling, his critics say, was the decrease in Swedish population from 1,376,000 at the beginning of his reign (1697) to 1,247,000 at his death (1718), a decrease of over 9 percent.

The strain of war was tremendous and was born principally by the peasant. It was he who had to supply the materials of war, the sons to fight, the wood for wagons and ships, and the surpluses that could be turned into cash to buy the weapons of war. The blockades did affect commerce, but much of the devastation was due to crop failures and famine.

Between 1696 and 1700 there were a series of famines followed by epidemics. The plague years of 1710–12 took their toll. There were severe crop failures in 1717 and again in 1718. In fact the latest calculations show that only 3 percent of the farms lay derelict at Karl's death. Recent estimates indicate Karl's wars resulted in the loss of less than 30,000 men during the war and about 8,000 of those eventually returned as repatriated prisoners of war from Russia. Even some war prisoners taken by Denmark and sold to Venice as galley slaves made it back to Sweden. While the losses were certainly significant, they do not represent the disastrous conditions sometimes presented for the age of greatness and certainly nothing like the devastation wrought in Germany by the Thirty Years' War. It must be remembered that after Karl XII's death the country still carried on the war for two and a half years, albeit in a different manner.

This period of development of the modern Sweden covered here and particularly the age of greatness (1632–1718) was one of almost constant warfare. Yet, except for Danish incursions into southern Sweden, the battles and associated destruction were on foreign soil, exempting the homeland from the worst aspects of seventeenth century warfare. The dominant Swedish navy kept the Baltic open and safe for commerce. Miners and agriculturalists had markets for their produce and merchants could trade freely anywhere along the Baltic rim. Therefore, the economy was generally healthy and at times booming. The period saw the incorporation of territories that make up modern Sweden, the results of war.

Except for Denmark, with about the same population, the country's enemies were much larger than Sweden. Gustav I's Sweden had about a million people and at its height under Karl X the Swedish Empire contained only about 3 million compared to Poland (about 7.5 million) or Russia (10 to 15 million). Sweden was sparsely populated by European standards of the day; consider England with 5 million people or France with 20 million. In order to compete on the battlefield, Sweden had to gear all her resources for war. Like ancient Sparta, Sweden became the archetype military state with the economy and her political and social systems organized for war. This gave her power and military dominance for a time, but also caused her neighbors to turn against her. In the end Sweden could not stand against so many enemies.

Karl XII died leaving no heir; indeed, he had never married. When the king was fatally shot, Frederick of Hesse, who was with the army, immediately passed the word to his wife, Ulrika Eleonora, the king's younger sister. He saw to the arrest of Görtz, who favored Duke Karl Fredrick of Holstein-Gottorp, son of Karl's older deceased sister, as heir to the throne. Görtz was soon tried on dubious charges, convicted and executed, having made enough enemies in the government and nobility to seal his fate. The Råd and Riksdag confirmed Ulrika Eleanora queen, but only upon acceptance of a limiting constitution. After Karl XI and Karl XII's absolutism, the aristocracy again insisted on sharing the power. The ghost of Erik Sparre had arisen. The divine right of the monarch was dead. What is called the Swedish age of freedom (1718–71) had begun.

With his wife on the throne, although in a reduced capacity, Frederick had a free hand in conducting the war. He found that most of the generals and the Råd were not in favor of the Norwegian war, so this campaign was abandoned. Sweden obtained England's help and a million *thalers* compensation in exchange for a treaty turning Bremen and Verden over to George I. Prussia took Pomerania up to and including Stettin for two million *thalers*. Sweden paid Denmark 600,000 riksdalers for the return of lost territories, but allowed Frederick VI to absorb Karl Fredrick's Holstein-Gottorp, extinguishing any hope the duke had of taking the Swedish throne. Sweden retained Wismar, Rügen and her ancient ally Stralsund.

Through this series of treaties Sweden reduced its wars to just one active enemy, Russia. England attempted to help settle this in Sweden's favor, even sending her fleet to the Baltic twice to intimidate the tsar. But Peter retaliated by dispatching his galley fleet to raid the coasts of Finland and Österbotten in 1719 and again in 1721, burning crops and homes. Finally, France stepped in and mediated a peace. During negotiations Russia continued to spread wanton destruction up and down the Bothnian coast, keeping the pressure on Sweden to give concessions. By the Treaty of Nystad, Sweden lost all her Baltic provinces, but kept Finland except for Kexholm, most of Karelia and the fortress of Viborg. The treaty signed in August 1721 finally ended the Great Northern War.

Sweden's age of greatness had been exemplified by her military prowess and territorial expansion. Yet, there was another side to this period and to the country so adept at war. During this period Sweden also commenced a cultural flowering in the arts and sciences which would continue through the next period, the age of freedom, and blossom particularly in the Gustavian period that followed.

As early as Gustav Vasa's rebuilding of Stockholm and Johan III's architectural and construction projects, Sweden began to advance in areas other than warfare. Cultural progress was heightened by Gustav Adolf's sending whole libraries and wagonloads of art to Uppsala University and other institutions. It was furthered with Christina's importation of illustrious scientists, artists and philosophers from all parts of Europe. By Karl XI's reign Sweden was producing its own outstanding figures in the arts and sciences. Many gained renown through-out Europe and their accomplishments are of note even today.

Christina's court poet was Georg Stjernhjelm, called the father of Swedish poetry. But he also excelled in the fields of law, science, mathematics, history, and philosophy. Architecture flourished with perhaps its highest achievement being the building of the majestic royal palace in Stockholm. The building of this structure (1693–97) was the work of Nicodemus Tessin. Some notables were eccentrics like Lars Johansson, the Swedish bard who was stabbed to death in a tavern brawl at only thirty-six. Gunn Dahlstierna composed the epic poem *Kunga-Skald* (1697) in Dante's meter to honor Karl XI.

Still honored is Karl Linnaeus (1707–1778), who developed the basis for the Latin naming system use in botany today. He made his living as a physician, but traveled through Lappland, England, the Netherlands, France and his native Gotland and Öland studying and classifying plant life. Born in Rashult, Småland, Linnaeus wrote widely in the field of botany and is still considered one of the world's great naturalists.

There was Emanuel Swedenborg (1688–1772), a physicist, astronomer, geologist, paleontologist, mineralogist, physiologist and psychologist, who was knighted by Queen Ulrica Eleonora in 1719 for designing a machine to convey boats overland from one waterway to another. He wrote extensively on a variety of scientific and engineering subjects. In later years he turned to religion writing, *Heaven and Hell* and *The Divine Love and Wisdom*.

A close friend of Swedenborg was Christopher Polhem (1661–1751), considered the father of Swedish engineering. It was Polhem who had invented the screw device to adjust the trajectory of artillery used so successfully in the last years of the Great Northern War. At the behest of Karl XI, he built a winchlike device to elevate ore from the copper mine at Falun. Versions of the machine were later used in various situations and industries throughout Sweden. He designed and built an automated mass production factory in Stjärnsund driven by water power. This facility, honored by Karl XII, produced a variety of items, but in 1734 a fire burned most of the plant. The factory continued to make clocks and padlocks (Polhem locks), a device he invented.

Anders Celsius (1701–1744), inventor of the centigrade thermometer used throughout the world today, was primarily an astronomer and atmospheric scientist. He designed the Uppsala observatory and studied the aurora borealis.

Along with achievements in the fields of literature, architecture, the arts and sciences, Sweden was constantly struggling to develop a government that would give all the people a voice. During this period the Riksdag had come to be one of the most broad-based national assemblies in Europe. Particularly important was the Estates Assembly of Vesteres (1527) where 4 bishops, 15 members of the Råd, 129 nobles, 32 burgesses, 14 miners and 104 peasant representatives gathered.

The Form of Government, drawn up under Oxenstierna's supervision in 1634 with its definition of the composition, powers and duties of each of the administrative departments of government, is the earliest known example of a written constitution, a precursor of the Constitution of the United States written a century and a half later.

Sweden's accomplishments were remarkable and many faceted during her age of greatness though the requirements of war undoubtedly retarded progress in these other fields. The Durants summed it up best perhaps:

> Sweden in this period had a remarkable succession of strong kings; for half a century (1654–1718) they were the wonder of the world, rivaled only by Louis XIV. Had they possessed a larger background of resources they might have equaled the power of France, and the Swedish people,

inspired by the achievements of two Gustavs, three Karls, and their great ministers, might have financed a cultural flowering commensurate with their victories and aspirations. But the wars that exalted their power exhausted their wealth, and Sweden emerged from this age heroic but consumed. It is astonishing that a nation so weak (in resources and population) should have accomplished so much.[1]

Sweden would remain a respected military force for some time to come and a contributor to European culture. She would supply energetic and skilled sons and daughters for the building of an American civilization, and lead Europe in industrialization and governmental reform. But never again would a Swedish warrior king ride at the head of his army producing brilliant victories, crushing all before him, extending Swedish domains and carving a position of supremacy in Northern Europe.

Notes

Chapter 3

1. Andrew A. Stomberg, *History of Sweden* (New York: Macmillan, 1931), p. 229.

Chapter 4

1. Ingvar Andersson, *A History of Sweden* (London: William Coves and Sons, 1956), p. 122–3.

Chapter 5

1. Franklin D. Scott, *Sweden: The Nation's History* (Carbondale: Southern Illinois University Press, 1988) p. 122.
2. Will Durant, *The Story of Civilization*, Vol. 6, *Reformation* (New York: Simon and Schuster, 1985), p. 624–5.

Chapter 6

1. Vilhelm Molberg, *A History of the Swedish People*, Vol. II (New York: Dorset Press, 1989), p. 236.
2. Ivan Svalenius, *Gustav Vasa* (Stockholm: Wahlström & Widstrand, 1963), pp. 236–238.
3. Molberg, p. 244.
4. Ibid.
5. Ibid., p. 263.
6. Nils Ahnlund, *Gustav Adolf the Great*. Translated by Michael Roberts. (Princeton: Princeton University Press and The American-Scandinavian Foundation, 1940), p. 143.

Chapter 10

1. Michael Roberts, *The Early Vasas* (Cambridge: Cambridge University Press, 1968), p. 360.
2. Ibid.

Chapter 12

1. Andrew A. Dow, *History of Sweden* (New York: Macmillan, 1931), p. 369.
2. Nils Ahnlund, *Gustav Adolf the Great*. Translated by Michael Roberts. (Princeton: Princeton University Press and The American-Scandinavian Foundation, 1940), p. 26.
3. Ibid., p. 29.
4. Ibid.
5. Ibid.
6. Ibid.
7. Ibid., p. 35.
8. Ibid., p. 43.

Chapter 13

1. Michael Roberts, *Gustavus Adolphus* (London and New York: Longman, 1992), p. 25.
2. Ibid., p. 25.
3. Ibid., p. 25.
4. Ibid., p. 25.
5. Bernard Pares, *A History of Russia* (New York: Alfred A. Knopf, 1953), p. 149.
6. Ibid, p. 150.
7. *Gustaf II Adolf* (http://members.tripod.com/strv 102r/gustaf_ii_adolf3.htm), p. 2.

Chapter 15

1. Martin Veibull and Magnus Höjer, *Sveriges Historia*, Vol. 4 (Stockholm: Hjalmar Linnströms Förlag, 1881), p. 188.
2. Michael Roberts, *Gustavus Adolphus* (London and New York: Longman, 1992), p. 72.
3. Ibid., p. 71.
4. Nils Ahnlund, *Gustav Adolf the Great*. Translated by Michael Roberts. (Princeton: Princeton University Press and The American-Scandinavian Foundation, 1940), p. 262.
5. Ibid., p. 264.
6. Ibid., p. 283.

7. Ibid.
8. Ibid., p. 284.
9. Roberts, p. 139.

Chapter 16

1. Michael Roberts, *Gustavus Adolphus* (London and New York: Longman, 1992), p. 177.

Chapter 17

1. Georgina Masson, *Queen Christina* (New York: Farrar, Straus & Giroux, 1969), p. 25.
2. Ibid., p. 27.

Chapter 19

1. Georgina Masson, *Queen Christina* (New York: Farrar, Straus & Giroux, 1969), p. 21.
2. Ibid.
3. Ibid.
4. Ibid., p. 40.
5. Faith Compton Mackenzie, *The Sibyl of the North* (London: Cossell, 1931), p. 14.
6. Curt Weibull, *Christina of Sweden* (Göteborg: Elanders Boktryckeri Aktiebolag, 1966), p. 19.
7. Ibid., p. 22.
8. Ibid., p. 28.
9. Ibid., p. 76.
10. Ibid.
11. Ibid., p. 77.
12. Ibid., p. 87.

Chapter 21

1. C.A. Weslager, *New Sweden on the Delaware* (Wilmington, DE: Middle Atlantic Press, 1988), p. 21.

2. John Munroe, *Colonial Delaware: A History* (New York: KTO Press, 1978), p. 3.
3. Ibid., p. 13.
4. Attributed to Benjamin Franklin at the signing of the Declaration of Independence. The Electric Franklin, http://*www.ushistory.org*.

Chapter 23

1. Voltaire, *Lion of the North* (East Brunswick, NJ: Associated University Press, 1981), p. 29.
2. Ibid.
3. Ibid., p. 22.
4. Ibid., p. 42.

Chapter 24

1. R.M. Hatton, *Charles XII of Sweden* (New York: Weybright and Talley, 1968), p. 179.
2. Frans G. Bengtsson, *The Life of Charles XII* (New York: Macmillan, 1960), p. 132.

Chapter 26

1. Will Durant and Ariel Durant, *The Story of Civilization*, Vol. 8, *The Age of Louis XIV* (New York: Simon and Schuster, 1991), p. 389.
2. Voltaire, *Lion of the North* (East Brunswick, NJ: Associated University Press, 1981), p. 19.

Epilogue

1. Will Durant and Ariel Durant, *The Story of Civilization*, Vol. 8, *The Age of Louis XIV* (New York: Simon and Schuster, 1991), p. 365.

Bibliography

Åberg, Alf. *Nils Dacke och Landsfadern.* Stockholm: LTs Förlag, 1960.

Acrelius, Israel. *A History of New Sweden.* Philadelphia: Historical Society of Pennsylvania, 1876.

Ahnlund, Nils. *Gustav Adolf the Great.* Translated by Michael Roberts. Princeton: Princeton University Press and The American-Scandinavian Foundation, 1940.

Åkerman, Susanna. *Queen Christina of Sweden and Her Circle.* New York: E. J. Brill, 1991.

Alin, Oskar. *Sveriges Historia.* Vol. 3. Stockholm: Aktiebolaget Hiertas Bokförlag, 1889.

Andersson, Hans, Peter Carelli, and Lars Ersgård. *Vision of the Past.* Stockholm: Central Board of Antiquities, 1997.

Andersson, Ingvar. *A History of Sweden.* London: William Coves and Sons, 1956.

Bain, Robert. *Charles XII.* Freeport: Books for Libraries Press, 1895.

Baudou, Evert. *Papers in Northern Archaeology.* Umeå, Sweden: University of Umeå, 1984.

Bengtsson, Frans G. *The Life of Charles XII.* New York: Macmillan, 1960.

Bjørklund, Oddvar, Berit Lie, Haakon Holmboe, and Anders Røhr. *Historical Atlas of the World.* New York: Barnes & Noble, 1970.

Brzezinski, Richard. *The Army of Gustavus Adolphus (2): Cavalry.* Oxford: Osprey, 1993.

_____. *Lützen 1632 — Climax of the Thirty Years' War.* Oxford: Osprey Military, 2001.

Bull, Stephen. *An Historical Guide to Arms and Armour.* New York: Facts on File, 1991.

Cederlöf, Olle. *Vapenhistorisk Handbook.* Stockholm: Bokförlaget Rediviva, 1975.

Cnattingius, Nanna, Jutta Waller, and Birgita Windahl-Clerborn. *The Cultural Heritage in Sweden.* Stockholm: Central Board of National Antiquities, 1981.

Croxton, Derek, and Anushka Tischer. *The Peace of Westphalia: A Historical Dictionary.* Westport: Greenwood Press, 2002.

Cunliffe, Barry. *The Oxford Illustrated Prehistory of Europe.* Oxford: Oxford University Press, 1994.

Davies, Norman. *A History of Europe.* Oxford: Oxford University Press, 1996.

Dow, Andrew A. *History of Sweden.* New York: Macmillan, 1931.

Dow, James. *Ruthven's Army in Sweden and Estonia.* Stockholm: Antikvitets Akademien, 1965.

Durant, Will. *The Story of Civilization.* Vol. 6, *Reformation.* New York: Simon and Schuster, 1985.

_____, and Ariel Durant. *The Story of Civilization.* Vol. 8, *The Age of Louis XIV.* New York: Simon and Schuster, 1991.

The Electric Franklin. http://*www.ushistory.org.*

Evans, Jack R. *The Swedes From Whence They Came.* Seattle: SCW, 1993.

Fisk, Jill. *The Struggle for Supremacy in the Baltic: 1600–1725.* New York: Funk & Wagnalls, 1967.

Fletcher, C. R. L. *Gustavus Adolphus and the Thirty Years' War.* New York: Capricorn Books, 1963.

Frost, Robert I. *After the Deluge: Poland-Lithuania and the Second Northern War.* Cambridge: Cambridge University Press, 1993.

_____. *The Northern Wars.* Essex: Pearson Education, 2000.

Glete, Jan. *Warfare at Sea: 1500–1650.* London: Routledge, 2000.

Goldsmith, Margaret. *Christina of Sweden.* Garden City: Doubleday, Doran, 1933.

Gould, Dennis E. *Historical Dictionary of Stockholm.* Lanham, MD: Scarecrow Press, 1997.

Guinchard, J. *Sweden Historical and Statistical Handbook.* Stockholm: Government Printing Office, 1914.

Guthrie, William. *Battles of the Thirty Years' War.* Westport, CT: Greenwood Press, 2002.

_____. *The Thirty Years' War.* Westport, CT: Greenwood Press, 2003.

Hallendorff, Carl, and Adolf Schück. *History of Sweden.* Stockhom: C. E. Fritze, 1929.

Hårdh, Brigitta. *Wikingerzeitliche Depotfunde Aus Südschweven.* Varberg, Schweden: Holms Grafiska AB, 1976.

Hatton, R.M. *Charles XII of Sweden.* New York: Weybright and Talley, 1968.

Haywood, John. *Encyclopedia of the Viking Age.* London: Thames & Hudson, 2000.

Herman, Bernard L. *The Stone House.* Charlottesville: University of Virginia Press, 1992.

Hildebrand, Hans. *Sveriges Historia.* Vol. 2. Stockholm: Aktiebolaget Hiertas Bokförlag, 1889.

Hill, Charles Edward. *The Danish Sound Dues and Command of the Baltic: A Study of International Relations.* Durham: Duke University Press, 1926.

Hoffecker, Carol E., Richard Waldron, Lorraine E. Williams, and Barbara E. Benson. *New Sweden in America.* Cranbury, NJ: University of Delaware Press, 1995.

Hogg, Ian V. *The Illustrated History of Firearms.* London: New Burlington Book, 1983.

Holm, Thomas. *Description of the Province of New Sweden.* Philadelphia: M'Carty & Davis, 1834.

Jacquemont, E. *Christine de Suede.* Lyon: Librairie Ancienne de Louis Brun, 1912.

Johannesson, Kurt. *The Renaissance of the Goths in Sixteenth-Century Sweden.* Berkeley: University of California Press, 1982.

Johnson, Amandus. *The Instructions for Johan Printz.* New York: Ira J. Friedman, 1930.

_____. *The Swedish Settlements on the Delaware: Their History and Relation to the Indians, Dutch and English, 1638–1664.* Philadelphia: Swedish Colonial Society, 1911.

Jones, Archer. *The Art of War in the Western World.* Champaign: University of Illinois Press, 1987.

Jones, Gwyn. *A History of the Vikings.* Oxford: Oxford University Press, 1984.

Keegan, John. *Battle at Sea.* Chatham: Mackays of Chatham, 1988.

Kiernan, V. G. *The Duel in European History.* Oxford: Oxford University Press, 1988.

Larsson, Lars, Johann Callmer, and B. Stjernquist, eds. *The Archaeology of the Cultural Landscape.* Lund: Bloms Boktryckeri AB, 1992.

Larsson, Thomas B., and Hans Lundmark. *Approaches to Swedish Prehistory.* Oxford: B.A.R., 1989.

Lepage, Jean-Denis G. G. *Castles and Fortified Cities of Medieval Europe.* Jefferson, NC: McFarland, 2002.

_____. *Medieval Armies and Weapons in Western Europe.* Jefferson, NC: McFarland, 2002.

Lindeström, Peter. *Geographia Americae, with an Account of the Delaware Indians.* Philadelphia: Swedish Colonial Society, 1925.

Lockhart, Paul Douglas. *Denmark in the Thirty Years' War.* London: Associated University Presses, 1996.

_____. *Sweden in the Seventeenth Century.* New York: Palgrave Macmillan, 2004.

Lundkvist, Sven. *Gustaf Vasa och Europa.* Stockholm: Svenska Bokforlaget, 1960.

Lynam, Edward. *The Cafta Marina of Olaus Magnus.* Portland: Anthoensen Press, 1949.

MacDonald, Malcom Ross. *Encyclopedia of Discovery and Exploration.* Vol. 2. London: Aldus Books, 1971.

MacDonald, Marie Peterson. *Öjebomåla: 1350–1950.* Glendive, MT: Gateway Press, 1972.

Mackenzie, Faith Compton. *The Sibyl of the North.* London: Cossell, 1931.

MacMunn, Sir George. *Gustavus Adolphus.* New York: Robert M. McBride, 1931.

Masson, Georgina. *Queen Christina.* New York: Farrar, Straus & Giroux, 1969.

Molberg, Vilhelm. *A History of the Swedish People.* Vol. 1. New York: Dorset Press, 1989.

_____. *A History of the Swedish People.* Vol. II. New York: Dorset Press, 1989.

Montelius, Oscar. *The Civilisation of Sweden in Heathen Times.* New York: Haskell House, 1969.

Munroe, John. *Colonial Delaware: A History.* New York: KTO Press, 1978.

Myatt, Maj. Frederick. *Illustrated Encyclopedia of Pistols and Revolvers.* London: Salamander Books, 1980.

Nilsson, Victor. *Sweden.* New York: Peter Fenelon Collier, 1899.

Nordstrom, Byron J. *The History of Sweden.* Westport, CT: Greenwood Press, 2002.

North, George. *The Description of Swedland, Gotland and Finland.* New York: Scholar's Facsimiles & Reprints, 1947.

Pares, Bernard. *A History of Russia.* New York: Alfred A. Knopf, 1953.

Parker, Geoffrey. *The Military Revolution.* Cambridge: Cambridge University Press, 1988.

Petri, Olavus. *Olai Petri Svenska Krönika.* Stockholm: Klemming, 1860.

Quick, John. *Dictionary of Weapons & Military Terms.* New York: McGraw-Hill, 1973.

Rink, Oliver. *Holland on the Hudson.* Ithaca, NY: Cornell University Press, 1986.

Roberts, Michael. *Essays in Swedish History.* London and Southampton: Camelot Press, 1953.

_____. *From Oxenstierna to Charles XII.* Cambridge: Cambridge University Press, 1991.

_____. *Gustavus Adolphus.* London and New York: Longman, 1992.

_____. *Sweden's Age of Greatness: 1632–1718.* New York: St. Martin's Press, 1973.

_____. *The Age of Liberty.* Cambridge: Cambridge University Press, 1986.

_____. *The Early Vasas.* Cambridge: Cambridge University Press, 1968.

_____. *The Swedish Imperial Experience 1560–1718.* London, Cambridge University Press, 1979.

Rose, Susan. *Medieval Naval Warfare.* London: Routledge, 2002.

Savage, Anne. *The Anglo-Saxon Chronicles.* London: Barnes & Noble, 2000.

Schenck, Earl. *Paradise Point.* New York: Spiral Press, 1968.

Schiller, Frederick. *History of the Thirty Years' War in Germany.* New York: A.L. Burt, n.a.

Scott, Franklin D. *Sweden: The Nation's History.* Carbondale: Southern Illinois University Press, 1988.

Slavin, Arthur J. *The New Monarchies and Representative Assemblies.* Boston: Heath, 1964.

Smith, Jerry C., and William L. Urban. *The Livonian Rhymed Chronicle.* Bloomington: Indiana University Press, 1977.

Söderqvist, O. *Johan III och Hertig Karl, 1568–1575*. Uppsala: Almqvist & Wiksell, 1898.

Spectre, Peter H., and David Larkin. *Wooden Ship: The Art, History and Revival of Wooden Boatbuilding*. Boston: Houghton Mifflin, 1991.

Stomberg, Andrew A. *History of Sweden*. New York: Macmillan, 1931.

Strindberg, August. *Gustav Adolf*. Seattle: University of Washington Press, 1957.

_____. *The Vasa Trilogy*. Translated by Walter Johnson. Seattle: University of Washington Press, Seattle, 1959.

Strömberg, Märta. *Ingelstorp Zur Siedlungsentwicklung Eines Sucschwedischen Dorfes*. Berlings: Arl_v, 1982.

Svalenius, Ivan. *Gustav Vasa*. Stockholm: Wahlström & Widstrand, 1963.

Svenström, Ragnar, and Carl-Fredrik Palmstierna. *A Short History of Sweden*. Oxford: Clarendon Press, 1934.

Troyat, Henri. *Terrible Tsarinas*. New York: Algora, 1999.

Upton, A.F. *Charles XI and Swedish Absolutism*. Cambridge: Cambridge University Press, 1998.

Veibull, Martin, and Magnus Höjer. *Sveriges Historia*. Vol. 4. Stockholm: Hjalmar Linnströms Förlag, 1881.

Voltaire, *Lion of the North*. East Brunswick, NJ: Associated University Press., Inc., 1981.

_____. *The History of Charles the Twelfth*. Philadelphia: J. B. Lippincott, 1865.

Weibull, Curt. *Christina of Sweden*. Göteborg: Elanders Boktryckeri Aktiebolag, 1966.

Weibull, Jörgen. *Swedish History in Outline*. Sweden: Skogs Boktryckeri AB, 1997.

Weslager, C.A. *Delaware's Buried Past*. New Brunswick, NJ: Rutgers University Press, 1944.

_____. *Dutch Explorers, Traders and Settlers of the Delaware Valley, 1609–1664*. Philadelphia: University of Pennsylvania Press, 1969.

_____. *New Sweden on the Delaware*. Wilmington, DE: Middle Atlantic Press, 1988.

_____. *The Swedes and Dutch at New Castle*. Wilmington, DE: Middle Atlantic Press, 1988.

Wolfram, Helwig. *The Roman Empire and Its Germanic Peoples*. Los Angeles: University of California Press, 1990.

Wordsworth, John. *The National Church of Sweden*. London: Mowbray, 1911.

Wuorinen, John. *The Finns on the Delaware*. New York: Columbia University Press, 1938.

Yela, Gary. *New Sweden*. Wilmington: University of Delaware Press, 1988.

Index